California Adoption Law and Procedure

California Adoption Law and Procedure

Everett L. Skillman

Professor of Law

Vandeplas Publishing

United States of America

California Adoption Law and Procedure

Skillman, Everett L.

ISBN 978-1-60042-179-2

Published by:

Vandeplas Publishing LLC – August 2012

801 International Parkway, 5th Floor
Lake Mary, FL. 32746
USA

www.vandeplaspublishing.com

This book is dedicated to the good people at Olive Crest, who introduced Shelley and me to our sons.

TABLE OF CONTENTS

LIST OF SELECTED ABBREVIATIONS

AACWA -- Adoption Assistance and Child Welfare Act
BCIS -- Bureau of Citizenship and Immigration Services
CDSS -- California Department of Social Services
ICPC -- Interstate Compact for the Placement of Children
ICWA -- Indian Child Welfare Act
INS -- Immigration and Naturalization Service
UCCJA -- Uniform Child Custody Jurisdiction Act
UCCJEA -- Uniform Child Custody Jurisdiction and Enforcement Act
UPA -- Uniform Parentage Act
USCIS -- United States Citizenship and Immigration Services

LIST OF SELECTED STANDARD FORMS

Published by the California Department of Social Services:

The standard forms – as configured at the time this book is being printed – which are provided for free downloading on the California Department of Social Services web site (www.dss.cahwnet.gov/cdssweb/PG164.htm#ad), and which are relevant to an adoption proceeding are as follows:

AAP 1	Request For Adoption Assistance Program Benefit
AAP 2	Payment Instructions Adoption Assistance Program
AAP 3	Reassessment Information - Adoption Assistance Program
AAP 4	Eligibility Certification Adoption Assistance Program
AAP 5	Adoptions Assistance Program Independent Adoptions Program
AAP 6	Adoption Assistance Program Negotiated Benefit Amount and Approval Instructions and Form
AAP 7	Adoptions Assistance Program Statement Of Acknowledgement
AD 1A	Consent To Adoption By Parent(s) (In California)
AD 1C	Parental Consent to Adoption (Outside California)
AD 1F	Consent To Adoption By Parent(s) Outside California In Armed Forces
AD 2	Stepparent Adoption (Consent To Adoption By Parent Retaining Custody)
AD 2A	Stepparent Adoption (Consent To Adoption By Parent In California Giving Custody To Husband Or Wife Or Domestic Partner Of Other Parent)
AD 2B	Consent To Adoption By Parent Outside California Giving Custody To Husband Or Wife Or Domestic Partner Of Other Parent
AD 2D	Stepparent Adoption Consent To Adoption By Parent Outside California In Armed Forces Giving Custody To Husband Or Wife Or Domestic Partner Of Other Parent
AD 8	Marriage/Divorce Verification (Combined With AD 19)
AD 9	Independent Adoption Questionnaire
AD 10	Request for Reference
AD 20	Refusal To Give Consent To Adoption
AD 20B	Refusal To Give Consent To Adoption - Alleged Natural Father
AD 22	Health Facility Minor Release Report
AD 28	Notification Of Subsequent Action
AD 29	Employment Verification
AD 40 1	Adoptions Worksheet
AD 42 I	Independent Adoptions Program (Individual Case Report)
AD 42R	Agency Adoption Program - Individual Case Report
AD 56A	Agency Adoption Program Quarterly Statistical Report (Combines AD 56A, AD 56C, And AD 56E)

AD 56D Independent Adoption Program & Adoption Set Asides
AD 65 Parent's Authorization For Medical And Surgical Care
AD 67 Information about The Birth Mother
AD 67A Information About The Birth Father
AD 90 Supporting Information For Issuance Of California Department Of Social Services Acknowledgement And Confirmation Of Receipt Of Child Freeing Documents
AD 100 Authorization For Use And/Or Disclosure Of Health Information Independent Adoption Program
AD 100A Authorization For Use And/Or Disclosure Of Health Information Agency Adoption Program
AD 165 Presumed Father's Consent To Adoption (In California)
AD 166 Consent To Adoption By Father Outside California (to be used when presumed father denies he is the natural father)
AD 196 Request For Release Of Information
AD 200 Request For Case Record/Documents
AD 202B Intercounty Adoption Program Quarterly Statistical Report
AD 501 Relinquishment In or Out-of-County (Birth Mother/Presumed Father in CA)
AD 501A Relinquishment Out-of-State (Birth Mother/Presumed Father)
AD 504 Relinquishment – Out of State In The Armed Forces (Birth Mother/Presumed Father)
AD 508 Rescission Request/Rescission Of Relinquishment
AD 512 Psychosocial And Medical History Of Child - English Version
AD 521 Application For Adoption Of A Child
AD 524 Physician's Examination Of Adoption Applicant/Petitioner
AD 551A Notification Of Procedure In Lieu Of Signing Relinquishment, Waiver or Denial (To Be Used For California Court Actions, Out-of-State Actions, And Foreign Born Children)
AD 558 Notice Of Placement (To Be Sent Within 15 Days of Placement)
AD 580 Notice of Removal Of Child From Adoptive Home
AD 583 Relinquishment In Or Out Of County - Presumed Father Denies He Is The Birth Father in California
AD 584 Relinquishment Out of State - Presumed Father Denies He is the Birth Father
AD 586 Relinquishment In or Out-of-County (Alleged Natural Father In California)
AD 588 Denial Of Paternity By Alleged Natural Father - In Or Out Of California
AD 590 Waiver Of Right To Further Notice Of Adoption Planning (Alleged Natural Father In Or Out Of California)
AD 590A Waiver Of Right To Further Notice Of Adoption Planning - Presumed Father In Or Out Of California
AD 590B Waiver Of Right To Further Notice Of Adoption Planning (Presumed Father In Or Out Of California) Indian Child

AD 591	Relinquishment Out-of-State (Alleged Natural Father)
AD 593	Relinquishment – Out of State in Armed Forces (Alleged Natural Father)
AD 594	Alleged Natural Father's Consent To Adoption (In Or Out Of California)
AD 824	Adoption Petition - Consent and Joinder
AD 830	Summary Claim For Reimbursement Private Adoption Agency Reimbursement Program (Welare Institutions Code Section 16122)
AD 836	Report Of Physician Attending Birth Of Child Placed For Adoption
AD 842	Consent To Adoptive Placement By Alleged Natural Father (Outside California In Armed Forces)
AD 859	Consent To Adoption Of Indian Child By Parent(s)
AD 860	Consent To Adoption Of Indian Child By Presumed Father
AD 861	Consent To Adoption Of Indian Child By Alleged Natural Father
AD 862	Relinquishment Of An Indian Child Out of State - Alleged Natural Father
AD 863	Relinquishment Of An Indian Child Out of State - Birth Mother/Presumed Father
AD 864	Relinquishment Of An Indian Child In Or Out-Of-County - Birth Mother/Presumed Father In California
AD 866	Relinquishment Of An Indian Child In Or Out-of-County - Presumed Father Denies He Is The Birth Father In California
AD 867	Relinquishment of an Indian Child - Out-of-State - Presumed Father Denies He is the Birth Father
AD 868	Relinquishment Of Indian Child - In/Out of County - Alleged Natural Father In California
AD 880	Declaration Of Mother (to be completed by all mothers not married to the father except when a relinquishment or consent has been obtained from the father)
AD 885	Mother Or A Presumed Father Of A Child Who Is Not Detained, A Juvenile Court Dependent In Out-of-home Care, Or The Ward Of A Legal Guardian
AD 885A	Mother or a Presumed Father of a Child Who is Detained, a Juvenile court Dependent in Out-of-home Care, or the Ward of a Legal Guardian
AD 885C	Statement of Understanding Agency Adoptions Program - Alleged Natural Father Of The Child Who Is Not Detained, A Juvenile Court Dependent In Out-Of-Home Care, Or The Ward Of A Legal Guardian
AD 885D	Alleged Natural Father of the Child Who is Detained, a Juvenile Court Dependent in Out-of-Home Care, or the Ward of a Legal Guardian
AD 887	Statement Of Understanding - Independent Adoptions Program
AD 887A	Statement Of Understanding - Parent Who Did Not Give Physical Custody (Non-Custodial Parent) Of The Child To The Petitioner(s)
AD 887B	Statement of Understanding - Alleged Natural Father

AD 899 Statement of Understanding - Mother or a Presumed Father of the INDIAN Child Who is Not Detained, a Juvenile Court Dependent in Out-of-home Care, or a Ward of a Legal Guardian
AD 899A Statement of Understanding - Mother or a Presumed Father of an INDIAN Child Who is Detained, a Juvenile Court Dependent in Out-of-home Care, or the Ward of a Legal Guardian
AD 899C Statement Of Understanding - Alleged Natural Father of the INDIAN Child Who is Not Detained, a Juvenile Court Dependent in Out-of-home Care, or the Ward of a Legal Guardian
AD 899D Statement Of Understanding - Alleged Natural Father of an INDIAN Child Who is Detained, a Juvenile Court Dependent in Out-of-home Care, or the Ward of a Legal Guardian
AD 900 Statement Of Understanding Independent Adoptions Program – Parent Who Gave Physical Custody (Custodial Parent) of the INDIAN Child to the Petitioner(s)
AD 900A Statement of Understanding Independent Adoptions Program - Parent Who Did Not Give Physical Custody (non-custodial) Of The Indian Child To The Petitioner(s)
AD 904 Consent For Contact
AD 904A Waiver of Rights to Confidentiality For Siblings
AD 904B Waiver Of Rights To Confidentiality For Siblings - Under The Age 18
AD 907 Adoptive Placement Agreement
AD 908 Adoptions Information Act Statement
AD 908A Adoptions Information Act Statement
AD 909 Photo Listing Data Sheet
AD 918 Family Assessment Questionnaire II
AD 922 Relinquishment Addendum For Parent Identifying Adopting Parent(s)
AD 924 Independent Adoption Placement Agreement
AD 925 Independent Adoption Placement Agreement - INDIAN Child
AD 926 Statement Of Understanding Independent Adoptions Program – Parent Who Places The Child With The Prospective Adoptive Parent(s)
AD 927 Statement Of Understanding - Independent Adoptions Program
AD 928 Revocation Of Consent Independent Adoption Program
AD 929 Waiver Of Right To Revoke Consent Independent Adoption Program
AD 930 Independent Adoption Placement Agreement Transmittal Report
AD 4310 Adoption Programs Notice Required By Information Practices Act
AD 4313 Letter Requesting Parent Be Interviewed
AD 4315 Recommendation Of Dismissal Of Petition Court Report Outline
AD 4317 Revocation Of Relinquishment
AD 4320 Adoption Assistance Program (AAP) Agreement
AD 4324 Adoption Questionnaire I This is a large PDF file. Click here if you have problems with it: Tips for Using Adobe PDF Files
AD 4328 Authorization For Release Of Personal Items

AD 4336	Presumed Father's Consent To Adoption (Outside California In Armed Forces)
AD 4339	Relinquishment – Out of State (Birth Mother/Presumed Father)
AD 4348	Private Adoption Agency Reimbursement Program (PAARP)
AD 4349A	The Private Adoption Agency Reimbursement Program (PAARP) Full Time Equivalent
AD 4349B	The Private Adoption Agency Reimbursement Program (PAARP) Full Time Equivalent
AD 4349C	The Private Adoption Agency Reimbursement Program (PAARP) Full Time Equivalent
AD 4349D	The Private Adoption Agency Reimbursement Program (PAARP) Full Time Equivalent
AD 4349E	The Private Adoption Agency Reimbursement Program (PAARP) Full Time Equivalent
ADM 36	Medical Report Regarding Child To Be Adopted

Published by the California Judicial Council:

The fillable standard forms which are available for downloading at no charge on the California Judicial Council's web site (www.courtinfo.ca.gov/cgi-bin/forms.cgi), and which are relevant to an adoption proceeding are:

ADOPT-200	Adoption Request
ADOPT-210	Adoption Agreement
ADOPT-215	Adoption Order
ADOPT-220	Adoption of Indian Child
ADOPT-225	Parent of Indian Child Agrees to End Parental Rights
ADOPT-230	Adoption Expenses
ADOPT-310	Contact After Adoption Agreement
ADOPT-315	Request to: Enforce, Change, End Contact After Adoption Agreement
ADOPT-320	Answer to Request to: Enforce, Change, End Contact After Adoption Agreement
ADOPT-325	Judge's Order to: Enforce, Change, End Contact After Adoption Agreement
ADOPT-330	Request for Appointment of Confidential Intermediary
ADOPT-331	Order for Appointment of Confidential Intermediary
FL-200	Petition to Establish Parental Relationship (Uniform Parentage)
FL-200 S	Petition to Establish Parental Relationships (Uniform Parentage) (Spanish)
FL-210	Summons (Uniform Parentage-Petition for Custody and Support)
FL-210S	Summons (Uniform Parentage—Petition for Custody and Support) (Spanish)
FL-220	Response to Petition to Establish Parental Relationship (Uniform Parentage)

FL-220S Response to Petition to Establish Parental Relationship (Uniform Parentage) (Spanish)
FL-230 Declaration for Default or Uncontested Judgment (Uniform Parentage—Custody and Support)
FL-235 Advisement and Waiver of Rights Re: Establishment of Parental Relationship (Uniform Parentage)
FL-235 S Advisement and Waiver of Rights Re: Establishment of Parental Relationship (Uniform Parentage) (Spanish)
FL-240 Stipulation for Entry of Judgment Re: Establishment of Parental Relationship (Uniform Parentage)
FL-240 S Stipulation for Entry of Judgment Re: Establishment of Parental Relationship (Uniform Parentage) (Spanish)
FL-250 Judgment (Uniform Parentage—Custody and Support)
FL-250S Judgment (Uniform Parentage—Custody and Support) (Spanish)
FL-260 Petition for Custody and Support of Minor Children
FL-260 S Petition for Custody and Support of Minor Children (Spanish)
FL-270 Response to Petition for Custody and Support of Minor Children
FL-270 S Response to Petition for Custody and Support of Minor Children (Spanish)
FL-272 Notice of Motion to Set Aside Judgment of Paternity (Family Law—Government)
FL-272S Notice of Motion to Set Aside Judgment of Paternity (Family Law—Government) (Spanish)
FL-273 Declaration in Support of Motion to Set Aside Judgment of Paternity (Family Law—Governmental)
FL-273S Declaration in Support of Motion to Set Aside Judgment of Paternity (Family Law—Governmental) (Spanish)
FL-276 Response to Notice of Motion to Set Aside Judgment of Paternity (Family Law—Governmental)
FL-276S Response to Notice of Motion to Set Aside Judgment of Paternity (Family Law—Governmental) (Spanish)
FL-278 Order After Hearing on Motion to Set Aside Judgment of Paternity (Family Law—Governmental)
FL-278S Order After Hearing on Motion to Set Aside Judgment of Paternity (Family Law—Governmental) (Spanish)
FL-280 Request for Hearing and Application to Set Aside Voluntary Declaration of Paternity (Family Law—Governmental)
FL-280S Request for Hearing and Application to Set Aside Voluntary Declaration of Paternity (Family Law—Governmental) (Spanish)
FL-285 Responsive Declaration to Application to Set Aside Voluntary Declaration of Paternity (Family Law—Governmental)

FL-285S	Responsive Declaration to Application to Set Aside Voluntary Declaration of Paternity (Family Law—Governmental) (Spanish)
FL-290	Order After Hearing on Motion to Set Aside Voluntary Declaration of paternity (Family Law—Governmental)
FL-290S	Order After Hearing on Motion to Set Aside Voluntary Declaration of paternity (Family Law—Governmental) (Spanish)
ICWA-010(A)	Indian Child Inquiry Attachment
ICWA-010(A)S	Indian Child Inquiry Attachment (Spanish)
ICWA-020	Parental Notification of Indian Status
ICWA-020 S	Parental Notification of Indian Status (Spanish)
ICWA-030	Notice of Child Custody Proceeding for Indian Child
ICWA-030 S	Notice of Child Custody Proceeding for Indian Child (Spanish)
ICWA-030(A)	Attachment to Notice of Child Custody Proceeding for Indian Child (Indian Child Welfare Act)
ICWA-030(A)S	Attachment to Notice of Child Custody Proceeding for Indian Child (Indian Child Welfare Act) (Spanish)
ICWA-040	Notice of Designation of Tribal Representative and Notice of Intervention in a Court Proceeding Involving an Indian Child
ICWA-050	Notice of Petition and Petition to Transfer Case Involving an Indian Child to Tribal Jurisdiction
ICWA-060	Order on Petition to Transfer Case Involving an Indian Child to Tribal Jurisdiction

Published by the Federal Government:

The relevant standard forms which are available for downloading at no charge on the web site of U.S. Citizenship and Immigration Services (www.uscis.gov/portal/site/uscis) are:

I-130	Petition for Alien Relative
I-600	Petition to Classify Orphan as an Immediate Relative
I-600A	Application for Advance Processing of Orphan Petition
I-601	Application for Waiver of Grounds of Inadmissibility
I-800	Petition to Classify Convention Adoptee as an Immediate Relative
I-800A	Application for Determination of Suitability to Adopt a Child from a Convention Country
I-824	Application for Action on an Approved Application or Petition
N-600	Application for Certificate of Citizenship.
N-600K	Application for Citizenship and Issuance of Certificate (Section 322)
G-884	Return of Original Documents
G-1145	E-Notification of Application/Petition Acceptance

INTRODUCTION TO ADOPTION LAW

Most adoption cases in California are uncontested. That is, all "parties" to the adoption are in agreement that the adoption should be confirmed by court order. Many such cases involve birth parents who have been correctly identified and have lawfully consented, a child who has been properly placed with the prospective adoptive parents, a social services agency who has conducted the appropriate home study and has approved the prospective adoptive parents, and the absence of any objecting third party. On the other hand, many adoption cases appear at first to be uncontested, but complications arise, and sometimes well after emotional bonds have formed between the child and the prospective adoptive parents. This book exists primarily for those cases.

In *Sharon S. v. Superior Court*, (2003) 31 Cal.4th 417, the California Supreme Court stated, "The right to adopt a child, and the right of a person to be adopted as the child of another, are wholly statutory." The foundational statute is California Family Code § 8600, which provides that an unmarried minor may be adopted by an adult as provided by statute. (Unless otherwise expressly noted, all references in this book to statutes are to California statutes.) In interpreting the adoption statutes, the California Supreme Court held in *In re Santos' Estate*, (1921) 185 Cal. 127, that the "main purpose of adoption statutes is the promotion of the welfare of children, bereft of the benefits of the home and care of their real parents, by the legal recognition and regulation of the consummation of the closest conceivable counterpart of the relationship of parent and child." It is that "counterpart," and the attendant procedures, which this book will attempt to describe, in terms of what the presently existing law provides. The subject of the adoption of children also includes a wide variety of issues, and this book will focus on the legal questions, as opposed to the social and psychological issues.

More than any other field, adoption law requires skills in multi-party dynamics. The individuals and entities involved in an adoption usually include the child, the prospective adoptive parent or parents, the birth mother, the birth father or a set of possible birth fathers, the child's siblings and other relatives, a social worker and the public agency he or she represents (such as the California Department of Social Services ("CDSS") and/or the county social services agency), possibly a representative of the private agency to whom the child may have been relinquished, possibly a representative from U.S. Citizenship and Immigration Services ("USCIS") in an intercountry adoption, the attorneys for these parties, and the court or courts. It is therefore no wonder that adoption law has grown to be so complicated.

This book is devoted to the adoption of children. While the adoption of adults, i.e., individuals 18 years of age and older, is provided for in Family Code §§ 9300, et seq., such practice is undertaken (pragmatically speaking) for estate planning and insurance purposes, and not so much for the purposes explained in *Santos*. In addition, one may adopt a disabled adult in order to better accommodate the care of the adoptee, but conservatorships are the more traditional vehicle for such purposes.

With certain exceptions, adoption is governed by state law; and adoption law varies significantly from state to state. For example, if a birth parent in California seeks to place his or her child for adoption in Wyoming with a Wyoming couple, that birth parent will have far fewer rights than if the adoption were completed in California. (See, *In re Adoption of MM*, (Wyo. 1982) 652 P.2d 974 [explained in Chapter 9 of this book].) Likewise, all states have updated their jurisdictional statutes so as to conform to the Uniform Child Custody Jurisdiction and Enforcement Act ("UCCJEA"), which governs almost all types of child custody orders. Vermont adopted the UCCJEA on July 1, 2011, and was the last state to do so. One of the provisions of the UCCJEA is that it does not apply to adoptions, however a handful of states have excluded that provision from their version of the UCCJEA. There are also many federal laws which touch upon adoption (e.g., tax law and immigration law), but they do not themselves authorize the filing of an adoption petition.

In addition to state statutes, the regulations of the CDSS are relevant in California adoption cases, and such rules are considered to have the force and effect of statute, as long as they are enacted "pursuant to a delegation of rulemaking authority by the Legislature." (See *Agricultural Labor Relations Bd. v. Superior Court*, (1976) 16 Cal.3d 392.). Even in instances where there is no express legislative delegation of rulemaking authority, the California Supreme Court recently stated in *Sharon S.* that while the courts take ultimate responsibility for the interpretation of statute, the courts give "great weight and respect to the administrative construction thereof." As explained in Chapter 11 of this book, these same maxims also apply in the federal context.

The California courts have long held (as have most other jurisdictions) that adoption is "purely statutory." (See *Estate of Pierce*, (1948) 32 Cal.2d 265.) All 50 states and the District of Columbia now have adoption statutes. It does not appear that any court has ever recognized a "common law" right to adopt or be adopted, with the exception of the posthumous recognition of the parent-child relationship in the context of a probate or wrongful death case. This is also true as to the federal immigration regulations dealing with adoption. Moreover, the court in *In re Timothy W.*, (1990) 223 Cal.App.3d 437, stated that "children have no constitutional right to be adopted." Since adoption law is "purely statutory," and since those statutes change like the weather, the reader is urged to always have a current edition of the California Family Code close at hand, and to always consult the relevant applicable statutes, regulations and case law before advising a client or providing written or oral statements to a court or agency.

Although adoption proceedings are wholly statutory, the California Supreme Court has held that the rule of the common law, that statutes in derogation thereof are to be strictly construed, has no application to adoption statutes, in that their provisions are to be liberally construed with a view to effect its objects and to promote justice. (*Adoption of Barnett*, (1960) 54 Cal.2d 370.) Moreover, while *Barnett* references "common law," there is no English common law on the subject of adoption, and England had no adoption statute until 1926. Perhaps that is why Charles Dickens had so much material to include in his novels.

California has had adoption statutes in effect since 1872. Therefore, while adoption law nationwide is diverse, the fundamentals can be learned by studying California's jurisprudence. Only Mississippi, Texas, Vermont and Massachusetts have had adoption laws in place longer than California, with Mississippi's 1846 law being the oldest. Also, since California has so many appellate courts, California case law covers adoption in greater detail than any of the 50 states. In addition, since the U.S. State Department's annual statistics show that California residents always complete more intercountry adoptions than those any other state, California is the best backdrop for a study of the federal and state laws relating to intercountry adoptions. Finally, the California Legislature has led the way in applying new concepts in adoption law.

As stated in *Santos*, the two main objects of California's adoption statutes are to promote the welfare of children, and to provide legal recognition for the closest conceivable counterpart of the relationship of parent and child. *Barnett* and *Santos* are the mainstays of California adoption law. These two decisions are cited in many recent appellate opinions, such as the 2003 *Sharon S.* decision. Therefore, since the underlying policies have remained relatively constant, most of the fundamental doctrines of adoption law are stable enough to allow for course study.

Effective in 1994, California's adoption statutes underwent wholesale re-codification, and were transferred from the "Civil Code" to the new "Family Code." However, the California Legislature enacted Family Code § 2 to express the Legislature's *general* intent to leave the law substantively unchanged. *Sharon S.* reiterates that there is no substantive difference between the relevant sections of the Family Code and their predecessors in the Civil Code.

In handling an adoption, agencies, courts and court clerks expect the parties to use the standard forms provided by the California Judicial Council, the CDSS, the USCIS, and other relevant entities. In many instances, papers will not be accepted for filing unless the appropriate standard form is used. The forms are provided at the web sites of the California Judicial Council (http://www.courtinfo.ca.gov/forms), the CDSS (http://www.dss.cahwnet.gov/cdssweb/on-linefor_271.htm) and the USCIS (http://www.immigration.gov). At the time this practice guide was written, the forms were available for downloading at no charge. The forms which are now available are too numerous to reprint in this practice guide, however specific forms will be referred to in this book according to the form number provided at the web sites. Most other states also provide standard forms as well, but the reader is warned that the laws of the other states are widely divergent, and the forms do not always explain these differences in the law.

Very little of this book is devoted to the history of adoption law. The ancient Romans had a form of adoption law, and several adopted children later became Roman emperors, but Roman adoption law is dissimilar to that which is applied modernly. See, Presser, *The Historical Background of the American Law of Adoption*, 11 J.FAM.L. 443 (1971); Huard, *The Law of Adoption: Ancient and Modern*, 9 VAND.L.REV. 743 (1956); Brosnan, *The Law of Adoption*, 22 COLUM.L.REV. 332 (1922). Since the contemporary jurisprudence makes no reference whatsoever to English or Roman law, a study of the history of adoption law should be reserved for another book.

Many aspects of juvenile dependency law, which includes foster care and is codified at California Welfare and Institutions Code § 300, et seq., is touched upon in this book. Guardianships are also discussed generally. However, guardianships, foster placements and adoptions are distinctly different. On the other hand, these three areas of law are inextricably intertwined. But in order to organize a text that can be meaningfully used in a one semester class that fully covers and primarily focuses on adoption law, such a text can only provide a brief survey of guardianship law and juvenile dependency law. Nonetheless, the law student's maxim still applies: "Whoever wishes to be a juris-consult, let him [or her] continually study, and desire to be taught by every one." (See *Black's Law Dict.*, 5th Ed., p.1125.)

Prof. Everett L. Skillman

Augustus Caesar was adopted by his great-uncle Gaius Julius Caesar in 44 BC by means of a testamentary adoption, which is not recognized in the State of California.

THE LEGAL EFFECT OF THE ADOPTION DECREE 1

In this chapter:

The boy originally named Leslie Lynch King, Jr. had his name changed to Gerald Rudolff Ford, Jr. by his mother and stepfather. He is commonly regarded as the first adopted person to become President, but he was never formally adopted. In 1975, he signed into law sweeping amendments to the immigration statutes, paving the way for international adoptions

I. THE CREATION OF THE NEW PARENT-CHILD RELATIONSHIP

A. The New Relationship of the Child –

1. – to the Adoptive Parents

After an adoption order is entered, the adopted child and the adoptive parents sustain towards each other the legal relationship of parent and child, and enjoy all of the rights and are subject to all of the duties of that relationship. (Family Code §§ 7601 and 8616; *In re Santos' Estate*, (1921) 185 Cal. 127.) For example, an adoption affects estate tax planning issues (such as credits or exemptions for property passed to a "family member"), insurance coverage issues (like the "family member" exclusion on homeowners policies), the right to recover for wrongful death, liability in personal injury cases for "negligent supervision," educational decision-making for the child, and other areas.

2. – to the Birth Parents

Family Code § 8617 states that the birth parents of an adopted child are, from the time of the adoption, relieved of all parental duties towards, and all responsibility for, the adopted child, and have no right over the child. However, in *Sharon S. v. Superior Court*, (2003) 31 Cal.4th 417, the California Supreme Court held that it is not mandatory to apply Family Code § 8617 in all adoptions, and that the birth parent's right to have her parental relationship terminated by the adoption may be waived, since it is not jurisdictional. Likewise, Family Code § 8548 provides for this same result in the context of a stepparent adoption.

Sharon S. approves of "second parent adoptions," i.e., independent adoptions that have the effect of a stepparent adoption, but which do not require the adopting parent to be the spouse or domestic partner of the custodial birth parent. However, the *Sharon S.* court stated that birth parents are otherwise presumed to desire to be relieved of all parental duties towards, and all responsibility for, the adopted child. Second parent adoptions are examined in Chapter 8.

B. In Rem Nature of the Adoption Decree

1. In Rem Jurisdiction in Adoption Cases

Adoption of Barnett, (1960) 54 Cal.2d 370, which concerned a petition for an independent adoption, held that an adoption proceeding creates a status and is therefore "in rem." In *County of Los Angeles v. Superior Court*, (1969) 2 Cal.App.3d 1059, the court held that the in rem nature of adoption applies to both independent adoptions and agency adoptions. As such, a court order granting an adoption petition constitutes a judicial declaration that is binding on the whole world, just as a divorce decree binds the whole world as to the parties' marital status.

2. What is "In Rem" Jurisdiction?

In rem jurisdiction is exercised in probate cases. In one probate case involving a disputed "equitable adoption," it was stated, "By giving the notice prescribed by the statute, the entire world is called before the court, and the court acquires jurisdiction over all persons for the purpose of determining their rights to any portion of the estate, and every person who may assert any right or interest therein is required to present his claim to the court for its determination. Whether he appears and presents his claim, or fails to appear, the action of the court is equally conclusive upon him, subject only to being reversed, set aside, or modified on appeal." *In re Radovich's Estate*, (1957) 48 Cal.2d 116.

In *Radovich*, the probate court held that the equitable status of the adoption of the son was established where the evidence showed a consent (oral agreement) by the birth parents and an acceptance by adoptive father, thereby giving rise to inheritance rights. The Supreme Court stated that even if the viability of the doctrine of equitable adoption is in doubt, the probate court's in rem decision was binding on the whole world, even as to a state taxing agency that was not a "party" to the probate proceeding.

C. Child Support Obligation

1. Generally

According to Family Code § 3900, the father and mother generally have an equal responsibility to support their child in the manner suitable to the child's circumstances. Under Family Code § 3901(a), this statutory duty requires a parent to support his or her unmarried child until the child attains the age of 18 years or graduates high school (whichever occurs last, if the child is a full-time high school student who is not self-supporting), unless the child has attained the age of 19 years. In addition, under Family Code § 3910(a), the father and mother have an equal responsibility to maintain, to the extent of their ability, a child of whatever age who is incapacitated from earning a living and without sufficient means.

2. Additional Support

Family Code § 3901(b) expressly states that a parent has the legal ability to agree to provide additional support, and the court has the power to inquire as to whether an agreement to provide additional support has been made.

3. Unconditional Duty to Support

Family Code § 3556 provides that a noncustodial parent's duty to support the child is not affected by the custodial parent's failure or refusal to implement any court-ordered custody or visitation rights.

4. Ending of Support Duty upon Termination of Rights

An adoption extinguishes the birth parent's obligation to support the child, since that is one of the "duties" that is terminated at the adoption under Family Code § 8617. However, although adoptions terminate child support duties, the Supreme Court declared in *Marshall v. Marshall*, (1925) 196 Cal. 761, that one may not complete an adoption of his or her own child for the purpose of terminating the other parent's support duty. Further, an adoption does not discharge the obligation to pay past child support in arrears.

Importantly, in *Helmig v. Dunmore*, (2000) 83 Cal.App.4th 1, the court held that an interlocutory ruling under Family Code § 8604 (that the birth parent's consent was not necessary for an adoption) did not relieve that birth parent of his child support obligation, since the adoption order had not yet been issued. The *Helmig* court also noted that a Family Code § 8604 finding that consent was unnecessary was not the equivalent of a termination of parental rights because of abandonment under Family Code § 7822.

Helmig held that there is a difference between a termination of parental rights and a judicial declaration that an alleged father's consent is not necessary to the adoption. In addition, the automatic termination of the duty to support becomes an issue in stepparent adoptions, which are discussed more fully in Chapter 8. Suffice it to say here that where a natural parent loses parental rights by virtue of a stepparent adoption, that natural parent's duty to pay all unmet past child support obligations remains in effect, but that that natural parent's continuing accrual of future child support obligations ends.

II. INHERITANCE RIGHTS

A. Intestate Succession between Adoptive Parent and Child

In determining intestate succession, the relationship of parent and child exists under Probate Code § 6450(b) between an adopted person and the person's adopting parent or parents. This rule applies with regard to intestate succession by, through, or from any person.

B. Severing Intestacy between Child and Natural Parent

With certain exceptions, Probate Code § 6451 states that the adoption severs the relationship between the child and the natural parents for the purpose of determining intestate succession. Probate Code § 6451(c) also states that a "prior adoptive parent and child relationship" (such as where one child was adopted on two different occasions) is treated as a natural parent and child relationship. The exceptions to the rule severing prior relationships are as follows:

1. Exception for Stepparent Adoption and the Death of a Natural Parent Prior to an Adoption

Probate Code § 6451(a) provides that the adoption does not sever the parent-child relationship between an adopted person and his or her natural parent where, (1) the natural parent and the adopted person lived together at any time as parent and child, or the natural parent was married to or cohabiting with the other natural parent at the time the person was conceived and died before the person's birth, and (2) the adoption was by the spouse of either of the natural parents or after the death of either of the natural parents. Probate Code § 6451(b) appears to require there to be a stepparent adoption in order to qualify under this exception. See *In re Estate of Dye*, (2001) 92 Cal.App.4th 966.

More specifically, Family Code § 9004 states that in a stepparent adoption, the form prescribed by the department for the consent of the birth parent shall state: "If you and your child lived together at any time as parent and child, the adoption of your child by a stepparent does not affect the child's right to inherit your property or the property of other blood relatives."

2. Exception for Wholeblood Sibling of the Adoptee

Probate Code § 6451(b) also carves out an exception for a wholeblood brother or sister of the adopted person or the issue of that brother or sister, stating that such a person's relationship to the adopted person is not severed by the adoption for intestate succession purposes.

C. Testamentary Provisions

1. Status under the Omitted Child Statutes

Probate Code § 21620 provides that if a will fails to provide for a child adopted after the will was created, the omitted child "shall receive a share in the decedent's estate equal in value to that which the child would have received if the decedent had died without having executed any testamentary instrument." In *Estate of Mowry*, (2003) 107 Cal.App.4th 338, the court held that Probate Code § 21620 does not apply to children adopted before the will was executed. Also, Probate Code § 21621 states that the child shall not receive a share if the omission of the child from the will was intentional and that that intent appears from the testamentary instruments.

2. Applicable Law Where Statutes Have Been Amended

Over the past few decades, the Probate Code has undergone several major revisions. In the context of interpreting a will to determine whether a person is a testamentary beneficiary by virtue of a parent-child relationship that was created by an adoption, the courts look to the law as it existed when the will was created in determining testamentary intent. In *Newman v. Wells Fargo Bank*, (1996) 14 Cal.4th 126, the Supreme Court held that the then-current version of what is now Probate Code § 6451(a), which allows adopted persons to inherit through their natural parents under certain circumstances, was not applicable in interpreting a will that was drafted at a time when that law did not exist in any form. The Supreme Court held that, in determining whether a person was a beneficiary of a class gift, the provisions of the law in effect when the decedent executed her will and died in 1972 controlled the interpretation of the will, and not the 1985 statutory amendments, since the former version of the law presumably would better carry out the testator's intent.

Further analysis of *Newman* tends to show that under most circumstances a person who was adopted would be considered "issue" of the adoptive parent in interpreting a will that was drafted under the current law of California.

D. Equitable Adoption

While Probate Code § 6455 assumes that there is a "judicial doctrine of equitable adoption," the law is unclear as to what an "equitable adoption" is. All 50 states and the District of Columbia generally require that the adoption be finalized in some way by a court order. On the other hand, a majority of the states make allowance for an equitable adoption to serve as the basis of an individual's right to inherit through an intestate decedent. However, where parent and child are both alive, it does not appear that any state allows a parent-child relationship to be recognized solely through an equitable adoption. (But see, *Kaho v. Ilchert*, (9th Cir. 1985) 765 F.2d 877 [recognizing an equitable adoption under the law of Tonga for immigration purposes].) Moreover, in *In re*

Grace's Estate, (1948) 88 Cal.App.2d 956, the court held that the determination of whether an equitable adoption occurred is determined by the laws of the state where it allegedly occurred.

1. Equitable Adoption vis-à-vis Adoptive Parent's Death

In *In re Estate of Ford*, (2004) 32 Cal.4th 160, the California Supreme Court interpreted Probate Code § 6455 and held that the doctrine of equitable adoption allows a foster child who was accepted and treated as a natural or adopted child, and as to whom adoption typically was promised or contemplated but never performed, to share in the inheritance of the foster parents' property. However, *Ford* also states that California's version of the doctrine of equitable adoption rests on "contract principles," and does not recognize an estoppel arising merely from the existence of a *de facto* "familial" relationship between the decedent and the claimant.

Ford ruled that while a California equitable adoption claimant need not prove all the elements of an enforceable contract to adopt, the claimant must demonstrate the existence of some direct expression, on the decedent's part, of an intent to adopt the claimant, and may show such intent by proof of (1) an unperformed express agreement, or (2) a promise to adopt, or (3) some other acts or statements directly showing that the decedent intended the child to be, or to be treated as, a legally adopted child. The intent to adopt the claimant may be proved by an attempt to adopt (even if invalid or unconsummated), the decedent's statement of his or her intent to adopt the child, or the decedent's representation to the claimant or to the community at large that the claimant was the decedent's natural or legally adopted child. *Ford* also holds that an equitable adoption claimant must show that the decedent acted consistently with that intent by forming with the claimant a close and enduring familial relationship. Finally, the *Ford* court ruled that the claimant has the burden to prove these matters by clear and convincing evidence.

2. Equitable Adoption in the Context of the Child's Death

In *Reynolds v. City of Los Angeles*, (1986) 176 Cal.App.3d 1044, the court held that the equitable adoption doctrine connotes an oral consensual agreement between parties not otherwise incapacitated from entering into a contract, who then agree that the child should be adopted. The *Reynolds* court reasoned that when the child "performs" the contract, a species of equitable estoppel results. It would appear that the "oral consensual agreement" language of *Reynolds* is superseded by *In re Estate of Ford*, (2004) 32 Cal.4th 160, although the California Supreme Court did not expressly overrule *Reynolds*. In any event, under the *Reynolds* analysis, the child is required to be a "party" to that consensual agreement.

Reynolds was a wrongful death case involving the demise of a 17-year-old boy in a car accident, and *Reynolds* appears to apply a formulation of the equitable adoption doctrine that was fashioned for a case involving the death of a parent. Consequently, the plaintiff in *Reynolds* could not satisfy the rule, since the child was an infant when the equitable adoption took place.

The putative adoptive father in *Reynolds* unsuccessfully argued that an equitable adoption had occurred by virtue of his reliance on the birth parents' consent to allow him to be the full custodial "father" of the child (who was an infant at that time) and an unsigned "order" from a court in England. However, the unsigned order appeared to only give him custody for the purpose of completing an adoption proceeding in the United States, which the putative adoptive father failed to do. *Reynolds* also rejects the argument that the child was the intended third party beneficiary of the contract between his caretakers and the court in Great Britain, since the right to make such an argument belongs only to the third party, in this case the child who died in the automobile accident.

The *Reynolds* court also examined *Steed v. Imperial Airlines*, (1974) 12 Cal.3d 115, in which the plaintiff in the wrongful death case was a minor who was the stepchild of the decedent, and who was never formally adopted by the decedent during his lifetime. While the *Steed* decedent's wife and legitimate child were permitted to pursue a wrongful death action, the stepchild was not allowed to sue for wrongful death, because no evidence was introduced of an oral consensual agreement on the part of the decedent to treat the stepchild as his own child.

Statutory adoptions are most often completed when the child is of tender years, and it is the rare case where the child's formal consent is required under Family Code § 8602 by virtue of the child being 12 years of age or older. Since the vast majority of statutory adoptions are completed without the child's formal consent, it is unclear why the plaintiff in *Reynolds* was told he failed to prove that the child "consented," especially since the child accepted all of the benefits of being raised by the putative adoptive father for a continuous period of 17 years.

3. De Facto Adoption through the Uniform Parentage Act

As explained in Chapter 3, Family Code § 7611(d), which is part of the Uniform Parentage Act, provides that one may be judicially recognized as the parent of a particular child simply by receiving the child in one's home and holding the child out as one's own, even in the absence of a biological connection with the child. This judicial recognition of parental rights in a non-biological parent, which is the essence of an adoption, can occur in a proceeding not brought for the primary purpose of an adoption.

In *In re Nicholas H.*, (2002) 28 Cal.4th 56, the California Supreme Court held that a man who was admittedly not the biological father of the child could still be deemed to be the child's presumed father pursuant to Family Code § 7611(d). Importantly, *Nicholas H.* did not involve a paternity contest between two men, but was a juvenile court proceeding under Welfare & Institutions Code § 300, et seq., in which the only man involved in the child's life was claiming parental rights. In *Nicholas H.*, Kimberly and Jason, who were not married, conceived Nicholas, and then separated. Kimberly then took up residence with Thomas. Kimberly and Thomas "wanted Thomas to act as a father to Nicholas, so Thomas participated in Nicholas's birth, was listed on Nicholas's birth certificate as his father, and provided a home for Kimberly and Nicholas for several years." However, Kimberly became involved in drug use, transiency and violence towards others, prompting the county social services agency to detain the child and place him in the foster care system. Since Jason could not be located, his paternity could not be established. During the proceedings, the juvenile court judge stated, "If I were to agree with County Counsel that Thomas's admission that he is not Nicholas's biological father rebuts the presumption, then what we would be doing is leaving Nicholas fatherless." The juvenile court determined that Thomas was the presumed father, and vacated its prior order that Jason must submit to a paternity test.

The *Nicholas H.* court noted that where the presumptions arising under the Uniform Parentage Act would give rise to conflicting conclusions, Family Code § 7612(b) requires the trier of fact to choose "the presumption which on the facts is founded on the weightier considerations of policy and logic." In *Nicholas H.*, the Supreme Court simply affirmed the juvenile court's finding that the man with no biological link was the child's presumed father.

A similar result occurred in *In re Marriage of Pedregon*, (2003) 107 Cal.App.4th 1284. However, *Pedregon* was a child support proceeding in which a man who was not the child's biological father was deemed, over his objection, to be the child's presumed father. The court held that the non-biological father's statements and conduct toward the child over the years gave rise to a kind of parenthood by estoppel. However, the doctrine of parentage by estoppel does not apply to man who mistakenly believed he was the child's father. (*County of San Diego v. Arzaga* (2007) 152 Cal.App.4th 1336.) Parentage by estoppel is different from parentage by collateral estoppel arising from a judgment. (See *Kristine H. v. Lisa R.* (2005) 37 Cal.4th 156.)

In *In re Karen C.*, (2002) 101 Cal.App.4th 932, the court held that a woman who was genetically unrelated to the child was entitled to the presumption of maternity since she had raised the child and held her out as her own. Karen (the child) was conceived by Alicia and Jose P., a married couple, but was said to be unwanted. Through an "intermediary," Alicia unsuccessfully attempted an "untherapeutic third-trimester abortion," and she ultimately "gave Karen to Leticia promptly after Karen was born" at a county hospital, where Alicia had falsely told hospital staff that her own name was Leticia, so that Leticia's name would be listed on Karen's birth certificate as Karen's birth mother. (The courts have the authority to correct an original birth certificate. (*Wynn v. Superior Court* (2009) 176 Cal.App.4th 346.))

The *Karen C.* facts also included that Leticia then raised Karen as her own child for more than a decade, and told Karen that Karen was adopted. Karen had no contact with her natural parents, who later moved to Guatemala. Leticia later suffered from alcoholism and Karen found herself in the foster care system. During the proceedings associated with the foster care (see Chapter 6), Leticia asserted that she was Karen's "parent" and was entitled to certain rights in that proceeding. The juvenile court disagreed. However, the appellate court reversed and directed the juvenile court to analyze Leticia's assertion of parental rights pursuant to the *Nicholas H.* decision. The *Karen C.* court issued a disclaimer that it was offering no opinion as to the enforceability of what it termed a "de facto adoption."

In *In re Estate of Chambers*, (2009) 175 Cal.App.4th 891, the court held that where a putative heir seeks to assert that he or she was the child of the decedent because the decedent "receive[d] the child into his home and openly [held] out the child as his natural child" (see Family Code § 7611(d)), the putative heir must prove these facts by clear and convincing evidence. This result is dictated by Probate Code § 6453(b) and Family Code § 7630(c).

E. Inheritance from or through a Foster Parent or Stepparent

1. Generally

There is no statute which allows a person to inherit by intestate succession merely by virtue of a stepparent-stepchild relationship. Until the stepparent adopts the child, there is no legally recognized parent-child relationship. The same is true with the foster parent-dependent child relationship, since the arrangement is at the mercy of the county social services agency and the court involved in the dependency proceeding. As explained in Chapter 6 of this book, foster parenting in California occurs where the agency first detains a child due to the natural parents' neglect or abuse of the child (as defined by Welfare & Institutions Code § 300), and then places the child in the foster parent care so as to simulate the kind of family setting that the child needs.

2. "Legal Barrier to Adoption"

On the other hand, Probate Code § 6454 states that, for the purpose of determining intestate succession, the relationship of parent and child exists between a person and his or her foster parent or stepparent, if two essential elements are satisfied: (a) The "relationship" began during the person's minority and continued throughout the joint lifetimes of the person and his or her foster parent or stepparent, and (b) it is established by clear and convincing evidence that the foster parent or stepparent would have adopted the person but for a legal barrier.

Estate of Joseph, (1998) 17 Cal.4th 203, holds that the "legal barrier" must have been the "necessary" cause of the failure to adopt. It also held that Probate Code § 6454 requires the "legal barrier" to adoption of the foster child or stepchild to have begun during the foster child or stepchild's minority, and to have continued throughout the joint lifetimes of the foster child or stepchild and the foster parent or stepparent. The Supreme Court stated that one such "legal barrier" would have consisted of the birth parent's refusal to consent to the adoption. However, the foster child in *Joseph* was an adult, and the decedent, who was a widower at his death, could have established a parent/child relationship with his former foster child by way of an adult adoption (which does not require consent of the natural parents).

Joseph also adds a judicially-created "intent" element to the Probate Code § 6454: Using the causation language of Probate Code § 6454(b) as support, the *Joseph* court held that the "intent to adopt must have continued" throughout the joint lifetimes of the parties.

F. Wrongful Death Suits

1. Statutory Basis for Standing

California's wrongful death statute (Code of Civil Procedure § 377.60(a)) gives several persons, including those "who would be entitled to the property of the decedent by intestate succession," standing to sue for damages. Based on Code of Civil Procedure § 377.60(a), it would appear that those who would qualify to inherit by intestate succession by virtue of any of the rules mentioned above would be able to sue for wrongful death. Of course, one who has standing to sue still must prove all of the other elements of the cause of action.

2. Standing to Sue Where Parental Rights are Terminated

In *Fraizer v. Velkura*, (2001) 91 Cal.App.4th 942, the court held that the natural grandmother of a child whose parent's rights were terminated under Welfare & Institutions Code § 366.26 had standing to sue for the alleged wrongful death of the child. Unlike the effect of a termination order vis-à-vis visitation rights, the *Fraizer* court refused to hold that the termination order operated as a universal termination of all legal bonds between the child and the birth family. On the other hand, the *Fraizer* court recognized that a grandparent would not have standing to sue if parental rights were still intact, for example where the child was merely in the custody of a guardian.

3. The "Children's" Standing to Sue

In addition to heirs, the wrongful death statute gives "children" standing. However, in *Phraner v. Cote Mart, Inc.*, (1997) 55 Cal.App.4th 166, the court held that an adopted child had no standing to sue for the alleged wrongful death of the child's biological mother.

Phraner reasons that an adoption severs the parent-child relationship with the natural mother, and that the allegation that the minor and the natural mother maintained a "close relationship" after the adoption does not confer standing to sue. None of the Probate Code exceptions allowed the child to be an intestate heir of the natural mother since: (a) the child was placed for adoption at birth and never lived with the natural mother, (b) neither adoptive parent was ever married to the minor's natural mother or father, and (c) the natural mother did not die before the minor's birth. Finally, *Phraner* held that its construction of the wrongful death statute did not violate equal protection, since the distinction drawn by the Legislature was not irrational.

As far as questioning the plaintiff's standing, *Scott v. Thompson*, (2010) 184 Cal.App.4th 1506, held that where the plaintiff is admittedly only the decedent's presumed father, the decedent's natural sister lacks standing. The court held that under the Uniform Parentage Act (i.e., Family Code §§ 7611(a) and 7630(a)), only the child, the child's natural mother, another man presumed to be the child's father, an adoption agency to whom the child has been relinquished, or a prospective adoptive parent of the child may challenge presumed fatherhood.

III. GUARDIANSHIPS

A. Contrasting Adoption with Guardianship Generally

One way to understand the nature of an adoption decree is to contrast it with a guardianship order. Guardianships are generally ordered for the purpose of protecting the ward during his or her period of incapacity to protect himself or herself. (See, *Oyama v. California*, (1948) 332 U.S. 633.) In addition, *In re Santos' Estate*, (1921) 185

Cal. 127, holds that the status of guardian and ward falls short of the close approximation to the relationship of parent and child which is attainable through an adoption, since the minor is in reality a ward of the court, and the guardian is in effect an arm of the court, and is subject to the control of the court in the discharge of his or her duties as guardian.

Santos also holds that since the adoptive parents acquire superior rights to the custody of the child, the reasons for the existence of the guardianship cease and the continuation thereof is no longer appropriate. However, *Santos* also states that even after the adoption, a "guardianship of the estate" of the child may remain in existence in the court's discretion. In the interest of staying within the subject of adoption law, this book will only briefly touch upon guardianships. In addition, this book will only deal with guardianships of the "person" of the child, and not merely of the "estate," as in *Suleman v. Superior Court*, (2010) 180 Cal.App.4th 1287.

While the statutes governing guardianship evince an intent to provide a temporary arrangement for the child, the case law interpreting those statutes could give rise to a more permanent custody order. In addition, guardianship law should not be ignored in that guardianships can play a major role in many adoption proceedings, especially independent adoptions, as will be seen in the following chapter, and in proceedings to dispense with the birth parent's consent to the adoption pursuant to Family Code § 7800.

1. Temporary v. Permanent

While the parent/child relationship continues after the adoption, even after the death of all of the parties, Probate Code § 1600(a) states that a guardianship terminates when the ward attains majority or dies. In addition, Probate Code § 1600(b) provides that a guardianship of the person terminates upon the adoption of the ward or upon the emancipation of the ward under Family Code § 7002. Furthermore, Probate Code § 1601 allows the guardian, a parent, or the ward to petition the court for an order terminating the guardianship if it is shown that it is no longer necessary that the ward have a guardian or that it is in the ward's best interest to terminate the guardianship.

2. Continuing Jurisdiction v. Final Order

As stated in *In re Guardianship of Simpson*, (1998) 67 Cal.App.4th 914, after the guardianship order has been issued, a motion may be filed in the same case to vacate the guardianship when it can be demonstrated that the parent is fit to reassume custody, and there is no statute of limitations restricting such a motion.

3. Whether there is a Need for Consent

The "consent" issue is treated differently in guardianships, as opposed to adoptions, as demonstrated by comparing the apparently summarily approved stipulation in *In re Guardianship of Simpson*, (1998) 67 Cal.App.4th 914, with the interviews, counseling, home studies and other formalities that accompany a consent to an adoption (as explained in Chapter 3 of this book). In addition, where there is an involuntary guardianship, there is no termination of parental rights, meaning that concerns about constitutional rights are not as critical.

4. Whether there is a Change in Inheritance Rights

There is no provision for intestate inheritance rights to or from a guardian. Of course, the guardian may execute a will leaving an inheritance to the child. In *Lewis v. Regional Center of the East Bay*, (1985) 174 Cal.App.3d 350, a guardian lacked standing to assert a wrongful death claim concerning the child, even though the guardians were also the child's grandparents.

5. Whether there is Restricted Access to Documents

Like adoptions, guardianship proceedings are closed to the public, and the records of a guardianship are not open for public inspection. However, the statutes dealing with access to documents are much more detailed in the context of adoption than they are with guardianships, as explained further in Chapters 10 and 12.

B. Relationship between Guardianships and Adoptions

1. Standing to File Petition for Independent Adoption

Family Code § 8802(a)(1)(D)(i) and (iii) state that a person who has been the legal guardian of the child for one year has standing to file a petition to adopt the child, but the guardianship is required to have been in place for three years if it was instituted for a purpose other than adoption or if it was instituted during the course of dependency proceedings (see Chapter 6). Family Code § 8802(a)(1)(D)(ii) provides that a guardian may have standing to file a petition for independent adoption if the guardianship has been in place for six months, and the child has been "abandoned" within the meaning of Family Code § 7822. According to Probate Code § 1516.5(a), the child's guardian may bring a proceeding, within the guardianship case itself, to free the child from the parents' control and custody pursuant to Family Code § 7800, et seq. The concept of "abandonment" is discussed in Chapter 6 of this book.

2. Exclusive Jurisdiction in Interstate Adoptions

In *Adoption of Zachariah K.*, (1992) 6 Cal.App.4th 1025, the court held that an Oregon couple who validly brought a newborn infant from California to Oregon with the birth mother's initial consent, and then obtained a guardianship order from the Oregon court with the birth mother's consent less than two months after the child's birth, thereby conferred exclusive jurisdiction upon the Oregon courts to decide issues concerning the child. Therefore, the birth mother's filing of a petition in a California court to withdraw her consent under laws then in existence was of no effect, pursuant to the federal Parental Kidnapping Prevention Act and what was then the Uniform Child Custody Jurisdiction Act. These jurisdictional statutes, plus Family Code § 9210 and the current Uniform Child Custody Jurisdiction and Enforcement Act, are discussed in Chapter 9.

3. Necessary Disclosures in the Petitions

Under Probate Code § 1510(f), if the petitioner has knowledge of any pending adoption, juvenile court, marriage dissolution, domestic relations, custody, or other similar proceeding affecting the proposed ward, the petition shall disclose the pending proceeding. The adoption statutes contain the mirror image of these provisions as explained in the chapters which follow.

Probate Code § 1510(g) states that if the petitioners have accepted or intend to accept physical care or custody of the child with intent to adopt, whether formed at the time of placement or formed subsequent to placement, the petitioners shall so state in the guardianship petition, whether or not an adoption petition has been filed.

In addition, Probate Code § 1510(h) provides that if the proposed ward is or becomes the subject of an adoption petition, the court shall order the guardianship petition consolidated with the adoption petition.

4. Issues in the Guardianship Proceeding

Probate Code § 1514(a) allows the court to appoint a guardian if, upon hearing the petition, it appears "necessary or convenient." In determining whether guardianship is necessary or convenient, the court is to be guided solely by what appears to be for the best interest of the child in respect to its temporal and mental and moral welfare. *San Diego County Dept. of Pub. Welfare v. Superior Court*, (1972) 7 Cal.3d 1. In *In re Case's Guardianship*, (1943) 57 Cal.App.2d 844, the court held that when the appointment of a guardian for a minor of tender years is found to be necessary, such appointment is actually a duty of the Superior Court. However, when it appears that a guardianship is no longer necessary for such ward, the court must thereupon remove the guardian. Inasmuch as a natural parent has a superior right to the custody of his child when possessed of such character as to make him a fit custodian thereof, the reason for the guardianship of the minor ceases and its continuance is improper. Also, Probate Code § 1514(b) states that in appointing a guardian of the person, the court is governed by Family Code § 3040, et seq., which states the "parental preference doctrine" relating to the custody of a minor.

On the other hand, *In re Guardianship of Simpson*, (1998) 67 Cal.App.4th 914, provides a different way of handling the termination of a guardianship by court order (as opposed to the termination of a guardianship by operation of the events described in Probate Code § 1600). The court stated that the burden in a contested guardianship termination proceeding is not upon the guardians to show that there would be detriment to the child if returned to the natural parent, but that it is upon the noncustodial parent to show "overall fitness" on his or her part "sufficient to overcome the inherent trauma of removing a successful caregiver."

In *Simpson*, a voluntary guardianship was established by stipulation for Sydney and Justin Simpson after their father, O.J. Simpson, was jailed on the charge of murdering Nicole Brown Simpson, their mother, and another victim, Ron Goldman. O.J.'s incarceration lasted 17 months, and when released upon his acquittal, he promptly filed a petition to terminate the guardianship pursuant to Probate Code § 1601, asserting that there was "no further need" for it. The *Guardianship of Simpson* court first explained there was no res judicata or collateral estoppel effect from the acquittal in the murder trial (which used a "beyond a reasonable doubt" burden of proof) or from the verdict against the father in the civil wrongful death trial (which used a "preponderance of the evidence" burden of proof). The major issue was whether evidence of the mother's murder should have been admitted in the guardianship case.

The *Simpson* court relied on *Guardianship of Smith*, (1957) 147 Cal.App.2d 686, wherein the appellate court upheld the trial judge's allowance of the entire record of a murder trial into evidence at a guardianship proceeding, despite the child's mother's acquittal on the murder charges, and the trial judge's use of the evidence contained in that record as the basis of its decision to maintain the guardianship. Also citing *Guardianship of Kassandra H.*, (1998) 64 Cal.App.4th 1228, the *Simpson* court stated that the totality of evidence bearing on the father's fitness should have been examined, with the burden upon him to show sufficient overall fitness to justify the termination of the guardianship. Pursuant to its ruling that the murder evidence should have been admitted, the *Simpson* court stated that Probate Code § 1601 provides the standards a court should analyze when terminating a voluntary guardianship; not the Family Code § 3041 parental preference doctrine.

5. Burden of Proof in a Guardianship Proceeding

As stated in *In re Guardianship of Simpson*, (1998) 67 Cal.App.4th 914, where the issues involve a contested request for a court-ordered termination of a guardianship, the burden is on the noncustodial parent to show by the totality of the evidence a sufficient overall fitness to justify the termination of the guardianship. The *Simpson* court took note of *In re B.G.*, (1974) 11 Cal.3d 679, which held that in the creation of a guardianship, the standard of proof would be for the guardians to show by clear and convincing evidence that it was detrimental to allow the child to stay with the natural parent, which is essentially the "parental preference doctrine" now codified at Family Code § 3041. The *Simpson* court distinguished *B.G.* by stating that this standard does not apply in a guardianship termination proceeding under Probate Code § 1601 following a voluntarily established guardianship.

However, there is a conflict in the case law. In *In re Case's Guardianship*, (1943) 57 Cal.App.2d 844, the noncustodial parent was in a naval prison at the time that the maternal grandmother was appointed guardian of the minor, and the noncustodial parent sought return of the child upon his release from the military and from incarceration. The appellate court held that it was incumbent upon the guardian to show that the guardianship was still "necessary or convenient" for the child.

THE BEST INTERESTS OF THE CHILD 2

In this chapter:

The biological mother of Steven Paul Jobs only wanted him to be adopted by college graduates. When she found out that Clara Jobs didn't graduate from college and that Paul Jobs only attended high school, she consented to the adoption only after they promised to encourage the boy to attend college.

I. GENERAL CONSIDERATIONS

A. The Child's Best Interests Are Paramount.

As set forth at Family Code § 8612(c), the court may only enter an order of adoption if it is satisfied that the interests of the child will be promoted by the adoption. The courts have held that the best interests of the child is the paramount consideration in any adoption proceeding. (*Matter of Bewley* (1914) 167 Cal. 8; *In re Adoption of Matthew B*., (1991) 232 Cal.App.3d 1239.) Furthermore, the best interests of the child is also significant for purposes of the Uniform Parentage Act (see Family Code § 7664(b), *Adoption of Kelsey S*., (1992) 1 Cal.4th 816), dependency proceedings (Welfare & Institutions Code § 366.26), and several other contexts, as explained in later chapters of this book. This chapter will analyze the specific pragmatic considerations taken into account in determining the best interests of the child.

B. Examples of the Priority of the Child's Best Interests

1. Statutory Requirements re Documentation

In *In re Adoption of Matthew B*., (1991) 232 Cal.App.3d 1239, and *Adoption of Barnett*, (1960) 54 Cal.2d 370, the courts held that the best interests of the child, which in those cases were to allow the children to remain with the only caretakers they had ever known and to continue to enjoy the stability of those family settings, overrode the statutory requirements concerning how the consent to the adoption was taken. The *Matthew B*. case dealt with a consent that was taken in light of what was then a questionable surrogacy contract, and *Barnett* dealt with the failure to notarize the natural mother's signature on the consent form.

2. Regulatory Requirements

In *Adoption of Michelle T*., (1975) 44 Cal.App.3d 699, the court held that the fact that the CDSS failed to comply with its own mandatory regulations and guidelines is not determinative of the best interests of the child. (See also, *Tyler v. Children's Home Society*, (1994) 29 Cal.App.4th 511.) *Tyler* involved a private agency's failure to provide certain counseling to the relinquishing birth parents as required by 22 California Code of Regulations § 35134(a), and held that the best interests of the child superseded these regulatory violations.

3. Stipulations

Although Family Code § 3011(e)(2) contemplates that the parties' written stipulations regarding custody or visitation supersede the court's consideration of various factors in a child custody proceeding, the same is not true in an adoption proceeding. In *In re Adoption of Matthew B*., (1991) 232 Cal.App.3d 1239, the court stated that the child's welfare is the controlling force in directing custody, and the courts will always look to this rather than to the subjective desires of the parties. The *Matthew B*. court held more specifically that the court is not required to award custody in conformity with such stipulations, since the courts are required to act in the child's best interests. *In re Marriage of Jackson*, (2006) 136 Cal.App.4th 980, holds that a court in a divorce case cannot enter a judgment terminating parental rights based solely upon the parties' stipulation that the child's mother or father relinquishes those rights, and that such a judgment is void for lack of subject matter jurisdiction.

4. Illegal Contracts and Unclean Hands

In *In re Adoption of Matthew B.*, (1991) 232 Cal.App.3d 1239, the court dealt with what was then the first impression issue of the validity of surrogacy contracts. The *Matthew B.* court stated that even if such contracts were assumed to be illegal (which they were later found not to be in *Johnson v. Calvert*, (1993) 5 Cal.4th 84), the state's paramount interest in the child's welfare overrides its interest in deterring illegal conduct. In a similar vein, in *San Diego County Dept. of Pub. Welfare v. Superior Court*, (1972) 7 Cal.3d 1, the Supreme Court held that in an adoption or guardianship proceeding, the question of unclean hands is subordinated to the primary concern, which is to determine what is in the best interest of the child.

It is unclear how far such statements can be applied. For example, baby selling and baby buying are criminal offenses. (see, Penal Code §§ 181 and 273; Family Code § 8610.) In *People v. Daniel*, (1987) 195 Cal.App.3d 623, the court upheld a felony conviction of a natural parent who violated Penal Code § 181. However, since *Daniel* was a criminal case, it did not answer any question about the child's fate. In addition, in some situations it may be in the best interests of the child to approve the adoption if the alternative of placing the baby back with the natural mother or father who "sold" the child is less favorable. One article posits that it is in the best interests of the child to provide an economic incentive to those birth parents who are ambivalent about keeping their child. See, Landes & Posner, *The Economics of the Baby Shortage*, 7 Journal of Legal Studies 323 (1978). This subject is discussed further in Chapter 3 with regard to the taking of the birth parent's consent to the adoption.

II. DETERMINING THE CHILD'S BEST INTERESTS

A. Generally

1. Relativity Standard

In *Adoption of Michelle T.*, (1975) 44 Cal.App.3d 699, the court held that the best interests of the child is an elusive guideline that belies rigid definition, but whose purpose is to "maximize a child's opportunity to develop into a stable, well-adjusted adult." The court also held that the concept of "best interests" presents a relative standard, in that the question is not whether a particular set of circumstances is in the best interest of the child, but whether a particular set of circumstances relative to an alternative set of circumstances is in the best interest of the child.

In *Michelle T.*, the alternatives presented were adoption by an aging couple or commitment of the two-year-old child to the foster care system. The court chose the adoption since there was a greater certainty that the child would be in a stable home. The court stated that the "best interest of the child" is a test which provides for "the least detrimental available alternative for safeguarding the child's growth and development," and that the "least detrimental alternative is that specific placement which maximizes, in accord with the child's sense of time and on the basis of short term predictions given the limitations of knowledge, his or her opportunity for being wanted and for maintaining on a continuing basis a relationship with at least one adult who is or will become his psychological parent."

2. Best Interests from the Standpoint of the Child

In re Adoption of Matthew B., (1991) 232 Cal.App.3d 1239, held that courts must weigh the best interests factors and make its findings solely from the standpoint of the child, and should not consider the feelings and desires of the contesting parties, except insofar as they affect the child's best interests. *In re Adoption of Schroetter*, (1968) 261 Cal.App.2d 365, states: "The purpose of adoption proceedings is to promote the welfare of the child; it is not to satisfy the desires of the proposed adoptive parents."

There is case law from other states providing that, without regard to age, the child's preferences are considered in ascertaining the best interest of the child. (See *Holley v. Adams*, (Tex. 1976) 544 S.W.2d 367, 371-372.) On the other hand, this is not to say that the child, no matter how young, is the decision-maker on the adoption petition. Rather, one could say that the trial judge, as the state's representative carrying out the state's *parens patriae* function in deciding what is best for the child, should want to know what the child desires, and why.

3. Factual Issues

Adoption of Michelle T., (1975) 44 Cal.App.3d 699, states that the issue of whether the adoption is in the best interests of the child is a fact question, and the decision of the trial court on this issue will not be set aside unless a clear abuse of discretion is shown. In addition, the court in *In re Adoption of Matthew B.*, (1991) 232 Cal.App.3d 1239, stated that the sum of intangibles which go into the "best interests" formula is also comprised in part of the demeanor, attitudes, intonation, sincerity and personality of the witnesses, which are factual issues. The *Matthew B.* court held that on the best interests issue, the substantial evidence test applies in reviewing the trial court's factual determinations, i.e., so long as substantial evidence supports the trial court's findings, its decision will be affirmed.

Along these lines, "best interests" could turn on factual conclusions drawn from conflicting evidence, i.e., expert testimony, which is what occurred in the *Matthew B.* case. The trial court's factual conclusions drawn from conflicting substantial evidence will be upheld on appeal. (*In re Adoption of Schroetter*, (1968) 261 Cal.App.2d 365.)

B. Factors Considered in the Best Interests Analysis

Although the paramount issue in any adoption is the child's best interests, there is no definitive California law which provides a discrete list of factors or essential elements used in determining those best interests. The closest the Legislature has come to doing so is Family Code § 3011, which applies in actions for custody or visitation. Importantly, the language of Family Code § 3011 clearly implies that its list of factors is not exhaustive. Further, additional factors are mentioned in the case law and in the regulations of various agencies, specifically as to the requirements for the home study and the agency assessment of the petitioners. In many instances, the child's best interests are completely dependent upon the suitability of the prospective adoptive parents and their home. These factors, and other factors drawn from case law, regulations and judicial decisions from other states, are explained in the text that follows.

Once the relevant factors are determined, the court must consider them all. A judge's emphasis upon one negative factor where all others are positive may constitute an abuse of discretion. (See *Adoption of Michelle T.*, (1975) 44 Cal.App.3d 699.) On the other hand, determining the weight assigned to each of the "best interests" factors is within the exclusive province of the trial court. (See *In re Adoption of Matthew B.*, (1991) 232 Cal.App.3d 1239.)

1. The Child's Emotional Needs

There is case law stating that family stability, continuity of environment, and loving relationships are the most important criteria for determining the best interests of the child. (See *In re Adoption of Matthew B.*, (1991) 232 Cal.App.3d 1239.)

a) Family Stability and Continuity of Environment

The importance of the continuity of the environment and the trauma to a young child caused by separation from its established home has been viewed by the courts as a serious consideration in adoption cases. (*Adoption of Michelle T.*, (1975) 44 Cal.App.3d 699.) The *Michelle T.* court relied heavily upon a work called "Beyond the Best Interests of the Child" by Goldstein, Freud & Solnit, and published in 1973, emphasizing the importance to a child of continuity of parental relationships. The Goldstein work states that changes or interruptions in this relationship cause the child to regress along the whole line of his affections, skills, achievements, and social adaptation, that upon separation, physical, emotional, intellectual, social, and moral growth does not happen without causing the child inevitable internal difficulties, and that the instability of all mental processes during the period of development needs to be offset by stability and uninterrupted support from external sources.

The court in *In re Adoption of Matthew B.*, (1991) 232 Cal.App.3d 1239, stated that the best interests determination also depends upon an inquiry into the heart of the parent-child relationship, and the ethical, emotional, and intellectual guidance the parent gives to the child throughout his formative years, and how best to provide continuity of attention, nurturing, and care. Thus, crucial to a best-interests determination is the importance of stability and continuity in the life of the child, and the harm that may result from disruption of established patterns of care and emotional bonds.

In addition, the courts have shown a significant amount of concern for sibling contact. (See, *In re Carmaleta B.*, (1978) 21 Cal.3d 482; *In re Melissa G.*, (1989) 213 Cal.App.3d 1082.) Also, Family Code § 8801(b), which deals with independent adoptions, requires disclosure as to whether other children or adults reside in the prospective adoptive home.

b) Emotional Bonding

In re Adoption of Matthew B., (1991) 232 Cal.App.3d 1239, states that the emotional and love attachments the parties have for the child and the child's mental and physical health are relevant to the "best interests" question. The *Matthew B.* court held that consideration of the best interests of the child shall include the extent of emotional bonding with the prospective adoptive parent or parents, as opposed to the extent of bonding or the potential to bond with the natural parent or parents.

c) Amount of Parental Contact with Child

Family Code § 3011(c) states that the court shall consider not only the nature of the parental contact, but the amount of the child's contact with the parents as well. This analysis therefore comprises a qualitative and quantitative examination.

2. Age of the Child

Family Code § 8602 states that the consent of a child, if over the age of 12 years, is necessary to the child's adoption. Otherwise, the child's consent is not legally required. However, there is no requirement that the adopted person be a minimum or maximum age. A newborn infant can be adopted, as can an adult (see Family Code §§ 9300, et seq.) As far as the relationship of the child's age to the best interests analysis, this would be a factor in determining the kind of bonding that would occur.

It does not appear that California law allows an unborn child to be adopted, based on the various requirements of the adoption statutes (the need to have the child physically "placed" with the prospective adoptive parents, the need to have the child present in the courtroom for examination at the adoption hearing, etc.). As explained in later chapters, a surrogacy arrangement is not considered to encompass an adoption.

3. The Child's Health, Safety and Welfare

Family Code § 3011(a) mentions the child's "health, safety, and welfare" as a factor. In addition, Family Code § 8801(b) states that the prospective adoptive parent's general area of residence is a relevant factor.

Pragmatically, this factor is investigated by looking for hazardous conditions in the prospective adoptive parents' home (exposed rusty nails, accessibility of dangerous cleaning solutions and other chemicals, incomplete fencing in the back yard, etc.), and their vehicles.

4. Any Threat of Abuse of the Child

Family Code § 3011(b) deals with the possibility of child abuse. It states that the court shall "consider" any history of abuse by one parent or any other person seeking custody against (1) any child to whom he or she is related by blood or affinity or with whom he or she has had a caretaking relationship, no matter how temporary, (2) the other parent, or (3) a parent, current spouse, or cohabitant, of the parent or person seeking custody, or a person with whom the parent or person seeking custody has a dating or engagement relationship.

a) Definition of "Abuse"

Family Code § 3011(b) defines its use of the term "abuse." The statute refers to the definition set forth in Penal Code § 11165.6, which states that "child abuse" is physical injury inflicted by other than accidental means, sexual abuse, neglect, willful cruelty or unjustifiable punishment, and unlawful corporal punishment or injury, but not including "a mutual affray between minors," or an injury caused by reasonable and necessary force used by a peace officer acting within the course and scope of his or her employment as a peace officer. Under Penal Code § 11165.3, "willful cruelty or unjustifiable punishment" is the causing of unjustifiable physical pain or mental suffering, or the endangering of the child's health or safety. According to Penal Code § 11165.4, "unlawful corporal punishment" is cruel or inhuman corporal punishment or injury resulting in a traumatic condition. However, Welfare & Institutions Code § 300(a) permits "reasonable and age-appropriate spanking to the buttocks where there is no evidence of serious physical injury."

Family Code § 3011(b) also provides that "abuse" against any of the adults that the statute identifies means "abuse" as defined in Family Code § 6203, which governs domestic violence cases. That statute essentially employs the classic definitions of injurious battery and assault, as well as a reference to sexual assault. Additionally, Family Code § 6203 refers to Family Code § 6320, which includes such things as harassment and annoying telephone calls. On the other hand, since this is only one factor in the best interests analysis, it would appear that a subjective reference to an "annoying" telephone call would most probably be outweighed by other more relevant factors.

b) Need for Corroborative Evidence of "Abuse"

Family Code § 3011(b) allows the court to require substantial independent corroboration of allegations of abuse, as a prerequisite to its consideration of the allegations. The language of the statute gives the court discretion as to how it will treat allegations of abuse. If the court requires evidence, the statute states that such evidence would include written reports by law enforcement agencies, child protective services or other social welfare agencies, courts, medical facilities, or other public agencies or private nonprofit organizations providing services to victims of sexual assault or domestic violence.

c) Conviction for Domestic Violence or Abuse

Family Code § 8811(c)(1), which governs independent adoptions, provides that under no circumstances shall the DSS or a county adoption agency give final approval for an adoptive placement in any home where the prospective adoptive parent or any adult living in the prospective adoptive home has (A) a felony conviction for child abuse or neglect, spousal abuse, crimes against a child, including child pornography, or for a crime involving violence, including rape, sexual assault, or homicide, but not including other physical assault and battery, or (B) a felony conviction that occurred within the last five years for physical assault, battery, or a drug- or alcohol-related offense.

As used in Family Code § 8811(c)(1)(A), the phrase "crime involving violence" appears to be very broad; and an "alcohol-related offense" as mentioned in Family Code § 8811(c)(1)(B) would appear to include a felony drunk driving conviction. The same essential rule applies to agency adoptions (Family Code § 8712(c)(1)) and intercountry adoptions even if finalized in a foreign country (Family Code § 8908(c)(1)). Also, the strong absolute wording of these statutes would appear to prevent a court from requiring the agency to modify a negative home study report where such a felony conviction exists.

5. Educational Opportunities and School Record

In *In re Adoption of Matthew B.*, (1991) 232 Cal.App.3d 1239, the court stated that the child's educational opportunities are relevant to the "best interests" question. Other states have held that the child's school record is relevant. (*Natural Mother v. Paternal Aunt*, (Miss. 1991) 583 So.2d 614, 619.) The child's school record can be examined to determine aptitudes.

C. Suitability of the Adoptive Parents

The laws of all 50 states and the District of Columbia require that an investigation of the adoptive parents take place before the adoption is approved. Statutes and regulations exist in California which provide factors to be examined in making the "suitability" determination:

1. Parenting Abilities

Family Code § 8801(b) states that one should consider whether there have been any removals of children from the care of the prospective adoptive parents due to child abuse or neglect. Case law from other jurisdictions states that the courts should examine the parental abilities of the individuals seeking custody, the programs available to assist these individuals to promote the best interest of the child, the plans for the child by these individuals or by the agency seeking custody, the acts or omission of the parent which may indicate that the existing parent-child relationship is not a proper one, and any excuse for the acts or omissions of the parent. (See *Holley v. Adams* (Tex. 1976) 544 S.W.2d 367, 371-372.)

2. Age of the Prospective Adoptive Parents

As far as a minimum age is concerned, Family Code § 8600 requires a prospective adoptive parent to be an adult, and Family Code § 8601(a) requires each prospective adoptive parent to be at least 10 years older than the child. On the other hand, in the context of stepparent adoptions and relative adoptions, Family Code § 8601(b) allows the court to approve an adoption without regard to the ages of the parties, if the court is satisfied that the adoption of the child is in the best interests of the parties and is in the public interest.

As for maximum age, in *Adoption of Michelle T.*, (1975) 44 Cal.App.3d 699, the court held that the age of the prospective adoptive parents is a relevant factor, but that age cannot be the sole determinant for recommending against an adoption, where all other factors favor the adoption. In *Michelle T.*, the prospective adoptive parents, ages 70 and 54 years respectively, sought to complete an independent adoption of a two-year-old girl who had lived with them for nine months at the time the adoption petition was filed, and the court held that the petition should have been granted.

There are cases in which the adoption was denied because of old age, but not as the sole determinant. In *Adoption of Driscoll*, (1969) 269 Cal.App.2d 735, the adoption was denied based on unfavorable age and health considerations. In *Adoption of Martin*, (1946) 76 Cal.App.2d 133, the adoption was denied based not only on age, but on the fact that the prospective adoptive parent was required to provide care to an adult with epilepsy.

3. Health of the Prospective Adoptive Parents

Family Code § 8801(b) requires disclosure of any health conditions on the part of the prospective adoptive parents which would curtail their normal daily activities or reduce their normal life expectancies. This would appear to include use of tobacco.

As for mental health, in *In re Adoption of Schroetter*, (1968) 261 Cal.App.2d 365, the appellate court upheld the trial court's denial of a couple's adoption petition, wherein a psychological expert testified that the wife was "previously depressed," "apprehensive, defensive, guarded," having feelings of inferiority and little or no "self image," attempting to present herself in the best possible light, having a "conflict between spontaneity and a fantasy 'right way to do things,' " seeking a "nonexistent perfectionism," and having a "long standing passive-aggressive character disorder" that supposedly would cause her to "develop psychiatric symptoms in the future and be in need of psychiatric care." Other states have also held that in determining the best interest of the child, the court may consider family stability and the mental and physical health of the parties. (*Petition of R.H.N.*, (Colo. 1985) 710 P.2d 482, 486.)

Today, *Schroetter* stands for the proposition that where only one of the two petitioners exhibits symptoms of mental illness or disability, the adoption should be denied if the child's exposure to the person with the mental illness or disability would not be in the child's best interests. However, as explained in Chapter 6, there is question as to whether *Schroetter* would be followed today, especially in light of modern developments in psychiatric care. Importantly, the *Schroetter* court attempted to distinguish itself from *Adoption of Lingol*, (1951) 107 Cal.App.2d 457, wherein the only psychiatric problem had been 12 years earlier, with no indication of the possibility of a recurrence.

4. Employment and Financial Resources

Family Code § 8801(b) mentions the prospective adoptive parents' employment. The statute also requires disclosure as to whether there are other children who do not reside in prospective adoptive home, the child support obligation for these children and any failure to meet these obligations. Also, while there is no law requiring the prospective adoptive parents to be "employed," the adoptive parents need to have a reliable and continuous source of income with which to pay for the child's upbringing.

5. Marriage and Family Stability

Family Code § 8601(b) expressly contemplates that an "unmarried person" may seek to adopt a child. Also, *County of Los Angeles v. Superior Court*, (1969) 2 Cal.App.3d 1059, holds that an agency cannot seek to dismiss an adoption petition merely by virtue of the post-petition divorce of the prospective adoptive parents. However, Family Code § 8801(b) mentions the length of the prospective adoptive parents' current marriage and their number of previous marriages as a relevant factor.

6. Criminal Record

Family Code § 8801(b) also discusses that any convictions for crimes other than minor traffic violations are a relevant factor. This factor is discussed in detail above.

7. Substance Abuse

Family Code § 3011(d) lists as a relevant factor (1) the "habitual or continual" illegal use of controlled substances (as defined in Health & Safety Code §§ 11000, et seq.) or (2) the habitual or continual abuse of alcohol. Thus, isolated instances (and therefore not "habitual or continual" uses or abuses), would not appear to be significant.

8. Race or Ethnicity

a) California Law

In 2003, Family Code § 8709 was amended to eliminate pre-existing references to race as a consideration in determining the best interests of the child. Pre-2003 Family Code § 8709 stated that a public or private adoption agency to which a child has been freed for adoption by either relinquishment or termination of parental rights may consider the cultural, ethnic, or racial background of the child and the capacity of the prospective adoptive parent to meet the needs of a child of this background as one of a number of factors used to determine the best interest of a child. Former Family Code § 8709 also appeared to allow agencies to place, or to delay or deny the placement of a child, in an adoptive home, and appeared to include the decision to seek termination of parental rights or otherwise make a child legally available for adoptive placement.

On the other hand, 22 California Code of Regulations § 35089(a)(1)(D) still requires the adoption agency to obtain "identifying information" concerning the race and ethnicity of the prospective adoptive parents, as well as every child and adult living in their home. However, there does not appear to be any statute which authorizes the CDSS to enact a regulation concerning race with regard to the assessment of the petitioners, and it is unclear what an agency could use such "identifying information" for.

b) Federal Statutes

Although 22 California Code of Regulations § 35089(a)(1)(D) ostensibly state that an agency must obtain "identifying information" regarding race, these rules may be of questionable validity, since they may violate the equal protection clause of the 14th Amendment of the U.S. Constitution, and may be pre-empted by 42 U.S.C. §§ 671, 674 and 996b (the Adoption Assistance and Child Welfare Act ("AACWA")) and 42 U.S.C. § 1996b(1). The AACWA (at 42 U.S.C. § 671) basically provides that an agency or entity that receives federal funding may not (1) deny any person the opportunity to become an adoptive or a foster parent on the basis of the race, color, or national origin of the person, or of the child; and (2) delay or deny the placement of a child for adoption, or into foster care, on the basis of the race, color, or national origin of the adoptive or foster parent, or the child. Likewise, 42 U.S.C. § 1996b(1) states that a person or government that is involved in adoption or foster care placements may not (A) deny any individual the opportunity to become an adoptive or a foster parent, based on the race, color, or national origin of the individual, or of the child, involved; or (B) delay or deny the placement of a child for adoption or foster care based on the race, color, or national origin of the adoptive or foster parent, or the child, involved.

Family Code § 8708 echoes these federal provisions, meaning it is unclear why the state regulations require the agency to obtain "identifying information" as to race. Moreover, 42 U.S.C. § 1996b contains no provision stating that race may be considered even as a "factor" in determining the best interests of the child. In addition, the Multi-Ethnic Placement Act (42 U.S.C. § 5115a), which once stated that an agency receiving federal funds may take race into consideration as a "factor" in the placement decision, was repealed in 1996, around the same time as the enactment of 42 U.S.C. § 1996b.

If a violation is established, 42 U.S.C. § 1996b(2) provides that racism in the context of adoptive or foster placement is deemed to be a violation of title VI of the Civil Rights Act of 1964 (42 U.S.C. § 2000d et seq.), which would thereby give the victims of the discrimination a private right of action in a federal suit. One exception to this provision is 42 U.S.C. § 1996b(3), which states that the rules against racial discrimination in adoptive or foster placement do not apply to children subject to the Indian Child Welfare Act (25 U.S.C. § 1901.)

c) Federal Constitution

As for whether 22 California Code of Regulations § 35089(a)(1)(D) is constitutional, one must note that the regulation only requires the gathering of certain information, and does not purport to guide the placement decision. Therefore, the regulation would not at first glance appear to give rise to an "injury in fact."

However, in determining whether there has been a violation of the federal constitution, one must ascertain what kind of adoption the case involves, since an actionable 14th Amendment violation only occurs where there has been "state action." (*Evans v. Newton*, (1966) 382 U.S. 296.) In an independent adoption, it is the birth parent who directly places the child with the prospective adoptive parents, and the investigative agency only provides a report to the court – the agency is not the entity which actually denies the right to complete an independent adoption. (Interestingly, 42 U.S.C. § 1996b covers "persons" who are involved in "adoptive placements," meaning that it is conceivable that the statute could apply in the context of an independent adoption.) Stepparent adoptions can only be sought by a spouse of a custodial parent, and then only with both natural parents' consent, unless there are grounds to dispense with the consent requirement – meaning that the agency's role is relatively less significant in these cases.

In contrast, in an agency adoption, the petition cannot even be filed unless the agency first places the child with the prospective adoptive parents, meaning that a constitutional violation can occur in such situations. Indeed, the California courts have held that in light of the extensive "public" functions that are performed by private adoption agencies, the conduct of a private agency is treated as "state action" for purposes of 14th Amendment analysis. (See, *Scott v. Family Ministries*, (1976) 65 Cal.App.3d 492.)

d) History of and Debate over Interracial Adoption

There is no California case law as to whether it is constitutional to consider race as part of the "best interests of the child" analysis. On the other hand, much has been published on the topic. (See M. Howard, *Transracial Adoption: Analysis of the Best Interests Standard*, (1984) 59 Notre Dame L. Rev. 503 ("the Howard article"); E. Bartholet, *Where Do Black Children Belong? The Politics of Race Matching in Adoption*, (May 1991) 139 U. Pa. L. Rev. 1163 ("the Bartholet article"); and J. Hanan, *The Best Interest of the Child: Eliminating Discrimination in the Screening of Adoptive Parents*, (1997) 27 Golden Gate U.L.Rev. 167 ("the Hanan article").

The Howard article recounts the history of the debate, and notes that the Child Welfare League of America ("the CWLA") stated in 1958 that while racial characteristics should not be determinative in placing a child for adoption, "children placed in adoptive families with similar racial characteristics, such as color, can become more easily integrated into the family group and community," and that "physical resemblances should not be a determining factor in the selection of a home, with the possible exception of such racial characteristics as color." Howard also recites that by 1968, the CWLA changed its position, asserting that racial background should not be determinative, and that it should not be assumed by an agency that difficulties will necessarily arise if adoptive parents and children are of different racial origin.

Howard then traces the history of the National Association of Black Social Workers ("the NABSW"), who in 1972 apparently condemned transracial adoption on the grounds that, "Black children belong, physically, psychologically and culturally in Black families in order that they receive the total sense of themselves and develop a sound projection of their future," and that "Black children in white homes are cut off from the healthy development of themselves as Black people." Howard also stated that the NABSW held that interracial adoptions were a "form of genocide," and that if they continued, "our children will not have the background and knowledge which is necessary to survive in a racist society. This is impossible if the child is placed with white parents in a white environment." Howard theorized that the NABSW statements were "so militant that transracial adoption fell by 39 percent in a single year." Howard opined that the NABSW position statements caused the CWLA to change its position second time, when in 1972 it began to approve the practice of racial matching.

This view was shared in one leading case, which stated: "It is a natural thing for children to be raised by parents of their same ethnic background." (*Drummond v. Fulton County Dep't of Family & Children's Services*, (5th Cir. 1977) 563 F.2d 1200.) The *Drummond* court upheld an order awarding custody of the daughters of a divorcing black father and white mother to their father because it was best if the girls stayed "among their own people." (*Ward v. Ward*, (Wash. 1950) 216 P.2d 755.)

Speaking to the contrary, Bartholet noted in 1991 that there is "evidence as to the apparent well-being of transracial adoptees." Professor Bartholet stated that the then-current racial matching policies "should be abandoned not simply because they violate the law but because they do serious injury to black children in the interest of promoting an inappropriate separatist agenda." However, Bartholet suggested that perhaps agencies should be allowed to exercise a "genuinely mild preference" for same-race adoptions, which she said "would mean that if an agency had qualified black and white families waiting to adopt, it could take race into account in deciding how to allocate the children waiting for homes. The agency could operate on the principle that all things being essentially equal, it would be better to assign black children to black parents and white children to white parents." On the other hand, Bartholet conceded that, "On a pragmatic level, there is a real question as to whether it is possible to create a genuinely mild preference for same-race placement--a real danger that if any racial preference is allowed, enormous weight will in fact be given to race no matter what the formal rule of law."

The Hanan article noted the difficulties of applying racial matching standards to children having mixed racial background. Hanan recounts that racial laws often categorized individuals with any trace of African ancestry as being black based on an old racist notion that even one drop of "non-white blood" contaminates "white blood." She also highlights the situation involving an interracial couple who want to become adoptive parents, or a single individual of mixed race wanting to adopt a child, thus showing that the practice of racial matching could become a barrier to adoption. The Hanan article also analyzes Family Code §§ 8708 and 8709 (as they then existed), and concludes that "it is very difficult if not impossible to know for certain which factors were crucial to a placement decision. Eliminating the use of race as a permissible factor would eliminate the possibility that race could remain a decisive factor in practice."

Modernly, the "factor" of race can creep into the decision-making process in connection with the safety and/or crime rate of the prospective adoptive parents' neighborhood, which is required to be analyzed under Family Code §§ 3011(a) and 8801(b). In addition, due to the randomness of certain kinds of crimes and the fact that criminals are able to travel easily from city to city, as are law abiding citizens, it would not appear that general area of residence should be a major factor in the "best interests" analysis.

9. Religion

Religion does not receive the same treatment as race or national origin. Under Family Code § 8709(a), a public or private adoption agency to which a child has been freed for adoption by either relinquishment or termination of parental rights may consider the religious background of the child and the capacity of the prospective adoptive parent to meet the needs of a child of this background as one of a number of factors used to determine the best interest of a child. Also, under 22 California Code of Regulations § 35089(a)(1)(E), the adoption agency is required to obtain information concerning the religion of the prospective adoptive parents, as well as that of every child and adult living in their home.

In *Scott v. Family Ministries* (1976) 65 Cal.App.3d 492, the court found these kinds of "religious matching" criteria to be constitutionally acceptable as one factor to be considered in the "best interests" analysis. However, *Scott* held that an adoption agency could not impose a religious eligibility requirement on prospective adoptive parents. Thus, the *Scott* court held that a Protestant agency could not deny a person the right to adopt a child in its care simply because the applicant was not a Protestant.

10. Language Barriers

There are no regulations concerning language differences, even re intercountry adoptions. If the child to be adopted is an infant, language should not be a factor.

11. Citizenship

There is no California law requiring the prospective adoptive parent to be a U.S. citizen. (See *Cabrillos v. Angel*, (9th Cir. 1922) 278 F. 174.)

12. Sexual Orientation

In California, the right to adopt may not be denied on the basis of sexual orientation. In addition, Family Code §§ 9000, et seq., expressly allows a stepparent adoption to be completed by the child's custodial parent's "domestic partner," as defined in Family Code § 297. On the other hand, the agency is empowered by 22 California Code of Regulations § 35089(a)(1)(H) to obtain information concerning the identity of any additional adult in the prospective adoptive parent's house. In addition, 22 California Code of Regulations § 35089(a)(2)(A) and (C) appear to allow the investigating agency to ask questions about the prospective adoptive parents' "general characteristics" and "social background," regardless of their sexual orientation.

III. EVIDENCE OF THE CHILD'S BEST INTERESTS – THE HOME STUDY

A. The Home Study Assessment and Investigative Report

1. The Duty to Investigate

The court in *In re Backhaus' Adoption*, (1962) 209 Cal.App.2d 13, held that the CDSS or investigating agency has the duty to ascertain whether the child is a proper subject for adoption and whether the proposed home is suitable for the child, prior to filing report with the court. As explained below, regulations which provide guidelines for meeting that duty currently exist.

2. Required Types of Documentation

To facilitate the assessment, 22 California Code of Regulations § 35087(a) requires the adoption agency (public or private) to obtain the following documentation for all petitioners:

a) Medical and Employment Records

The adoption agency obtains an authorization for the release of medical and employment information on the petitioner pursuant to 22 California Code of Regulations § 35087(a)(1), and then independently obtains those records from the applicable third parties.

b) Financial Records

The adoption agency also obtains an authorization for the release of financial information, pursuant to 22 California Code of Regulations § 35087(a)(2), if necessary. For example, such an authorization would allow the agency to discover if the petitioner's home is in foreclosure.

c) Medical Examination Report

A medical examination report on the petitioner is to be provided to the agency pursuant to 22 California Code of Regulations § 35087(a)(3). The regulation also states that, (A) the report shall be signed by a licensed physician or a nurse practitioner practicing under licensed physician, (B) the examination shall have been conducted no earlier than six months prior to the filing of the adoption petition, and (C) the agency shall waive the medical report when the petitioners are members of a religious sect, denomination, or organization which, in accordance with its creeds or tenets, relies on faith and prayer for healing. Since the regulation does not state that a third party may set aside the adoption due to a failure to have a medical examination performed on the petitioners, it appears that the agency also has authority to waive this requirement in all cases.

d) Communicable Tuberculosis

Under 22 California Code of Regulations § 35087(a)(5), the petitioners provide to the agency a "certificate" for each adult residing in the petitioner home, stating that these adults are free from communicable tuberculosis. It would appear such a "certificate" would be provided by a facility that is permitted to make such an evaluation, and that the adults in the petitioner's home would have to submit to a blood sample, so that a true certificate could be issued.

e) School Records

A "school report" for all school age children residing in the petitioner's home must be provided to the agency under 22 California Code of Regulations § 35087(a)(4). The petitioner's existing children's grades in school would not appear to be highly significant, but the school records would reveal information concerning behavior in class and disciplinary action.

f) References

The petitioner is to provide at least three letters of reference regarding the suitability of the petitioner as an adoptive parent pursuant to 22 California Code of Regulations § 35087(a)(6). The regulation also states that face-to-face interviews with individuals providing references shall be permitted as a substitute for letters of reference, as long as these interviews are documented.

g) State Criminal Record and Fingerprints

Under 22 California Code of Regulations § 35087(a)(7), the agency is to obtain the full state criminal record, if any, from the California Department of Justice ("DOJ"). To do so, the regulation requires the adoption agency to submit one set of fingerprints for each petitioner to the DOJ, and shall clearly indicate "Adoption" on the request to inform the DOJ of the purpose of the criminal record clearance. The agency is also required under 22 California Code of Regulations § 35087(a)(7)(C) to contract with the DOJ for the Subsequent Arrest Notification Service in order to receive arrest information subsequent to the original DOJ criminal record sent to the agency and pending the court order granting the completion of the adoption. Under 22 California Code of Regulations § 35087(a)(7)(D), the agency must notify the DOJ when the adoption has been finalized, denied, or dismissed to discontinue receiving subsequent arrest information on a subject previously fingerprinted for adoption purposes, unless the petitioner is being assessed or investigated by the agency for another adoption. Pursuant to 22 California Code of Regulations § 35087(a)(7)(E), the agency shall require new sets of fingerprints and shall make new requests for state criminal records to the DOJ in the event of subsequent adoptions, unless the Subsequent Arrest Notification Service is still in effect.

Importantly, there is no provision allowing the adoption agency to obtain documents or ask questions concerning the petitioner's juvenile record or school record, both of which are confidential under California law. In addition, for some reason the regulations do not require the adoption agency to obtain fingerprints of the adults living in the petitioner's home, although identifying information on such adults must be disclosed.

h) Federal Criminal Record

Under 22 California Code of Regulations § 35087(a)(8), the FBI criminal record, if any, of the petitioner, must be obtained from the DOJ when the petitioner has resided in California for less than two years, or when information gathered in the assessment has given the agency reason to believe that the petitioner may have committed a crime in another jurisdiction. The regulation also provides that even mere employment in another state may validly give the adoption agency reason to believe that the person may have committed a crime in another jurisdiction. Therefore, employment outside California should be fully explained.

3. Required Interviews and Evaluations

Under 22 California Code of Regulations § 35089(a), the investigating agency must conduct a series of interviews and make several evaluations in making its assessment, pursuant to certain criteria stated below. The weighing of that information is guided by the statutes and case law mentioned above. This particular regulation also provides the laundry list of the kinds of data that must be gathered:

a) Identifying Information

According to 22 California Code of Regulations § 35089(a)(1), the adoption agency is to obtain the following identifying information on the petitioner and any children and adults residing in the petitioner's home:

(A) Name, date of birth and sex.

(B) Current address and telephone number.

(C) Blood relationship to child, if any.

(D) Race and ethnic background information.

(E) Religion.

(F) Current employment information.

(G) Verification of marital status, if relevant, including verification of the termination of all prior marriages, if any. (The regulation also provides that when verification of the dissolution of any marriage of a petitioner is not possible, a marriage prior to a verified divorce decree shall be assumed to have been validly dissolved, and that a valid divorce presupposes that that marriage was valid.)

(H) Personal and/or biological relationship of the petitioner to other individuals residing in the petitioners home.

b) Criteria in Making the Assessment

The adoption agency may take into account any criminal record on the part of the petitioners. (See 22 California Code of Regulations § 35089(a)(3).) However, importantly, there is no provision allowing the adoption agency to investigate the petitioner's juvenile record or school record, both of which are confidential under California law. In addition, according to 22 California Code of Regulations § 35089(a)(2), the adoption agency is to evaluate the petitioner, as well as any children and adults residing in the home, under the following criteria:

(A) General characteristics.

(B) Feelings and attitudes which may impact the adoption.

(C) Social background.

(D) Educational background.

(E) Financial stability.

(F) Work adjustment.

(G) Adequacy of housing.

These criteria do not lend themselves to mathematical precision. In addition, there is no requirement that a prospective adoptive parent have a particular level of education, or a particular level of income, or a particular size of home. The important thing to determine is whether there are adequate resources available to raise the child in a safe, loving and stable home.

4. Home Study Fee

To fund the home study, Family Code § 8810(a) allows the CDSS or county adoption agency to charge a fee for handling the investigation of the adoption petition.

Under Family Code § 8810(a)(2), a non-refundable fee of $775 may be charged if there is already a valid preplacement evaluation in existence at the time of filing the adoption petition. However, Family Code § 8810(a)(1) otherwise allows a non-refundable fee of $2,950 to be charged. Under Family Code § 8810(c), the agency may waive the fee for prospective adoptive parents of low income.

B. Preplacement Evaluations

Family Code § 8811.5(a) states that a licensed private adoption agency may certify prospective adoptive parents by a preplacement evaluation that contains a finding that an individual is suited to be an adoptive parent. According to Family Code § 8811.5(c), the preplacement evaluation shall be completed no more than one year prior to the signing of an adoption placement agreement. In addition, Family Code § 8811.5(c) contemplates that the preplacement evaluation may be renewed, in which case the private agency may charge a fee to cover the extent of the work required to prepare the renewal that is attributable to changes in family circumstances.

Under Family Code § 8811.5(b), the preplacement evaluation shall include an investigation pursuant to standards included in the CDSS's regulations governing independent adoption investigations, and the private agency may charge an investigation fee that is comparable to the fees charged by the CDSS or a delegated licensed county adoption agency.

As explained further in Chapter 11, a primary purpose of a pre-placement evaluation in the context of intercountry adoptions is the expedited processing of the visa application for the child with the U.S. Bureau of Citizenship and Immigration Services. The California agency completes the home study assessment and evaluation even if the adoption is finalized abroad.

C. Submitting the Home Study Report to the Court

1. Authority to Reject the Agency's Recommendation

In *Adoption of McDonald*, (1954) 43 Cal.2d 447, the Supreme Court rejected the contention that the consent of a licensed adoption agency, to which the subject child had been relinquished, was a jurisdictional prerequisite to an adoption decree. As explained below and in other chapters, the *McDonald* rule has been interpreted to require the court to be the final decision-maker as to what is in the child's best interests.

In re Backhaus' Adoption, (1962) 209 Cal.App.2d 13, provides that the trial court has jurisdiction by statute to review an unfavorable home study report, and to make its own independent determination of the suitability of the home of petitioners for the adoption. *Backhaus* also holds that the statutes governing adoption proceedings do not require that all of the statutory prerequisites to an effective adoption decree (i.e., the child being available to appear in court, the consents having been signed, etc.) need to be satisfied at the time of judicial review of that report. The court also held there was no provision stating that such review could only be made at the time of, or as a part of, the final hearing on the adoption petition.

Backhaus (which was decided before Family Code §§ 8900, et seq. was enacted) involved an intercountry adoption of a German-born child. The CDSS investigated the home and made an unfavorable recommendation to the federal immigration agenyc, which precluded the child from entering the U.S. under the then-existing quotas. After that, even though the child was still in Germany, and even though the natural father's consent had still not been obtained, an adoption petition was filed in a California court. In that case, the CDSS filed an unfavorable report and an adverse recommendation. The petitioners then filed a petition seeking judicial review of the report and a motion to strike alleged extraneous matter contained in it. The CDSS filed a motion for summary judgment on the grounds there was no jurisdiction to proceed on the merits of the adoption petition, since the child was not yet free for adoption, and since the child could not appear before the court as statutorily required. The motion was granted for lack of jurisdiction. On appeal, the *Backhaus* court held there were three prerequisites to the court's jurisdiction to review the report: (1) there must be an adoption petition on file with the court; (2) the department must have conducted its investigation and filed its report and recommendation with the court clerk; and (3) the report and recommendation must be unfavorable to the petitioners. The court held that all three elements concurred in its case, and reversed the summary judgment.

In deciding upon litigation strategy, choosing the "judicial bias" tactic is rarely wise. However, in *Adoption of Richardson*, (1967) 251 Cal.App.2d 222, the trial judge indicated his bias against deaf mutes by writing to the adoption bureau director before the hearing that "this adoption should be nipped in the bud." In *Richardson*, those physical defects, while entitled to be considered, were clearly not determinative of fitness.

2. Time for Submitting the Report

a) 180-day Rule

As for independent adoptions, Family Code § 8807(a) states that within 180 days after the filing of the petition, the CDSS or a delegated county adoption agency shall investigate the proposed adoption and submit to the court a full report of the facts disclosed by its inquiry with a recommendation regarding the granting of the petition. The court has discretion pursuant to Family Code § 8807(c) to allow additional time for the filing of the report, provided that the petitioner or petitioners have been given at least five days' notice and an opportunity to be heard with respect to the request for additional time. In interpreting Family Code § 8807(a), the court in *Adoption of Baby Girl B.*, (1999) 74 Cal.App.4th 43, held that the 180-day time limit is directory, not mandatory, meaning that the failure to meet the 180-day deadline does not force the trial court to grant the adoption petition, no matter who is "at fault."

In an independent adoption, Family Code § 8807(b) provides that where the investigation establishes that there is a serious question concerning the suitability of the petitioners or the care provided the child or the availability of the consent to adoption, the report shall be filed immediately. In *Adoption of Michelle T.*, (1975) 44 Cal.App.3d 699, the court held that in cases of serious question, the CDSS must shorten the 180-day time frame in which to submit a "full report of the facts disclosed by its inquiry," but that this rule does not authorize the Department to file an incomplete report.

b) Service upon the Petitioners

According to Family Code § 8821, when any report or findings are submitted to the court by the CDSS or a delegated county adoption agency, a copy of the report or findings, whether favorable or unfavorable, shall be given to the petitioner's attorney in the proceeding, if the petitioner has an attorney of record, or to the petitioner.

CONSENT TO THE ADOPTION 3

In this chapter:

John Joseph Nicholson is the most nominated male actor in the history of the Academy Awards. His biographer has asserted that Nicholson's father was Edgar Kirschfeld, even though Donald Furcillo had bigamously married Nicholson's mother six months before Nicholson was born, and offered to take care of the child. Nicholson was brought up believing that his grandparents were his parents.

I. THE FUNDAMENTAL REQUIREMENTS OF NOTICE AND CONSENT

This chapter explores the constitutional and statutory foundation of the consent issue, and will discuss exactly what "consent" is, whose consent must be obtained, how and when it must be obtained, and how it may be revoked. As will become clear, the concept of "consent" goes hand in hand with the issue of who must be given notice of the adoption proceedings.

Relinquishments for agency adoptions will be touched upon here, and will be discussed more fully in Chapter 5. While a consent to an independent adoption is analogous to a "relinquishment" of the child to a licensed adoption agency for the purpose of adoption, the statutes treat relinquishments somewhat differently than consents, and an agency relinquishment is actually a ground for dispensing with the need for "consent" in the technical sense. This chapter will attempt to isolate the concept of consent, which is most easily done by describing it in the context of an independent adoption.

A. Constitutional Considerations

1. General Rule

As stated in *Lehr v. Robertson*, (1983) 463 U.S. 248, and many other cases explained in this book, a parent's relationship with his or her child is a liberty interest which is protected as a substantive due process right, and the right to be consulted about an adoption necessarily entails the right to be notified, which is the essence of procedural due process. The Supreme Court also held in *Armstrong v. Manzo*, (1965) 380 U.S. 545, that the failure to give the birth father notice of a pending adoption proceeding violates "the most rudimentary demands of due process of law." The *Armstrong* court also stated, "An elementary and fundamental requirement of due process in any proceeding which is to be accorded finality is notice reasonably calculated, under all the circumstances, to apprise interested parties of the pendency of the action and afford them an opportunity to present their objections."

In *Armstrong*, the child was born during the marriage of the birth parents; the birth mother and father then divorced; and the birth mother was awarded legal custody of the child. She remarried, and the new couple desired to complete a stepparent adoption. To do so, they filed an adoption petition in Texas, which is where they resided. They also filed an affidavit stating that the birth father had failed to support the child for a period in excess of the statutory period in which a birth parent's consent rights may be lost. No notice was given to the birth father of the filing of this affidavit, nor of the adoption petition, although the petitioners knew his precise whereabouts. The court then granted the adoption petition without the birth father's consent. The birth father soon learned of the adoption. He then filed a motion asking that the adoption decree be set aside based on lack of notice. As to his motion, the Texas courts ruled that the birth father failed to meet his burden of proving that the adoption should be set aside, and that any constitutional infirmity was cured by the hearing that was afforded to him on his motion.

The U.S. Supreme Court in *Armstrong* held that this shifting of the burden of proof, which resulted from the initial lack of notice, violated the birth father's procedural due process rights. It held that if the birth father had been given timely notice, it would have been the stepparent's burden to prove not only that he was a suitable adoptive parent, but also why the birth father's consent to the adoption was not required, and that if "neither side offered any evidence, those who initiated the adoption proceedings could not have prevailed." *Armstrong* is an example of the many U.S. Supreme Court cases recognizing the parent-child relationship as a "liberty" interest that is protected under the Due Process clause.

2. Consent is a Jurisdictional Issue

In *Arnold v. Howell*, (1950) 98 Cal.App.2d 202, the court stated that, "consent lies at the foundation of statutes of adoption," and that "with certain statutory exceptions, consent to an adoption is considered a jurisdictional prerequisite." This passage from *Arnold* is cited with approval in *In re Adoption of Barnett*, (1960) 54 Cal.2d 370. *Arnold* also provides that where consent to an adoption actually does not exist, the jurisdictional prerequisite to a valid adoption is lacking, thereby opening up the adoption decree to direct or collateral attack. (See Chapter 9 regarding direct and collateral attacks on adoption orders.)

On the other hand, in *San Diego County Dept. of Pub. Welfare v. Superior Court*, (1972) 7 Cal.3d 1, the Supreme Court cited *Barnett* and stated that "the consent of the natural parents, except in those situations excepted by statute, is a jurisdictional prerequisite to an adoption with the caveat that such consent requirements are no longer to be construed strictly in favor of the rights of the natural parent. As we have pointed out, such requirements are to be liberally construed in order to effect the object of the adoption statutes in promoting the welfare of children, bereft of the benefits of the home and care, of their real parents."

3. Consent, When Required, Supersedes All Issues

While the child's welfare is the paramount consideration (see Chapter 2), the California Supreme Court held in *Adoption of Kelsey S.*, (1992) 1 Cal.4th 816, that "consent is required of a mother and a presumed father regardless of the child's best interest." "Consent" is an issue of constitutional law, while the "best interests" rule originates in state law.

In *In re Timothy W.*, (1990) 223 Cal.App.3d 437, the court stated, "when a natural mother refuses to consent to an independent adoption within a reasonable time after placing the child with prospective adoptive parents, and six months will always be a reasonable time, the court may not consider whether returning the child to the birth mother will be in the minor's best interests." (The child was in the home of the prospective adoptive parents since the day the child was born, and the birth mother's first written notification of the refusal to consent, which consisted of a letter to the court, came just four days before the child turned six months old.)

The *Timothy W.* court also stated, "When consent is refused, the law does not permit a court to examine the best interests of the child in making a custody determination. Issues of bonding and lifestyles of the birth parents and their families are totally irrelevant in a proceeding which is to be limited only to effectuating the unconditional return of the child to his or her birth mother." *Timothy W.* further held that where the birth mother has never consented to an adoption and has formally refused to give her consent, the child must be returned to the birth mother. There is simply no discretion to consider whether the child has bonded to the prospective adoptive family or who will provide a better home."

In *Adoption of Parker*, (1948) 31 Cal.2d 608, the Supreme Court determined that since the birth mother never formally consented to the adoption of her child, it would order the child to be returned to her, even though the child had bonded with the adoptive parents for eight years. It also held that "consent by estoppel" will not be recognized, and that the facts of the case did not give rise to an abandonment.

B. Situations Where Consent is Not Required

1. Family Code § 8606

Family Code § 8606 provides that the consent of a birth parent is not necessary where (a) that birth parent has been judicially deprived of the custody and control of the child pursuant to Family Code § 7800, et seq., or Welfare & Institutions Code § 366.26 or by a similar order of a court of another jurisdiction (see Chapter 6 of this book); (b) the birth parent has, in a judicial proceeding in another jurisdiction, voluntarily surrendered the right to the custody and control of the child; (c) the birth parent has deserted the child without provision for identification of the child (desertion is discussed in Chapter 6); (d) the birth parent has relinquished the child for adoption as provided in Family Code § 8700 (relinquishments are examined in Chapter 5); or (e) the birth parent has relinquished the child for adoption to a licensed or authorized child-placing agency in another jurisdiction pursuant to the law of that jurisdiction. (Interstate adoptions are the subject of Chapter 9 of this book.)

As will be discussed more fully in Chapter 6, the U.S. and California Supreme Courts have upheld the constitutionality of terminations of parental rights where certain requirements have been satisfied, and consent is not constitutionally required where a parent has had parental rights lawfully terminated.

2. Family Code § 8604(b)

Family Code § 8604(b) defines certain "birth parents" whose consent to the adoption is unnecessary. It states that if one birth parent has been awarded custody by judicial order, or by agreement of both parents, and the other birth parent for a period of one year willfully fails to communicate with and to pay for the care, support, and education of the child when able to do so, then the birth parent having sole custody may alone consent to the adoption, but only after the birth parent not having custody has been lawfully served with a copy of a citation that requires the non-custodial birth parent to appear at the time and place set for the appearance in court under Family Code §§ 8718, 8823, 8913, or 9007. Family Code § 8604(c) then states that the failure of a birth parent to pay for the care, support, and education of the child for the period of one year or failure of a birth parent to communicate with the child for the period of one year is prima facie evidence that the failure was willful and without lawful excuse, which effectively shifts the burden of proof on the issue of willfulness. This code section will also be discussed more fully in Chapter 6 of this book.

It appears that Family Code § 8604(b) passes constitutional muster. In *Caban v. Mohammed*, (1978) 441 U.S. 380, the U.S. Supreme Court stated, "In those cases where the father never has come forward to participate in the rearing of his child, nothing in the Equal Protection Clause precludes the State from withholding from him the privilege of vetoing the adoption of that child." See also, *Lehr v. Robertson*, (1983) 463 U.S. 248. It is also important to note that *Armstrong v. Manzo*, (1965) 380 U.S. 545, only dealt with the notice issue, and not whether the trial court could find that consent is unnecessary where proper notice has been served. Thus, Family Code § 8604(b) does not violate *Armstrong*. In addition, although the U.S. Supreme Court in *Stanley v. Illinois*, (1972) 405 U.S. 645, held that the Fourteenth Amendment due process clause entitled an unmarried father to a hearing on his fitness as a parent before his children were taken from him, *Stanley* implicitly recognizes that parental rights could be terminated where due process is given.

Helmig v. Dunmore, (2000) 83 Cal.App.4th 1, contrasts a finding that consent is not necessary from a judicial deprivation of parental rights. The decision appealed from in *Helmig* was the trial court's order concerning whose consent was necessary, which came before the ultimate order granting the adoption. The *Helmig* court stated that the finding under Family Code § 8604 that consent was unnecessary was not equivalent to an order terminating parental rights under Family Code § 7822. The *Helmig* court also stated that while an adoption extinguishes the birth parent's obligation to support the child, as well as all other duties and rights of the birth parent, a ruling under Family Code § 8604 that the birth parent's consent was unnecessary for an adoption did not relieve that birth parent of his child support obligation.

II. WHAT IS "CONSENT?"

A. Definition

There is no California or U.S. Supreme Court case defining "consent" in the context of an adoption. Nor is there any Family Code provision defining "consent," although there are many California statutes defining "consent" in other contexts. Black's Law Dictionary states that "consent" is the "voluntary agreement by a person in the possession of and exercise of sufficient mental capacity to make an intelligent choice to do something proposed by another." There is nothing in the Black's saying who must initiate the communication between the two persons.

In *Arnold v. Howell*, (1950) 98 Cal.App.2d 202, the court held that the agreement must be "free and voluntary and include consent to all the legal consequences of adoption." *Arnold* also states that a consent obtained by misrepresentation, fraud, duress, undue influence or other overreaching practices of the adopting parents or others, is not a true consent. In *Arnold*, the child was formally adopted after the birth father, who was about to be shipped overseas as part of his military service in World War II, was allegedly told that custody of the child would be returned to him after he returned. The birth father did return some years later, but the child was not given back to him upon his request. The *Arnold* court ruled that the pleadings were sufficient, especially due to the birth father's allegations of his distress and anxiety over his orders to go overseas to war.

Thirty years later, in *Adoption of Jennie L.*, (1980) 111 Cal.App.3d 422, the court stated that, "Fraud or duress practiced by the adoptive parents *or known to them* may constitute grounds for invalidating consent." [emphasis added] In *Jennie L.*, the trial court invalidated a consent based on evidence that the birth parent had been pressured by *her* family to place the child for adoption. The evidence included her father's anger, physical abuse, efforts to obtain an abortion, and efforts to induce the birth mother to place her child for adoption, and her testimony that she did not voluntarily sign the consent to adoption. On the other hand, the appellate court reversed, holding that the birth parent failed to show that the adoptive parents had knowledge of the birth parent's family's improper statements and conduct, and that there was no evidence of fraud or duress by either the adoptive parents or the adoption services representatives.

As for the law in other states, in *Anonymous v. Anonymous*, (Ariz.App. 1975) 530 P.2d 896, the court held that a birth mother's consent to have her three-day-old child adopted could not be invalidated on the basis of the mother's post-partum depression. The Arizona appellate court also held that the birth mother's taking of an empirin compound with codeine and seconal three hours before signing the consent was insufficient grounds to invalidate consent. There is no analogous California case law.

B. Contrasting "Consent" with "Contractual Intent"

In *In re Duarte's Adoption*, (1964) 229 Cal.App.2d 775, the court held that a consent to adoption is not in the nature of a bilateral contract and that a mother need not receive consideration in order to be bound by such consent. The court rejected the contention that the mother's consent to the adoption was invalid because she received "no consideration." As explained herein, there are other specific rules that highlight the differences between "consent" and "contractual intent."

1. Consent Does Not Involve a Contractual Exchange

a) Criminality of "Selling" and "Buying" Children

Penal Code § 181 makes it a felony to sell or attempt to sell any person to another, or to receive money or anything of value in consideration of placing any person in the custody or under the power or control of another, or to buy or attempt to buy any person, or to pay money or deliver anything of value to another in consideration of having any person placed in his custody or under his power or control. Likewise, Penal Code § 273(a) makes it a misdemeanor for any person or agency to pay, offer to pay, or to receive money or anything of value for the placement for adoption or for the consent to an adoption of a child. Also, Penal Code § 273(f) expressly allows for prosecution of any person for a misdemeanor or felony pursuant to Penal Code § 487 (which defines "grand theft") and other provisions of law.

In *People v. Daniel*, (1987) 195 Cal.App.3d 623, the court held that Penal Code § 181 made it unlawful for a birth father, who had four months previously placed his 17-month-old daughter with the prospective adoptive parents for purposes of adoption, to then demand money from the prospective adoptive parents in exchange for the right to continue the placement. The court held that demanding money to consent to an adoption constitutes an attempted sale and is a violation of Penal Code § 181.

The human trafficking laws do not appear to criminalize "baby selling" and "baby buying" for adoption purposes. The federal definition of human trafficking (22 U.S.C. § 7102(8) and (9)) deals with the recruitment, harboring, transportation, provision, or obtaining of a person for commercial sex acts or for involuntary servitude, peonage, debt bondage or slavery. The California statutes (Penal Code § 236.1 and Civil Code § 52.5) also makes it a felony to engage in such conduct, but they do not reference the trafficking of persons solely for purposes of adoption. Of course, if an intercountry adoption were used for the purpose of obtaining preferential status for an immigrant visa to bring a person into the United States in order to perform commercial sex acts or involuntary servitude, the adoption would not appear to provide a defense to charges of human trafficking.

People v. Daniel was a criminal case, and therefore did not say whether the unlawful payment of a sum of money should negate an adoption which might be in the best interests of the child. However, Penal Code § 181 also makes it a felony to "buy" a child, and a prison sentence imposed on the prospective adoptive parents would clearly impede the adoption.

b) Exception for Maternity-Related Expenses

Not all payments of money to the birth parents are illegal. Penal Code § 273(b) provides an exception for the payment or receipt of funds for maternity-connected medical or hospital or necessary living expenses of the mother preceding and during her hospital stay as an act of charity, as long as the payment is not contingent upon placement of the child for adoption, consent to the adoption, or cooperation in the completion of the adoption.

On the other hand, Penal Code § 273(c) makes it a misdemeanor for any parent to intentionally receive such financial benefits with the intent to either not complete or not consent to the adoption. In addition, Penal Code § 273(d) makes it a misdemeanor for a parent to obtain such financial benefits from two or more prospective adopting families or persons concerning the same child, if either parent knowingly fails to disclose the existence of all prospective adopting families or persons interested in adopting the child (with knowledge that there is an obligation to disclose that information), and knowingly accepts said financial benefits if the aggregate amount exceeds the reasonable maternity-connected medical or hospital and necessary living expenses of the mother preceding and during the pregnancy.

c) Exception for Adoption-Related Fees

Penal Code § 273(a) also provides an exception for the adoption services fees paid to the CDSS, a licensed adoption agency, adoption services providers (see Family Code § 8502) or an attorney providing adoption legal services.

d) Accounting for Expenses

To monitor compliance with Penal Code §§ 181 and 273, the Legislature enacted Family Code § 8610, which provides that certain accountings that must be filed during the adoption proceedings. These accounting procedures will be discussed more fully in Chapter 10.

2. Legal Capacity to Consent to an Adoption

a) Minors

Family Code § 8814(d) specifically states, "A birth parent who is a minor has the right to sign a consent for the adoption of the birth parent's child and the consent is not subject to revocation by reason of minority." The hornbook rule that minors have no capacity to enter into contracts is a matter of state law (as Civil Code § 1556). Since consent to an adoption is not a contract, Civil Code § 1556 does not apply.

b) Diminished Mental Capacity

According to 22 California Code of Regulations § 35097(a), a consent to an adoption cannot be accepted if the birth parent does not have the ability to understand the content, nature, and effect of signing a consent to adoption. There is also no provision allowing a grandparent or other person to vicariously consent to the adoption. In such situations, it would appear that parental rights of a birth parent having diminished mental capacity would have to be terminated pursuant to Family Code § 7826 and/or Family Code § 7827 in order to dispense with the consent requirement.

III. WHOSE CONSENT IS REQUIRED? – UNIFORM PARENTAGE ACT

Family Code § 8604(a) states, "Except as provided in subdivision (b), a child having a presumed father under Section 7611 may not be adopted without the consent of the child's birth parents, if living." Family Code § 8512 defines "birth parent" as "the biological parent or, in the case of a person previously adopted, the adoptive parent." Family Code § 8605 then states that a child not having a presumed father may not be adopted without the consent of the child's mother, if living. Therefore, the statutes provide that a female has consent rights if she is the mother, but that a male only has consent rights if he is a "presumed" father.

Status as a "presumed" father is governed largely by the Uniform Parentage Act, which became law in California in 1975, and which is now codified at Family Code §§ 7600-7730. The Uniform Parentage Act abolished the concept of legitimacy (or illegitimacy) and replaced it with the concept of parentage. The Act was drafted following the U.S. Supreme Court's decisions in *Levy v. Louisiana*, (1968) 391 U.S. 68, and *Glona v. American Guarantee Co.*, (1968) 391 U.S. 73, which declared that laws that discriminate against illegitimate children and their parents violate equal protection. Family Code § 7602 now states that the parent and child relationship extends equally to every child and to every parent, regardless of the marital status of the parents. Also, in *Adoption of Michael H.*, (1995) 10 Cal.4th 1043, the California Supreme Court stated that the Uniform Parentage Act "provides a comprehensive scheme for judicial determination of paternity, and was intended to rationalize procedure, to eliminate constitutional infirmities in then existing state law, and to improve state systems of [child] support enforcement."

Since it is the "Uniform" Parentage Act, Family Code § 3 requires that it "shall be construed to effectuate the general purpose to make uniform the law in those states which enact that provision." In the case of the Uniform Parentage Act, that means all 50 states, the District of Columbia, and several territories. Moreover, although the Uniform Parentage Act was originally part of the Civil Code, but was then transferred to the new Family Code, the Legislature stated in Family Code § 2 that the transfer of a statute to the new code book is not deemed to be a new enactment, but a continuation of the previous statutory language.

The Act treats males and females differently. The text below explains how the courts have reconciled these statutes with the due process and equal protection clauses of the U.S. Constitution, so as to give rise to the concept of a "*Kelsey S.* father," who has consent rights pursuant to the Constitution and apart from the Uniform Parentage Act. See also, *Quilloin v. Walcott*, (1978) 434 U.S. 246. In interpreting the statutes, the California Supreme Court in *Adoption of Kelsey S.*, (1992) 1 Cal.4th 816, identified "three classifications of parents: mothers, biological fathers who are presumed fathers, and biological fathers who are not presumed fathers (i.e., natural fathers)," and stated that "consent is required of a mother and a presumed father regardless of the child's best interest." In addition to the four Family Code § 7611(a)-(d) categories of presumed fathers, the *Kelsey S.* court identified another category arising under Family Code § 7664(b), i.e., that a natural father's consent to an adoption of his child by a third party is required if the natural father makes the required evidentiary showing that retention of his parental rights is in the child's best interest (as explained below and in Chapter 2 of this book).

A. "Presumed Fathers" (v. "Alleged Fathers")

According to Family Code § 7611, a male "is presumed to be the natural father of a child if he meets the conditions provided in," (1) Family Code § 7540, et seq. (i.e., the conclusive presumption of paternity as to a child of the marriage), (2) Family Code § 7570, et seq. (dealing with paternity declarations as explained below), or (3) one or more of the four categories of Family Code § 7611(a)-(d), as explained below.

As set forth in *Tyler v. Children's Home Society*, (1994) 29 Cal.App.4th 511, an "alleged father" is a male who is claimed to be the child's father but who does not meet the statutory definition of a "presumed father." The *Tyler* court also held that an alleged father does not have automatic physical custody rights, nor is his consent required for an adoption unless he demonstrates a full commitment to parental responsibility – emotional, financial, and otherwise – under the *Kelsey S.* model (as explained below).

1. Categories of Presumed Fathers (Family Code § 7611)

a) Child of the Marriage

Family Code § 7611(a) states that a male is presumed to be the child's father if he and the child's natural mother are or have been married to each other and the child is born during the marriage, or within 300 days after the marriage is terminated by death, annulment, declaration of invalidity, or divorce, or after a judgment of separation is entered by a court. Likewise, Family Code § 7540 states, "Except as provided in Section 7541 [which deals with the blood tests mentioned above], the child of a wife cohabiting with her husband, who is not impotent or sterile, is conclusively presumed to be a child of the marriage." In other words, where the biological paternal link has not been scientifically negated, the child of the marriage cannot be adopted without the husband's consent, unless other grounds exist to dispense with his consent.

In *In re Melissa G.*, (1989) 213 Cal.App.3d 1082, the court tackled the question of the constitutionality of the conclusive presumption arising under what is now Family Code § 7540. The *Melissa G.* court relied on the plurality decision in *Michael H. v. Gerald D.*, (1989) 491 U.S. 110, and Justice Brennan's dissenting opinion, which summarized the common ground shared by a majority of the High Court: "Five Members of the Court refuse to foreclose the possibility that a natural father might ever have a constitutionally protected interest in his relationship with a child whose mother was married to and cohabiting with another man at the time of the child's conception and birth. Five Justices agree that the flaw inherent in a conclusive presumption that terminates a constitutionally protected interest without any hearing whatsoever is a procedural one."

In *Melissa G.*, the child was born during the marriage but only eight days before the mother and father separated, and then lived with her mother and a second man who became the mother's second husband four months later. After the separation, the first husband never visited the child. Blood tests showed that the second husband was the child's father. The mother and the second husband then had another child, and sibling bonding occurred over the course of two years. The court held that this sibling bonding was the child's "most important psychological relationship." The second husband then engaged in spousal abuse against the mother, causing the children to be detained in protective custody. Over the first husband's objection, the court held that the second husband would be treated as the child's father in the ensuing juvenile dependency proceedings. The *Melissa G.* court thus decided against a man who asserted his parental claim pursuant to the conclusive presumption, and said that applying the presumption in this instance would violate the child's constitutional rights.

b) Child of an Apparently Valid Marriage

Family Code § 7611(b) allows a male to be a presumed father if, before the child's birth, he and the child's natural mother have attempted to marry each other by a marriage solemnized in apparent compliance with law, although the attempted marriage is or could be declared invalid, and either of the following is true: (1) the attempted marriage could be declared invalid only by a court, the child is born during the attempted marriage, or within 300 days after its termination by death, annulment, declaration of invalidity, or divorce, or (2) the attempted marriage is invalid without a court order, the child is born within 300 days after the termination of cohabitation.

c) Child of Couple Marrying After the Child's Birth

Family Code § 7611(c) allows a male to be a presumed father if, after the child's birth, he and the child's natural mother have married, or attempted to marry, each other by a marriage solemnized in apparent compliance with law, although the attempted marriage is or could be declared invalid, and either of the following is true: (1) with his consent, he is named as the child's father on the child's birth certificate, or (2) he is obligated to support the child under a written voluntary promise or by court order. Importantly, there is no time limit as to when the subsequent marriage must occur. It would appear that one legislative purpose for the latter two alternative conditions is to obviate those sham marriages which are entered into only to thwart a proposed adoption.

d) Child Received into the Alleged Father's Home and Held out as His Natural Child

Family Code § 7611(d) allows a male to be a presumed father if he receives the child into his home and openly holds out the child as his own natural child. *In re Nicholas H.*, (2002) 28 Cal.4th 56, held that such presumed fatherhood could exist even if the man admitted he was not child's biological father. Also, Family Code § 7602 states that the parent and child relationship extends equally to every child and to every parent, regardless of the marital status of the parents.

In interpreting what is now Family Code § 7611(d), the California Supreme Court held in *Adoption of Kelsey S.*, (1992) 1 Cal.4th 816, and *Adoption of Michael H.*, (1995) 10 Cal.4th 1043, that the statutes requires actual receipt of the child into the natural father's home – not a mere "constructive receipt" of the child – even if the child's mother hinders actual receipt of the child into the father's home. There is dicta in *Kelsey S.* suggesting that receipt into the home for only one day might be sufficient to establish presumed father status. (The *Michael H.* decision acknowledges that *Kelsey S.* contains some dicta.) There is no statute or case law setting forth a minimum amount of time that the child must be in the putative father's home to perfect presumed father status. On the other hand, the dicta from *Kelsey S.* failed to consider the Legislature's treatment of "token efforts" to communicate with the child, which under Family Code § 7822(b) are insufficient to overcome a presumption of abandonment. (See Chapter 6 of this book.) *Kelsey S.* also fails to consider the relationship between the act of receiving the child into the home and the timing of the open and public admission of paternity.

As far as what constitutes "openly holding out the child as one's own natural child," the court in *In re T.R.* (2005) 132 Cal.App.4th 1202, held that the court's look to such factors as whether the man actively helped the mother in prenatal care; whether he paid pregnancy and birth expenses commensurate with his ability to do so; whether he promptly took legal action to obtain custody of the child; whether he sought to have his name placed on the birth certificate; whether and how long he cared for the child; whether there is unequivocal evidence that he had acknowledged the child; the number of people to whom he had acknowledged the child; whether he provided for the child after it no longer resided with him; whether, if the child needed public benefits, he had pursued completion of the requisite paperwork; and whether his care was merely incidental. The *T.R.* court also held that the presumption may be rebutted by evidence of molestation of the child and failure to disclose "sex offender" status, since the purpose of the presumption is to safeguard the relationship of the child to the "individual who has demonstrated a commitment to the child and the child's welfare."

e) Child of a Rapist?

Family Code § 7611.5 states, "Where Section 7611 does not apply, a man shall not be presumed to be the natural father of a child if either of the following is true: (a)

The child was conceived as a result of an act in violation of Section 261 of the Penal Code [rape] and the father was convicted of that violation. (b) The child was conceived as a result of an act in violation of Section 261.5 of the Penal Code [statutory rape], the father was convicted of that violation, and the mother was under the age of 15 years and the father was 21 years of age or older at the time of conception."

The introductory phrase of Family Code § 7611.5, i.e., "Where Section 7611 does not apply," is a source of concern. As worded, the statute appears to provide that if a man otherwise qualifies as a presumed father, his consent to the adoption would be required, even if the child was conceived as a result of a rape. Therefore, unless the father's parental rights could be terminated under Family Code § 7825 or some other relevant statute, his consent to the adoption would technically appear to be necessary, if he could establish presumed father status.

As to constitutional considerations, the court in *Adoption of Kelsey S.*, (1992) 1 Cal.4th 816, held that its decision afforded no protection, constitutional or otherwise, to a male who impregnates a female as a result of nonconsensual sexual intercourse. On the other hand, *Kelsey S.* affords parental rights on constitutional grounds, and not under the Uniform Parentage Act.

2. Two Additional Categories of Fathers with Rights

a) Paternity Declarations

Family Code § 7573 states, "Except as provided in Sections 7575, 7576, and 7577, a completed voluntary declaration of paternity, as described in Section 7574, that has been filed with the Department of Child Support Services shall establish the paternity of a child and shall have the same force and effect as a judgment for paternity issued by a court of competent jurisdiction. The voluntary declaration of paternity shall be recognized as a basis for the establishment of an order for child custody, visitation, or child support."

A paternity declaration signed in another state is entitled to full faith and credit. (*In re Mary G.* (2007) 151 Cal.App.4th 184.) On the other hand, *H.S. v. Superior Court*, (2010) 183 Cal.App.4th 1502, holds that a paternity declaration is voidable if it is signed by a married woman and a man who is not her husband.

In addition, the introductory language of Family Code § 7611 indicates that a male "is presumed to be the natural father of a child if" he satisfies all the conditions for a paternity declaration as provided in Family Code § 7570, et seq. That being the case, such a person would be a "presumed father" with consent rights based solely on the paternity declaration. The courts have also held that a man who signs a paternity declaration has greater rights than a man who is a Family Code § 7511(d) presumed father by virtue of having received the child into his home and held out the child as his natural child, even if the man who signed the paternity declaration had not taken meaningful steps to maintain contact with the child or provide for his support. (See *Kevin Q. v. Lauren W.* (2009) 175 Cal.App.4th 1119.)

Family Code § 7574 provides for the format of the declaration of paternity; Family Code § 7575 deals with rescission of a paternity declaration; Family Code § 7576 sets forth how the presumptions from a paternity declaration may be rebutted; and Family Code § 7577 covers declarations signed by minors. The court in *In re J.L.*, (2008) 159 Cal.App.4th 1010, applied Family Code § 7575(b)(3)(A), and held that a motion to set aside a paternity declaration can be filed by a local child support agency, the mother, the man who signed the paternity declaration, a participant in a Family Code § 7630 paternity action, or a participant in any action to establish an order for child custody, visitation, or child support based upon the paternity declaration. Family Code § 7575(b)(3)(A) also allows for such an interested party to file a motion for genetic tests for the purpose of contesting the paternity declaration, if the motion is filed not later than two years from the date of the child's birth. *County of Orange v. Superior Court*, (2007) 155 Cal.App.4th 1253, also holds that the court has equity jurisdiction (Family Code § 7575(c)(4)) to entertain such a motion where it is alleged that the moving party is the victim of extrinsic fraud.

b) "Best Interests" Where Paternity Is Claimed

Family Code § 7664(b) provides the court with the substantive framework for determining whether an alleged father is a presumed father. The statute begins by saying that if the natural father or a man representing himself to be the natural father claims parental rights, the court shall determine if he is the father, and "then determine if it is in the best interest of the child that the father retain his parental rights, or that an adoption of the child be allowed to proceed." As explained in Chapter 2, the "best interests" criteria set forth in Family Code § 3011 are to be applied in a Uniform Parentage Act case.

Importantly, Family Code § 7664(c) states that "nothing in this part [which consists of the entire Uniform Parentage Act, including Family Code § 7664(b)] changes the rights of a presumed father under Section 7611." Therefore, it would appear that where a male has proven that he is a "presumed father" as defined by Family Code § 7611, the "best interests" analysis is inapplicable to the question of whether he has consent rights.

On the other hand, an additional category of persons with consent rights exists under Family Code § 7664(b), which requires the consent of a man who is not a presumed father, where it is in the best interests of the child that that man retain his parental rights. Where the "best interests" analysis under Family Code § 7664(b) applies, the statute provides that in making that determination, the court may consider all relevant evidence, including the efforts made by the father to obtain custody, the age and prior placement of the child, and the effects of a change of placement on the child. If the court finds that it is in the best interest of the child that the father should be allowed to retain his parental rights, it shall order that his consent is necessary for an adoption. If the court finds that the man claiming parental rights is not the father, or that if he is the father it is in the child's best interest that an adoption be allowed to proceed, it shall order that that person's consent is not required for an adoption. The statute clarifies that a Family Code § 7664(b) finding that a person's consent is not required for an adoption "terminates all parental rights and responsibilities with respect to the child." *Quilloin v. Walcott*, (1978) 434 U.S. 246, provides that where the child is in the custody of prospective adoptive parents and the natural father merely wants to block the adoption, the court is "not required [by the equal protection clause] to find anything more than that the adoption, and denial of legitimation, [are] in the best interests of the child." But if the alleged father meets his burden of proof , *Adoption of Kelsey S.*, (1992) 1 Cal.4th 816, states that the court may issue not only a declaration of parentage, but also a custody award to the natural father.

Family Code § 7664(b) also states that Family Code § 3041, which codifies the "detriment" rule applicable to child custody determinations in a marital dissolution or separation, "does not apply to a proceeding under this chapter (which is entitled 'termination of parental rights in adoption proceedings')." (See also, *Adoption of Kelsey S.*, (1992) 1 Cal.4th 816, and *Adoption of Christopher S.*, (1987) 197 Cal.App.3d 433.) In other words, according to Family Code § 7664(b), the court is only to determine whether it is in the best interests of the child that the father retain his parental rights, as opposed to allowing the adoption to be finalized. The court need not and must not inquire as to whether awarding custody to the alleged father would be "detrimental" to the child.

3. "*Kelsey S.* Fathers"

a) Summary of the *Kelsey S.* Decision

In *Adoption of Kelsey S.*, (1992) 1 Cal.4th 816, the California Supreme Court held that pursuant to the federal constitutional guarantees of equal protection and due process, the father of a child born out of wedlock may not properly be denied the right to withhold his consent to his child's adoption by a third party, where he has undertaken diligent and legal attempts to obtain custody of his child and to rear it himself, and where there is no showing of the father's unfitness as a parent. *Kelsey S.* involved a natural father who was hindered in his efforts to become a presumed father as defined by Family Code § 7611(d). Indeed, an attorney advising a custodial birth parent to hinder such efforts could be held liable for punitive damages to the natural father. See *Kessel v. Leavitt*, (W.Va. 1998) 511 S.E.2d 720.

Importantly, both *Kelsey S.* and the later case of *Adoption of Michael H.*, (1995) 10 Cal.4th 1043, state that an unwed father has no federal constitutional right to withhold consent to an at-birth, third party adoption unless he shows that, "within a short time after he learned or reasonably should have learned" that the biological mother was pregnant with his child, he promptly came forward and demonstrated as full a commitment to his parental responsibilities as the biological mother allowed and the circumstances permitted. Applying this rule, the court must therefore examine the natural father's conduct even before the child is born.

In *Kelsey S.*, it appears that at the time of the child's birth, the prospective adoptive parents had the natural mother's permission to take the child home from the hospital. Two days after the child's birth, the undisputed natural father filed an action to establish his parental relationship and to obtain custody of the child. The court immediately issued a temporary restraining order awarding custody of the child to the natural father, who then filed a copy of the order with law enforcement officials, but was unsuccessful in his attempts to personally serve the order on the prospective adoptive parents, who had actual custody of the child. The order also stayed all adoption proceedings and prohibited any contact between the child and the prospective adoptive parents. Apparently since there was no service of the order, the prospective adoptive parents filed a petition for adoption and to declare that there was no presumed father. Two days later, the court modified its order and awarded temporary custody of the child to its mother, and prohibited contact with either the natural father or the prospective adoptive parents. The following week, the prospective adoptive parents filed a petition under what is now Family Code §§ 7660-7666 to terminate the natural father's parental rights. The trial court ruled that the natural father was not a "presumed father" under the Uniform Parentage Act. After four days of hearings, the trial court found by a preponderance of the evidence that the child's best interests required termination of his parental rights, pursuant to what is now Family Code § 7664(b).

The California Supreme Court did not overturn the trial court's interpretations of the statutes nor its findings. Instead, it concluded that since the language of what is now Family Code § 7664(a)(2) did not require any showing of unfitness on the part of the natural father, the statutes appeared to conflict with *Stanley v. Illinois*, (1972) 405 U.S. 645, which states that the Due Process clause requires a particularized finding of unfitness. The natural father in *Kelsey S.* was never found to be unfit. The *Kelsey S.* court also reviewed *Lehr v. Robertson*, (1983) 463 U.S. 248, which held that the significance of the biological link is that it offers the natural father an opportunity that no other male possesses to develop a relationship with his offspring, and that if he grasps that opportunity and accepts some measure of responsibility for the child's future, he may enjoy the blessings of the parent-child relationship and make valuable contributions to the child's development. But if he has never established a substantial relationship with his child, statutory non-recognition of his paternity does not operate to deny equal protection.

After reviewing these cases, the *Kelsey S.* court held, "If an unwed father promptly comes forward and demonstrates a full commitment to his parental responsibilities--emotional, financial, and otherwise--his federal constitutional right to due process prohibits the termination of his parental relationship absent a showing of his unfitness as a parent. Absent such a showing, the child's well-being is presumptively best served by continuation of the father's parental relationship. Similarly, when the father has come forward to grasp his parental responsibilities, his parental rights are entitled to equal protection as those of the mother. [¶] A court should consider all factors relevant to that determination. [1] The father's conduct both before and after the child's birth must be considered. [2] Once he knows or reasonably should know of the pregnancy, he must promptly attempt to assume his parental responsibilities as fully as the mother will allow and his circumstances permit. [3] In particular, the father must demonstrate a willingness himself to assume full custody of the child -- not merely to block adoption by others. [4] A court should also consider the father's public acknowledgement of paternity, [5] payment of pregnancy and birth expenses commensurate with his ability to do so, and [6] prompt legal action to seek custody of the child." As far as what constitutes "prompt," the court in *In re Baby Boy V.*, (2006) 140 Cal.App.4th 1108, held that it is possible that a man could be deemed to be a *Kelsey S.* father even if that man came forward when the child was eight months old, as long as he did so as soon as he first heard of the child's existence.

The *Kelsey S.* court then held that if the natural father meets his burden of proof such that the case is reduced down to the issue of whether the natural father is an "unfit parent," any finding of unfitness must be supported by clear and convincing evidence, the burden of which is on the party arguing that the natural father has no parental rights. In *Adoption of Michael H.*, (1995) 10 Cal.4th 1043, the California Supreme Court stated that the father's constitutional interest is merely inchoate and does not ripen into a constitutional right that he can assert to prevent adoption unless he proves that he has promptly come forward and demonstrated a full commitment to his parental responsibilities, "because the mere existence of a biological link does not merit constitutional protection; rather, the federal Constitution protects only the parental relationship that the unwed father has actively developed by coming forward to participate in the rearing of his child and acting as a father." On the other hand, the court in *In re Adoption of Arthur M.*, (2007) 149 Cal.App.4th 704, held that the biological father's fear of being prosecuted for rape does not excuse him from his duty to come forward to meet his parental responsibilities.

In a footnote, the *Kelsey S.* court held that its decision affords no protection, constitutional or otherwise, to a male who impregnates a female as a result of nonconsensual sexual intercourse. However, nothing in the opinion put the burden on the natural father to prove that "consensual" intercourse had taken place.

b) The Impact of *Kelsey S.* upon the Attorney

The practitioner would be wise to give notice to anyone who would be even marginally considered as a possible father under the Uniform Parentage Act and the *Kelsey S.* case, even if it is thought that that person might not consent to the adoption. There is nothing in the law saying that the giving of notice is an admission that the person receiving notice has parental rights. To the contrary, once notice is given, the responsibility then falls on the alleged father to substantiate his parental rights.

c) Non-Retroactivity of the *Kelsey S.* Decision

The court in *Adoption of Kelsey S.*, (1992) 1 Cal.4th 816, emphasized that its decision was only to be applied prospectively: "Our decision shall therefore have no effect in adoption proceedings in which a final judgment has been entered. Such judgments cannot be challenged either directly or collaterally." For example, it would appear that a pre-1992 adoption decree cannot be collaterally attacked in a probate proceeding on the grounds that *Kelsey S.* was violated in obtaining the adoption order.

4. The Evidentiary Effect of the Presumption of Paternity

a) Rebutting the Statutory Presumption

Family Code § 7612(a) states that except as to the paternity presumptions arising under Family Code § 7540 (child of the marriage) and Family Code § 7570 (paternity declarations), a presumption under Family Code § 7611 is a rebuttable presumption affecting the burden of proof and may be rebutted in an appropriate action by clear and convincing evidence. However, in *In re Nicholas H.*, (2002) 28 Cal.4th 56, the California Supreme Court held that a man who was the child's presumed father pursuant to Family Code § 7611(d), and who had admitted that he was not the biological father of the child, was not required to be adjudicated as a non-father since the provisions of Family Code § 7612(a) were not mandatory. Importantly, *Nicholas H.* did not involve a paternity contest between two men, but was a dependency proceeding in which the only man involved in the child's life was claiming parental rights.

As to how the presumption may be overcome, Family Code § 7612(c) states that the Family Code § 7611 presumption is rebutted by a judgment establishing paternity of the child by another man. Importantly, the statute does not limit such judgments to those issued by California courts, and does not limit such judgments to those issued in paternity proceedings. However, it would seem that such a judgment would have to satisfy the elements of the doctrine of collateral estoppel (see *Pacific Lumber Co. v. State Water Resources Control Bd.* (2006) 37 Cal.4th 921, 943) before the presumption could be automatically overcome by that judgment.

b) Conflicting Presumptions of Parentage

Family Code § 7612(b) states that if the facts give rise to two or more of the statutory presumptions that conflict with each other, "the presumption which on the facts is founded on the weightier considerations of policy and logic controls." Since the statute uses the word "controls," it would appear the court must choose one man as the father of the child in the eyes of the law. There is no provision stating that a child may have two fathers, and in fact, Family Code § 7610(b) speaks in terms of "the" natural father of the child. For purposes of resolving conflicting presumptions under Family Code § 7612(b), a *Kelsey S.* father is the equivalent of a statutorily presumed father. (*In re M.C.* (2011) 195 Cal.App.4th 197.)

In *In re Melissa G.*, (1989) 213 Cal.App.3d 1082, the court did in fact make a choice between two men claiming presumed father status. The child in *Melissa G.* was conceived and born during the mother's marriage to a man (who is thus presumed to be the father under Family Code § 7611(a)), but the couple separated and the mother and child then moved to the home of another man, who held the child out as his own (making the second man a presumed father under Family Code § 7611(d), since under Family Code § 7541 he established that there was no biological link between the child and the first man). The court weighed a great number of considerations, including not only the emotional aspects of the parent-child relationships, but sibling contact as well, and held that the child's mother's husband was not the presumed father.

In *Johnson v. Calvert*, (1993) 5 Cal.4th 84, which was a case involving a surrogacy agreement, the court enforced the agreement, thus deciding to make a choice between two women claiming to be the child's "natural mother."

On the other hand, in *Elisa B. v. Superior Court*, (2005) 37 Cal.4th 108, the Supreme Court held that the child had two mothers. The court stated, "a woman who agreed to raise children with her lesbian partner, supported her partner's artificial insemination using an anonymous donor, and received the resulting twin children into her home and held them out as her own, is the children's parent under the Uniform Parentage Act." On the other hand, *Elisa B.* was a child support action, and not an adoption case.

c) Three Parents?

In *K.M. v. E.G.*, (2005) 37 Cal.4th 130, the California Supreme Court held that a child could have two legally recognized "mothers" within the meaning of the Uniform Parentage Act. However, *K.M. v. E.G.* involved a mere sperm donor who could not acquire any legally recognized parental rights. But in *In re M.C.*, (2011) 195 Cal.App.4th 197, the biological father was deemed to be a *Kelsey S.* father, while the birth mother's wife (The two women married each other on October 15, 2008, when same-sex marriage was legal in California.) was deemed to be a "presumed mother" pursuant to Family Code § 7611(a) and (d).

In *Elisa B. v. Superior Court*, (2005) 37 Cal.4th 108, the California Supreme Court rejected the notion that a child could have three legally recognized parents. Therefore, the *M.C.* court held that the trial court erred in finding that the child had three parents, and remanded for the purpose of determining which two of the three should be accorded parental rights.

5. Procedure for Determining Presumed Father Status

a) Petition to Terminate Parental Rights

A person thought to be a mere "alleged" father may later be deemed to be a presumed father having the power to veto the adoption. However, Family Code § 7662 provides a way to prevent that from happening, and a way to rebut a presumption of such a man's parenthood.

Family Code § 7662 states that if a mother relinquishes for or consents to, or proposes to relinquish for or consent to, the adoption of a child who does not have a presumed father under Section 7611, or if a child otherwise becomes the subject of an adoption proceeding and the alleged father, if any, has not, in writing, denied paternity, waived his right to notice, or voluntarily relinquished for or consented to the adoption, the agency or person to whom the child has been or is to be relinquished, or the mother or the person having physical or legal custody of the child, or the prospective adoptive parent, shall file a petition to terminate the parental rights of the father, unless either of the following occurs: (a) the father's relationship to the child has been previously terminated or determined not to exist by a court, or (b) the father has been served as prescribed in Family Code § 7666 with a written notice alleging that he is or could be the natural father of the child to be adopted or placed for adoption and has failed to bring an action for the purpose of declaring the existence of the father-child relationship pursuant to Family Code § 7630(c) within 30 days of service of notice or the birth of the child, whichever is later. In *In re Andrew V.*, (1991) 232 Cal.App.3d 1286, this 30-day rule was deemed to be a type of statute of limitations which could be subject to various exceptions; not a jurisdictional statute.

Importantly, Family Code § 7662 only deals with the adoption of children who either do not have a presumed father, or who have a presumed father but where several conditions exist. In many cases, the prospective adoptive parents do not know whether the child has a presumed father or not, especially since presumed father status may exist under Family Code § 7611(d) but not be readily apparent.

There is also nothing in the statutes which prohibits pleading in the alternative, meaning that there is nothing to prevent a prospective adoptive parent to, on the one hand, seek a declaration of the nonexistence of paternity, and on the other hand, seek a termination of parental rights, and do so all in the same petition. If two different petitions are used, there is nothing to prevent the two petitions from being served at the same time and later consolidated.

b) Standing to File Petition

Under Family Code § 7630(b), an "interested party" may bring an action to determine the existence or nonexistence of a Family Code § 7611(d) father-child relationship. However, where presumed father status is asserted under Family Code § 7611(a), (b) or (c), the provisions of Family Code § 7630(a) state that only the child, the child's natural mother, or the child's presumed father under Family Code § 7611(a), (b) or (c) may bring such an action. In *Said v. Jegan*, (2007) 146 Cal.App.4th 1375, the court held that a man who was only an alleged father had standing to bring a Family Code § 7630(b) petition to determine the nonexistence of a father-child relationship. Family Code § 7630(a)(2) states that after the paternity presumption has been rebutted, another man's paternity may be established in the same action if he is joined as a party.

In addition, Family Code § 7631 states that, if the mother relinquishes for, consents to, or proposes to relinquish for or consent to, the adoption of the child, a man who is not a presumed father may bring an action for the purpose of declaring that he is the natural father of a child having a presumed father under Section 7611, except in cases where a man is conclusively presumed to be the child's father pursuant to Family Code § 7540. Family Code § 7631 states that the commencement of the action suspends a pending proceeding in connection with the adoption of the child until a judgment in the action is final.

c) Identifying Persons to be Named and Served

(1) Due Diligence

The identification of persons to be named and served with a petition to determine parental rights under Family Code § 7630 should be made after the due diligence procedures of Family Code § 7663 have been completed. (The identification of persons to be named and served as parties to the adoption proceedings is explained in Chapter 10.)

Family Code § 7663(a) states that in an effort to identify the natural father, the court shall cause inquiry to be made of the mother and any other appropriate person by any of the following: (1) the CDSS, (2) a licensed county adoption agency, (3) the licensed adoption agency to which the child is to be relinquished, or (4) in the case of a stepparent adoption, at the option of the board of supervisors, a licensed county adoption agency, the county department designated by the board of supervisors to administer the public social services program, or the county probation department. Thus, counsel should suggest that the court initiate this statutory process where these entities have not done so already. Also, there is no prohibition against the prospective adoptive parents from hiring an investigator to locate the natural father, and even though Family Code § 7663(c) states that the official investigative findings shall be reported to the court, there is no prohibition against reporting to the court the results of a private investigation.

As for the methodology, Family Code § 7663(b) states that the inquiry shall include all of the following: (1) whether the mother was married at the time of conception of the child or at any time thereafter, (2) whether the mother was cohabiting with a man at the time of conception or birth of the child, (3) whether the mother has received support payments or promises of support with respect to the child or in connection with her pregnancy, and (4) whether any man has formally or informally acknowledged or declared his possible paternity of the child.

(2) Serving Notice and the Consequences for Failing to Respond to Notice

Family Code § 7664(a) states that if, after the inquiry, the natural father is identified to the satisfaction of the court, or if more than one man is identified as a possible father, each shall be given notice of the proceeding in accordance with Family Code § 7666, unless he has been served with a written notice alleging that he is or could be the natural father of the child to be adopted or placed or relinquished for adoption and has failed to bring an action pursuant to subdivision (c) of Section 7630 to declare the existence of the father and child relationship within 30 days after service of the notice or the birth of the child, whichever is later.

Family Code § 7666(a) provides that notice of the proceeding shall be given to every person identified as the natural father or a possible natural father in accordance with the Code of Civil Procedure for the service of process in a civil action in this state, except that publication or posting of the notice of the proceeding is not required. Proof of giving the notice shall be filed with the court before the petition is heard. Family Code § 7666(b) states that if a person identified as the natural father or possible natural father cannot be located or his whereabouts is unknown or cannot be ascertained, the court may issue an order dispensing with notice to that person. However, in practice, it is advisable to seek an order allowing service by publication where a possible father cannot be located.

Family Code § 7662(a)(2) and the second sentence of Family Code § 7664(a) provide that if any of the possible fathers fails to appear or, if appearing, fails to claim parental rights, his parental rights with reference to the child shall be terminated. In *Adoption of Aaron H.*, (2000) 84 Cal.App.4th 786, the court upheld a termination of parental rights resulting from the birth father's failure to timely respond to notice, and stated that any motion to set aside that type of termination of rights on grounds of mistake, inadvertence, surprise or excusable neglect as defined in Code of Civil Procedure § 473 would have to present evidence that the moving party sought relief "with reasonable diligence." The *Aaron H.* court found no abuse of discretion in an order denying Code of Civil Procedure § 473 relief to a birth father who took 39 days after notice to assert his alleged paternity rights.

(3) Unknown Fathers

Family Code § 7665 states that if, after the inquiry (see Family Code § 7663), the court is unable to identify the natural father or any possible natural father and no person has appeared claiming to be the natural father and claiming custodial rights, the court shall enter an order terminating the unknown natural father's parental rights with reference to the child.

d) Deadline to File Petition for Declaration of Existence of Parental Relationship

(1) Non-Presumed Fathers Claiming Rights

An action under Family Code § 7631 "shall be brought" within 30 days after (1) the man is served as prescribed in Section 7666 with a notice that he is or could be the father of the child or (2) the birth of the child, whichever is later. This would appear to create a method by which to terminate alleged parental rights of any male who is "not a presumed father." Indeed, the termination of rights by virtue of the alleged father's failure to formally asserts parental rights is also demonstrated at Family Code § 7664(a), as explained above.

(2) Presumed Fathers and Interested Parties

Importantly, Family Code § 7630(b) expressly states that an action for the purpose of determining the existence or nonexistence of the father and child relationship presumed under Family Code § 7611(d) may be brought "at any time." Family Code § 7633 even allows it to be brought before the child's birth. However, where presumed father status is asserted pursuant to Family Code § 7611(a), (b) or (c), such an action must be brought "within a reasonable time after obtaining knowledge of relevant facts" if the petitioner is seeking to establish the nonexistence of the father-child relationship.

If the petitioner is seeking to establish the existence of a father-child relationship, such an action may be brought "at any time" against a person who is asserted as being a presumed father under Family Code § 7611(a), (b) or (c). *In re Shereece B.*, (1991) 231 Cal.App.3d 613, holds that where there is no presumed father, a proceeding to terminate an alleged natural father's parental rights may be brought before formal commencement of an adoption proceeding.

e) The Hearing on the Petition

Family Code § 7667(a) states that an action to terminate the parental rights of a father of a child under Family Code § 7600, et seq. shall be set for hearing not more than 45 days after filing of the petition and completion of service thereof or the entry of an order dispensing with notice of the proceedings. The petition shall either specify the date of the hearing or state that it will be held on a date which shall be separately noticed.

As for the evidence at the hearing, the U.S. Supreme Court held in *Rivera v. Minnich*, (1987) 483 U.S. 574, that the issue of paternity need only be decided under the "preponderance of the evidence" standard, whereas the issue of the termination of a presumed father's parental rights is determined under the "clear and convincing evidence" standard. A distinction should therefore be drawn at the hearing between a determination that a man is not a presumed father versus a determination that a presumed father's parental rights are being terminated.

f) Establishing the Biological Link

(1) Blood or Genetic Tests

Family Code § 7541(a) states that notwithstanding Section 7540 [which deals with a husband's conclusive presumption of paternity of the child of the marriage], if the court finds that the conclusions of all the experts, as disclosed by the evidence based on blood tests performed pursuant to Chapter 2 (commencing with Section 7550), are that the husband is not the father of the child, the question of paternity of the husband shall be resolved accordingly.

However, Family Code § 7541(e) states that blood tests may not be used to challenge paternity where, (1) paternity had already been established by way of a final judgment on or before September 30, 1980 (which would now relate only to situations where the "child" is an adult and the adoption is being challenged for example in a probate case), (2) the child was conceived by artificial insemination, as described in Family Code § 7613, or (3) the child was conceived by means of a surgical procedure wherein the wife had her husband's consent.

(2) Procedure for Seeking Tests

Family Code § 7541(b) and (c) contemplate the bringing of a noticed motion for blood tests under this section, but establish that it must be filed no later than two years from the child's date of birth. Family Code § 7541(b) and (c) also contemplate that a motion for blood tests may be brought by the husband, the child's "presumed father" as defined in Family Code §§ 7611 and 7612, the child's mother if the child's biological father has filed an affidavit with the court acknowledging paternity of the child, and even by the child through or by a guardian ad litem. In addition, Family Code § 7551 only requires the court to entertain the motion if it is made "at a time so as not to delay the proceedings unduly." Family Code § 7551 also allows the court to *sua sponte* order the mother, child and alleged father to submit to genetic tests. (*Gabriel P. v. Suedi D.* (2006) 141 Cal.App.4th 850.)

However, a trial court's power to order genetic testing to assist it in determining whether someone is the biological father of the child extends only to parties over whom the court has personal jurisdiction. (*San Mateo County Dept. of Child Support Services v. Clark* (2008) 168 Cal.App.4th 834.) Also, when a man who is not a Family Code §

7611 presumed father seeks to establish his paternity, the trial court may not order blood tests under Family Code § 7541 to defeat the conclusive Family Code § 7540 "child of the marriage" presumption. (*In re Elijah V.* (2005) 127 Cal.App.4th 576.)

Interestingly, Family Code § 7551 states that the court "shall" grant a timely motion for genetic tests. However, Family Code § 7541(d) requires that the motion for blood tests be supported by the moving party's declaration under oath stating the factual basis for placing the issue of paternity before the court.

Although Family Code § 7541 speaks in terms of a noticed motion, Family Code § 7551 states that where paternity is a relevant fact, the court "may" upon its own initiative or upon suggestion made by or on behalf of any person who is involved order the mother, child, and alleged father to submit to genetic tests. If a party refuses to submit to the tests, the court may resolve the question of paternity against that party or enforce its order if the rights of others and the interests of justice so require. A party's refusal to submit to the tests is admissible in evidence in any proceeding to determine paternity. For the purposes of this chapter, "genetic tests" means any genetic test that is generally acknowledged as reliable by accreditation bodies designated by the United States Secretary of Health and Human Services.

(3) Expert Testimony re Paternity

Family Code § 7554(a) states, "If the court finds that the conclusions of all the experts, as disclosed by the evidence based upon the tests, are that the alleged father is not the father of the child, the question of paternity shall be resolved accordingly." Family Code § 7554(b) then states, "If the experts disagree in their findings or conclusions, or if the tests show the probability of the alleged father's paternity, the question, subject to Section 352 of the Evidence Code, shall be submitted upon all the evidence, including evidence based upon the tests."

(4) No Rights for Mere Sperm Donor

Under Family Code § 7613(b), the donor of semen provided to a licensed physician and surgeon for use in artificial insemination of a woman other than the donor's wife is treated in law as if he were not the natural father of a child thereby conceived. The statute says nothing about anonymity. Thus, even if the sperm bank or a female recipient or some other interested person breached an agreement to maintain confidentiality or anonymity, nothing Family Code § 7613(b) would allow the donor to acquire parental rights. The court in *Steven S. v. Deborah D.*, (2005) 127 Cal.App.4th 319, held that a mere sperm donor acquires no parental rights, even if he had an intimate relationship with the child's mother.

Family Code § 7613(a) provides that if, under the supervision of a licensed physician and surgeon and with the signed written consent of her husband, a wife is inseminated artificially with semen donated by a man not her husband, the husband is treated in law as if he were the natural father of a child thereby conceived. Therefore, if the mother of the child is married at the time of the artificial insemination, the husband will always be the presumed father. It does not appear that the provisions of Family Code § 7613(a) are dependent upon Family Code § 7613(b), or vice versa. But if the female recipient is not married, Family Code § 7613 does not appear to prevent the sperm donor from later becoming a presumed father under *Adoption of Kelsey S.*, (1992) 1 Cal.4th 816, or one of the subsections of Family Code § 7611, meaning that under either of these two latter scenarios, the sperm donor would acquire consent rights.

It should be noted that Family Code § 7613 does not apply to the donor of ova. In *K.M. v. E.G.*, (2005) 37 Cal.4th 130, the Supreme Court held that where a woman provided ova to her lesbian partner for in vitro fertilization and the partner then gave birth to twins who had a genetic link to the donor, both women were "parents" of those children. The court held that the approach of *Johnson v. Calvert*, (1993) 5 Cal.4th 84, i.e., to choose one of the two women to be the child's mother, did not apply, because *Johnson* involved a surrogate whom the parties did not intend to act as the child's parent after the birth. Also, the children in *K.M. v. E.G.* were conceived through the aid of a sperm donor, meaning that the child did not have three parents.

g) Appealability of Order

Family Code § 7669 provides that an order requiring or dispensing with a father's consent for the adoption of a child is separately appealable.

B. Natural Mother

1. Proving Maternity

As set forth in Family Code §§ 8604(a) and 8605, the mother of the child has consent rights even if she cannot establish that she is a "presumed" mother. In most cases, the identity of the birth mother is clearly stated on the birth certificate. (But see *In re Karen C.*, (2002) 101 Cal.App.4th 932 [birth mother used false identity at the hospital].) Problems in identifying the birth mother could arise in the case of an abandonment, or where a child in the custody of a foreign orphanage is sought for adoption.

Family Code § 7610 states that a female may establish the mother-child relationship by proof of her having given birth to the child, or by applying the provisions of the Uniform Parentage Act. Additionally, Family Code § 7650 states, "Any interested person may bring an action to determine the existence or nonexistence of a mother and child relationship. Insofar as practicable, the provisions of this part applicable to the father and child relationship apply."

Based on the references in these two statutes to the Uniform Parentage Act, it would appear that a female could establish maternity not only through the birth certificate, but also by establishing one or more of the presumptions set forth at Family Code § 7611. In *Elisa B. v. Superior Court*, (2005) 37 Cal.4th 108, the court held that a female who had received the child into her home and held the minor out as her own offspring could be a Family Code § 7611(d) presumed mother, even though she was not a blood relative. Also, the court in *K.M. v. E.G.* (2005) 37 Cal.4th 130, held that a set of twins had "two mothers," since one "mother" supplied the ova that were fertilized in vitro (with donated sperm) and implanted in the other "mother," and the two women agreedly raised the children in their joint home.

2. Assisted Reproductive Technology – Surrogacy

In *Johnson v. Calvert*, (1993) 5 Cal.4th 84, the California Supreme Court addressed the question of identifying the child's "natural mother" under California law "when, pursuant to a surrogacy agreement, a zygote formed of the gametes of a husband and wife is implanted in the uterus of another woman, who carries the resulting fetus to term and gives birth to a child not genetically related to" the woman who gave birth. In *Johnson*, the surrogate claimed parental rights under the constitution and what is now Family Code § 7610 by virtue of having undisputedly given birth to the child. The wife who had contributed the egg pursuant to the surrogacy agreement was claiming parental rights under what is now Family Code §§ 7540, 7541 and 7611(a) by virtue of the genetic link between the child and both herself and her husband.

The *Johnson* court first determined that surrogacy agreements do not offend the state or federal Constitution or public policy. *Johnson* holds, "It is not the role of the judiciary to inhibit the use of reproductive technology when the Legislature has not seen fit to do so; any such effort would raise serious questions in light of the fundamental nature of the rights of procreation and privacy." The court also stated that since both women presented acceptable proof of maternity, the case could not be decided without inquiring into the parties' intentions as manifested in the surrogacy agreement. (see Family Code § 7612(b) [handling conflicting presumptions].)

The *Johnson* court then ruled that although the Uniform Parentage Act recognizes both genetic consanguinity and giving birth as means of establishing a mother and child relationship, "when the two means do not coincide in one woman, she who intended to procreate the child--that is, she who intended to bring about the birth of a child that she intended to raise as her own--is the natural mother under California law." In applying this rule, the court held that since at the time of contracting the parties contemplated that the wife would raise the child, the wife would be deemed the natural mother. The court held that a "best interests of the child" analysis would not be used in such a situation, since parentage had to first be determined. The court also rejected an argument made pursuant to the constitutional right of privacy, stating "A woman who enters into a gestational surrogacy arrangement is not exercising her own right to make procreative choices; she is agreeing to provide a necessary and profoundly important service without (by definition) any expectation that she will raise the resulting child as her own."

A footnote in *Johnson* makes a distinction between a surrogacy agreement and a "true 'egg donation' situation," where a woman receives the fertilized egg of another female with the intent to carry, give birth and raise the child as her own. The *Johnson* court held that the woman who gave birth in an egg donation situation is the natural mother under California law. *Johnson* made no reference whatsoever to instances where one woman who expressly intends to raise the child as her own contracts to have a second woman act as a surrogate mother where the egg is provided by the surrogate or a third woman. Importantly, *Johnson* expressly avoided answering the question of who had the constitutional right to decide whether to terminate the pregnancy, or whether the parties could contractually agree to transfer those constitutional rights.

The field of assisted reproductive technology is now very "cutting edge," scientifically speaking, and literally dozens of different kinds of arrangements that go well beyond a simple surrogacy are physically viable. Indeed, California law (see Family Code § 7611(g) and Probate Code § 249.5) now recognizes posthumous assisted reproduction. A full review of assisted reproductive technology is thus beyond the scope of this book. Suffice it to say that agreements to employ assisted reproductive technology are legally recognized in a variety of different contexts. (See Family Code § 7606 and *Robert B. v. Susan B.* (2003) 109 Cal.App.4th 1109.)

C. Adoptive Parents

Family Code § 7601 provides that the "parent and child relationship" as used in this part (i.e., the Uniform Parentage Act) means the legal relationship existing between a child and the child's natural or adoptive parents incident to which the law confers or imposes rights, privileges, duties, and obligations. The term includes the mother and child relationship and the father and child relationship. Family Code § 7610(c) states that the parent and child relationship between a child and an adoptive parent may be established "by proof of adoption." Likewise, Family Code § 8512 provides that " 'Birth parent' means the biological parent or, in the case of a person previously adopted, the adoptive parent."

The most compelling "proof of adoption" would be a certified copy of the adoption decree. However, the statute does not require a copy of the adoption order. For example, proof of adoption could consist of the revised birth certificate (see Chapter 12), or copies of the checks received from the CDSS pursuant to the Adoption Assistance Act (see Chapter 5). One cannot receive such payments unless there has been an adoption of a "special needs child."

D. The Consent of Others

1. The Prospective Adoptive Parent

Family Code § 8612(b), which applies to all adoptions, states, "The prospective adoptive parent or parents shall execute and acknowledge an agreement in writing that the child will be treated in all respects as their lawful child." The California Judicial Council has developed the Adopt-210 Form for purposes of executing this agreement.

2. The Spouse of the Prospective Adoptive Parent

Under Family Code § 8603, a married person, not lawfully separated from the person's spouse, may not adopt a child without the consent of the spouse, provided that the spouse is capable of giving that consent.

3. The Child

Family Code § 8602 states that the consent of a child, if over the age of 12 years, is necessary to the child's adoption. As explained in Chapter 10, the child and all parties are required to appear in court for the adoption hearing, the court is required to examine all parties appearing in court, and the child is to be examined in chambers. If the child is over 12 years old, the child may also sign the Adopt-210 Form.

4. Agencies?

In *Adoption of McDonald*, (1954) 43 Cal.2d 447, the Supreme Court rejected the contention that the consent of a licensed adoption agency, to which the subject child had been relinquished, was a jurisdictional prerequisite to an adoption decree. Although agency consent is not required, "placement" of the child is statutorily required before a petition for an agency adoption can be filed, as discussed in Chapter 5.

On the other hand, Family Code § 8814(c) provides that in certain situations where the natural mother or presumed father is located outside California, their consent may be signed before a notary, and in that case the consent of the CDSS or of the delegated county adoption agency is also necessary. In addition, Family Code § 8816 provides that, in an independent adoption proceeding, where the consent of the birth parent or parents is not necessary, agency consent shall be filed with the court before the hearing of the adoption petition, but that the consent may not be given unless the child's welfare is promoted by the adoption. This topic is covered in more detail in Chapter 4.

5. The Child's Guardian or Foster Parent?

In *In re Santos' Estate*, (1921) 185 Cal. 127, the Supreme Court stated that the consent of a lawfully appointed guardian is unnecessary to the adoption. There is likewise no provision in the statutes requiring the consent of a foster parent to the adoption, although a foster parent may have priority with regard to an adoptive placement by an agency, as explained in Chapter 5.

IV. TAKING THE CONSENT IN AN INDEPENDENT ADOPTION

A. Non-Delegability of the Right to Consent

Family Code § 8801(a) provides that the selection of a prospective adoptive parent or parents shall be personally made by the child's birth parent or parents and may not be delegated to an agent, and that the selection shall be based upon the birth parent or parents personal knowledge of the prospective adoptive parent or parents. However, if the child has been declared a dependent of the juvenile court, *M.L. v. Superior Court*, (2009) 172 Cal.App.4th 520, holds that the court has an independent obligation to determine the best interests of the child, and therefore is not required to defer to Mother's selection of adoptive parents for her child.

Family Code § 8801(b) defines "personal knowledge" as "substantially correct knowledge of all of the following regarding the prospective adoptive parents: their full legal names, ages, religion, race or ethnicity, length of current marriage and number of previous marriages, employment, whether other children or adults reside in their home, whether there are other children who do not reside in their home and the child support obligation for these children and any failure to meet these obligations, any health conditions curtailing their normal daily activities or reducing their normal life expectancies, any convictions for crimes other than minor traffic violations, any removals of children from their care due to child abuse or neglect, and their general area of residence or, upon request, their address."

B. Requirement of Pre-Consent Counseling – Involvement of Agencies and/or Adoption Service Providers

Family Code § 8806 states that the CDSS or delegated county adoption agency shall accept the consent of the birth parents to the adoption of the child by the petitioners and, before filing its report with the court, shall ascertain whether the child is a proper subject for adoption and whether the proposed home is suitable for the child. Before that, Family Code § 8808 and 22 California Code of Regulations § 35095(a), requires the CDSS or delegated county adoption agency to interview the petitioners and all persons from whom consent is required as soon as possible and, in the case of residents of this state, within 45 working days, excluding legal holidays, after the filing of the adoption petition. However, Family Code § 8808 and 22 California Code of Regulations § 35095(c) also provide that such counseling need not duplicate certain tasks (specified below) that may have already been performed and documented by a licensed adoption service provider (whose functions are described further in Chapter 4).

The interview with the placing parent or parents shall include, but not be limited to, discussion of any concerns or problems that the parent has with the placement and, if the placing parent was not interviewed as provided in Section 8801.7 (relating to the adoption service provider's interview), the content required in that interview. At the interview, the agency shall give the parent an opportunity to sign either a statement revoking the consent, or a waiver of the right to revoke consent, as provided in Section 8814.5.

In order to facilitate these interviews, at the same time the petition is filed with the court, the petitioners shall file with the district office of the CDSS or with the delegated county adoption agency responsible for the investigation of the adoption, a copy of the petition together with the names, addresses, and telephone numbers of all parties to be interviewed, if known. (In most cases, one must have received placement of the child in order to have standing to file the adoption petition. "Placement" will be discussed in Chapter 4 of this book.)

According to 22 California Code of Regulations § 35097(a), the agency shall determine that the consenting parent has the ability to understand the nature, content and effect of signing a consent to adoption. If the agency determines that the parent may not have the ability to understand the content, nature, and effect of signing a consent to adoption, the agency shall refer the parent to a licensed physician or to a licensed clinical psychologist for an evaluation of the parent's ability to so understand. The agency shall accept the consent to adoption only after the evaluation establishes that the parent has the ability to understand the nature, content, and effect of signing a consent to adoption.

C. Required Elements of Pre-Consent Counseling

The regulations provide at 22 California Code of Regulations § 35095(b) that prior to accepting a consent to adoption or a waiver of right to revoke consent, the following information shall be obtained:

1. Child's Background – Reasons for Choosing Adoption

The CDSS or county adoption agency must obtain information from the birth parent regarding the child's background, the birth parents' reasons for choosing adoption, and the birth parents' attitude toward the adoption. (22 California Code of Regulations § 35095(b)(1).) This is a task that may be performed by a licensed adoption service provider according to 22 California Code of Regulations § 35095(c). This inquiry involves having the birth parents provide medical and family background information on the AD 67 and AD 67A forms (see the CDSS web site), taking the consent to the adoption in accordance with 22 California Code of Regulations § 35375 if the child comes within the Indian Child Welfare Act's provisions, and documenting the name of any report, document, or information described in 22 California Code of Regulations § 35000(m)(2) that could not be obtained, and the reasons for not obtaining them.

2. Authorization for Release of Medical Information

The CDSS or county adoption agency must obtain written authorization from the birth parent for the release of medical information. See 22 California Code of Regulations § 35095(b)(2). This task may be performed by a licensed adoption service provider. 22 California Code of Regulations § 35095(c).

3. Authorization for Medical Treatment of the Child

The CDSS or county adoption agency must obtain written authorization from the birth parent for the petitioners to obtain medical care and/or treatment for the child. See 22 California Code of Regulations § 35095(b)(3). This may be obtained by a licensed adoption service provider according to 22 California Code of Regulations § 35095(c).

4. Verifying the Birth Mother's Marital Status

According to 22 California Code of Regulations § 35095(b)(4), the CDSS or county adoption agency must verify the marriages and dissolutions of marriage of the birth mother as required by 22 California Code of Regulations § 35023(b)(5).

5. Interviewing the Prospective Adoptive Parents

22 California Code of Regulations § 35095(b)(5) requires an interview of the petitioners unless the birth parent has requested that he or she be interviewed within 10 working days as provided in Family Code § 8814.5(a)(2)(C), and the agency's schedule precludes interviewing the petitioners prior to the interview with the birth parent. Additionally, Family Code § 9201(c) provides that prior to the placement of a child for adoption, the CDSS or a licensed adoption agency may, upon the written request of both a birth and a prospective adoptive parent, arrange for future contact between the birth and prospective adoptive parents that may include the sharing of identifying information regarding these parents.

6. Determining the Voluntariness as to Child Placement

Under 22 California Code of Regulations § 35095(b)(6), the CDSS or county adoption agency must determine that the birth parent voluntarily chose to place the child with the petitioners for the purpose of an independent adoption under Family Code § 8801 (see above). This regulation contains four requirements:

First, under 22 California Code of Regulations § 35095(b)(6)(A), the agency must document in the court report whether the birth parent voluntarily selected the petitioners and placed the child according to Family Code § 8801. Next, according to 22 California Code of Regulations § 35095(b)(6)(B), if the agency determines that the birth parent has not demonstrated substantially correct knowledge of all elements of personal knowledge regarding the petitioners (see Family Code § 8801(b)), a consent cannot be taken. Also, 22 California Code of Regulations § 35095(b)(6)(C) states that the agency shall advise the birth parent when the placement does not satisfy the statutory definition of an "adoptive placement." Finally, 22 California Code of Regulations § 35095(b)(6)(D) requires the agency to immediately report to the court if the adoptive placement is not made in accordance with the provisions of Family Code §§ 8609, 8801 or 8801.3 (which all relate to placement, and which are explained in Chapter 4).

7. Inquiring Whether Child Will Benefit from Adoption

The CDSS or county adoption agency must determine whether the child and the adoptive family can benefit from adoption. See 22 California Code of Regulations § 35095(b)(7).

8. Explaining Appropriate Statement of Understanding

The CDSS or county adoption agency must provide the parent with an explanation of information contained within the appropriate Statement of Understanding form prescribed by the CDSS. See 22 California Code of Regulations § 35095(b)(8). The CDSS publishes literally dozens of different "Statements of Understanding" to cover different types of situations, and they are all referred to at 22 California Code of Regulations §§ 35095.1 and 35095.2. The explanation of the appropriate Statement of Understanding may be performed by a licensed adoption service provider. See 22 California Code of Regulations § 35095(c). The Statements of Understanding are available on the CDSS web site.

9. Signature on the Statement of Understanding

Under 22 California Code of Regulations § 35095(b)(9), the CDSS or county adoption agency must obtain the birth parent's signature on the Statement of Understanding form after he or she has affirmed his or her understanding of the consent process by reading and initialing each explanatory statement on the Statement of Understanding.

10. Witnessing Signature on Statement of Understanding

According to 22 California Code of Regulations § 35095(b)(10), the CDSS or county adoption agency must sign the Statement of Understanding form certifying that the parent's signature has been properly witnessed. Under 22 California Code of Regulations § 35095(c), this task may be performed by a licensed adoption service provider.

D. The Use of Standard Forms

1. Manner of Obtaining Signatures on Consent Form

Family Code § 8814(a) states that, "Except as provided in Section 7662 [which describes situations where a child has no 'presumed father'], the consent of the birth parent or parents who did not place the child for adoption, as described in Section 8801.3 [which describes the technical requirements for a formal placement of a child for purposes of adoption], to the adoption shall be signed in the presence of an agent of the CDSS or of a delegated county adoption agency on a form prescribed by the CDSS. The consent shall be filed with the clerk of the appropriate superior court."

Concerning the forms that must be used, the State of California CDSS web site (see specifically, http://www.dss.cahwnet.gov/cdssweb/FormsandPu_271.htm) provides hundreds of different free forms and related publications too numerous to republish here. In addition, there are dozens of different forms just on the subject of "consent." Family Code § 8814(a) in essence requires that when the child's mother or presumed father has not formally placed the child for adoption (see Chapter 4 concerning "placement"), the consent of that mother or presumed father must be memorialized by use of the standard form. The tradeoff is that when the consent form is properly used, the consent becomes irrevocable after 30 days, as described below.

As far as who must be present at the signing of the consent form, the court in *In re Duarte's Adoption*, (1964) 229 Cal.App.2d 775, held that the consent was executed in compliance with the statutory prerequisites when it was acknowledged by a social worker with the Alameda County Welfare Department. The *Duarte* court applied a series of statutory presumptions and stated, "Although it is not apparent from the face of the form that the Alameda County Welfare Department was a licensed county adoption agency, WIC [Welfare & Institutions Code], section 1640, provides that 'any county agency' may, upon application by the county, become a licensed county adoption agency. Since it must be presumed that the transaction was 'fair and regular' and that the law was obeyed, it must accordingly be presumed that the Alameda County Welfare Department was a licensed county adoption agency." It would appear that such a process is in accord with the spirit of *Adoption of Barnett*, (1960) 54 Cal.2d 370, as explained above.

In addition, Family Code § 8814(b) provides that the consent form is prima facie evidence of the right of the person making it to the sole custody of the child and that person's sole right to consent where (1) the consent form is properly executed, (2) when the form recites that the person giving the consent is entitled to the sole custody of the child, and (3) when that fact is acknowledged before the agent. This presumption arises only if Family Code § 8814(a) has been satisfied.

2. Adoptive Placement Agreement May Become Consent

Family Code § 8801.3(c)(2) provides that if the birth parent takes no action after validly signing a proper adoption placement agreement, the agreement shall become a permanent and irrevocable consent to the adoption on the 31st day after signing the agreement. This statute was upheld in *Sharon S. v. Superior Court*, (2003) 31 Cal.4th 417. The particulars concerning placement agreements are discussed in Chapter 4.

E. Out-of-State Birth Parents

Family Code § 8814(c) provides that if the natural mother or presumed father is located outside California for an extended period of time unrelated to the adoption at the time of signing the consent, the consent may be signed before a notary or other person authorized to perform notarial acts, and in that case the consent of the CDSS or of the delegated county adoption agency is also necessary. Interjurisdictional adoptions will be discussed more fully in Chapter 9.

F. Consent for and Adoptive Placement of an "Indian Child"

1. The Manner of Taking the Consent

Family Code § 8606.5(a) and 25 U.S.C. § 1913(a) provide that consent to adoption given by the parent of an "Indian child" is not valid unless (1) the consent is executed in writing at least 10 days after the child's birth and is recorded before a judge, and (2) the judge certifies that the terms and consequences of the consent were fully explained in detail in English and were fully understood by the parent or that they were interpreted into a language that the parent understood. At 25 U.S.C. § 1903(4), the federal Indian Child Welfare Act defines "Indian child" as any unmarried person under 18 years old who is either (a) a member of an Indian tribe or (b) eligible for membership in an Indian tribe and is the biological child of a member of an Indian tribe. The Indian Child Welfare Act is discussed more fully in Chapter 9 of this book.

Unlike an adoption involving a non-Indian child, Family Code § 8606.5(b) and 25 U.S.C. § 1913(c) allow the parent of an Indian child to withdraw his or her consent to adoption for any reason at any time prior to the entry of a final decree of adoption, thus requiring return of the child to the parent.

2. Initial Pre-Placement Inquiry re "Indian Child" Status

Family Code § 8620(a)(1) provides that if a parent is seeking to place a child for purposes of adoption, the DSS, licensed adoption agency, or adoption service provider, as applicable, shall ask the child and the child's parent or custodian whether the child is, or may be, a member of, or eligible for membership in an Indian tribe or whether the child has been identified as a member of an Indian organization. The DSS, licensed adoption agency, or adoption service provider, as applicable, shall then complete the DSS forms provided for this purpose and make this completed form part of the file. If there is any information indicating that the child is or may be an Indian child, Family

Code § 8620(a)(2) requires the DSS, licensed adoption agency, or adoption service provider, as applicable, to obtain the following information:

> (A) The name of the child involved, and the actual date and place of birth of the child.
>
> (B) The name, address, date of birth, and tribal affiliation of the birth parents, maternal and paternal grandparents, and maternal and paternal great-grandparents of the child.
>
> (C) The name and address of extended family members of the child who have a tribal affiliation.
>
> (D) The name and address of the Indian tribes or Indian organizations of which the child is, or may be, a member.
>
> (E) A statement of the reasons why the child is, or may be, an Indian.

Family Code § 8620(a)(3)(A) then requires the DSS, licensed adoption agency, adoption service provider, or attorney for the prospective adoptive parents, to send a notice, which shall include the above information, and a request for confirmation of the child's Indian status, to any parent and any custodian of the child, and to any Indian tribe of which the child is, or may be, a member or eligible for membership. If any of the above information cannot be obtained, the notice shall indicate that fact. (Please see Family Code § 180 and Chapter 9 of this book concerning sending notices to Indian tribes.) Family Code § 8620(a)(3)(B) requires the notice to describe the nature of the proceeding and advise the recipient of the Indian tribe's right to intervene in the proceeding on its own behalf or on behalf of a tribal member relative of the child.

V. REVOCATION, RESCISSION AND WITHDRAWAL OF CONSENT

A. Limited Revocability of Consent

Family Code § 8814.5 currently provides that a valid consent to an adoption may only be revoked (with or without cause) within 30 days after the consent form is signed. According to Family Code § 8814.5(a)(3) and (b), consent may indeed be revoked within the 30-day period for no particular reason. On the other hand, Family Code § 8815(a) states, "Once the revocable consent to adoption has become permanent as provided in Section 8814.5, the consent to the adoption by the prospective adoptive parents may not be withdrawn."

Prior to 1995, the statutes formerly set forth a procedure whereby a birth parent could petition the court to allow a consent to an adoption to be withdrawn. See generally, *Adoption of Jennie L.*, (1980) 111 Cal.App.3d 422. Those statutes were repealed and were never replaced with any kind of similar statute. While Family Code §§ 8814.5 and 8815 were upheld by the California Supreme Court in *Sharon S. v. Superior Court*, (2003) 31 Cal.4th 417, the lower court in that case was still instructed to decide whether the consent had been obtained by fraud or undue influence. Therefore, a distinction must be drawn between the revocation of revocable consent, and a finding that true consent was never validly obtained in the first place.

Family Code § 8801.3(c)(2) also provides that if the birth parent takes no action after validly signing a proper adoption placement agreement (see Chapter 4 of this book concerning placement agreements), the agreement shall become a permanent and irrevocable consent to the adoption on the 31st day after signing the agreement.

B. Exercising the Right to Revoke Consent

Family Code § 8814.5(a)(1) provides that after a consent to the adoption is signed by the birth parent or parents pursuant to Section 8801.3 [dealing with placement agreements (see Chapter 4 of this book)] or 8814 [dealing with consents signed in the presence of an agency representative], the birth parent or parents signing the consent only has 30 days to "sign and deliver to the department or delegated county adoption agency a written statement revoking the consent and requesting the child to be returned to the birth parent or parents."

Importantly, Family Code § 8814.5(a)(1) requires the birth parent to say in writing both that consent is revoked and that the child must be returned. A mere oral statement is insufficient, and a mere attempt to block an adoption without seeking return of the child is insufficient. However, Family Code § 8815(b) provides that where the birth parent or parents request return of the child before the end of the 30 days, "the child shall immediately be returned to the birth parent or parents so requesting."

Even if the prospective adoptive parents have concerns that the birth parent or parents requesting return of the child are unfit or present a danger of harm to the child, the express language of Family Code § 8815(c) states that their "only option is to report their concerns to the investigating adoption agency and the appropriate child welfare agency," but that, "These concerns shall not be a basis for failure to immediately return the child."

C. Waiving the Right to Revoke Consent

Family Code § 8814.5(a)(2) states that within 30 days after signing the consent form or placement agreement, the birth parent may also "sign a waiver of the right to revoke consent on a form prescribed by the department in the presence of a representative of the department or delegated county adoption agency." Under Family Code § 8814.5(b), the consent may not be revoked after a waiver of the right to revoke consent has been signed. The CDSS web site provides forms for this purpose.

Family Code § 8814.5(a)(2) goes on to provide that the waiver must be signed in the presence of an agency representative, or if one is not reasonably available, in the presence of a judicial officer if the birth parent is represented by independent legal counsel. In certain circumstances, an adoption service provider may assist in this regard and may be present at the time the waiver is signed. The waiver form may only be validly signed after an interview has been completed by the agency representative, unless the waiver of the right to revoke consent is signed in the presence of a judicial officer, in which case the interview is to be conducted by the judicial officer. Family Code § 8814.5(a)(2) requires the agency representative or the court, as the case may be, to interview the birth parent within 10 days after his or her request.

In the case of a birth parent residing outside of California, the interview, and the witnessing of the signing of a waiver of the right to revoke consent of a birth parent may be conducted in the state where the birth parent is located, by (a) a representative of a public adoption agency in that state, (b) a judicial officer in that state where the birth parent is represented by independent legal counsel, or (c) an adoption service provider.

D. Invalidation of Consent

As set forth in *In re Timothy W.*, (1990) 223 Cal.App.3d 437, and *Arnold v. Howell*, (1950) 98 Cal.App.2d 202, an adoption cannot be recognized where there is no consent and there are no grounds for dispensing with consent. In *Timothy W.*, the appellate court held that the adoption order should have never been issued since a valid consent had not been obtained. In *Arnold*, the court approved of a collateral attack against an unappealable adoption order, holding that a valid consent did not exist due to fraud and undue influence.

A distinction must be made between the revocation of a consent, and the invalidation of a consent as was adjudicated in *Arnold*. While the Legislature has repealed the statutes providing for judicial approval of a withdrawal of consent, replacing them with a 30-day statutory right to revoke consent as set forth below, *Arnold* and *Timothy W.* remain binding case precedent. Thus, a court may deny an adoption petition where it finds that there was never a valid consent to the adoption, even if the 30-day period for revoking a consent has passed.

As for the completed adoption of an Indian child, Family Code § 8606.5(c) and 25 U.S.C. § 1913(d) provide that the Indian child's parent may "withdraw consent" to the adoption within two years after the adoption is finalized upon the grounds that the consent was obtained through fraud or duress, and may petition the court to vacate such decree on that basis. If the court agrees, it shall return the child to the parent or the "prior Indian custodian" pursuant to Family Code §§ 8606.5(c) and 8619.5.

OTHER ISSUES IN INDEPENDENT ADOPTIONS 4

In this chapter:

Larry Ellison is America's third wealthiest person. He was born in 1944 in New York, and lived there briefly with his biological mother. His biological father was a U.S. Air Force pilot who was stationed abroad at the time of young Larry's birth. He was adopted in Illinois by his biological mother's sister and brother-in-law. His adoptive father is a Russian immigrant whose last name is derived from having entered the U.S. at Ellis Island.

I. WHAT IS AN "INDEPENDENT ADOPTION"?

Under Family Code § 8600, "An unmarried minor may be adopted by an adult as provided in this part [i.e., Family Code §§ 8600-9212]." These laws provide for four kinds of adoptions: agency adoptions, independent adoptions, intercountry adoptions, and stepparent adoptions. This chapter of the book deals with independent adoptions.

Family Code § 8524 defines an "independent adoption" as "the adoption of a child in which neither the department [of social services] nor an agency licensed by the department is a party to, or joins in the adoption petition." In its simplest form, with the exception of adoptions of children 12 years old or older, whose consent would be necessary to the adoption (see Family Code § 8602), the law views an independent adoption as essentially a two-sided transaction, the natural parents being one party and the prospective adoptive parents as the other.

In contrast, an "agency adoption" (see Family Code § 8506 and Chapter 5 of this book), can be viewed as a three-sided transaction since at some point the agency is actually vested with custody rights over the child. On the other hand, even in the simplest of independent adoptions, several other persons and entities are involved for the purpose of facilitating the transaction according to California law. This chapter covers those additional issues involved in the independent adoption, including statutory capacity to file an adoption petition, the significance of having a child "placed" for purposes of an adoption, how "placement" is secured, the role of adoption service providers, attorneys and agencies, and the liabilities they may incur.

II. INDIVIDUALS WHO MAY FILE FOR AN INDEPENDENT ADOPTION

Family Code § 8802(a)(1) sets forth the four categories of individuals who may file a petition for an "independent adoption." However, it sets forth no rule concerning how to decide between competing adoption petitions. The four categories are:

A. Person with Whom Child Has Been Placed for Adoption

Family Code § 8802(a)(1)(C) states that "a person with whom a child has been placed for adoption" may file a petition for an independent adoption. Since this subsection operates independently of the others, it is possible for a person who is not a guardian nor a family relative to pursue an adoption, as long as the requirements for a "placement" have been satisfied. This is discussed below more fully.

B. Person Named in Parent's Will as Intended Adoptive Parent

Under Family Code § 8802(a)(1)(B), "a person named in the will of a deceased parent as an intended adoptive parent where the child has no other parent" may file a petition for independent adoption. Since this provision is independent of Family Code § 8802(a)(1)(A), it is not necessary for such a person to be a blood relative of the child. Since this provision is independent of Family Code § 8802(a)(1)(C), the will essentially takes the place of a placement agreement signed by the birth parent.

Although most modern estate planning uses living trusts, there is no case law stating whether being named solely in the deceased parent's living trust as the intended adoptive parent is sufficient to confer standing to file an adoption petition. On the other hand, the incorporation of the terms of the living trust into the will or a codicil should be sufficient to satisfy Family Code § 8802(a)(1)(B).

On the subject of deceased birth parents, Family Code §§ 8604(a) and 8605 both state that the consent of the birth parent is only necessary if he or she is living. A pre-death consent to the adoption is therefore not required by the statutes. Therefore, it would appear that the prospective adoptive parents would only need to complete the home study and the interviews with the social services agency, to assure the court of the suitability of the adoptive parents. This is explained more fully in Chapter 2.

In addition, under these circumstances, Probate Code § 6451(a)(1) provides that inheritance rights between the child and the deceased natural parent are not terminated in most circumstances, in the event of a subsequent adoption.

C. Blood Relative of the Child or the Child's Half-Sibling

What if the birth parent dies without leaving a will? Family Code § 8802(a)(1)(A) provides that a petition may be filed by "an adult who is related to the child or the child's half sibling by blood or affinity, including all relatives whose status is preceded by the words 'step,' 'great,' 'great-great,' or 'grand,' or the spouse of any of these persons, even if the marriage was terminated by death or dissolution." Family Code § 8802(a)(1)(A) operates independently of Family Code § 8802(a)(1)(C), meaning that a family relative meeting the statutory definition may file an adoption petition even if the child has not been "placed" with him or her for purposes of adoption. However, that family relative must still obtain all of the required consents in the statutorily required manner, and still must cooperate with the appropriate social services agency in connection with the home study and other matters.

It is also important to note that while a stepparent would qualify to file a petition for an "independent adoption" of the child of his or her spouse, it is much easier for the stepparent to proceed pursuant to Family Code § 9000, which specifically governs stepparent adoptions, which are talked about more in Chapter 8 of this book.

Family Code § 8714.5 provides for a "relative adoption," which appears to be almost indistinguishable from an independent adoption pursuant to Family Code § 8802(a)(1)(A). The identification of individuals who have standing to file the adoption petition are identical in both statutes, meaning that such persons could seek either "kind" of adoption. Also, the effect of the adoption decree under both statutes is identical -- the petitioner becomes the parent of the child subject to the petition. Indeed, although the statute attempts to focus (in a somewhat ambiguous manner) on children who are in the dependency or foster care system (which is discussed more in Chapter 6 of this book), Family Code § 8714.5(b) appears to allow for the filing of a petition for relative adoption even as to children who are not in the dependency system.

D. The Child's Legal Guardian for the Specified Period

According to Family Code § 8802(a)(1)(D)(i), a petition for independent adoption may be filed by a legal guardian who has been the child's legal guardian for more than one year. (*In re Charlotte D.* (2009) 45 Cal.4th 1140.) However, Family Code §

8802(a)(1)(D)(iii) provides that if the parent nominated the guardian for a purpose other than adoption for a specified time period, or if the guardianship was established pursuant to Welfare & Institutions Code § 360 (which deals with dependency proceedings as explained in Chapter 6 of this book), the guardianship must have been in existence for three years before the petition for independent adoption may be filed by the legal guardian.

On the other hand, Family Code § 8802(a)(1)(D)(ii) allows a petition for independent adoption to be filed by one who has been the child's legal guardian for more than six months, if the court finds that the child has been abandoned within the meaning of Family Code § 7822 (which is also explained in Chapter 6 of this book).

Based on these provisions, the securing of a guardianship in connection with an independent adoption can be useful. As discussed more fully in Chapter 6, one may become the caretaker of a child by way of a long term guardianship that was ordered in a dependency proceeding. In such a case, the birth parent's rights may or may not have been terminated in the dependency proceeding. If they have been, then the guardian may apply Family Code § 8606(a) to complete the adoption without that birth parent's consent. If the birth parent's rights were not terminated, then the prospective adoptive parent must either obtain the birth parent's consent or successfully bring a petition to terminate parental rights pursuant to Family Code § 7822 or upon some other basis, thus dispensing with the need to obtain the birth parent's consent.

Family Code § 8802(d) states that if the child is the subject of a guardianship petition, the adoption petition shall so state and shall include the caption and docket number or have attached a copy of the letters of the guardianship or temporary guardianship. The petitioners shall notify the court of any petition for guardianship or temporary guardianship filed after the adoption petition. The guardianship proceeding shall be consolidated with the adoption proceeding.

III. PLACEMENT OF THE CHILD BY THE BIRTH PARENT

A. What is "Placement"?

Family Code § 8539 defines the verb "place for adoption" as, "in the case of an independent adoption, the selection of a prospective adoptive parent or parents for a child by the birth parent or parents and the completion of an adoptive placement agreement on a form prescribed by the department by the birth parent or parents placing the child *with* prospective adoptive parents." [emphasis added] By use of the word "with," it appears that the child has to be physically in the prospective adoptive parents' custody in order to be considered "placed."

Family Code § 8814(a) contemplates that the placement may be authorized by only one birth parent. Therefore, where the identity or whereabouts of the birth father for example is unknown, the placement of the child may still be completed by the birth mother. If the non-placing birth parent is ultimately located or identified, and if that birth parent's consent is required, the adoption itself cannot be finalized without that consent.

B. Distinguishing "Placement" from "Release" from a Health Care Facility – the AD-22 Form

In many cases, the parties to an independent adoption reach an informal understanding before the child is born that the prospective adoptive parents will be given immediate or nearly immediate "custody" of the child at the time of birth. Health & Safety Code § 1283(a) sets forth the requirements that the prospective adoptive parents must fulfill in order to secure the right to take the child home from the hospital. That statute provides, "No health facility shall surrender the physical custody of a minor under 16 years of age to any person unless such surrender is authorized in writing by the child's parent, the person having legal custody of the child, or the caregiver of the child who is a relative of the child and who may authorize medical care and dental care under Section 6550 of the Family Code."

To accommodate these purposes, the CDSS has published Form AD-22 on their website, thereby providing a way, free of charge, to comply with the "authorized in writing" provision of the statute. Logistically, while the prospective adoptive parents have the child at their home pursuant to the AD-22 form and with the birth parents' permission, all of the other adoption-related functions (such as the necessary counseling of the birth mother, the signatures on the consent and placement forms, and the filing of the adoption petition) must still be completed.

The AD-22 form is also governed by Family Code § 8607, which states that such forms adopted by the CDSS "shall contain a statement in boldface type delineating the various types of adoptions available, the birth parents' rights with regard thereto, including, but not limited to, rights with regard to revocation of consent to adoption, and a statement regarding the authority of the court under . . . [Family Code § 7800, et seq.] to declare the child abandoned by the birth parent or parents." The AD-22 form does this.

Notably, the birth parent's signature on the AD-22 form does not constitute a "placement" of the child for purposes of adoption nor a consent to an adoption. See *San Diego County Dept. of Public Welfare v. Superior Court*, (1972) 7 Cal.3d 1. Also, in *In re Timothy W.*, (1990) 223 Cal.App.3d 437, the court recognized that the form itself states that it is not a relinquishment or consent for adoption, and informs the parties about the basic ways a child may be placed for adoption. The *Timothy W.* court also recognized that even though the AD-22 form authorizes the prospective adoptive parents to make provisions for medical and surgical care for the child for a period not to exceed six months from the date of the child's release from the hospital, the form itself provides that the birth mother retains all parental rights to the child's custody. Viewed in this way, the AD-22 form is properly characterized as merely permission to take the child home from the hospital and to authorize medical care for the child for a fixed period. The *Timothy W.* court also stated that in spite of the existence of a fully executed AD-22 form, the prospective adoptive parents' temporary physical custody of the child actually "becomes unlawful when they refuse to return the child upon the birth mother's request."

C. Required Pre-Placement Counseling of Placing Birth Parent

Family Code § 8801(a) states that the selection of a prospective adoptive parent or parents shall be personally made by the child's birth parent or parents, based upon his, her, or their personal knowledge of the prospective adoptive parent or parents, and expressly prohibits the use of a delegated agent to make the placement decision. Family Code § 8801(b) defines that "personal knowledge" to include the birth parent's knowledge about all different aspects of the prospective adoptive parents' names, addresses, ages, employment, races, religions, marital status, home life, health, and many other subjects.

In order to ensure that the birth parent acquires this personal knowledge about the prospective adoptive parents, as well as about the birth parent's rights, Family Code § 8801.3 imposes statutory prerequisites before a child may be considered to have been placed for adoption. They are as follows:

1. Advice of Rights pursuant to Family Code § 8801.5

Family Code § 8801.3(a) states that a child shall not be considered to have been placed for adoption unless "Each birth parent placing the child for adoption has been advised of his or her rights, and if desired, has been counseled pursuant to Section 8801.5." Importantly, Family Code § 8801(a) contemplates that a legally recognized placement may occur by one birth parent alone, meaning that Family Code § 8801.3(a) may be satisfied even if only the placing birth parent was advised of rights. One must remember that the non-placing birth parent, if that parent has enforceable parental rights (see Chapters 3 and 6 of this book) may still demand to have custody of the child. Family Code § 8801.3(b)(1) provides that the advice of rights shall occur at least 10 days before the signing of the placement agreement, unless the adoption service provider finds that exigent circumstances require a shorter time.

As for the rights of which the birth parent must be informed, Family Code § 8801.5(c) requires the CDSS to prescribe the format and process for advising birth parents of their rights (which would include the matters covered by 22 California Code of Regulations § 35095(b) as discussed in Chapter 3 in connection with obtaining consent to the adoption), and states that those rights also include the following:

a) "Alternatives to Adoption"

Family Code § 8801.5(c)(1) states that the placing birth parent must be advised of his or her "alternatives to adoption." Those alternatives obviously include the right to keep the child and raise the child with the birth parent's own funds or through public or private financial assistance, and to have the child adopted by some other set of prospective adoptive parents.

b) "Alternate Types of Adoption"

Family Code § 8801.5(c)(2) provides that the placing birth parent must be advised about "the alternative types of adoption, including a description of the full procedures and timeframes involved in each type." The alternative types of adoption would include the independent adoption, where the child is transferred directly from the birth parent to the adoptive parent, and the agency adoption, where the agency actual acquires legal custody of the child. As far as "open adoptions" are concerned, the birth parent may be advised that Family Code § 8616.5 provides for the enforceability of a "post-adoption contact agreement," where the parties agree to such an arrangement. (Post-adoption contact agreements are discussed in Chapter 8.)

c) "Rights and Responsibilities of Birth Parent"

Under Family Code § 8801.5(c)(3), the placing birth parent must be advised of "the full rights and responsibilities of the birth parent with respect to adoption, including the need to keep the department informed of his or her current address in case of a medical emergency requiring contact and of providing a full health history." The rights of the birth parent are explained throughout this book. The birth parent's responsibilities with respect to the adoption would include the duty to provide medical information concerning himself or herself, as well as that of the child (as discussed in Chapter 7).

d) "Right to Separate Legal Counsel"

Family Code § 8801.5(c)(4) states that the placing birth parent must be advised of, "the right to separate legal counsel paid for by the prospective adoptive parents upon the request of the birth parent, as provided for by Section 8800." The role of attorneys is discussed below.

e) "Three Separate Counseling Sessions"

Family Code § 8801.5(c)(5) states that the placing birth parent must be advised of "The right to a minimum of three separate counseling sessions, each to be held on different days, to be paid for by the prospective adoptive parents upon the request of the birth parents, as provided for by subdivision (d)." The counseling sessions are explained in Chapters 2 and 3 of this book, in addition to the following text.

2. Adoption Service Provider's Assistance

Family Code § 8801.5(d) states that each placing birth parent shall be offered at least three separate counseling sessions, to be held on different days, and that each counseling session shall be not less than 50 minutes in duration. The counseling may be provided by the adoption service provider who has informed the birth parent of his or her rights, or by another adoption service provider, or by a licensed psychotherapist, as defined by Evidence Code § 1010, as elected by the person, and after having been informed of these choices. The law does not prohibit these counseling sessions from taking place before the child is born. However, the placement agreement cannot be signed until after the child's birth.

Family Code § 8801.3(b) requires the adoption service provider to sign the adoption placement agreement, along with each prospective adoptive parent, and each birth parent placing the child, at least 10 days after advising the placing birth parent of his or her rights. Although Family Code § 8801.3(b)(1) allows for a shorter time when the adoption service provider finds that exigent circumstances exist, that statute requires that those exigent circumstances be stated in the placement agreement. In any case, Family

Code § 8801.3(b)(3) requires the placing birth parent and the prospective adoptive parents to sign the agreement in the presence of the adoption service provider.

In addition, Family Code § 8801.7(a) provides that an adoption service provider shall offer to interview the birth parent after the placement of the child with the prospective adoptive parents. The interview shall occur within "10 working days" after the placement of the child for adoption and shall include a consideration of any concerns or problems the birth parent has with the placement, a readvisement of the rights of the birth parent, and the taking of the health and social history of the birth parent, if not taken previously. Also, if there are any concerns regarding the placement, or if the birth parent wishes to revoke the consent to the adoption, Family Code § 8801.7(b) requires the adoption service provider to immediately notify the CDSS or delegated county adoption agency and assist the birth parent.

The advisement and counseling fees shall be paid by the prospective adoptive parents at the request of the birth parent pursuant to Family Code § 8801.5(f). On the other hand, Family Code § 8801.7(c) provides, "No adoption service provider shall have a contractual relationship with prospective adoptive parents, an attorney or representative for prospective adoptive parents, or any individual or organization providing services of any type to prospective adoptive parents for which the adoptive parents are paying a fee, except as relates to the payment of the fees for the advising and counseling of the birth parents." (See also, Family Code § 8801.5(e).)

D. Statutorily Required Use of Placement Forms

Family Code § 8801.3(b) and (c) contemplate that the CDSS is to publish standard form placement agreements, and that the placement agreement is to be memorialized on those standard forms. The CDSS's web site provides many different placement agreements and related papers, which are designed for different specific situations.

1. Required Contents of the Placement Agreement

Family Code § 8801.3(c) states that the adoption placement agreement form shall include statements that (1) the birth parent received the advisement of rights and the date upon which it was received, (2) the birth parent understands that the placement is for the purpose of adoption and that the adoption placement agreement shall become a permanent and irrevocable consent to the adoption if the birth parent takes no further action before the 31st day after signing, (3) the birth parent signs the agreement having personal knowledge of certain facts regarding the prospective adoptive parents pursuant to Family Code § 8801, and (4) the adoptive parents have been informed of the basic health and social history of the birth parents.

Although Family Code § 8801.3(c)(5) states that the placement agreement shall contain the placing birth parent's actual consent to the adoption, it does not appear that the absence of this element would void the placement. The current versions of the CDSS's standard adoption placement agreement forms (e.g., the AD 907, AD 924 and AD 925 forms) do not contain the actual consent to the adoption. Instead, they state that the placement agreement will become a consent on the 31st day after signing if no further action is taken. The actual consent (if needed) is provided on other forms as explained in Chapter 3 of this book.

In *Sharon S. v. Superior Court*, (2003) 31 Cal.4th 417, the California Supreme Court stated that the placement agreement may provide that the birth parent shall retain the parental right of control of the child. In so holding, the *Sharon S.* court approved of a CDSS form "addendum" that allowed the parties to memorialize this understanding. However, at the time this book was compiled, the addendum did not appear on the CDSS web site, nor did the AD-924 form placement agreement refer to an "addendum." On the other hand, Family Code § 8801.3 does not exclude any matter from being included on the placement agreement, nor does it bar the parties from adding interlineations to the placement agreement. In any event, *Sharon S.* also held that even this unconventional placement agreement could become an irrevocable consent to an adoption pursuant to Family Code §§ 8801.3(c)(2) and 8814.5 over the birth parent's objection.

In the case of an interstate placement, which is one way to complete an independent adoption, Family Code § 8801.3(d) requires the adoption placement agreement to "meet the requirements of the Interstate Compact on the Placement of Children in Section 7901." However, the notion of a "placement agreement" between the birth parent and the prospective adoptive parent does not appear in the ICPC, and it is unclear that the ICPC even applies to independent adoptions at all. The ICPC and interstate adoptions are discussed in more detail in Chapter 9 of this book.

2. Signing and Witnessing of the Placement Agreement

Under Family Code § 8801.3(b)(5), "the child is not deemed to be placed for adoption with the prospective adoptive parents until the adoption placement agreement has been signed and witnessed." Family Code § 8801.3(b) states that the adoption service provider, each prospective adoptive parent, and each birth parent placing the child must sign the adoption placement agreement, and that it must be signed in the presence of an adoption service provider. See also Family Code § 8801.7(a).

3. Time of Signing the Placement Agreement

As set forth above, Family Code § 8801.3(b)(1) provides that the placement agreement cannot be signed until at least 10 days after the placing birth parent has been counseled, unless exigent circumstances exist. In addition, Family Code § 8801.3(b)(2) provides that the placement agreement may not be signed by either the birth parents or the prospective adoptive parents until the birth mother is discharged from the hospital, unless the birth mother remains hospitalized longer than the child, in which case the agreement may be signed by all parties at the time of the child's discharge from the hospital if the birth mother's competency to sign is verified by her attending physician and surgeon before she signs the agreement.

Importantly, the statutes do not state that the placing birth parent, the prospective adoptive parents and the adoption service provider all must sign the adoption placement agreement at the same time. In fact, Family Code § 8801.3(b)(6) states that if the birth parent is not located in this state or country, the adoption placement agreement shall be signed "before an adoption service provider or, for purposes of identification of the birth parent only, before a notary or other person authorized to perform notarial acts in the state or country in which the birth parent is located." In other words, it appears the adoption service provider may travel out of the state or the country to witness the signing.

4. Processing of the Placement Agreement

Family Code § 8801.3(b)(4) requires the adoption service provider who witnessed the signatures of the placing birth parent and the prospective adoptive parents on the adoption placement agreement to immediately forward the original of the agreement and the supporting documentation to the CDSS or delegated county adoption agency. In addition, the prospective adoptive parents should demand a copy of the adoption placement agreement, since they are required by Family Code § 8802(a)(2) to attach a copy to the adoption petition.

5. Legal Effect of the Placement Agreement

As stated above, the completion of a written placement agreement is one way that the prospective adoptive parents may secure the right under Family Code § 8802(a)(1)(C) to file an adoption petition with the court. In addition, as explained below and in Chapters 8 and 9, the prospective adoptive parents acquire certain procedural rights upon receiving the child pursuant to a fully executed written placement agreement.

Certain duties also arise. For example, the AD 924 form requires the prospective adoptive parents to arrange for all of the necessaries of life, such as necessary medical care for the child, including immunizations. It requires them to also to file the adoption petition within 10 days after signing the agreement, to return the child if a consent is not given or lawfully revoked, to not conceal the child, and to keep the parties apprised of current addresses.

In addition, signing the placement agreement may have lasting consequences even if the adoption is not finalized by court order. In *In re Marriage of Bonifas*, (Colo. App. 1994) 879 P.2d 478, the Colorado appellate court held that a prospective adoptive parent's written agreement to support the child, as memorialized on an adoptive placement agreement, was enforceable by the child (for child support) when the prospective adoptive parents (who had somehow kept actual custody of the child following an unsuccessful adoption proceeding) petitioned for divorce. It does not appear that the AD 924 form is identical to the *Bonifas* agreement, and placement agreements must be examined on a case-by-case basis. The *Bonifas* court avoided using the common law adoption theory as a model for its decision, but instead ruled that the language of the placement agreement created contractual obligations for the intended benefit of a third party beneficiary, i.e., the child. It does not appear that any California court has incorporated the reasoning of *Bonifas* in any published decision.

E. Location of the Child During the Adoptive Placement

By virtue of the word "with" in Family Code § 8802(a)(1)(C), the child resides with the prospective adoptive parents during the pendency of the adoptive placement.

Additionally, there are times in which it is appropriate to allow the child to accompany the prospective adoptive parents on extended trips to other counties and states for outings, vacations and family visits. This is part of the bonding process between the child and the prospective adoptive parents. For such cases, Family Code § 8803(a)(2) states that the child may be removed from the county in which the adoption proceeding is pending (which is usually the same county where the prospective adoptive parents reside (Family Code § 9211(a))) if the petitioners or other interested persons first obtain permission from the court, after giving advance written notice of intent to obtain the court's permission to the CDSS or delegated county adoption agency responsible for the investigation of the proposed adoption. Upon proof of giving notice, permission may be granted by the court if, within a period of 15 days after the date of giving notice, no objections are filed or if the court finds that the objections lack good cause.

On the other hand, Family Code § 8803(b)(1) provides that no such permission is needed if the child is absent for 30 or fewer days from the county in which the adoption proceeding is pending, unless a notice of recommendation to deny the petition has been personally served on the petitioners, or the court has issued an order prohibiting the child's removal from the county pending consideration of any of (A) the suitability of the petitioners, (B) the care provided the child, or (C) the availability of the legally required consents to the adoption.

Family Code § 8803(a)(1) states that during the pendency of an adoption proceeding the child proposed to be adopted may not be "concealed" either within or outside the county in which the adoption proceeding is pending. According to Family Code § 8803(c), to do so would constitute a violation of Penal Code § 280, which provides for incarceration in county jail or state prison. As stated above, the prospective adoptive parents are to keep the agency apprised of the child's whereabouts upon request. Since they are also to file the adoption petition in the county in which they reside, and have the child live in their home, the child will also normally be within the county in which the adoption proceeding is pending. Of course, where the child has been returned to and remains in the custody and control of the child's birth parent or parents, these rules do not apply, as expressly stated in Family Code § 8803(b)(2).

Since Family Code § 8803 only deals with situations where an "adoption proceeding" is pending, it does not appear that court approval would be necessary before the petition is filed. Although the Family Code § 110 definition of "proceeding" is not specifically limited to dealings with the court, the language of Penal Code § 280 differentiates between a "proceeding" and a "placement." On the other hand, common sense dictates that the prospective adoptive parents should obtain the permission of the birth parent, since transporting the child out of county without notice might cause the birth parent to revoke consent to the adoption or refuse to give consent. In addition, failure to give notice to the agency might later give rise to a negative home study report, which the prospective adoptive parents would then have to refute in court, perhaps at great monetary expense to themselves. To be safe, some level of written consent to transport the child out of the county should be obtained beforehand. If such consent is not forthcoming, the prospective adoptive parents would then have to file the adoption petition and seek court approval of the travel plans.

IV. THE ROLE OF ADOPTION SERVICE PROVIDER

A. The Functions of an Adoption Service Provider

1. Interviewing and Counseling Birth Parents

The adoption service provider is a counselor for the placing birth parent. Under Family Code § 8801.5(a) and (b), each birth parent placing a child for adoption shall be advised of his or her rights by an adoption service provider in a face-to-face meeting in which the birth parent may ask questions and have questions answered, in the manner provided by Family Code § 8801.3 (as explained above). In addition, under Family Code § 8808, certain aspects of the counseling of the birth parent in connection with taking the consent to an adoption may be given by an adoption service provider (as explained in Chapter 3). Furthermore, Family Code § 8814.5(a)(2) states that an adoption service provider may assist the birth parent or parents in any activity where the primary purpose of that activity is to facilitate the signing of the waiver of the right to revoke consent, and be present at the signing of the waiver (as explained in Chapter 3). On the other hand, Family Code § 8801.7(b) requires the adoption service provider to contact the CDSS and assist the birth parent if there are any concerns about the placement or the consent.

Family Code § 8801.3(b)(6) contemplates that adoption service providers may travel out-of-state to perform their services where the birth parent is not located in this state or country. In such an instance, the adoption service provider may still witness the signing of the adoption placement agreement.

2. Adoption Service Provider Has No Duty to Investigate

Family Code § 8801.7(c) states that an adoption service provider's duties "specifically do[] not include a duty to investigate information provided by the birth parents, prospective adoptive parents, or their attorneys or agents." As stated in Chapters 2 and 3, the investigative duties are imposed on the CDSS or the licensed county adoption agency. Therefore, the adoption service provider has no duty to interview the prospective adoptive parents, conduct a home study, or exercise due diligence in locating the birth father (e.g., if the client is the birth mother).

3. Intercountry Adoptions

There is a seeming conflict between state and federal law with regard to the phrase "adoption service provider." Under longstanding California law (Family Code §§ 8715(a) and 8811.5(a)), a mere adoption service provider has never been authorized to complete a home study of a prospective adoptive parent. However, new federal law enacted pursuant to the Hague Convention on Intercountry Adoption allows an "adoption service provider" to perform home studies. As explained in Chapter 11, only an adoption agency that is licensed for intercountry adoption may complete a home study for a California resident seeking to adopt a foreign child.

B. Qualifications to Operate as an Adoption Service Provider

Family Code § 8502(a) provides a list of those persons and entities who are qualified to carry out the functions of an adoption service provider: (1) a licensed private adoption agency (which is itself highly regulated, as explained in Chapter 5 of this book), (2) a licensed clinical social worker with five years' experience providing professional social work services while employed by a licensed California adoption agency or the CDSS, (3) as to entities outside California, an adoption agency that is licensed or otherwise approved under the laws of its state, or an individual who is licensed or otherwise certified as a clinical social worker under that state's laws, or (4) a licensed marriage, family, and child counselor with five years' experience providing professional adoption casework services while employed by a licensed California adoption agency or the CDSS. Where a person asserts qualifications under Family Code § 8502(a)(2) or (4), he or she is to present evidence of their experience to the CDSS, which then reviews the qualifications of each individual to determine if they have the requisite experience. On the CDSS websites, adoption service providers are listed.

There does not appear to be any statutory requirement that adoption service providers take a State examination, or that they be issued a license. (In contrast, as set forth in Chapter 5 of this book, adoption agencies must be licensed.) The statutes never use the phrase "licensed adoption service provider." On the other hand, all four subsections of Family Code § 8502(a) contemplate that the person will already have some sort of license, either as an adoption agency, a social worker or a marriage, family, and child counselor. (Also, Family Code § 8801.5(d) allows a licensed psychotherapist to perform the "counseling" function of the adoption service provider.)

C. When an Attorney May Act as an Adoption Service Provider

Family Code § 8502(b) states that if, in the case of a birth parent located in California, at least three adoption service providers are not reasonably available, or, in the case of a birth parent located outside of California who has contacted at least three potential adoption service providers and been unsuccessful in obtaining the services of an adoption service provider who is reasonably available and willing to provide services, independent legal counsel for the birth parent may serve as an adoption service provider pursuant to Family Code § 8801.5(e), which provides that an adoption service provider advise the placing birth parent of his or her rights, as mentioned above as to the placement agreement and in Chapter 3 with regard to consent.

Family Code § 8502(b) then states that an adoption service provider is "reasonably available" only if he or she is (1) available within five days for a Family Code § 8801.5 advisement of rights, or within 24 hours for the signing of the placement agreement, (2) within 100 miles of the birth mother, and (3) available for a cost not exceeding $500 to make an advisement of rights and to witness the signing of the placement agreement. It would appear that these three conditions would most likely exist when the birth parent is located out-of-state, since there are numerous qualified adoption service providers in California. Family Code § 8502(c) provides that where an attorney acts as an adoption service provider, the fee for an advisement of rights and to witness the signing of the placement agreement shall not exceed $500. This of course does not exclude other fees that the attorney may charge for performing legal services.

D. Consequences of Adoption Service Provider's Negligence

The adoption service provider statutes mentioned above impose duties of care, the violation of which would constitute negligence per se as defined by Evidence Code § 669, but which would not constitute grounds to set aside the adoption. Family Code § 8801.5(g) expressly states, "Failure to fulfill the duties specified in this section [which expressly governs adoption service providers] shall not be construed as a basis for setting aside the consent or the adoption, but may give rise to a cause of action for malpractice or negligence against those professionals or agencies serving as adoption service providers that are responsible for fulfilling the duties." Also, Family Code § 8801.7(c) states that the adoption service provider "owes a very high duty of care to the birth parent being advised, regardless of who pays the provider's fees." Therefore, the adoption service provider's negligence would give rise to a cause of action for damages, but would not vitiate consent.

Regarding the adoption service provider's role as counselor, Family Code § 8801.5(e) states that the counselor owes a duty of care to the birth parent being counseled, similar to the duty of care established by a psychotherapist-patient relationship, regardless of who pays the fees of the counselor. No counselor shall have a contractual relationship with the adoptive parents, an attorney for the adoptive parents, or any other individual or an organization performing any type of services for the adoptive parents and for which the adoptive parents are paying a fee, except as relates to payment of the birth parents' fee.

V. THE FUNCTIONS OF ADOPTION FACILITATORS

According to Family Code § 8623, an adoption facilitator is a person or entity who is not an adoption agency (see Chapter 5) and who either (a) advertises for the purpose of soliciting parties to an adoption or locating children for an adoption or acting as an intermediary between the parties to an adoption, or (b) charges a fee or other valuable consideration for services rendered relating to an adoption.

Family Code § 8637 expressly allows an attorney to perform the work of an adoption facilitator, and states that in doing so, the attorney's legal duties are limited to "those provisions of law regulating the practice of law." There is no clear line between what constitutes the work of an adoption facilitator and the practice of law. Although an adoption facilitator apparently "facilitates" adoptions, there is no statute defining the word "facilitate."

A. No State Licensing Requirements for Adoption Facilitators

There is no law saying that an adoption facilitator must be licensed by the State of California as such. The only "licensing" requirement concerning adoption facilitators is that which is contained in Family Code § 8636(a), which mandates that one must obtain a business license and a $25,000 bond. However, Family Code §§ 8632.5 and 8639 require adoption facilitators to be registered with the State DSS.

B. The Adoption Facilitator's Advertising and Communications

Under Family Code § 8624, the adoption facilitator's advertising must (a) identify the name of the party placing the advertisement and state that that party is an adoption facilitator, (b) be subject to Business & Professions Code § 17500 [which prohibits misleading advertising], (c) provide the required disclosures in the advertisement in the same font size as the facilitator's name, (d) provide the required disclosures in the most prominent color used in the advertisement, (e) provide the required disclosures in a readily understandable manner, and if the advertisement is a television advertisement, at the same speed and volume as the rest of the advertisement.

In addition, Family Code § 8626 provides that the adoption facilitator must disclose, in the first oral communication in which there is a description of services, that the facilitator is not a licensed adoption agency. The law also specifically states, at Family Code § 8625, that an adoption facilitator shall not (a) mislead any person into believing that the adoption facilitator is a licensed adoption agency [see Chapter 5 of this book], or (b) represent that he or she is able to provide services for which the facilitator is not properly licensed.

C. The Adoption Facilitator's Contract

1. Who May Be the Adoption Facilitator's Client?

Unlike the laws governing adoption service providers (see Family Code § 8801.7(c)), the adoption facilitator is not prohibited from entering into a contract with the adoptive parents. Family Code § 8631(b) only requires that the adoption facilitator's contract state in writing on whose behalf the facilitator is acting. Furthermore, Family Code § 8632 requires the adoption facilitator to explain the terms of the written contract verbally to the prospective adoptive parents and the birthparents, meaning that the facilitator's contract may be with both the prospective adoptive parents and the birthparents. On the other hand, as explained herein, if the attorney to perform the work of an adoption facilitator as allowed by Family Code § 8637, the attorney's ability to engage in dual representation is expressly limited by Family Code § 8800.

2. Adoption Facilitator Representing Multiple Clients

Family Code § 8627 contemplates that an adoption facilitator may "act[] on behalf of more than one party." However, Family Code § 8627 also states that where an adoption facilitator is acting on behalf of more than one party, all parties must sign a written agreement authorizing the facilitator to do so. With regard to an attorney acting as an adoption facilitator acting on behalf of more than one party, refer to the discussion below as to the role of attorneys.

3. Required Terms in the Adoption Facilitator's Contract

The adoption facilitator's contract is required by Family Code § 8631(a) to state that the facilitator is not a licensed adoption agency, and is required by Family Code § 8631(d) to state that the facilitator cannot provide any services for which the facilitator is not properly licensed, such as legal or therapeutic counseling.

The adoption facilitator's contract must also state, pursuant to Family Code § 8631(e), a list of all the services that the adoption facilitator is contractually required to provide, and pursuant to Family Code § 8631(b), a written statement disclosing on whose behalf the adoption facilitator is acting.

4. 72-Hour Right to Rescind the Contract

Family Code § 8629 provides for a 72-hour rescission period in which either the birthparents or the prospective adoptive parents may revoke the contract and request the return of any fees paid, without penalty, except for any reasonable fees actually earned by the facilitator and which are supported by written records or documentation. This right to rescind is required under Family Code § 8631(f) to be disclosed in the contract.

D. The Potential Liabilities of an Adoption Facilitator

1. Prohibited Activities

Family Code §§ 8625, 8631(a) and 8631(d) state that an adoption facilitator cannot hold himself or herself out as a adoption agency, or as an attorney (unless licensed as such), or as one licensed to perform "therapeutic counseling" (unless licensed as such). Since a pure adoption facilitator is barred from performing these kinds of services, the facilitator would therefore have no duty to perform these kinds of services. It is unclear whether the adoption facilitator, in the appropriate case, would have a duty to refer the client to a person or entity who is licensed to perform such services.

With regard to performing the work of an adoption service provider, the adoption facilitator is prohibited by Family Code § 8625(b) from representing that he or she is able to provide services for which the facilitator is not properly licensed. Although an adoption service provider is not required to take a State examination or receive a license to practice as an adoption service provider, all four subsections of Family Code § 8502(a) contemplate that the adoption service provider will already have some sort of license, either as an adoption agency, a social worker or a marriage, family, and child counselor. It would therefore appear that an adoption facilitator cannot perform the work of an adoption service provider.

Recently, Family Code § 8625(c) was added for the purpose of prohibiting adoption facilitators from "mak[ing] use of photolisting to advertise minor children for placement in adoption." Also, Family Code § 8625(d) now bars adoption facilitators from posting specific information in any "advertising" about particular minor children who are available for adoption placement. There is not yet any case law defining the words "advertise" or "advertising" in the context of this statute.

Also, a mere adoption facilitator may not offer, provide, or facilitate any adoption service in connection with a Hague Convention intercountry adoption. (Family Code § 8921.) However, a person who happens to be an adoption facilitator may have additional qualifications that allow him or her to provide services in connection with a Hague Convention adoption.

2. Duty to Disclose to the Adoptive Parents

Family Code § 8628 states that the adoption facilitator shall report in writing to the prospective adoptive parents all information that is provided to the facilitator by the birthparents concerning a particular child. Based on the Legislature's use of the phrase "all information," it would not appear that there is any confidentiality between birth parent and adoption facilitator. (See also Family Code § 8631(c).)

3. Remedies for Breach of Contract, Fraud or Negligence

Family Code § 8634 states that an adoption facilitator's contract "is subject to the rules and remedies relating to contracts generally." In addition, Family Code § 8638 states very broadly that the Attorney General, a district attorney, a city attorney or any aggrieved person may bring a civil action for damages, for rescission, or for any other civil or equitable remedy as the case may be for violation of the adoption facilitator statutes.

In most cases, it is the prospective adoptive parents who are named as parties to the adoption facilitator's contract. The question would then arise whether the birth parents who are not named as parties to the adoption facilitator's contract could be deemed to be third party beneficiaries of the adoption facilitator's contract. The adoption facilitator's bond is required by Family Code § 8636(b) to name as a beneficiary "any person damaged by fraud, misstatement, misrepresentation, unlawful act or omission, or failure to provide the services." In addition, Family Code § 8638 gives "any person" who is aggrieved the right to sue the adoption facilitator.

VI. RESPONSIBILITIES OF ATTORNEYS IN AN ADOPTION CASE

A. The Attorney for the Prospective Adoptive Parents

The attorney for the prospective adoptive parents owes his or her clients the duties of care and the fiduciary duties that any attorney would owe any client. In the context of independent adoptions, Family Code § 8800(h) also imposes on the prospective adoptive parents' attorney the duty to inform them in writing that (1) the birth parent or parents can revoke consent to the adoption pursuant to Family Code § 8814.5 (30-day revocation period), and (2) any moneys expended in negotiations or proceedings in connection with the adoption are not reimbursable. (Such expenditures are described in Family Code § 8610 and Penal Code § 273(a) and (b), and in Chapter 3 of this book.) Family Code § 8800(h) also requires the attorney to have the prospective adoptive parents sign a statement of their understanding of these facts. It appears that the statutes allow these matters to be completed at the time of signing the retainer agreement.

B. Birth Parent's Statutory Right to Paid Independent Counsel

Family Code § 8801.5(c)(4) states that the placing birth parent must be advised of "the right to separate legal counsel paid for by the prospective adoptive parents upon the request of the birth parent, as provided for by Section 8800." Family Code § 8800(g) guarantees the birth parent the right to independent counsel, but states that it is possible to waive the right to a paid independent attorney. Likewise, Family Code § 8800(d) states that notwithstanding any other law, it is unethical for an attorney to undertake the representation of both the prospective adoptive parents and the birth parents of a child in any negotiations or proceedings in connection with an adoption "unless a written consent is obtained from both parties." In such an instance, Family Code § 8800(i) requires that any written consent to dual representation shall be filed with the court before the filing of the birth parent's consent to the proposed adoption.

1. When Dual Representation Is Not Permitted

According to Family Code § 8800(c), "in an independent adoption proceeding, whether or not written consent is obtained, multiple representation by an attorney should be avoided whenever a birth parent displays the slightest reason for the attorney to believe any controversy might arise." Based on the phrase "slightest reason," it would appear unwise for an attorney to engage in dual representation before consent has been given or during the 30-day period in which consent is revocable, even if the birth parent did not ask the attorney to take any formal action.

2. Consequences of Improper Dual Representation

In *In re Baby Boy S.*, (1987) 194 Cal.App.3d 925, an attorney represented both the birth parent and the adoptive parent. The court held that an actual conflict of interest arose when the birth mother made certain statements manifesting her mere "ambivalence" about the adoption. The attorney then failed to diligently address the birth mother's legal needs. Under these circumstances, the *Baby Boy S.* court held that the attorney's improper conduct affected the substantive factual issue of whether the birth parent had abandoned the child, and that the attorney's conduct actually negated the birth parent's alleged intent to abandon.

On the other hand, in *In re Duarte's Adoption*, (1964) 229 Cal.App.2d 775, the court rejected the contention that the birth parent's consent was void because it was gained through the ineffective assistance of counsel. Importantly, the *Duarte's Adoption* case did not present facts demonstrating that a conflict of interest existed.

3. Requirements for Birth Parent's Written Consent to Dual Representation Where It Is Permitted

Family Code § 8800(d) provides that consent to dual representation shall be in writing and "shall include all of the following:" (1) a notice to the birth parents in the specified form of their right to have an independent attorney advise and represent them at the expense of the prospective adoptive parents (up to $500, unless a higher fee is agreed to by the parties), (2) a notice to the birth parents that they may waive their right to an independent attorney and may be represented by the attorney representing the prospective adoptive parents, (3) the waiver itself, and (4) an agreement that the attorney representing the prospective adoptive parents shall represent the birth parents.

Although the statute ostensibly permits the attorney to represent both the birth parent and the adoptive parent, the court in *In re Baby Boy S.*, (1987) 194 Cal.App.3d 925, warned of the "hazards of dual representation in adoption proceedings." It stated that while the predecessor to Family Code § 8800 allowed for written consent authorizing dual representation, there is an "almost inevitable impossibility of" avoiding an actual conflict of interest.

4. Withdrawal as Counsel for the Birth Parent

Family Code § 8800(c) provides that whenever a birth parent displays the slightest reason for the attorney to believe any controversy might arise, it is the attorney's duty to withdraw promptly from any case, advise the parties to retain independent counsel, refrain from taking positions in opposition to any of these former clients, and thereafter maintain an impartial, fair, and open attitude toward the new attorneys.

In addition, Family Code § 8800(b), as well as Rule 2-111(A)(2) of the California Rules of Professional Conduct provide that an attorney, upon withdrawal, shall take reasonable steps to avoid foreseeable prejudice to the rights of the client, including giving due notice to the client, allowing time for employment of other counsel, delivering to the client all papers and property to which the client is entitled, and complying with applicable laws and rules. As for substitute counsel, Family Code § 8800(e) allows the court, either on motion or *sua sponte*, to appoint an attorney to represent the birth parent in connection with the proposed adoption.

5. Award of Attorney's Fees

Family Code § 8800(f) states that the birth parent or parents may retain an attorney to represent them in negotiations or proceedings in connection with the child's adoption, and that the court may award attorney's fees and costs for just cause and based upon the ability of the parties to pay those fees and costs. It would appear that such a fee award for the birth parent would be justified if the birth parent were the prevailing party in a contested adoption. The statute does not extend the right to fees to agencies or to individuals other than birth parents.

C. Liability for Wrongful Termination of Parental Rights

In *Kessel v. Leavitt*, (W.Va. 1998) 511 S.E.2d 720, the West Virginia Supreme Court upheld a $7 million jury verdict for a birth father against a California attorney on causes of action for intentional interference with parental relations and fraudulent concealment, based on allegations that the attorney intentionally aided the birth mother (who was the attorney's client) in arranging an independent adoption in a Canadian jurisdiction (Alberta) that allegedly, unlike West Virginia and essentially all American jurisdictions, required no notice to the natural father.

The facts as described by the West Virginia court in *Kessel* were that the California attorney's client sought to keep the biological father, a West Virginia resident who had filed a West Virginia paternity action, from locating his newborn child or intervening in the adoption proceeding. (For some reason, the client came to California to give birth, and she did so in 1991, which was before *Adoption of Kelsey S.*, (1992) 1 Cal.4th 816, was decided.) The California attorney arranged for a private Canadian adoption in alleged defiance of a West Virginia temporary injunction prohibiting his client from placing the child for adoption while the natural father's paternity action was pending in West Virginia. The California attorney also allegedly allowed the prospective adoptive parents to withhold the biological father's name and misinform the Canadian adoption court that there were no other custody actions involving the child. When the biological father sued the California attorney in California to find his child and learn where the adoption was taking place, the California attorney allegedly withheld that information, citing attorney-client privilege. After finally discovering the information through other means, the biological father filed a Canadian paternity action but was unable to derail the adoption. The biological father then successfully sued the California attorney for damages in West Virginia's courts, which held that it had personal jurisdiction over the California attorney. (In an unpublished and thus unciteable California appellate decision (*Kessel v. Leavitt*, (1998) 75 Cal.Rptr.2d 639), the court agreed that West Virginia had personal jurisdiction over the attorney, so as to facilitate the sister-state judgment enforcement proceedings commenced in California.)

VII. THE INVOLVEMENT OF GOVERNMENTAL AGENCIES

As explained in Chapter 2, the CDSS or an authorized county adoption agency investigates whether the prospective adoptive parents and their home are suitable for the child. In addition, as discussed in Chapter 3, a representative of the CDSS or an authorized county adoption agency interviews the birth parents to make sure that their consent, where it is required, is provided voluntarily and with full knowledge of the ramifications of the adoption.

A. Identifying the Government Agency Involved in the Case

Throughout the second, third and fourth chapters of this book, one can see that the statutes speak repeatedly in terms of the CDSS or a "licensed" or "delegated" county adoption agency. However, quite often, it is the CDSS itself which handles the investigative functions of an independent adoption. Moreover, the government agency becomes involved in the adoption by way of Family Code § 8808, which requires the adoption petition to be filed with the district office of the CDSS or with the delegated county adoption agency responsible for the investigation of the adoption, at the same time the adoption petition is filed with the court. That triggers the agency's investigative process. Those agencies are listed on the CDSS's website.

There have been cases where a county agency that is not primarily concerned with adoptions is able to act as the licensed county adoption agency. In *In re Duarte's Adoption*, (1964) 229 Cal.App.2d 775, the court held that the Alameda County Welfare Department was qualified as such an agency, and was authorized to take a birth parent's consent to the adoption. The *Duarte* court recognized that certain statutes (see Welfare & Institutions Code § 16100) provide that any county agency may, upon application by the county, become a licensed county adoption agency. The *Duarte* court then applied the statutory presumptions that "transactions are fair and regular" (see now Civil Code § 3545) and that "the law has been obeyed" (see now Civil Code § 3548), and presumed that the Alameda County Welfare Department was a licensed county adoption agency, thereupon holding that the consent was "executed in strict compliance with" the statutes.

B. The Agency's Investigation and Reporting

Family Code § 8808 states that, at the same time the adoption petition is filed with the court, the petitioners shall file a copy of the petition with the district office of the CDSS or with the delegated county adoption agency responsible for the investigation of the adoption, together with the names, addresses, and telephone numbers of all parties to be interviewed. The CDSS or delegated county adoption agency shall then interview the petitioners and all persons from whom consent is required and whose addresses are known as soon as possible and, in the case of residents of this state, within 45 working days, excluding legal holidays, after the filing of the adoption petition. The interview with the placing parent or parents shall include, but not be limited to, discussion of any concerns or problems that the parent has with the placement and, if the placing parent was not interviewed as provided in Family Code § 8801.7, the content required in that interview. At the interview, the agency shall give the parent an opportunity to sign either a statement revoking the consent, or a waiver of the right to revoke consent, as provided in Family Code § 8814.5.

The agency is then to investigate the parties and the home of the prospective adoptive parents. According to Family Code § 8802(b), the prospective adoptive parents are required to promptly file with the agency the information it requires in its investigation of the proposed adoption. (It would appear that the state's compelling interest in the welfare of the child would supersede most assertions of privacy rights by the prospective adoptive parents.) Within 180 days after the filing of the petition, the agency is to submit to the court a full report of the facts disclosed by its inquiry with a recommendation regarding the granting of the petition, as required by Family Code § 8807(a), although the court does have discretion pursuant to Family Code § 8807(c) to allow additional time for the filing of the report. Family Code § 8821 provides that when any report or findings are submitted to the court by the agency, a copy of the report or findings, whether favorable or unfavorable, shall be given to the petitioner's attorney in the proceeding, if the petitioner has an attorney of record, or to the petitioner.

C. Judicial Review of the Agency's Report

In *In re Backhaus' Adoption*, (1962) 209 Cal.App.2d 13, it was held that the trial court had statutory jurisdiction to review the CDSS's report and make its own independent determination of the suitability of the home of the petitioners for the adoption. The *Backhaus* court stated that there are three prerequisites to the court's jurisdiction to review the report: (1) there must be an adoption petition on file with the court (meaning in most cases that there has to be a signed placement agreement); (2) the CDSS must have conducted its investigation and filed its report and recommendation with the court; and (3) the report and recommendation must be unfavorable to the petitioners.

Backhaus also holds that the statutes do not require that, at the time of judicial review, all consents required by the adoption statutes or by foreign law must have been obtained, nor that the child appear in court, nor that the judicial review of the adverse report take place at the time of, or as a part of, the final hearing on the adoption petition. The *Backhaus* court stated it had "no doubt that the Legislature intended judicial review of an unfavorable report to be a separate and distinct function of the court which may, but need not, be considered contemporaneously with the adoption petition." As such, *Backhaus* holds that the court may review an adverse report even before the birth parents' consents to the adoption are received or dispensed with.

D. Is the Consent of the Agency Required?

Under Family Code § 8806, the CDSS or delegated county adoption agency shall accept the consent of the birth parents to the adoption of the child by the petitioners and, before filing its report with the court, shall ascertain whether the child is a proper subject for adoption and whether the proposed home is suitable for the child.

In those independent adoptions where the consent of the birth parent or parents is not necessary, Family Code § 8816 provides that the CDSS or delegated county adoption agency shall, before the hearing of the petition, file its consent to the adoption with the clerk of the court in which the petition is filed, but that the consent may not be given unless the child's welfare will be promoted by the adoption. Although this statute appears to give the agency some discretionary authority over the adoption, the Supreme Court in *Adoption of McDonald*, (1954) 43 Cal.2d 447, emphatically held (concerning an agency adoption in which the subject child had been relinquished to the agency) that the consent of the agency was not a jurisdictional prerequisite to an adoption decree.

This would appear to apply equally to independent adoptions. In addition, if the agency withheld its "consent," the child would have no one who could make a legal claim to parenthood, since Family Code § 8816 applies in only the limited situations where parental consent to the adoption is unnecessary. Therefore, it would appear that Family Code § 8816 should only be applied in those instances where the prospective adoptive parents subject the child to conditions which would warrant putting the child into dependency proceedings pursuant to Welfare & Institutions Code § 300 (see Chapter 6 of this book).

AGENCY ADOPTIONS 5

In this chapter:

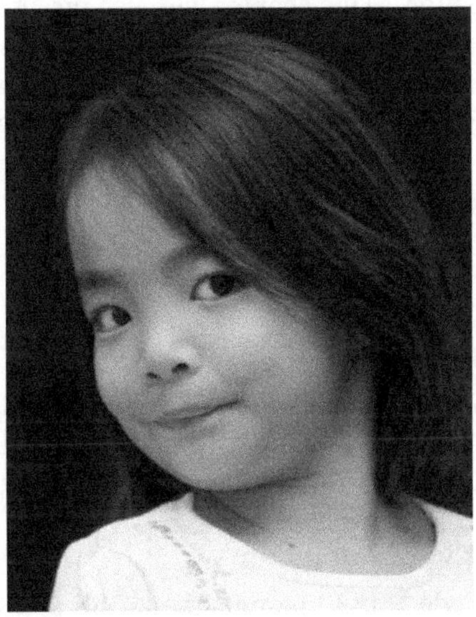

"Pure and genuine religion in the sight of God the Father means caring for orphans and widows in their distress." (James 1:27)

I. WHAT IS AN "AGENCY ADOPTION"?

As explained below, an agency adoption is the adoption of a child who is in the legal custody of a licensed adoption agency. Family Code § 8506 defines "agency adoption" as the adoption of a minor, other than an intercountry adoption, in which the CDSS or a licensed adoption agency is a party to, or joins in, the adoption petition. Under Welfare & Institutions Code § 16120(c), an agency adoption is the only type of adoption which will allow the adoptive parents to seek to receive continuing post-adoption financial aid under the Adoption Assistance Program ("AAP") for a "special needs" child.

An agency may acquire custody when a child is validly relinquished to the agency by a birth parent (thus dispensing with that birth parent's consent to any adoption, pursuant to Family Code § 8606(d) and (e)), or when a court terminates the birth parents' rights in a dependency proceeding brought and concluded pursuant to Welfare & Institutions Code §§ 300 and 366.26 (dispensing with consent under Family Code § 8606(a)), of if the child is referred to the CDSS or an agency after the child has been declared freed from parental custody under Family Code § 7893. An agency which does everything but assume the care, custody, and control of children would be classified by Family Code § 8533 as a "noncustodial adoption agency," although the statutes do not clearly identify what role a "noncustodial adoption agency" actually plays in a true agency adoption. This chapter will discuss relinquishments, while an overview of dependency proceedings is provided in Chapter 6.

In addition, since, prior to the adoption, the child is in the legal custody of the agency, the agency may exercise its discretionary authority over the placement of the child for purposes of adoptions, and thus control a statutory prerequisite to the filing of a petition for an agency adoption. This chapter will also discuss placements of children in the custody of agencies. In addition, while adoption agencies may be private or public, the California courts have consistently held that all are generally governed by the same rules, and that the conduct of even a private agency may constitute "state action" for purposes of constitutional issues, due to the Legislature's delegation of many state functions to private agencies, as is explained below.

II. THE ADOPTION AGENCY AS AN ARM OF THE STATE -- LICENSING

A. Licensing

Family Code § 8530 states that a "licensed adoption agency" is a county agency or a private agency that is licensed by the CDSS to provide adoption services. Health & Safety Code § 1298 prohibits operating an adoption agency without a license.

1. Private Agencies

Health & Safety Code § 1530 permits the CDSS to issue regulations concerning the licensing of adoption agencies. The bulk of the law governing the licensing of private agencies is provided through the CDSS's regulations. However, there are some statutory guidelines.

Family Code § 8521(a) and Health & Safety Code § 1502(9) contemplate that the adoption agency, or more specifically the "full-service adoption agency," will (1) assume the care, custody, and control of a child through a relinquishment of the child to the agency or the involuntary termination of parental rights to the child, (2) "assess" the birth parents, the prospective adoptive parents, or the child, (3) place children for adoption, and (4) "supervise" adoptive placements.

The CDSS regulations require that licensee applicants show proof of experience, education and competency in these four areas. See 22 California Code of Regulations §§ 89143, 89146, 89152 and 89155. In addition, Health & Safety Code § 1502.6 provides experience requirements similar to those listed in the regulations for the agency's executive director.

Moreover, Family Code §§ 8521(b) and 8533(b) require that private adoption agencies be organized and operated on a nonprofit basis. However, these statutes do not expressly require that the private agency demonstrate full compliance with the provisions of 26 U.S.C. § 501(c)(3) and other laws that govern non-profit entities. For private agencies who desire to provide intercountry adoption services, federal law requires them to operate on a nonprofit basis. (42 U.S.C. § 14922(a)(2)(A).)

To obtain the license, 22 California Code of Regulations § 89019(b) allows a private agency to submit an application signed by its executive officer and its chairman of the board of directors. Under 22 California Code of Regulations § 89019(d)(1), every application for a license shall be accompanied by a written plan of operation that covers the agency's program goals and description of services, administrative organization, personnel, physical facilities and office arrangement, budget and financing, and forms and clerical system. According to 22 California Code of Regulations § 89019(d)(2), the applicant agency must also provide a statement of facts on which the need for its service was determined and its plans for coordination with other community welfare services. If the applicant is a private agency, 22 California Code of Regulations § 89019(d)(3) requires submission of a copy of its constitution and bylaws and, if it is incorporated, a list of membership of the governing board and any advisory committee showing lengths of term and interest or qualifications on which selection was based and indicating which persons serve as officers and in which position, a copy of the articles of incorporation and bylaws, a copy of the proposed budget and plan for financing the agency.

Under 22 California Code of Regulations § 89019(d)(4), private agency applicants must also submit a statement as to how the agency will provide for (A) assistance with maternity care for mothers not eligible for Medi-Cal benefits or other means, (B) services and assistance to mothers not eligible for public services and funds, and (C) coordination and utilization of public social services as required by the CDSS's policy and procedures. In addition, Health & Safety Code § 1522 requires fingerprinting and a criminal record check of the applicant's personnel, and Health & Safety Code § 1522.1 states where any sort of license to care for children is being sought, a search through the Child Abuse Registry is required.

2. Government Agencies

Family Code § 8506 allows the CDSS to be the "agency" in an agency adoption. For example, in the smaller counties, the CDSS would be the entity which would take a relinquishment of a child or would prosecute a dependency proceeding. In addition, the State maintains a web site (http://www.cakidsconnection.com) that provides a "find a child" matchmaking software program, as well as photo listings of the children in their custody who are waiting for prospective adoptive parents to provide them with homes.

As for the agencies in the more populated counties, Welfare & Institutions Code § 16100 and 22 California Code of Regulations § 89019(a) provide that a county agency may obtain a "license" to provide adoption services. For a county agency, the process is relatively simple, since the regulations place less stringent requirements on the county agency seeking licensure. Indeed, the courts have even held that a county agency may, in certain circumstances, be presumed to have obtained a license to provide adoption services. See, *In re Duarte's Adoption*, (1964) 229 Cal.App.2d 775.

B. The Private Agency's Conduct Deemed "State Action" – the Case of *Scott v. Family Ministries*

In *Scott v. Family Ministries*, (1976) 65 Cal.App.3d 492, the court held that that by reason of the role of private licensed adoption agencies in California's adoption statutes and the extent to which the California law delegates to such agencies various governmental functions in a judicially authorized adoption, the activity of a private agency is in fact "state action." This proposition was also accepted in *Tyler v. Children's Home Society*, (1994) 29 Cal.App.4th 511. After the *Scott* court reached this conclusion, it held that pursuant to the U.S. Constitution, as interpreted in *Lemon v. Kurtzman*, 403 U.S. 602 (1971), a licensed private adoption agency could not impose a religious eligibility requirement upon persons seeking to adopt children in its care and custody.

1. The Facts of the *Scott* Case

In April 1975, World Vision, a Christian relief organization working in Cambodia with the consent of the Cambodian government, had 20 needy children at its child care center in the capital city of Phnom Penh. The Cambodian government had also authorized the center to find homes for the children in its care. The circumstances in Cambodia then escalated to crisis proportions when the capture of Phnom Penh by a rebel faction – the "Khmer Rouge" – became imminent. World Vision then decided to evacuate the 20 children in its care to Thailand. After that, the 20 children were "paroled" into the United States by the Attorney General for the purpose of adoption, in compliance with U.S. immigration law. (See Chapter 11 of this book concerning children in "parole status.") When they arrived, World Vision transferred the children to the custody of Family Ministries, a licensed private adoption agency in California, with instructions to place the children in Christian homes.

At that time, Family Ministries was a Protestant organization that placed children for adoption only in Protestant homes. Toup Ven was one Cambodian child. Although there was no evidence as to Toup Ven's religion, the court recognized that Cambodia is 92% Buddhist. The Scotts, who were Episcopalians, informed Family Ministries that they desired to adopt Toup Ven. The court also recognized that Episcopalians and Buddhists are not considered to be Protestants. Family Ministries informed the Scotts they only place children in Protestant homes.

The Scotts then filed a complaint for an injunction against Family Ministries. After a bench trial (as well as a series of temporary restraining orders), the court issued a permanent injunction on December 2, 1975 against Family Ministries enjoining, among other things, the religious eligibility requirement, any efforts by Family Ministries to place any of the 20 children with other families, and any effort to transfer the 20 children to other private adoption agencies. The injunction also vacated any adoptive placements made by Family Ministries, and required that custody of the 20 children be immediately transferred to the Los Angeles County Department of Adoptions, except that those children who had been placed for adoption could remain in the homes of their prospective adoptive parents. There was no evidence that Toup Ven had lived with the Scotts at any time, nor that Toup Ven had formed any emotional bond with the Scotts. Nevertheless, Dr. Scott was appointed guardian ad litem for Toup Ven and the other 19 children, who were joined as plaintiffs. The court did not vacate any final adoption order. Also, although the Scotts had filed a petition to adopt Toup Ven, the court never ruled on the adoption petition.

2. *Scott*'s View of the Private Agency's Functions

On the appeal by Family Ministries, the court in *Scott v. Family Ministries*, (1976) 65 Cal.App.3d 492, held that a private adoption agency acts as an arm of the state by virtue of (1) the statutory requirement that adoption agencies be licensed by the state, (2) the provisions now codified at Family Code § 8704(b) (which only allow a petition to adopt a child in the care of an adoption agency to be filed by the prospective adoptive parents with whom the child has been placed for adoption by that agency), and (3) the statutes and administrative regulations that "delegate" certain responsibilities to both county and private licensed adoption agencies. The *Scott* court identified those responsibilities, which included the duty to care for the child, the obligation to counsel and obtain information from the natural parents to determine their health and social history and other relevant data and to ensure the voluntariness of their relinquishment (if applicable), the duty to carefully study each child accepted for adoption to determine his or her needs and capacities in order to select the most appropriate adoptive family, the power and obligation to evaluate applicants desiring to adopt a relinquished child with respect to all the criteria prescribed by statute and regulations, the power to terminate a pre-petition placement for adoption at its discretion; and the right, after the adoption petition has been filed, to ask the court for removal of a child from the adoptive parents with whom the child has been placed.

The *Scott* court also considered that many of the requirements for independent adoptions are not involved in agency adoptions. For example, a party filing a petition for an agency adoption need only obtain the joinder of the agency, and does not need to notify the CDSS, since a private agency may submit the required report to the court under Family Code § 8715. Also, while an independent adoption requires a government agency to determine the voluntariness of the consent of the birth parents (see 22 California Code of Regulations § 35095(b)(6)), a relinquishment for an agency adoption may be taken solely by a private agency.

3. *Scott's* Rejection of "Agency *In Loco Parentis*"

Family Ministries argued that since World Vision, who originally had custody of the children with the permission of the Cambodian government, stood in the relationship of "in loco parentis" (Latin for "in the place of the parents"), World Vision validly expressed the "parental" religious preference. The implied factual premise was that Family Ministries and World Vision agreed that Episcopalians were not Christians, while Protestants were. However, without engaging in this religious discussion, the *Scott* court rejected this argument on the grounds that such a conclusion would be tantamount to requiring agency consent to an adoption, which had already been rejected in *Adoption of McDonald*, (1954) 43 Cal.2d 447.

III. RELINQUISHMENTS

A. Generally

As explained in Chapter 3, Family Code § 8606(d) provides that the "consent" of the birth parent is not required when that individual has relinquished the child to an adoption agency. Since a relinquishment is a voluntary act, it takes the place of the consent of the relinquishing parent. On the other hand, the rules for taking a relinquishment are different from those governing the taking of a consent. In *In re Bridget R.*, (1996) 41 Cal.App.4th 1483, the court held that Family Code sections 8804 and 8815 "are part of the statutory scheme governing independent adoptions and have no application outside of that scheme."

In addition, the relinquishment process is subject to the regulations of the CDSS (see 22 California Code of Regulations §§ 35128 et seq.), who has the legislative authority to enact such regulations. (See Family Code §§ 8621 and 8700(k), and Welfare & Institutions Code § 10553.)

B. The Legal Effect of Filing an Enforceable Relinquishment

1. The Relinquishing Parent's Loss of Parental Rights

Family Code § 8700(j) states that the filing of the relinquishment with the CDSS terminates all parental rights and responsibilities with regard to the child, except as provided in subdivisions (g) and (h), which deal with relinquishments for the purpose of adoption by a specifically identified person. Also, the effect of a relinquishment by a birth parent is to allow adoption of the child without further consent of that birth parent. (See Family Code § 8606.)

2. The Agency's Acquisition of "Vested Rights"

In *In re Adoption of Graham*, (1962) 58 Cal.2d 899, the case involved a "concededly proper relinquishment." The court held that the filing of the relinquishment with the State created rights which could not be involuntarily divested by means of a *nunc pro tunc* order in a marital dissolution case. It ruled that while the power of the court to issue a *nunc pro tunc* order is to be liberally construed, but its operation may not destroy the "vested rights" that arise by virtue of the relinquishment. It also held that the legislative scheme for the placement of relinquished children contemplates that the statutory proceedings will progress unhampered by extrinsic matters (such as the divorce of the birth parents), and with assurance that proper proceedings may consummate a valid adoption. The *Graham* decision also envisioned "the further situation wherein a proper adoption, based upon valid relinquishments, could be set aside by the simple expedient of a nunc pro tunc final decree which would invalidate the relinquishments."

Consequently, under *Graham*, the agency acquires "vested rights" by virtue of a valid relinquishment. On the other hand, the Supreme Court has held that a relinquishment is not enforceable unless all relevant statutory procedures have been followed in obtaining it. See *San Diego County Dept. of Public Welfare v. Superior Court*, (1972) 7

Cal.3d 1. And as set forth above in *Scott v. Family Ministries*, (1976) 65 Cal.App.3d 492, those rights are subject to constitutional restrictions. As set forth below, the Legislature and the courts have further narrowed those rights in various aspects.

3. The Effect on Related Dependency Proceedings

Dependency proceedings are expressly mentioned in Family Code § 8700(i), which states that if the parent has relinquished a child who has been found to come within the jurisdiction of the juvenile court under Welfare & Institutions Code § 300, the CDSS or agency accepting the relinquishment shall provide written notice of the relinquishment within five court days to (1) the juvenile court having jurisdiction of the child, (2) the child's attorney, if any, and (3) the relinquishing parent's attorney, if any. Although it would appear that there would be nothing for the court in the dependency proceedings to decide once the relinquishment becomes enforceable (since the filing of the relinquishment terminates all parental rights), the court must still determine if dismissal of the dependency case is in the child's best interests (see Chapter 6).

C. Procedures for Obtaining an Enforceable Relinquishment

1. Interviews, Counseling and Required Disclosures

While there are no statutory provisions mandating interviews or counseling with the relinquishing parent, interviews and counseling are required by the CDSS regulations. One of the regulations is 22 California Code of Regulations § 35133, which provides: "Prior to accepting the parent's relinquishment of the child for adoption, the agency shall provide counseling as appropriate to the category of parents as described at Section 35134 [which is explained below] who reside in California." In addition, 22 California Code of Regulations § 35129 provides that "The agency shall provide a minimum of two face-to-face interviews with parents who are considering relinquishment and who reside in California. ¶ (1) The required interviews shall be provided over a period of two or more days. ... ¶ (3) During the interview the agency shall explain to the parent the purpose of the agency and the services it provides." Likewise, 22 California Code of Regulations § 35135 provides: "(a) Prior to accepting the parent's relinquishment of a child for adoption, the agency shall determine: ¶ (1) That the parent has chosen the plan of adoption for the child and freely chooses to relinquish the child. ... [and] ¶ (4) That the parent, if residing in California, has received required counseling as appropriate to the category of parents commencing with Section 35134."

In *Tyler v. Children's Home Society*, (1994) 29 Cal.App.4th 511, the court held that nothing in this regulation requires both interviews to occur before the signing of the relinquishment documents, nor that there are any requirements as to the location or duration of the meeting, nor as to who else may be present during the interviews. The *Tyler* court also held that the regulations may validly allow the adoption agency to provide differing types of counseling for the birth father, depending on whether he is a "presumed father" or an "alleged father." (See Chapter 3.)

The Statement of Understanding forms that are provided on the CDSS web site set forth the information that must be conveyed to the relinquishing parent(s) in "written form," as required by 22 California Code of Regulations § 35147. The *Tyler* court also had to answer the question of whether the relinquishing parents had to also be orally told the information contained in the Statements of Understanding. *Tyler* did not set forth a per se rule, but instead noted factually that there had been some human interaction, that the relinquishing parents were "intelligent and strong-minded," and that there was no evidence of prejudice from the lack of verbal communication as to the right, in that particular instance, to independent counsel.

a) Availability of Legal Counsel

Under 22 California Code of Regulations § 35134(a)(2) and (e)(2), "the agency shall inform the parent that he/she has the right to seek legal counsel to assist him/her in the relinquishment process when appropriate the agency shall make referral to legal resources." *Tyler* holds that the relinquishing parent must show that prejudice resulted from the alleged failure to inform as to the right to independent legal counsel.

b) Availability of Resources

22 California Code of Regulations § 35134(a)(4) provides that the agency shall "inform the parent of at least the following resources and make a referral when appropriate: Financial resources, Employment resources, Education resources, Child care resources, Housing resources, and Health service resources." Financial resources would include benefits received in programs such as Aid to Families with Dependent Children (AFDC) and even student loans. Housing resources would include dormitories and other college/university housing, along with housing provided under various federal programs. Although this regulation appears to direct the agencies to provide very specific information, the *Tyler* court held that a failure to fully to comply with this regulation does not constitute grounds for rescission, unless the relinquishing parent shows prejudice.

c) The Option of an Independent Adoption

While 22 California Code of Regulations § 35134(a)(6) requires the agency to advise the mother and presumed father of the option of an independent adoption, there is no such provision pertaining to alleged fathers. However, the alternative of an independent adoption is mentioned in the standard Statements of Understanding, which are distributed to all. *Tyler* holds that if independent adoptions are not discussed, there still cannot be a rescission of the relinquishment unless prejudice is established, even if there was no discussion of the significance of the distinction between independent adoption and agency adoption.

d) Other Options and Alternative Plans

According to 22 California Code of Regulations § 35134(a)(3), the agency must "provide all available information regarding alternative plans for the child, with a complete description of each alternative, including keeping the child, placement with extended family members, and/or foster care and reunification services." Such alternative plans could include receiving financial and child care help from grandparents and other family.

e) Holding the Relinquishment Prior to Filing

Pursuant to 22 California Code of Regulations § 35141, the agency representative shall inform all parents of the time frame options for the filing of the signed relinquishment form with the department. It also states that (A) the parent shall be permitted to request that the signed relinquishment form be filed without a holding period, and (B) the parent shall be permitted to have the signed relinquishment form held for a specified period of up to 30 days before the agency submits it to the department for filing. The *Tyler* court held that this regulation does not allow an indefinite hold, but that the indefinite hold applies only where there are unresolved questions about custody rights of other parents not involved in the relinquishment. (22 Cal. Code Regs. § 35141(a)(2).) *Tyler* also states that the adoption worker may verbally advise the birth parents about "holds."

f) Availability of Rescission of Relinquishment

Under 22 California Code of Regulations § 35169, the agency must follow certain procedures when it receives a request for rescission of a relinquishment. However, *Tyler* held that the failure to follow such procedures after the signing of the relinquishment cannot be used to demonstrate the signing itself was not knowing and voluntary.

g) Counseling Regarding "Feelings"

The agency is required, under 22 California Code of Regulations § 35134(a)(5) and (e)(6), to "provide counseling services as needed to assist the parent with his/her feelings regarding the child and the long-range implications of relinquishing the child for adoption." *Tyler* holds that this regulation confers discretion on the adoption worker to determine what counseling is needed. *Tyler* also states that the failure to comply with this regulation does not constitute grounds for rescinding the relinquishment without establishing prejudice, and that the mere fact that the birth parent is crying while signing the relinquishment does not establish prejudice.

h) Information re Medical History

Under Family Code §§ 8608 and 8706, the agency must obtain medical histories from relinquishing parents. However, *Tyler* holds that the purpose of this requirement is not to protect relinquishing parents, but to provide the prospective adopting parents with the kinds of information which may reasonably influence their decision whether to adopt the child. Thus, noncompliance does not prejudice the relinquishing parents.

2. Signing and Witnessing of Relinquishment Papers

a) Formal Requirements

Family Code § 8700(a) states that either birth parent may relinquish a child to the CDSS or a licensed adoption agency for adoption by a written statement signed before two subscribing witnesses and acknowledged before an authorized official of the CDSS or agency. That code section also provides that the relinquishment, when reciting that the person making it is entitled to the sole custody of the child and acknowledged before the officer, is prima facie evidence of the right of the person making it to the sole custody of the child and the person's sole right to relinquish.

b) Capacity to Relinquish Child

Family Code § 8700(b) provides that a relinquishing parent who is a minor has the right to relinquish his or her child for adoption to the CDSS or a licensed adoption agency, and the relinquishment is not subject to revocation by reason of the minority. There is no provision stating that a parent with diminished mental capacity is competent to sign a relinquishment. It would appear that an adoption under these circumstances would require a termination of parental rights, subject to the child's best interests.

c) Relinquishments Naming Adoptive Parents

Family Code § 8700(f) allows the relinquishing parent to name the specific person or persons with whom he or she intends that the agency place the child for adoption. As set forth below, a birth parent acquires certain revocation rights when such a relinquishment is executed. However, it does not appear that the intended adoptive parents acquire any vested rights solely by virtue of this type of relinquishment. On the other hand, the intended adoptive parents may acquire enforceable rights by virtue of other circumstances, as described further in this chapter.

3. Filing with the State Department of Social Services

Family Code § 8700(e) states that a relinquishment has no effect until a certified copy is filed with the CDSS. Upon filing with the CDSS, the relinquishment is final and may be rescinded only by the mutual consent of the CDSS or licensed adoption agency to which the child was relinquished and the birth parent or parents relinquishing the child.

4. State's Refusal to Acknowledge the Relinquishment

In *Adoption of Baby Boy D.*, (2001) 93 Cal.App.4th 1, it was held that where the CDSS refuses to acknowledge the validity of a relinquishment, a court should do more than to merely review the action of the CDSS and determine if all the boxes on the relinquishment form were properly checked off; it should determine whether the relinquishment was in fact valid, i.e., whether it was a knowing, voluntary and intelligent waiver of parental rights. The *Baby Boy D.* court also held that the CDSS's refusal to acknowledge a relinquishment is not determinative of whether or not it is valid, but that the court should examine the evidence to determine whether the birth parent in fact intended to relinquish the child for purposes of adoption. If so, the relinquishment operates to terminate the relinquishing parent's rights in spite of the CDSS's rejection of the document. The *Baby Boy D.* court also applied a kind of "substantial compliance with law" rule.

5. Providing Copies of Documents

Under 22 California Code of Regulations § 35151(a)(3)(D), upon the signing of the forms the agency must "give the parent a copy of the completed relinquishment document," and under 22 California Code of Regulations § 35153(a)(6), the agency must "send the parent a copy of the filed relinquishment form," after it is filed with the CDSS. The court in *Tyler v. Children's Home Society*, (1994) 29 Cal.App.4th 511, held that the failure to give the parents copies of the signed documents does not constitute grounds for rescission of the relinquishment without a showing of prejudice, and that the providing of the documents before the signing vitiates prejudice. *Tyler* also held that events occurring subsequent to the signing, such as the failure to provide copies of documents, cannot be used to demonstrate that the signing itself was tainted.

6. Relinquishment to Private Agency (Dependency Case)

Where the child is the subject of ongoing dependency proceedings, the child is actually in the legal custody of the juvenile court, as explained in Chapters 6 and 9. However, in *Teresa J. v. Superior Court*, (2002) 102 Cal.App.4th 366, the court held that a birth parent of a child in dependency proceedings not only has the right to execute a valid relinquishment, but may relinquish the child to a private agency. On the other hand, in response to the argument that the public social services agency involved in the dependency proceeding must be involved in the taking of the relinquishment, the *Teresa J.* reiterated that the juvenile court retains broad power to limit the parent's ability to relinquish the dependent child.

7. Interstate Relinquishments

a) Parents Coming to California to Relinquish

Family Code § 8700(c) states that if the relinquishing parent resides outside California and the child is being cared for and is or will be placed for adoption by the CDSS or a California-licensed adoption agency, the relinquishing parent may relinquish the child to the CDSS or agency by a written statement signed by the relinquishing parent before a notary on a form prescribed by the CDSS, and previously signed by an authorized official of the CDSS or agency, that signifies the willingness of the CDSS or agency to accept the relinquishment.

b) Parents Relinquishing Child outside California

Under Family Code § 8700(d), if a relinquishing parent and child reside outside California and the child will be cared for and will be placed for adoption by the CDSS or a licensed adoption agency, the relinquishing parent may relinquish the child by a written statement signed by the relinquishing parent, after that parent has satisfied the following requirements: (1) Prior to signing the relinquishment, the relinquishing parent shall have received, from a representative of an agency licensed or otherwise approved to provide adoption services under the laws of the relinquishing parent's state of residence, the same counseling and advisement services as if the relinquishing parent resided in this state. (2) The relinquishment shall be signed before a representative of an agency licensed or otherwise approved to provide adoption services under the laws of the relinquishing parent's state whenever possible or before a licensed social worker on a form prescribed by the CDSS, and previously signed by an authorized CDSS or agency official, that signifies the willingness of the CDSS or agency to accept the relinquishment.

8. Statutorily Required Inquiry re "Indian Child" Status

Family Code § 8620(a)(1) provides that if a parent is seeking to relinquish a child the DSS or licensed adoption agency, as applicable, shall ask the child and the child's parent or custodian whether the child is, or may be, a member of, or eligible for membership in an Indian tribe or whether the child has been identified as a member of an Indian organization. The DSS or licensed adoption agency, as applicable, shall then complete the DSS forms provided for this purpose and make this completed form a part of the file.

If there is any information indicating that the child is or may be an Indian child, Family Code § 8620(a)(2) requires the DSS or licensed adoption agency, as applicable, to obtain the following information:

> (A) The name of the child involved, and the actual date and place of birth of the child.
>
> (B) The name, address, date of birth, and tribal affiliation of the birth parents, maternal and paternal grandparents, and maternal and paternal great-grandparents of the child.
>
> (C) The name and address of extended family members of the child who have a tribal affiliation.
>
> (D) The name and address of the Indian tribes or Indian organizations of which the child is, or may be, a member.
>
> (E) A statement of the reasons why the child is, or may be, an Indian.

Family Code § 8620(a)(3)(A) then requires the DSS, licensed adoption agency, or attorney for the prospective adoptive parents, to send a notice, which shall include the above information, and a request for confirmation of the child's Indian status, to any parent and any custodian of the child, and to any Indian tribe of which the child is, or may be, a member or eligible for membership. If any of the above information cannot be obtained, the notice shall indicate that fact. (Please see Family Code § 180 and Chapter 9 of this book concerning sending notices to Indian tribes.) Family Code § 8620(a)(3)(B) requires the notice to describe the nature of the proceeding and advise the recipient of the Indian tribe's right to intervene in the proceeding on its own behalf or on behalf of a tribal member relative of the child.

D. Rescission or Revocation of a Relinquishment

1. General Rule of Irrevocability

Family Code § 8700(e) sets forth the general rule that once a certified copy of the relinquishment is filed with the CDSS, it is final and may be rescinded only by the mutual consent of the CDSS or licensed adoption agency to which the child was relinquished and the birth parent or parents relinquishing the child.

2. Revocation of a Party-Specific Relinquishment

Just as a consent to an independent adoption may be revoked within 30 days (see Chapter 3), a relinquishment that specifically identifies the intended adoptive parents may be rescinded within 30 days under certain circumstances. Family Code § 8700(g) sets forth an exception to the rule of irrevocability, and states that if the relinquishment names the person or persons with whom placement by the CDSS or licensed adoption agency is intended (as permitted by Family Code § 8700(f)) and the child is (1) not placed in the home of the named person or persons or (2) the child is removed from the home prior to the granting of the adoption, then the CDSS or agency shall mail a notice by certified mail, return receipt requested, to the birth parent signing the relinquishment within 72 hours of the decision not to place the child for adoption or the decision to remove the child from the home.

Family Code § 8700(h) then provides that the relinquishing parent has 30 days from the date on which the Family Code § 8700(g) notice was mailed to rescind the relinquishment. On the other hand, under Family Code § 8700(h)(2), if the relinquishing parent does not request rescission during the 30-day period, the CDSS or licensed adoption agency is free to select other adoptive parents for the child.

As an alternative, under Family Code § 8700(h)(3), if the relinquishing parent and the CDSS or licensed adoption agency wish to identify a different person or persons during the 30-day period with whom the child is intended to be placed, the initial relinquishment shall be rescinded and a new relinquishment identifying the person or persons completed. Based on the manner in which this statute is structured and phrased, it would appear that the relinquishing parent has a right to substitute the name of a new intended adoptive parent(s).

The California Supreme Court in *Sharon S. v. Superior Court*, (2003) 31 Cal.4th 417, acknowledged the possibility of effectuating a second parent adoption by way of an agency adoption. It would be accomplished by the custodial birth parent relinquishing the child to an agency, wherein that birth parent states in the relinquishment that he or she intends herself or himself to become the adoptive parent, along with another person designated by the birth parent.

3. Rescission Based on Mutual Agreement

Family Code § 8700(e) states that there can be a rescission of the relinquishment based on the mutual agreement of the relinquishing parent and the agency. Under 22 California Code of Regulations § 35169(b), after a relinquishment has been filed with the CDSS, the agency shall treat an oral or written declaration by the relinquishing parent, that he or she wishes to rescind the relinquishment or to have the child returned as a request for rescission.

Once an oral or written request to rescind has been made, 22 California Code of Regulations § 35169(b)(3) requires the agency to (A) cease all adoptive planning for the child until the agency reaches a decision regarding the request, (B) give the relinquishing parent the AD 508 form [which is very short and deals only with rescission requests], (C) advise the parent that he or she has 14 days from the date the agency provides the rescission form in which to give the agency a written request for rescission, (D) specify the date by which the parent must complete and return the AD 508 to the agency, and (E) inform the parent that if the form is not completed and returned to the agency by the specified date, the request for rescission shall be nullified. However, the court in *Tyler v. Children's Home Society*, (1994) 29 Cal.App.4th 511, held that the failure to abide by such procedures does not indicate that the original relinquishment was not voluntary.

4. Rescission for Fraud or Undue Influence

In spite of the legislative policy of Family Code § 8700(e) mandating the finality of a filed relinquishment, there exist judicially-created grounds by which a birth parent may bring an action in equity to set aside a relinquishment for cause, such as for fraud or undue influence. In *Brooks v. Los Angeles County Bureau of Adoptions*, (1963) 218 Cal.App.2d 732, the court reversed the sustaining of a demurrer and held that the then-existing statutes, which are substantially similar to those that now exist, were not specific enough to negate the independent rule of equity allowing rescission for fraud. Also, *In re Cheryl E.*, (1984) 161 Cal.App.3d 587, held that there could be a rescission based on a finding of undue influence where the adoption worker has misrepresented certain material facts to the birth parent.

In *Hall v. Department of Adoptions*, (1975) 47 Cal.App.3d 898, the court recognized that fraud, force or duress exerted by a third party (such as the birth parent's spouse) may be grounds to rescind a relinquishment. However, the *Hall* court said that there still must be proof that the fraud, force or duress caused the relinquishment to be involuntary. Furthermore, *Hall* cites Civil Code § 1689 in holding that there must be evidence that the agency participated in or had reason to know of the third party's duress or fraud. *Hall* deals with a case of extensive spousal abuse and child abuse by the husband/father, while the mother relinquished the child for adoption after the child was in the foster care system for a short time. She did not prove that her act was the result of her husband's wrongful persuasion or his threat of harm to herself or child if she did not agree to relinquish the child to appellant, and the complaint charged only the husband and not the county adoption agency with the wrongful conduct.

The *Hall* court reviewed the testimony showing that the mother was unhappy and at times wavering on her decision to relinquish the child for adoption, but stated that it "is manifestly clear that the decision was clearly her own and she freely arrived at that decision." The court also considered the statement by the mother that she felt that the adoption worker was "pushing her," but that such a statement was a mere characterization of what was otherwise proper conduct by the adoptions worker. In addition, the court found it significant that the mother never asked to have her relinquishment cancelled or to have her child returned to her, until the complaint was filed and served.

Hall also states that the rules requiring very definite and specific allegations in a pleading stating a fraud claim apply with equal force in an action to rescind a relinquishment, and that it is insufficient to merely say that "it will all be resolved at trial" or that "the testimony and evidence will tell us what the fraud is."

5. Rescission for Constructive Fraud – the *Tyler* case

In *Tyler v. Children's Home Society*, (1994) 29 Cal.App.4th 511, the court reviewed Family Code § 8700, 22 California Code of Regulations §§ 35167, and other statutes and regulations, and held that once a relinquishment is filed with the CDSS, it is final and cannot statutorily be rescinded except under narrow circumstances, such as by the mutual consent of the adoption agency and the relinquishing parent or parents.

However, in *Tyler*, the court held that there could be rescission for "construction fraud." *Tyler* cited Civil Code § 1573, which states, "constructive fraud consists: ¶ 1. In any breach of duty which, without an actually fraudulent intent, gains an advantage to the person in fault, or anyone claiming under him, by misleading another to his prejudice, or to the prejudice of anyone claiming under him; or, ¶ 2. In any such act or omission as the law specially declares to be fraudulent, without respect to actual fraud."

Tyler also held that "constructive fraud arises on a breach of duty by one in a confidential or fiduciary relationship to another which induces justifiable reliance by the latter to his prejudice," and that "actual reliance and causation of injury must be shown." The court held that an agency has no "fiduciary" duties because its concurrent responsibilities to the other parties, the child and prospective adoptive parents (whose interests may potentially conflict with those of the birth parents), negate a fiduciary relationship with the birth parents. Furthermore, *Tyler* merely assumed *arguendo* that a confidential relationship existed (citing *Cheryl E.*, (1984) 161 Cal.App.3d 587), based on the birth parent's allegations that she was young and inexperienced, in a weakened condition, and had placed trust in the private agency.

In further defining "constructive fraud," the *Tyler* court held that while noncompliance with the CDSS regulations does not automatically invalidate a relinquishment, noncompliance will constitute a ground for rescission of a relinquishment, regardless of the lack of fraudulent intent, if the noncompliance rises to the level of constructive fraud, i.e., if the violation causes prejudice to the relinquishing parents by affecting their decision to relinquish. The specific violations in the *Tyler* case consisted of the failure to (1) discuss the option of placing the baby with extended family members, (2) discuss educational or employment resources, (3) give the relinquishing parents copies of the executed documents, and (4) obtain the birth father's medical history. *Tyler* rejects the notion that there can be "presumed prejudice" from regulatory violations, but states that the birth parent must prove that actual prejudice resulted from the violations. *Tyler* also held that there is no shifting of the burden of proof to prove that the transaction was voluntary, as occurs in undue influence cases, based on the legislative policy according finality to relinquishments, as stated in Family Code § 8700(d) and confirmed in *In re Adoption of Graham*, (1962) 58 Cal.2d 899. The *Tyler* court emphasized that the case did not present issues of deliberate misconduct by the agency personnel, but rather at most negligent omissions of regulatory requirements, and did not involve a "wholesale disregard of the regulations," but rather certain specific violations.

The heart of the *Tyler* decision was its holding that "the manifest overall purpose of the regulations is to assure that relinquishments are given voluntarily and knowingly, and that purpose is served by a rule of substantial compliance," which means "actual compliance in respect to the substance essential to every reasonable objective of the provisions." The *Tyler* court borrowed from *Adoption of Barnett*, (1960) 54 Cal.2d 370, and held that strict adherence to the statutes and regulations was not essential to the completion of the adoption, since the main objective of the statutes and regulations is to promote the welfare of children. On the other hand, as noted in *Tyler*, the best interests of the child are not at issue in a rescission action, since constitutionally-protected parental rights are at stake.

6. Rescission for Lack of Due Process

Tyler v. Children's Home Society, (1994) 29 Cal.App.4th 511, also holds that an adoption agency's noncompliance with regulations does not necessarily constitute a deprivation of procedural due process. *Tyler* notes that parenting is a fundamental right, that parents enjoy a fundamental liberty interest in the care, custody and control of their children, and that parental rights cannot be terminated except according to procedures that satisfy due process. However, it also noted that constitutionally-mandated requirements of procedural due process are found in the constitution, as interpreted by the courts, and not in state statutes and regulations. Since a failure to comply with state law procedural requirements does not necessarily constitute a denial of due process, the mere fact that a state agency violates its own procedures does not, *ipso facto*, mean that it has contravened federal due process.

Tyler also confirmed that constitutional rights may generally be waived, provided the waiver is knowing, voluntary and intelligent, with sufficient awareness of the relevant circumstances and likely consequences, and that due process may require that certain procedures be followed to insure that a waiver of constitutional rights is accomplished knowingly, voluntarily, and intelligently. *Tyler* held that the four regulatory violations it cited did not amount to a violation of due process.

7. Incomplete Enforceability If Relinquishment Is Taken During Pendency of a Guardianship or Adoption Case

a) The *San Diego Public Welfare* Case

In *San Diego County Dept. of Public Welfare v. Superior Court*, (1972) 7 Cal.3d 1, the Supreme Court held that adoption is preferred over guardianship. However, the court also held that where a guardianship petition is filed by the persons having lawful physical custody of the child, the birth parent's subsequent signing of a relinquishment to an agency may not be valid where the best interests of the child dictate in favor of the proposed guardians. The court stated that adoption statutes may not reasonably be interpreted as depriving such a child of the protection afforded by guardianship proceedings in a proper case.

Likewise, *San Diego Public Welfare* held that where there is a pre-existing and ongoing petition for an independent adoption, the court's jurisdiction over that proceeding is not terminated by a subsequent relinquishment of the child to an agency. In the words of the Supreme Court, an agency "cannot deprive the court of jurisdiction to consider the pending adoption petition simply by the device of obtaining a relinquishment from the natural mother."

In *San Diego Public Welfare*, the child had already been placed by the birth parent with the persons who later became the guardians, and for the purpose of allowing their immediate filing of an independent adoption petition, which they did indeed file. The Supreme Court stated that, "the social worker in the instant case may have been a little over zealous in an attempt to induce the natural mother to refuse to consent to the adoption by the [proposed guardians/ adoptive parents] . . . and to relinquish the child to Department." For these reasons, it is unclear how far *San Diego Public Welfare* can be taken, based on its unique facts.

On the other hand, the *San Diego Public Welfare* court rejected the proposition that "the relinquishment signed by the natural mother is of no force and effect because it was obtained during the pendency of the guardianship proceedings." In fact, the *San Diego Public Welfare* court held that the signing and filing of the relinquishment operated to dispense with the need to obtain the natural mother's consent in the pending independent adoption proceeding. The court merely limited the agency's rights arising from the relinquishment.

b) The Status of the *Graham* "Vested Rights" Rule

The case of *In re Adoption of Graham*, (1962) 58 Cal.2d 899, which involved a "concededly proper relinquishment," holds that the agency acquires "vested rights" by virtue of the relinquishment. However, the Supreme Court decided *San Diego Public Welfare* after *Graham*, meaning that the agency might not acquire "vested rights" if it takes the relinquishment in less than complete good faith, and for the purpose of hindering a previously-filed petition for an independent adoption. It would appear that the *San Diego Public Welfare* court could have simply interpreted the language of what is now Family Code § 8700(a) to say that only a parent with legal and actual custody may execute a valid relinquishment, but it did not use this rationale.

On the other hand, it should be noted that *San Diego Public Welfare* confirms that "in the absence of a showing that the agency is unfit to have the temporary custody of the child or that it is improbable that the child will be adopted, the appointment of a guardian is neither 'necessary' nor 'convenient' [which is the applicable standard under Probate Code § 1514(a) in a guardianship proceeding]." See also, *Guardianship of Henwood*, (1958) 49 Cal.2d 639, which held that the Legislature's comprehensive plan for the adoption of relinquished children would be frustrated, if at any time the court could determine in the exercise of its independent judgment and discretion that a guardian should be appointed and custody removed from the agency or the prospective adoptive parents selected by it.

8. Required Joinder of Both Birth Parents

In *Hall v. Department of Adoptions*, (1975) 47 Cal.App.3d 898, the court held that in an action to rescind a relinquishment, it is error to allow the matter to proceed without the joinder of both natural parents, where both parents had signed the relinquishment. The court held that the error exists even if both parents are witnesses at trial, since there are rights and duties affecting both parent that very well may be changed or possibly entirely removed. The court held that the failure to join both birth parents could result in uncertainty as to parental obligations, especially with regard to child support duties.

9. Validity of Relinquishment Signed in another State Where a Dependency Case is Pending in California

In *Taylor M. v. Superior Court*, (2003) 106 Cal.App.4th 97, the infant child was the subject of a dependency proceeding in California, while the birth father executed a relinquishment to a Texas adoption agency in contemplation of an adoption proceeding that was to be completed in Texas. The birth father thereafter sought to revoke the relinquishment, whereupon a proceeding was initiated in Texas to terminate the birth father's rights, albeit after the California juvenile court had taken jurisdiction over the child under the Uniform Child Custody Jurisdiction and Enforcement Act (see Chapter 9) by virtue of a detention order in the dependency proceedings (see Chapter 6). The California appellate court in *Taylor M.* held that the Texas court (which was also bound by the UCCJEA) had no jurisdiction over the child, and it was the duty of the California juvenile court to determine the validity of the relinquishment.

10. Rescission of Relinquishment of an "Indian Child"

Under Family Code § 8620(b) and 25 U.S.C. § 1913(c) allow the parent of an Indian child to rescind a relinquishment for any reason at any time prior to the entry of a final decree of adoption, thus requiring return of the child to the parent.

IV. PLACEMENT OF THE CHILD BY THE AGENCY

A. Placement Confers Standing to File an Adoption Petition

Family Code § 8704(b) states that no petition may be filed to adopt a child that has been relinquished to the CDSS or a licensed adoption agency, or is in the legal custody and control of the CDSS or a licensed adoption agency for adoptive placement, except by the prospective adoptive parents with whom the child has been placed for adoption by that agency.

In interpreting a substantially similar predecessor to Family Code § 8704(b), the court in *In re Adoption of Runyon*, (1969) 268 Cal.App.2d 918, applied the plain language of the statute, and rejected an "equal protection" challenge. In *Runyon*, the petitioners had had the child in their home in foster placement continuously for 8 years before the agency removed the child from them, which occurred prior to their filing of an adoption petition. The court ruled that the law did not give them standing to file an adoption petition after the child was taken from them, since the procedures are "entirely statutory." It also rejected an argument made pursuant to *Adoption of Barnett*, (1960) 54 Cal.2d 370, that the statutes should be liberally construed so as to preserve what was virtually a family unit. The court held that the rules relating to standing to file for an independent adoption did not apply where the child was in the agency's legal custody.

The case of *Mullins v. State of Oregon*, (9th Cir. 1995) 57 F.3d 789, is also significant. Even though it deals with Oregon law, *Mullins* holds that a grandparent has no federal constitutional right to adopt a child in agency custody merely by virtue of a biological connection with the child. In *Mullins*, the grandparent admittedly had not had a significant amount of actual contact with the child, meaning that the court had no means by which to determine whether a constitutional right to adopt might arise by virtue of the emotional bonding between child and caregiver. As stated above, *Runyon* dealt with an equal protection challenge and did not discuss whether there was a substantive due process right to file the adoption petition.

B. What Constitutes "Placement" by an Agency?

Unlike the statutes governing independent adoptions (see Chapter 4), there are no clear agency adoption statutes requiring a placement agreement to be fully executed before the child is considered "placed" for purposes of adoption. (In practice, agencies do of course require the prospective adoptive parents to sign a placement agreement. In addition, the CDSS web site provides a standard "notice of placement" as Form 558, which the agency is required to file with the CDSS within 15 days of the placement.) Also, the court in *Jinny N. v. Superior Court*, (1987) 195 Cal.App.3d 967, reviewed the statutes now codified at Family Code § 8700, et seq., and stated that they do not define exactly what constitutes a placement for purposes of adoption.

In *Jinny N.*, the county agency (the Orange County Social Services Agency or "the SSA") had previously placed the child for purposes of foster care with the person who later applied to become the adoptive parent. The child thereafter remained in that home at all relevant times. The SSA had also sent letters to the foster parent praising her efforts in raising the child. Once the natural parents' rights were finally terminated in dependency proceedings, the SSA later encouraged the foster parent to adopt the child "under its auspices." The foster parent then filed a petition for an agency adoption, but the agency was unwilling to file a joinder due to the delay on the part of the CDSS in formally recognizing the juvenile court's order terminating the birth parents' rights and in the processing of other items of paperwork. Finally, when the SSA learned that the child had bruises on her buttocks (see Welfare & Institutions Code § 16001.9, which prohibits corporal punishment of a foster child), the SSA filed a motion to dismiss the adoption petition and remove the child from the home.

The trial court granted the motion pursuant to *In re Adoption of Runyon*, (1969) 268 Cal.App.2d 918, saying that there was no placement because no placement agreement had been signed. However, the appellate court in *Jinny N.* reversed, and held that the SSA's "actions and words altered her status to that of a prospective adoptive parent," and that "the SSA had indeed placed Teresa with her for purposes of adoption." Since there was a "placement," standing to file the adoption petition existed, making it reversible error to dismiss the petition. The *Jinny N.* court also stated, "Common sense tells us, however, that a placement can originally have one purpose--i.e., foster care--and metamorphose into an adoptive placement, even absent formal paperwork. The intent of the parties must surely be evaluated, along with the objective indicia of adoption proceedings." The court also stated, "No talismanic words or documents were required at that point [after the SSA invited the petitioner to become the adoptive parent] to cement petitioner's rights." It also held, "where, as here, the agency verifiably solicits, nurtures, and confirms an adoptive placement, the mere lack of what the agency deems to be a necessary final document cannot deprive the would-be parent of all statutory protection." In a footnote, the *Jinny N.* opinion treated the agency's lack of a formal joinder to the adoption petition in the same way it treated the absence of a placement agreement.

C. Agency Authority re Placement before Filing of Petition

Family Code § 8704(a) states, "The department or licensed adoption agency to which a child has been freed for adoption by either relinquishment or termination of parental rights is responsible for the care of the child, and is entitled to the exclusive custody and control of the child until an order of adoption is granted. Any placement for temporary care, or for adoption, made by the department or a licensed adoption agency may be terminated in its discretion at any time before the granting of an order of adoption. In the event of termination of any placement for temporary care or for adoption, the child shall be returned promptly to the physical custody of the department or licensed adoption agency."

There is also a similar provision which applies to children whose parents' rights were terminated in dependency proceedings. Welfare & Institutions Code § 366.26(j) provides, "The State Department of Social Services or licensed adoption agency shall be responsible for the custody and supervision of the minor and shall be entitled to the exclusive care and control of the minor at all times until a petition for adoption is granted. With the consent of the agency, the court may appoint a guardian of the minor, who shall serve until the minor is adopted." As set forth herein, these two statutes have been interpreted to apply to the period prior the filing of the adoption petition only, due to the apparent conflict in the language of Family Code § 8704(b) referring the court's authority after the filing of the petition.

D. Agency Discretion re Placement – Home Studies

All 50 states and the District of Columbia require that the prospective adoptive parents be investigated before the adoption is finalized. Some states have more stringent investigative requirements than others, and California appears to require a more detailed investigation than most. This investigation, called the "home study" or "family assessment," is undertaken for the purpose of allowing the agency to make a reasoned decision concerning whether and where to place the child for adoption. This section of the book will analyze the home study and the degree of discretion that an agency may exercise in making its placement decision.

1. The Agency's Authority and Duty to Investigate

According to Family Code § 8715(a), "The department or licensed adoption agency, whichever is a party to or joins in the petition, shall submit a full report of the facts of the case to the court." Obviously, one cannot submit a "report of the facts" unless one learns of the facts. That is accomplished through the "assessment" authorized by 22 California Code of Regulations § 35180(a), which states, "The agency shall assess each applicant seeking to adopt a child for whom the agency needs adoptive parents in order to determine the applicant's suitability as a prospective adoptive parent."

2. The Matters Which Are the Subject of the Investigation

a) Identifying Information

Under 22 California Code of Regulations §§ 35180(a)(1)(A) and 35181(b)(1), (2) and (7), the required information shall include identifying information about the applicant and any children and adults residing in the home, including their name, address, telephone number, date of birth, sex, and relationship, if any, to the child to be adopted.

Further, 22 California Code of Regulations § 35181(b)(3) and (4) require the applicant to inform the agency about matters of race, ethnicity and religion. As to race and ethnicity, it is unclear what relevance these matters have, and federal law (42 U.S.C. §§ 671, 674 and 1996b, as explained in other chapters) prohibits the denial of an adoption application on the basis of race. As to religion, Family Code § 8709(a) and *Scott v. Family Ministries*, (1976) 65 Cal.App.3d 492, allow the agency to engage in "religious matching," but not "religious discrimination."

b) Commitment and Capability to Raise the Child

According to 22 California Code of Regulations § 35180(a)(1)(D), the assessment must state whether the applicant appears committed and capable to meet the child's needs. Likewise, 22 California Code of Regulations § 35181(c)(2) requires the agency to ascertain and consider the applicant's commitment and capability to meet the needs of a child, not only as to children generally but as to the specific needs of an identified child for the adoption.

This determination is to include a description of the age, race, gender and characteristics of children that this family, in the agency's judgment, is likely to be willing and able to parent, and whom the agency will consider for placement with the applicant. It must also include any characteristics of a child for which, in the agency's judgment, the applicant would be unsuitable. The agency is also required under 22 California Code of Regulations § 35181(c)(6) to analyze the applicant's "social support system," apparently with regard to whether the applicant can draw upon such "social support system" (which is undefined) to meet the child's needs.

c) Marital Status

Under 22 California Code of Regulations § 35181(b)(6), the applicants are required to provide the agency with documentation concerning marital status. It would appear that this regulation impliedly allows the agency to take marital status into consideration in assessing the applicant(s). On the other hand, in *County of Los Angeles v. Superior Court*, (1969) 2 Cal.App.3d 1059, the court held that a petition for an adoption may go forward even if the prospective adoptive parents file for a divorce after the filing of the adoption petition. Family Code § 8601(b) expressly contemplates that an "unmarried person" may seek to adopt a child. However, in *Marten v. Thies*, (1979) 99 Cal.App.3d 161, the court held that the failure to inform the adoption agency, prior to filing the adoption petition, of the existence of marital difficulties in the home, constituted grounds for the agency to terminate the adoptive placement. Importantly, in *Marten v. Thies*, the social worker in that case "found nothing to indicate that the child was physically suffering or that she was in any immediate danger; she appeared well cared for."

d) Other Children of Prospective Adoptive Parents

In addition to the children living in the home, the applicants are also required under 22 California Code of Regulations § 35181(b)(8) to provide the agency with the names, dates of birth and location of any minor child of the applicant who is not living in the home. This would appear to prompt the agency to ask why the applicant's minor child is not living in the home.

e) Motivation of the Prospective Adoptive Parents

In assessing the applicant, 22 California Code of Regulations § 35181(c)(4) requires the agency to ascertain and consider the applicant's motivation for seeking adoption and for the willingness to assume permanent responsibility for the care, guidance and protection of a child through adoption. This would not seem to be of major concern, since it is generally accepted that the desire to be a parent is a natural instinct and is held in high moral regard. On the other hand, the agency must look into the prospective adoptive parent's reasons, since there are isolated instances where the desire to adopt arises from improper motives.

f) Legal and Financial Factors

According to 22 California Code of Regulations §§ 35180(a)(1)(F) and 35181(c)(3) and (7), the assessment shall include information as to the applicant's understanding of the legal and financial rights and responsibilities in adoption, as well as a statement as to whether the applicant has been provided information about the Adoption Assistance Program (a financial aid program which is further described in Chapter 7). In this same vein, 22 California Code of Regulations §§ 35180(a)(1)(G) and 35181(f) requires the assessment to mention any "resources, services or training which would assist the adoptive applicant in meeting the needs of a child." As set forth in Chapter 1 of this book, once the order granting the adoption petition is entered, the adoptive parents assume the legal duty to support the child. On the other hand, there is no set minimum monthly income under which the adoptive parents must qualify.

In addition, 22 California Code of Regulations § 35181(c)(9) requires the agency to consider the preparation or plan that the applicant has made for care of the minor in the event of death or incapacity of the adoptive parent or parents. A parent does not have a duty to purchase life insurance, but the agency is required to see to it that the best interests of the child are served, including provision for the child in the event of the adoptive parent's death.

g) Safety and Adequacy of the Home

Under 22 California Code of Regulations §§ 35180(a)(1)(E) and 35181(c)(5), the assessment must set forth a determination that the applicant's home is safe and adequate. As an anecdote, the author of this book is an adoptive parent and was formerly a foster parent, and was required by the county social services agency to place a fire extinguisher in his kitchen, along with a map of fire escape routes, even though no fire had ever occurred. The county social services agency also required the author to install latches and locks on every cupboard and closet in his garage, and to take his vehicles to an independent mechanic to have them certified as being in proper working condition.

h) Fingerprinting, Criminal Record and Child Abuse Data

Under 22 California Code of Regulations §§ 35180(a)(1)(C) and 35184, the assessment must include information about the applicant's "social history," which here includes the results of a screening for any criminal background and any referrals for child abuse or neglect, and must set forth a determination as to whether any child has been abused or neglected by the applicant. Also, Family Code § 8712(a) provides that the agency shall require each person filing an application for adoption to be fingerprinted, and shall secure from an appropriate law enforcement agency any criminal record of that person to determine whether the person has ever been convicted of a crime other than a minor traffic violation, and may also secure the person's full criminal record, if any. Family Code § 8712(b) requires the agency take whatever criminal record into consideration, and assess the effects of any criminal history on the applicant's ability to provide adequate and proper care and guidance to the child, all of which must be included in the agency's report to the court. The statute also says that the fee charged for the fingerprinting or for checking or obtaining the criminal record shall be paid by the applicant, but that the agency may defer, waive, or reduce the fee under certain circumstances.

i) Postadoption Contact with Birth Parents and Natural Siblings

Family Code § 8715(b) states that if the child has been freed for adoption by the juvenile court in a dependency proceeding brought pursuant to Welfare & Institutions Code § 300, the agency's report must describe if the requirements of Welfare & Institutions Code § 16002(e), which deal with the agency's duty to facilitate "ongoing" sibling contact unless the juvenile court orders that such contact is detrimental to the child, have been completed and what, if any, plan exists to facilitate postadoptive contact between the child and his or her siblings and half-siblings. In addition, Family Code § 8715(c) provides that if the adoption petition has been filed with a Family Code § 8616.5 postadoption contact agreement, the agency's report shall address whether the postadoption contact agreement has been entered into voluntarily, and whether it is in the best interests of the child who is the subject of the petition. (Postadoption contact agreements are discussed at length in Chapter 8.)

Importantly, there is no provision in Family Code § 8715 or Welfare & Institutions Code §§ 300, et seq. or 16002 requiring the adoptive parent to allow ongoing sibling contact with the child. As far as the adoption case is concerned, these sections only require the agency to report this information to the court. In addition, while sibling contact is an important factor in the best interests of the child analysis, it should be emphasized that the court is to ascertain what is in the best interests only of the child which is the subject of the adoption petition, and not of the siblings or half-siblings of that child.

Where the adoptive applicant is a relative, the agency must also consider, under 22 California Code of Regulations §§ 35181(d) and 35183(e) and (f), the nature of the relationship that the relative or caregiver has with the birth parent or other extended family members, along with whether he or she would consider entering into a kinship adoption agreement and, if so, what kind of post-adoption contact the relative or caregiver would have with the birth parent or other family members.

j) Factors Relating to Dependency Proceedings

As for children who are dependents of the juvenile court following a Welfare & Institutions Code § 300 proceeding, 22 California Code of Regulations § 35181(c)(10), requires the agency to consider, in assessing the adoptive applicant (with respect to the examining the applicants and any children or other adults residing in their home), the ability of the child welfare agency to support an adoptive case plan for the child, and whether the applicant is willing and able to be a "permanency planning family." (See Chapter 6 for a short explanation of these terms and of dependency proceeding.)

k) "General Characteristics"

22 California Code of Regulations § 35181(c)(8) allows the agency, in assessing the adoptive applicant, to consider the "general characteristics" of the applicant and any children or other adults residing in the home. There is no definition of "general characteristics," and it is unclear how far this provision can be taken, if anywhere at all. The same could be said of 22 California Code of Regulations § 35181(c)(1), which apparently requires the agency to consider the applicant's "social history," "personal characteristics" and "current functioning," which are not adequately defined in the regulations.

3. Conduct of the Investigation

The CDSS web site states, "Depending on the workload of the agency selected, it can take anywhere from six months to a year to complete an adoption family assessment. Most adoptive placements occur one to several months after the family assessment has been approved."

a) Contacts with the Prospective Adoptive Parents

According to 22 California Code of Regulations § 35181(a), the agency shall have at least 3 separate face-to-face contacts with each applicant for the purpose of interviewing the applicant for the assessment. However, up to 2 contacts may be adoption training or preparation class sessions. On the other hand, the contacts shall include, at least, one interview with the applicant in the home, a separate face-to-face interview with each applicant, a joint interview when there are two applicants, a face-to-face interview with all other individuals residing in the home, and "additional interviews as necessary."

b) Documentation from the Applicants

Under 22 California Code of Regulations § 35181(b), the applicants must provide to the agency "verification of employment or income," a "marriage certificate, if married," and "verification of termination of prior marriages" if applicable. 22 California Code of Regulations § 35181(b)(6) also states that "when verification of the dissolution of all marriages of the applicants is not possible, the marriages preceding a verified divorce decree shall be assumed to be validly dissolved."

Medical documents must also be provided. According to 22 California Code of Regulations § 35181(b)(9), the agency shall obtain from the applicant a report of a medical examination of each applicant, said report having been completed by a licensed physician or a nurse practitioner or physician's assistant practicing under a licensed physician, and having been completed no more than 6 months before the date of the adoption application. However, in lieu thereof, 22 California Code of Regulations § 35181(b)(9)(C) allows the agency to have the applicant complete a health questionnaire if the applicant is the current care giver of the child or a relative seeking to adopt a specific child, and the completed questionnaire does not, in the agency's judgment, identify indicators requiring further evaluation or report. Furthermore, 22 California Code of Regulations § 35181(b)(9)(C)(2)(a) states that, "if in the agency's judgment, sufficient additional information is obtained from the physician who has been treating a specific condition identified in the questionnaire, additional medical examination is not necessary." On the other hand, 22 California Code of Regulations § 35181(b)(10) specifically requires the applicant to obtain "a certificate, for each adult residing in the home, stating that the individual is free from communicable tuberculosis."

With regard to other documents, the applicants are required to provide authorization for information from additional sources to be released to the agency, as necessary, to complete the assessment (22 California Code of Regulations § 35181(b)(14)), authorization for the adoption agency to release a copy of the written assessment to other adoption and child welfare agencies for the purpose of matching the applicant with a child (22 California Code of Regulations § 35181(b)(15)), and the names of three individuals to be contacted by the agency for the purpose of obtaining references (22 California Code of Regulations § 35181(b)(11)).

c) Independently Obtained Information

22 California Code of Regulations § 35181(b)(12) requires the agency to examine the results of a screening for any criminal background of the applicant and any other adults residing in the home and, if required by Section 35184(e)(1) [dealing with indications of criminal activity in other jurisdictions], the FBI criminal record, if any, from the DOJ. Along the same lines, 22 California Code of Regulations § 35181(b)(13) requires the agency to examine the results of a screening for child abuse or neglect.

d) Abbreviated Home Studies

(1) Foster Parents and Relative Caregivers

According to 22 California Code of Regulations § 35183(a), the agency may conduct an "abbreviated assessment" where (1) the applicant is the child's foster parent caregiver, (2) the applicant is documented as being an existing relative caregiver who was assessed pursuant to Welfare & Institutions Code § 361.3, or (3) the applicant has successfully completed a prior agency, independent or intercountry adoption in California within the last five years and the written assessment is available. However, comparing 22 California Code of Regulations § 35183 with the other regulations providing the standard rules for assessments, it appears that the meaningful differences are only that the applicant is excused from having to participate in the two adoption training classes, that additional disclosure concerning the applicant's minor children who are not living in the home is not required, and that only one reference is required (instead of three). Other than these minor differences, the abbreviated assessment is legally the same as the standard assessment.

Family Code § 8730 states that if the prospective adoptive parent of a child is a foster parent with whom the child has lived for a minimum of six months or a relative caregiver who has had an ongoing and significant relationship with the child, then the assessment may, at the discretion of the agency, or unless the court with jurisdiction over the child orders otherwise, require only (a) a criminal records check of the relative caregiver or foster parent, (b) a determination of sufficient financial stability (including verification of employment records or income) and that any government assistance to which the child is entitled is used exclusively to meet the child's needs, (c) a determination that the relative caregiver or foster parent has not abused or neglected the child (including a review of disciplinary practices) and has fostered the healthy growth and development of the child, (d) a determination that there is no likelihood that the relative caregiver or foster parent will abuse or neglect the child in the future, that the caregiver or foster parent can protect the child, ensure necessary care and supervision, and foster the child's healthy growth and development, (e) a determination that the relative caregiver or foster parent can address racial and cultural issues, and (f) an interview with the relative caregiver or foster parent, an interview with each individual residing in the home and an interview with the child to be adopted.

Family Code § 8731 states that if the prospective adoptive parent of a child has been the child's foster parent, the assessment described in Family Code § 8730 shall not be initiated until the child to be adopted has resided in the foster parent's home for at least six months. This gives the foster parent the chance to qualify for the abbreviated assessment.

(2) Updating Prior Home Studies

Where the applicant had already been assessed under Welfare & Institutions Code § 361.3 or had completed a prior adoption, the agency is to consider any and all changed circumstances. Furthermore, 22 California Code of Regulations § 35183.1(b) requires the agency to obtain authorization from the applicant to obtain the prior assessment, while 22 California Code of Regulations § 35183.1(c) and (d) require the prior assessment to be updated.

4. Preferential Status in Adoptive Placement

a) Preferential Status for Foster Parents

Where the child's natural parents' rights have been terminated in a Welfare & Institutions Code § 300 proceeding, the foster parent generally has preferential status with regard to adoptive placement. Welfare & Institutions Code § 366.26(k) states that, "Notwithstanding any other provision of law, the application of any person who, as a relative caretaker or foster parent, has cared for a dependent child for whom the court has approved a permanent plan for adoption, or who has been freed for adoption, shall be given preference with respect to that child over all other applications for adoptive placement if the agency making the placement determines that [1] the child has substantial emotional ties to the relative caretaker or foster parent and [2] removal from the relative caretaker or foster parent would be seriously detrimental to the child's emotional well-being." The statute goes on to state that "preference" means that the application shall be processed and, if satisfactory, the family study shall be completed before the processing of the application of any other person for the adoptive placement of the child.

The law does allow for the birth parent in such a situation to attempt to again become the child's legal parent. According to 22 California Code of Regulations § 35181(e), if the adoptive applicant is a birth parent of the child to be adopted, and if the child was a dependent of the juvenile court, the agency must assess whether the conditions which led to the child's removal from the parent still exist. On the other hand, even though the birth parent may apply to adopt the child that is in the agency's custody, the birth parent does not have preferential status for purposes of placement.

b) Preferential Status for Relatives

Family Code § 8710 states that in cases where the child has *not* been adjudged a dependent of the juvenile court pursuant to Welfare & Institutions Code § 300, the agency shall first consider adoptive placement in the home of a relative where the child is being considered for adoption. (Where the child has not been adjudged a dependent of the juvenile court, it is unlikely that the child is in foster care.) The statute goes on to provide that for children who were with a foster parent for at least four months, that foster parent shall be considered with respect to the child along with all other prospective adoptive parents, if a relative is not available, if placement with an available relative is not in the child's best interest, or if placement would permanently separate the child from other siblings who are being considered for adoption or who are in foster care and an alternative placement would not require the permanent separation. This category of preferential status for foster parents only applies where the child has substantial emotional ties to the foster parent, the child's removal from the foster home would be seriously detrimental to the child's well-being, and the foster parent has made a written request to be considered to adopt the child.

Where the child is a dependent of the juvenile court, the "relative placement preference" (Welfare & Institutions Code § 361.3) only applies when a new placement becomes necessary after reunification services are terminated but before parental rights are terminated. (*In re Lauren R.* (2007) 148 Cal.App.4th 841.) *Lauren R.* holds that there is no such thing as "relative placement preference" vis-à-vis _adoptive_ placement.

5. Writ of Administrative Mandate Directed to the Agency

a) Court's Pre-Filing Authority over the Agency

Family Code § 8704(a), which speaks of the agency's "exclusive custody and control" over the child prior to the filing of the petition, does not by itself require the agency to provide notice and a hearing when terminating adoptive placement and removing the child prior to the filing of the adoption petition. Nor do the agency adoption statutes themselves provide for judicial review of such agency action. However, to guard against the possibility of arbitrary agency action, the court in *Rodriguez v. Superior Court*, (1971) 18 Cal.App.3d 510, held that an agency's decisions in a pre-adoption placement are subject to judicial review pursuant to the administrative writ of mandate provisions of Code of Civil Procedure §§ 1084, 1085 and 1094.5.

In *Cain v. Adoption Agency*, (1976) 54 Cal.App.3d 1127, the court set forth the standard for petitions for administrative writs, and held that where the agency terminates the placement before the adoption petition is filed, the prospective adoptive parents have the burden to show that there was no substantial evidence showing that the agency's action served the best interests of the child. Also, even though the agency is vested with discretion as to placement of the child, the court in *C.V.C. v. Superior Court*, (1973) 29 Cal.App.3d 909, held that the superior court conducts a de novo review of the agency's actions, based on the fundamental rights that the prospective adoptive parents have in the continuation of the family unit.

The *C.V.C.* court further held that the 14th Amendment's guarantee of due process requires that prospective adoptive parents be given notice and an opportunity to be heard before the removal of the child from the pre-adoptive placement, except in extraordinary circumstances, such as where summary deprivation is justified by the government's interest in preventing imminent danger to the child. On the other hand, a *post*-removal hearing was held to be sufficient in *Marten v. Thies*, (1979) 99 Cal.App.3d 161, since an imminent danger to the child apparently existed in that case by virtue of the fact that there were recently discovered and undisclosed marital difficulties on the part of the prospective adoptive parents, and an absence of a father figure in the home (although the social worker's report stated that the child was not in danger and was given adequate care). In the *Marten* court's opinion, such circumstances warranted giving the prospective adoptive parents a mere post-removal hearing as to the propriety of terminating the adoptive placement. The *Marten* court rejected the contention that the phrase "imminent danger" means "immediate physical danger." The effect of the *C.V.C.* decision was also limited in *Department of Social Services v. Superior Court*, (1997) 58 Cal.App.4th 721, which essentially held that the child's sibling relationships with children in another household did not give rise to a "fundamental right" to be placed for purposes of adoption in that other household.

The *Marten* court also held that there is no separate right to independent counsel for the child in proceedings for a writ of administrative mandate, and that it is the agency which is charged with the responsibility of representing the child's interests. (See Chapter 10 of this book concerning procedural issues in an adoption case.)

b) Court Lacks Authority to Make New Placement.

In *Department of Social Services v. Superior Court*, (1997) 58 Cal.App.4th 721, the court recited that Family Code § 8704(a) and Welfare & Institutions Code § 366.26(j) give the adoption agency the exclusive custody, control and supervision of the minor referred for adoptive placement, and that this exclusive authority includes the "discretion" to place the minor in, and if necessary, to remove the minor from, a prospective adoptive home or the child's foster care placement pending adoptive placement. The court also took account of Welfare & Institutions Code § 366.3, which states that the juvenile court retains jurisdiction over the minor to ensure the adoption is completed as expeditiously as possible and to determine the "appropriateness of the placement," but held that this still does not give the juvenile court the power to substitute its independent judgment for that of the agency. *Department of Social Services v. Superior Court* instead holds that the juvenile court is limited to reviewing whether the agency abused its discretion in placing the child or in terminating a placement, but that absent a showing that the agency's decision is "patently absurd or unquestionably not in the minor's best interests," the court may not interfere and disapprove of the placement or the removal.

The *Department of Social Services v. Superior Court* decision reversed the juvenile court's act of vetoing the agency's separation of a five-member sibling group and subsequent "judicial" placing of all five children in one house. The decision also disagrees with *In re Robert A.*, (1992) 4 Cal.App.4th 174, and *In re Danielle W.*, (1989) 207 Cal.App.3d 1227, neither of which were adoption cases, and rejected the argument that the CDSS is merely an "arm of the court" acting in the best interests of the minor and therefore subject to the court's supervision. The *Department of Social Services* court reasoned that the making of a placement decision is not a court function since it does not constitute "declaring the law" or "determining the rights of the parties to a controversy."

c) Exhaustion of Administrative Remedies

Where a writ administrative mandate is available, the petitioners must first exhaust all of the potential remedies they have with the agency itself. One such administrative remedy is at 22 California Code of Regulations § 35215, which provides for a grievance review hearing.

According to 22 California Code of Regulations § 35215(a), upon the applicant's written request, the "agency shall provide for a grievance review hearing on any action taken by the agency before a petition for adoption is filed." The written request must (A) be signed by the applicant or his or her authorized representative, (B) state specifically the facts surrounding the action complained of, and (C) be submitted to the agency within thirty days of the agency action which is the subject of the complaint, or be submitted to the Adoptions Branch of the CDSS if the grievance concerns an action taken by a licensed private adoption agency based on the petitioner's FBI criminal record. This regulation would appear to apply to private agencies.

On the other hand, 22 California Code of Regulations § 35215(a)(2) states that no request for a grievance review hearing shall be granted if the request is based solely on (A) agency action taken in compliance with a court order, (B) a question regarding the validity of a statute or a regulation, or (C) any issue for which a state hearing is available under Welfare & Institutions Code § 10950 (which deals with grievance hearings concerning the actions of public agencies).

If one is seeking a writ of administrative mandate, the petitioner should refer directly to the statutes and practice guides covering the general procedures in administrative writ cases. A detailed explanation of the various deadlines, procedures for procuring the administrative record, and other relevant aspects of administrative writ cases, is beyond the scope of this book.

E. Court's Authority over Placement after Filing of Petition

1. Removal of the Child from the Petitioner's Home

Family Code § 8704(b) states, "After the adoption petition has been filed, the department or licensed adoption agency may remove the child from the prospective adoptive parents only with the approval of the court, upon motion by the department or licensed adoption agency after notice to the prospective adoptive parents, supported by an affidavit or affidavits stating the grounds on which removal is sought." Consequently, by statute, the language of *Marten v. Thies*, (1979) 99 Cal.App.3d 161, which authorizes mere *post*-removal notice in cases of "imminent danger," would not appear to apply where the adoption petition has been filed with the court. On the other hand, as explained in Chapter 6 of this book, Welfare & Institutions Code §§ 305 and 306 authorizes a social worker to take custody of any child if there is "reasonable cause" to believe that that child is in immediate danger.

2. Removal of Child from County by Petitioner or Others

Family Code § 8713(b)(2) states that during the pendency of the adoption proceedings, the child may not be removed from the forum county unless the petitioners or other interested persons first obtain permission for the removal from the court, after giving advance written notice to the responsible agency of the intent to obtain the court's permission. If the agency objects, the matter is set for a hearing, at which time the court is authorized to grant the requested permission to removed of the child over the agency's objection, subject to any limitations that the court feels are in the child's best interest.

As for persons other than the petitioners, Family Code § 8713(a) states that a child who has been freed for adoption may not be removed from the county in which the child was placed by any person who has not petitioned to adopt the child, without first obtaining the written consent of the agency responsible for the child. There does not appear to be any statutory right to judicial review of the agency's decision under these circumstances, unless one can show standing as an "interested person." Likewise, Family Code § 8713(b)(1) prohibits anyone from concealing the child proposed to be adopted, and there is no judicial review over a finding that a person concealed the child. The child has to be made reasonably available to the agency.

According to Family Code § 8713(d), a violation of these rules is punishable by imprisonment under Penal Code § 280.

Family Code § 8713(c) provides three exceptions to these rules. First, a child may be freely taken out of the forum county pursuant to Family Code § 8713(c)(3), where the responsible agency has given written consent. Second, a child may also be freely taken out of the county under Family Code § 8713(c)(2) where the child has been returned to and remains in the custody and control of the child's birth parent or parents. Third, Family Code § 8713(c)(1) allows the child to be freely taken out of the forum county for periods of less than 30 days, unless the agency has personally served a notice of recommendation of denial of the petition or the court has issued an order prohibiting the child's removal from the county pending consideration of an issue concerning (A) the suitability of the petitioners, (B) the care provided the child, or (C) the availability of the legally required agency consents to the adoption. (It appears that the word "consent" in Family Code § 8713(c)(1)(C) refers the agency's recommendation concerning the adoption, since agency consent to the adoption is not needed, as explained below.)

F. Court's Authority to Grant Petition over Agency's Objection

Family Code § 8704(b) states, "If the department or licensed adoption agency refuses to consent to the adoption of a child by the person or persons with whom the department or licensed adoption agency placed the child for adoption, the court may nevertheless order the adoption if it finds that the refusal to consent is not in the child's best interest."

In interpreting this language, the Supreme Court held that "once a child has been relinquished, since the consent of the agency to which it has been relinquished is not required, the only determination for the court to make upon a petition for adoption properly filed before it, is whether or not granting the petition will promote the welfare, and is in the best interest, of the child." (See *San Diego County Dept. of Pub. Welfare v. Superior Court*, (1972) 7 Cal.3d 1.) The *San Diego Public Welfare* court also held that while the agency's expertise is to be accorded due weight, this does not mean that its recommendation is binding. The Supreme Court also held in *Adoption of McDonald*, (1954) 43 Cal.2d 447, that agency consent is not required for the adoption. It would thus appear that the word "consent" as it appears in Family Code § 8704(b) is treated more like a concurrence or a recommendation than the kind of consent which a birth parent would give in an independent adoption.

As mentioned above, Family Code § 8715(a) requires the agency to provide the court with a full report of the facts. In addition, Family Code § 8715(d) allows the CDSS to submit a report in an agency adoption case. Under Family Code § 8720(a), the court clerk upon receipt of the report shall immediately refer it to the court for review if the CDSS or the agency finds that the petitioner's home is not suitable for the child, or that the "required" agency consents are not available and the CDSS or agency recommends that the petition be denied, or if the petitioners desire to withdraw the petition and the CDSS or agency recommends that the petition be denied. Family Code § 8720(b) then requires the court to set a date for a hearing on the petition and give reasonable notice of the hearing to the petitioners, the CDSS or agency, and if necessary the birth parents, by certified mail, return receipt requested. (The conduct of the hearing is described in Chapter 10 of this book.)

DISPENSING WITH THE NEED FOR CONSENT 6

In this chapter:

"Too many children in foster care are falling through cracks. Be a hero, take the time learn about adoption today." – Bruce Willis

I. INTRODUCTION

Family Code § 8606(a) states that there is no need to obtain the consent of a birth parent whose parental rights have been terminated in dependency proceedings brought pursuant to Welfare & Institutions Code §§ 300 and 366.26, or where the child has been freed from parental custody pursuant to Family Code § 7893. This chapter will discuss these two situations, as well as the specific subject of abandonment and desertion, which is covered in Family Code §§ 7822, 8604(b) and 8606(c). (The loss of consent rights is also discussed in Chapter 3 with regard to parentage proceedings.)

II. TERMINATION OF PARENTAL RIGHTS IN DEPENDENCY CASES

Dependency proceedings are initiated under Welfare & Institutions Code § 300 when there is probable cause to believe that the child's safety or health is in danger. At that point, an officer of the social services agency (with the help of law enforcement officers) physically takes the child; a petition to terminate parental rights is filed with the juvenile court; and a complicated court proceeding is commenced by the public agency. This chapter will briefly describe dependency proceedings. While the case is pending, the child is placed in a shelter and/or a foster home, and the birth parent is given the opportunity and the resources to "reunify" with the child. If the birth parent "fails to reunify" with the child, the court may terminate parental rights.

This process occurs with unfortunate frequency. In 1999 in Los Angeles County alone, 64,656 children of all ages and ethnicities were under the supervision of the county social services agency, and 5,192 of those were considered "freed children-parental rights terminated" and in the "adoptions caseload." Los Angeles County is not an isolated example, and there are staggering numbers of children who are at risk nationwide. Most states have developed systems for handling endangered children, and Family Code § 8606(a)(2) thus dispenses with the birth parent's consent where parental rights have been terminated "by a similar order of a court of another jurisdiction, pursuant to a law of that jurisdiction authorizing the order."

A. Grounds to Declare the Child a Dependent of the Court

Welfare & Institutions Code § 300 sets forth several specific risk categories justifying an order declaring the child to be within the "jurisdiction" of the juvenile court and a dependent of the court. Since these situations occur thousands of times per year statewide, the Judicial Council has published standard forms by which the applicable social services agency may allege the grounds for detaining the child. The ten headings which follow are verbatim recitations [with additional descriptive language in brackets] of the headings used on the forms that describe these risk categories. (Each of the forms also contains blank space for the social services official to set forth the specific facts supporting these pre-printed contentions.)

1. Serious [Nonaccidental] Physical Harm

The preprinted allegations from Judicial Council Form JV-120 provide, "The child has suffered, or there is a substantial risk that the child will suffer, serious physical harm inflicted nonaccidentally upon the child by the child's parent or guardian." This is identical to the the first sentence of Welfare & Institutions Code § 300(a).

a) "Substantial Risk"

Welfare & Institutions Code § 300(a) also states that "a court may find there is a substantial risk of serious future injury based on the manner in which a less serious injury was inflicted, a history of repeated inflictions of injuries on the child or the child's siblings, or a combination of these and other actions by the parent or guardian which indicate the child is at risk of serious physical harm."

b) Legal Corporal Punishment

Welfare & Institutions Code § 300(a) provides that, " 'serious physical harm' does not include reasonable and age-appropriate spanking to the buttocks where there is no evidence of serious physical injury." The Legislature also enacted the following statutory language which appears in the paragraph immediately after Welfare & Institutions Code § 300(j): "It is the intent of the Legislature that nothing in this section disrupt the family unnecessarily or intrude inappropriately into family life, prohibit the use of reasonable methods of parental discipline, or prescribe a particular method of parenting." Likewise, Health & Safety Code § 1531.5 expressly allows an individual to become a foster parent even if he or she has administered "corporal punishment not constituting child abuse" to his or her own child, or will continue to do so to his or her own child. In light of the Legislature's use of the phrase "corporal punishment not constituting child abuse," there necessarily must exist, as a matter of law, forms of corporal punishment that do not amount to child abuse.

c) Reporting Child Abuse

The law imposes a duty on certain professionals to report instances of suspected child abuse. In return, the law protects those individuals from suit for defamation and other causes of action. For example, in *Storch v. Silverman*, (1986) 186 Cal.App.3d 671, the court enforced the provisions of Penal Code § 11172, which makes physicians and other medical practitioners immune from liability for reporting child abuse (as they must under Penal Code §§ 11164, et seq.), even if the report is mistaken. Where someone other than an enumerated professional undertakes to report suspected child abuse, it would appear that the only immunity would be the general First Amendment protection given to citizens who, in good faith, report suspected wrongdoing to law enforcement authorities. (See, *Briggs v. Eden Council for Hope & Opportunity*, (1999) 19 Cal.4th 1106; Civil Code § 47(b); Code of Civil Procedure § 425.16.)

2. Failure to Protect [due to Negligence or Inability]

Judicial Council Form JV-121 begins by stating, "The child has suffered, or there is a substantial risk that the child will suffer, serious physical harm or illness, . . ." The form then provides four check boxes, the first one indicating, "as a result of the failure or inability of his or her parent or legal guardian to supervise or protect the child adequately." The second box states, "as a result of the willful or negligent failure of the child's parent or legal guardian to supervise or protect the child adequately from the conduct of the custodian with whom the child has been left." The third box then states, "by the willful or negligent failure of the parent or legal guardian to provide the child with adequate food, clothing, shelter, or medical treatment." Next to the fourth box is printed, "by the inability of the parent or legal guardian to provide regular care for the child due to the parent's or legal guardian's mental illness, developmental disability, or substance abuse." This four-part configuration mirrors the four alternative grounds set forth in Welfare & Institutions Code § 300(b), which allows the child to be detained based on the parent's mere negligence or inability to care for the child.

a) Mental Illness

Concerning the Welfare & Institutions Code § 300(b) rule dealing with "mental illness" and "developmental disability," one must also note the statutory language in the paragraph immediately following Welfare & Institutions Code § 300(j): "The Legislature further declares that a physical disability, such as blindness or deafness, is no bar to the raising of happy and well-adjusted children and that a court's determination pursuant to this section shall center upon whether a parent's disability prevents him or her from exercising care and control."

The courts have applied limited definitions of "mental illness" and "developmental disability" in these cases. In *In re Carmaleta B.*, (1978) 21 Cal.3d 482, the Supreme Court held that the definitions set forth in Welfare & Institutions Code §§ 5550 and 5590 are to be used in determining whether a parent fits within this risk category. These statutes describe persons who are incapable of managing themselves or their affairs independently, with ordinary prudence, and who require supervision, control and care for their own welfare, or for the welfare of others or for the welfare of the community, and who are of such mental condition that they are in need of supervision, treatment, care or restraint to prevent danger to themselves or others. The *Carmaleta B.* court rejected a proposed definition that was based primarily on the welfare of the child, stating that "family rights, both the parent's and the child's rights, should not be vulnerable to a too easy finding of mental illness. Indeed, the strictness of this definition of mental illness has acted as a safeguard to protect the primacy of the family." It also held that an order to free a child from parental custody and control must rest on present circumstances as well as past acts although such prior acts are evidence which may be considered by the court in deciding whether there is sufficient showing to justify the order.

Another example of this strict definition is *In re Kimberly F.*, (1997) 56 Cal.App.4th 519, where the trial court had terminated reunification services and parental rights based on a psychologist's opinion that the mother had a "narcissistic" personality, and based on evidence that her home was dirty and unsanitary. The appellate court reversed, holding that that particular diagnosis was an insufficient basis for the removal of, or retention of, children from their parents, and that an unkempt house is likewise insufficient grounds. The *Kimberly F.* court stated, "the government cannot separate children from their parents based on a psychologist's estimation that a parent is 'narcissistic, egocentric, and self-centered,' 'cynical, passive-aggressive, rigid, easily argumentative,' 'sullen, mistrustful, and generally self-indulgent.' We are not dealing here with real mental illness, but with a description of human personality."

b) Developmental Disability

In applying the predecessor to Welfare & Institutions Code § 300(b), the courts have used the Welfare & Institutions Code § 4512 definition of "developmental disability" to govern these cases. (See *In re Victoria M.*, (1989) 207 Cal.App.3d 1317.) The latter statute includes individuals who suffer from mental retardation, cerebral palsy, epilepsy or autism, or related disabling conditions, but not from "other handicapping conditions that are solely physical in nature." The developmental disability must cause an "inability of the parent or legal guardian to provide regular care for the child."

c) Substance Abuse

There is no subsection of Welfare & Institutions Code § 300 merely saying that one's parental rights may be taken away if one is found in possession of an illegal substance. Instead, Welfare & Institutions Code § 300(b) requires proof that the child has suffered, or that there is a substantial risk that the child will suffer, serious physical harm or illness because of a parent's inability to provide regular care for the child due to the parent's substance abuse. Importantly, the statute does not require proof of addiction to an illegal substance. Also, alcoholism is a form of "substance abuse" and could provide grounds under the statute.

d) Parental Homelessness

Welfare & Institutions Code § 300(b) also states, "No child shall be found to be a person described by this subdivision solely due to the lack of an emergency shelter for the family." By use of the word "emergency" in describing the lack of shelter, it would appear that temporary homelessness, by itself, is not grounds to detain the child. However, where the homelessness is more permanent, concern over the welfare of the child would focus on either the disability of the parent or the willfulness or negligence in refusing to provide for the child.

e) "Spiritual Treatment through Prayer"

Welfare & Institutions Code § 300(b) also provides, "Whenever it is alleged that a child comes within the jurisdiction of the court on the basis of the parent's or guardian's willful failure to provide adequate medical treatment or specific decision to provide spiritual treatment through prayer, the court shall give deference to the parent's or guardian's medical treatment, nontreatment, or spiritual treatment through prayer alone in accordance with the tenets and practices of a recognized church or religious denomination, by an accredited practitioner thereof, and shall not assume jurisdiction unless necessary to protect the child from suffering serious physical harm or illness. In making its determination, the court shall consider (1) the nature of the treatment proposed by the parent or guardian, (2) the risks to the child posed by the course of treatment or nontreatment proposed by the parent or guardian, (3) the risk, if any, of the course of treatment being proposed by the petitioning agency, and (4) the likely success of the courses of treatment or nontreatment proposed by the parent or guardian and agency. The child shall continue to be a dependent child pursuant to this subdivision only so long as is necessary to protect the child from risk of suffering serious physical harm or illness."

3. Serious Emotional Damage [to the Child]

The Judicial Council uses the following language on Form JV-122: "The child is suffering, or is at substantial risk of suffering, serious emotional damage evidenced by severe anxiety, depression, withdrawal or untoward aggressive behavior toward self or others . . ." Two check boxes then follow, the first providing, "as a result of the conduct of the parent or guardian," and the second, "because the child has no parent or guardian capable of providing appropriate care." This language is derived from the two alternative bases set forth in Welfare & Institutions Code § 300(c). The statute also states, "No child shall be found to be a person described by this subdivision if the willful failure of the parent or guardian to provide adequate mental health treatment is based on a sincerely held religious belief and if a less intrusive judicial intervention is available." While Welfare & Institutions Code § 300(b) deals with the mental condition of the parent, subsection (c) deals with the child's emotional condition.

4. Sexual Abuse [of the Child by Parent or Others]

Judicial Council Form JV-123 provides two check boxes, the first one indicating, "The child has been sexually abused, or there is a substantial risk that the child will be sexually abused, as defined in subdivision (b) of section 11165.1 of the Penal Code [which states that 'sexual abuse' means 'sexual assault or sexual exploitation' according to very specific and detailed definitions], by his parent or guardian or a member of the child's household." The second box indicates, "The parent or guardian has failed to protect the child adequately from sexual abuse and the parent or guardian knew or reasonably should have known that the child was in danger of sexual abuse." This language is the same as the two bases set forth in Welfare & Institutions Code § 300(d), which refer to the Penal Code § 11165.1 definition of sexual abuse.

5. Severe Physical Abuse [Caused by Others]

The preprinted language from Judicial Council Form JV-124 provides, "The child is under the age of five and has suffered severe physical abuse by a parent, or by any person known by the parent, and the parent knew or reasonably should have known that the person was physically abusing the child." This language is identical to the first sentence of Welfare & Institutions Code § 300(e). It is unclear why the Legislature chose to only protect children under five years old with this statute. It is also unclear why this subdivision was enacted separately from subdivision (a) which deals with "serious physical nonaccidental harm," and subdivision (i) which deals with "cruelty." Other than the "five-year-old" cut-off, the only substantive difference between the three subdivisions is that (e) and (i) include a broader group of perpetrators. In addition, there is significant cross-over with subdivision (d) as well.

Welfare & Institutions Code § 300(e) also states, " 'severe physical abuse' means any of the following: any single act of abuse which causes physical trauma of sufficient severity that, if left untreated, would cause permanent physical disfigurement, permanent physical disability, or death; any single act of sexual abuse which causes significant bleeding, deep bruising, or significant external or internal swelling; or more than one act of physical abuse, each of which causes bleeding, deep bruising, significant external or internal swelling, bone fracture, or unconsciousness; or the willful, prolonged failure to provide adequate food."

The statute purports to make the parent liable for the wrongdoing of third parties. On the other hand, *Wallis v. Spencer*, (9th Cir. 2000) 202 F.3d 1126, held that the state has no interest whatever in protecting children from parents unless it has some evidence that the parent is unfit and the child is in imminent danger. Accordingly, *Wallis* held that the state may not, consistent with the Constitution, interpose itself between a fit parent and her children simply because of the conduct of the other parent. It would therefore appear that where a social worker believes that a parent is neglecting or abusing a child, the social worker must first inquire whether the other parent is available to take safe custody of the child before the social worker can detain the child.

6. Caused Another Child's Death via Abuse or Neglect

The Judicial Council has provided the following on Form JV-125: "The child's parent or guardian has caused the death of another child through abuse or neglect." This language is identical to Welfare & Institutions Code § 300(f). Importantly, this code section does not require that the deceased child be a sibling, and does not require the deceased child to have been in the parent's custody at the time of the death.

Based on the overly broad wording of Welfare & Institutions Code § 300(f), which goes well beyond what constitutes an "unfit parent," it would appear that the courts should severely limit the definition of "neglect" as used in the statute. For example, in one actual dependency case, a married couple went to a retirement dinner and left their child with a babysitter. The child's next-door-neighbor friend then came into the home to play with the child. The next-door-neighbor friend then died due to complications from appendicitis because the babysitter did not timely seek medical attention for the friend. When emergency personnel finally arrived on the scene when the child died, a social worker came and detained the married couple's child. Soon thereafter, a dependency petition was filed pursuant to Welfare & Institutions Code § 300(f).

7. No Provision for Support [of the Child]

The preprinted language from Judicial Council Form JV-126 provides, "The child has been left without any provision for support; or the child's parent has been incarcerated or institutionalized and cannot arrange for the care of the child; or a relative or other adult custodian with whom the child resides or has been left is unwilling or unable to provide care or support for the child, the whereabouts of the parents is unknown, and reasonable efforts to locate the parent have been unsuccessful." This is essentially the same as Welfare & Institutions Code § 300(g), which generally covers abandonments and "voluntary surrenders" of newborn infants at a health care facility. (However, Welfare & Institutions Code § 300(g) does not use the words "abandon," "abandonment," "desert" or "desertion," which appears to obviate the need to prove an intent to abandon.)

The subject of a Health & Safety Code § 1255.7 "voluntary surrender" is discussed further near the end of this chapter.

8. Freed for Adoption

Judicial Council Form JV-127 states, "The child has been freed for adoption from one or both parents for 12 months by either relinquishment or termination of parental rights and . . ." After that, the form provides two check boxes, the first one indicating, "an interlocutory decree has not been granted pursuant to section 224n of the Civil Code [which consisted of the adoption statutes that are now codified at Family Code § 8500, et seq.]." The second box indicates, "an adoption petition has not been granted."

To the extent that Judicial Council Form JV-127, which essentially mirrors Welfare & Institutions Code § 300(h) [but without the reference to former Civil Code § 224n], deals with children who have been freed for adoption by both parents, it would appear that the sole purpose of the JV-127 form is to make the child a dependent of the court where adoption efforts have failed. Where rights have been terminated as to only one parent, this form serves to inform the court of the status of that parent, while another form would have to be used to terminate the rights of the custodial parent.

9. Cruelty

Two check boxes appear on Judicial Council Form JV-128, along with the following pre-printed language: Next to the first box is stated, "The child has been subjected to an act or acts of cruelty by the parent or guardian or a member of the child's household." Next to the second box is stated, "The parent or guardian has failed to protect the child adequately from an act or acts of cruelty, and the parent or guardian knew or reasonably should have known that the child was in danger of being subjected to an act or acts of cruelty." These two alternative grounds for terminating parental rights restate the language of Welfare & Institutions Code § 300(i). "Cruelty" is undefined, and it is not clear how Welfare & Institutions Code § 300(i) differs from the similar subsections mentioned above.

10. Abuse of Sibling [of the Child]

The preprinted language from Judicial Council Form JV-129 states, "The child's sibling has been abused or neglected, as defined in subdivision (a) [dealing with serious nonaccidental physical harm inflicted by parent or guardian], (b) [failure to protect due to negligence or inability of the parent or guardian], (d) [sexual abuse by parent or guardian or member of the household], (e) [intentional severe physical abuse of child under six years old by any person] or (i) [cruelty by a parent or guardian or member of the household], and there is a substantial risk that the child will be abused or neglected, as defined in those subdivisions." This language, with the exceptions of the matters placed in brackets, is the same as the first sentence of Welfare & Institutions Code § 300(j).

Subsection (j) goes on to state that in determining whether there is a "substantial risk" to the child, "the court shall consider the circumstances surrounding the abuse or neglect of the sibling, the age and gender of each child, the nature of the abuse or neglect of the sibling, the mental condition of the parent or guardian, and any other factors the court considers probative." Although a court might construe "sibling" to mean only a brother or sister, one should also note that many of the other subdivisions of Welfare & Institutions Code § 300 only require evidence of "substantial risk" to the child, and that abuse of a half-sibling or a cousin for example would constitute evidence of such a substantial risk.

B. Procedural Aspects of Dependency Proceedings

1. Detention of the Child and Notice to Parents

Under Welfare & Institutions Code §§ 305 and 306, if there is "reasonable cause" to believe the child is in immediate danger of one of the kinds of harm that are listed in Welfare & Institutions Code § 300 (described above), any social worker in a county welfare department or any "peace officer" (see Penal Code § 830) may physically take the child away from the parent or guardian (or from school or some other location away from the home), without a warrant, and place the child in protective custody. Welfare & Institutions Code §§ 307.4 and 308 then require the peace officer or the social worker to immediately to inform the parent through the most efficient means available that the child is in protective custody. In *In re Kobe A.*, (2007) 146 Cal.App.4th 1113, the court interpreted the dependency statutes as requiring notice even to parents who are incarcerated on felony charges for multi-year sentences. Notice on parents who reside outside the United States must comply with the international treaty governing service of process. (*In re Jorge G.*, (2008) 164 Cal.App.4th 125 [service of notice on parents residing in Mexico had to comply with the Hague Service Convention].)

The constitutionality of these provisions was upheld in *U.S. v. Bradley*, (9th Cir. 2003) 321 F.3d 1212. In *Bradley*, sheriff's deputies made a warrantless entry into a private residence in Northern California to locate a nine-year-old boy whose mother they had just arrested on drug charges. At that time, the officers saw illegal firearms in the house, and obtained a warrant for their seizure based on their observations there. The firearms were seized, and were introduced as evidence in a trial in which an individual was convicted on felony charges. The court upheld the validity of the initial entry in the home pursuant to the 4th Amendment in light of the "emergency doctrine" that was triggered by the "genuine concern for the welfare of the child inside."

2. The Filing of the Dependency Petition

Welfare & Institutions Code §§ 311 and 325 require that within 48 hours of the removal of the child, a petition must be filed with the court, seeking to declare the child a dependent of the court. As stated above, the Judicial Council provides several preprinted forms which facilitate this process, in light of the sheer number of children in the system and the speed with which the social services agency must move in this regard. In addition, where it is determined in these early stages that a proceeding should not be commenced, Welfare & Institutions Code § 307 and several other statutes give the officer or the social worker the option of immediately returning the child to the parent.

a) Standing to File the Dependency Petition

Under Welfare & Institutions Code § 325, the petition is filed by a probation officer. In practice, the petition is filed by the "county counsel" on behalf of the applicable social services agency. There is no provision allowing for a private person to file a dependency petition. Concerned citizens are only permitted to contact the social services agency and report suspected child abuse where such citizens have a good faith belief in the truth of the facts reported.

b) Mooting by Relinquishment or Adoption

Family Code § 8700(j) states that parental rights are terminated upon the filing of a signed relinquishment with the CDSS. In addition, the relinquishment must be provided under Family Code § 8700(i)(1) to the juvenile court within five days. At that point, there is nothing left for the juvenile court to adjudicate as to the relinquishing parent, since the relinquishment also operates to give the agency legal custody of the child for purposes of adoptive placement. In similar fashion, Family Code § 8616.5(f) and Rule 5.730(g) of the California Rules of Court expressly provide that an adoption of the child requires the juvenile court to dismiss the dependency proceeding and terminate its jurisdiction over the child.

However, in *Taylor M. v. Superior Court*, (2003) 106 Cal.App.4th 97, the court held that a dependency proceeding in California could not be dismissed *sua sponte* based on a relinquishment that was completed in Texas. The *Taylor M.* court stated that there were substantial jurisdictional questions as well as issues concerning the validity of the relinquishment that had to be fully litigated in the dependency proceeding, in light of the juvenile court's duty to act in the child's best interests and protect the child's welfare.

3. The Detention Hearing

Under Welfare & Institutions Code §§ 315 and 319, the next court day after the filing of the petition, the court must hold a hearing and decide three issues: (a) does the child fall into any of the risk categories listed in Welfare & Institutions Code § 300, (b) if so, were reasonable efforts made to prevent the removal of the child, and (c) if the child is to be detained, what kind of interim reunification services must be afforded to the parent. In answering these questions, the court determines whether prima facie evidence has been submitted by the social services agency in support of its allegations. "Reunification services" are explained below. Also, in *In re Jasmon O.*, (1994) 8 Cal.4th 398, the court held that the burden of proof is on the social services agency to show that an out-of-home placement is needed at the commencement of the proceedings.

4. The Jurisdictional Hearing

Within a maximum of 15 days after the detention hearing is held, Welfare & Institutions Code §§ 334 and 355 require a "jurisdictional hearing" to be held. In practice, the detention and jurisdictional hearings are many times held simultaneously. At the jurisdictional hearing, the court decides the following issues: (a) does the dependency petition set forth allegations bringing the child within the jurisdiction of the juvenile court, and (b) are the allegations true. To meet this burden, the social services agency need only satisfy the preponderance of the evidence standard. As stated above, Welfare & Institutions Code § 300 substantively governs whether the child is under the juvenile court's "jurisdiction," by virtue of the child falling within one of the ten risk categories.

5. The Disposition Hearing and the Reunification Plan

Welfare & Institutions Code §§ 358 and 361 provide for a disposition hearing to be held within 10 or 45 days of the jurisdictional order (depending on whether the child is in detention or not), at which time the court decides (a) whether to declare the child a dependent of the juvenile court, (b) if so, whether the child should be removed from the parents' home, and if so (c) what kind of reunification plan to order. The court also notifies the parents that parental rights will be terminated if there is no compliance with the reunification plan within 12 months. Also, these statutes provide that the social services agency has the burden at this hearing of proving up the first two issues by clear and convincing evidence.

The reunification plan is simply the roadmap for the parent(s) of the reunification services that are designed to lead him and/or her back to the point where they can once again be able to properly function as parents and enjoy a healthy parent-child relationship. As described in Welfare & Institutions Code § 361.5(e)(1), examples of "reunification services" include (A) maintaining contact between the parent and child through collect telephone calls; (B) transportation services, where appropriate; (C) "visitation services, where appropriate;" and (D) reasonable services to extended family members or foster parents providing care for the child if the services are not detrimental to the child. They may also include counseling, parenting classes, and vocational training programs. Rehabilitation programs for drug and alcohol addiction are also often provided. Only the child's mother and presumed father are entitled to the benefit of a reunification plan. (See *In re J.O.* (2009) 178 Cal.App.4th 139.) Interestingly, a man named as the father in a paternity judgment pertaining to child support duties is not necessarily deemed a presumed father in a dependency case. (*In re E.O.* (2010) 182 Cal.App.4th 722.)

In *In re Jasmon O.*, (1994) 8 Cal.4th 398, the Supreme Court interpreted the above mentioned provisions and confirmed that from the beginning of the dependency case to at least the time of the disposition hearing, the statutes express a presumption in favor of keeping parents and children together. Therefore, the purpose of reunification services, i.e., to "reunify" parent and child on all levels of their relationship, is served by providing a pragmatic plan to carry out this legislative goal. However, *Jasmon O.* also holds that 18 months is the maximum length of time that reunification services are provided to the parent, since at some point the state must turn its focus to the long term interests of the child.

6. The "6-Month" Review Hearing

Under Welfare & Institutions Code §§ 366, 366.21 and 366.22, the juvenile court is to hold a review hearing six months after the disposition hearing, at which time the court is to determine whether return of the child to the parents will cause a substantial risk of detriment to the physical or emotional well-being of the child. At this 6-month hearing, the statutes place the burden on the social services agency to prove by a preponderance of evidence that it would be detrimental to the child to return him or her to the parents. In *In re Jasmon O.*, (1994) 8 Cal.4th 398, the court held that at all of the semi-annual review hearings, the presumption is that the child should be returned to the parent unless the social services agency meets its burden of proof as set forth in the statutes described above.

7. The "12-Month" and "18-Month" Review Hearings

a) The Agency's Burden of Proof

According to Welfare & Institutions Code §§ 366, 366.3, 366.21 and 366.22, the court is to hold additional semi-annual hearings after the disposition order. At the 12-month and 18-month hearings, the court is to re-address the same questions discussed at the six-month hearing, plus whether to terminate reunification services and set a permanency planning hearing, where parental rights may ultimately be terminated. The social services agency must show by clear and convincing evidence that it offered adequate reunification services to the parent.

b) The Agency's Change of Purpose upon the Termination of Reunification Services

In *In re Jasmon O.*, (1994) 8 Cal.4th 398, and several other cases, the courts clearly acknowledge that the due process clauses of the federal and state Constitutions clearly protect a parent's interest in the companionship, care, custody and management of his or her children, as well as the child's fundamental right to belong to a family unit, to be protected from abuse and neglect and to have a placement that is stable, permanent, and that which allows the caretaker to make a full emotional commitment to the child. During the time in which the reunification plan is in effect, the social services agency is to make a good faith attempt to satisfy these objectives. However, where this is not possible for reasons beyond the social services agency's control, the court is to terminate the provision for reunification services.

In interpreting the statutes, specifically Welfare & Institutions Code §§ 352(a), 361.5(f), 366, 366.21, 366.22, 366.25, 366.26 and 366.3, the *Jasmon O.* court held that the turning point at which the child's interest may outweigh that of the parent is reached no later than 18 months after the child has been removed from the parental home, based on the 18 month maximum for the provision of reunification services to the parent. Likewise, the Supreme Court in *In re Marilyn H.*, (1993) 5 Cal.4th 295, stated that in such cases, "once family reunification services are terminated, the welfare agency's focus shifts from monitoring the parents' progress toward reunification to determining the appropriate placement plan for the child." *Marilyn H.* also holds that "although a parent's interest in the care, custody and companionship of a child is a liberty interest that may not be interfered with in the absence of a compelling state interest, the welfare of a child is a compelling state interest that a state has not only a right, but a duty, to protect."

8. The Section 366.26 Permanency Planning Hearing

a) Overview

As stated above, if at the disposition hearing the court finds by clear and convincing evidence that the child is a dependent of the court and should be removed from the parents' home, and if at the 18-month review hearing, at the latest, the court finds by clear and convincing evidence that appropriate reunification services were offered but that the parents have not actually reunified with the child, the court is to set a permanency planning hearing to be held at least 120 days later. Permanency planning hearings are governed by Welfare & Institutions Code § 366.26, which allows the court at that time to terminate parental rights if necessary and make one of three permanency plans for the child: The first option is adoptive placement under Welfare & Institutions Code § 366.26(b)(1) and (3), the second option is guardianship under Welfare & Institutions Code § 366.26(b)(2) and (4), and the third option is long-term foster care under Welfare & Institutions Code § 366.26(b)(5).

In *In re Jasmon O*., (1994) 8 Cal.4th 398, the Supreme Court confirmed that "reunification with the parent is not a subject of reconsideration in a termination of parental rights proceeding pursuant to section 366.26." However, as to the involvement of the birth parents at the Section 366.26 hearing, there is conflicting case law. In *In re Johnny M*., (1991) 229 Cal.App.3d 181, the court held that, at the permanent planning hearing, as a fundamental due process right the parent is allowed to contest the social services agency's recommendations for adoption. However, in *Jones T. v. Superior Court*, (1989) 215 Cal.App.3d 240, it was held that in a permanency planning hearing, due process does not require the court to consider guardianship or other less permanent alternatives to termination of parental rights if it finds that the minors are adoptable.

b) Criteria for Adoption as the Permanency Plan

In choosing among the three alternatives (adoption, guardianship or long-term foster care), Welfare & Institutions Code § 366.26(h) requires the court to consider the child's wishes and act in the child's best interests. More specifically, Welfare & Institutions Code § 366.26(b) and (c)(1) state that parental rights may be terminated only if the court finds by clear and convincing that it is likely the child will be adopted. This rule has been characterized as a "low threshold." (*In re K.B*. (2009) 173 Cal.App.4th 1275.) Under this standard, evidence regarding a specifically identified prospective adoptive parent is relevant, but not controlling on the issue of whether the child is adoptable. (*In re G.M.* (2010) 181 Cal.App.4th 552.) On the other hand, the *K.B*. court held that if a child has special needs which render the child not generally adoptable, a finding of adoptability can nevertheless be upheld if a prospective adoptive family has been identified as willing to adopt the child and the evidence supports the conclusion that it is reasonably likely that the child will in fact be adopted within a reasonable time. Also, *In re Jasmon O*., (1994) 8 Cal.4th 398, held that at a hearing on the termination of parental rights, such as a permanency planning hearing, the court may rely on evidence that the disruption of the child's bond with foster parents will cause the child serious, long-term emotional damage in determining whether it would be detrimental to return the child to the natural parent.

Under Welfare & Institutions Code § 366.26(c)(1)(B), adoption is not to be chosen if the court finds that termination of rights would be detrimental to the child due to a compelling reason such as (i) the child would benefit from continuing the relationship with the parents due to their history of regular visitation and contact with the child, (ii) the child is at least 12 years old and objects to termination of parental rights, (iii) the child is placed in a residential treatment facility, adoption is unlikely or undesirable, and continuation of parental rights will not prevent finding the child a permanent family placement if the parents cannot resume custody when residential care is no longer needed, (iv) the child is living with a relative or foster parent who is unable or unwilling to adopt the child because of exceptional circumstances, that do not include an unwillingness to accept legal or financial responsibility for the child, but who is willing and capable of providing the child with a stable and permanent environment and the removal of the child from the physical custody of his or her relative or foster parent would be detrimental to the emotional well-being of the child, (v) there would be substantial interference with a child's ongoing sibling relationship, and (vi) the child is an Indian child and termination of parental rights would interfere with his or her connection to the tribe. (Native American children and the Indian Child Welfare Act are discussed in more detail in Chapter 9 of this book.)

In *In re Celine R.*, (2003) 31 Cal.4th 45, the California Supreme Court interpreted the Welfare & Institutions Code § 366.26(c)(1)(B)(v) provision concerning sibling relationships, and held that the juvenile court may reject adoption under this provision only if it finds that adoption would be detrimental to the child whose welfare is being considered. The *Celine R.* opinion also states that the juvenile court may not prevent a child from being adopted solely because of the effect the adoption may have on a sibling. The Supreme Court affirmed the order setting adoption as the children's permanent plan.

c) Agency's Rights under the Permanency Plan

If the court terminates parental rights and orders adoption as the child's permanency plan, Welfare & Institutions Code § 366.26(j) requires the court to refer the child to the CDSS or to a licensed adoption agency (public or private) for adoptive placement by the agency. Once that occurs, "the State Department of Social Services or licensed adoption agency shall be responsible for the custody and supervision of the child and shall be entitled to the exclusive care and control of the child at all times until a petition for adoption is granted." Welfare & Institutions Code § 366.26(j) also allows the court to appoint a guardian for the child, but only "with the consent of the agency."

d) Finality of the Section 366.26 Order

According to Welfare & Institutions Code § 366.26(i), "Any order of the court permanently terminating parental rights under this section shall be conclusive and binding upon the child, upon the parent or parents and upon all other persons who have been served with citation by publication or otherwise as provided in this chapter. After making the order, the court shall have no power to set aside, change, or modify it, but nothing in this section shall be construed to limit the right to appeal the order."

David B. v. Superior Court, (1994) 21 Cal.App.4th 1010, held that the juvenile court in a dependency proceeding has no power to vacate orders on the ground of lack of personal jurisdiction after an order terminating parental rights has become final. In *David B.*, while it was known that the child's mother had essentially deserted the child, nothing was known by the court about the child's father. The social services agency had completed its due diligence in attempting to learn the identity and whereabouts of the father. Although the county family support collections department knew that the father was in the United States Marine Corps and was stationed in Seattle, Washington, the county social services agency reported to the juvenile court around the time of the disposition hearing that it did not know anything about the father. The social services agency did report to the juvenile court at the time of the permanency planning hearing that it knew the father's name and whereabouts, but the social services agency relied on its prior service of notice by publication, instead of attempting to effectuate personal service of notice to the father. The juvenile court then terminated the father's rights at the permanency planning hearing, and the father's right to appeal lapsed before he filed anything.

The *David B.* court recognized that a judgment is void for lack of jurisdiction of the person where there is no proper service of process on or appearance by a party to the proceedings, and that this principle applies to juvenile dependency proceedings. The *David B.* court also recognized that service by publication is sufficient to meet the requirements of jurisdiction only when a person's whereabouts remain unknown despite reasonably diligent inquiry, and that the social services agency's efforts were not reasonable, given the information in the possession of the district attorney's office.

However, in upholding the statutory language in what is now Welfare & Institutions Code § 366.26(i), the *David B.* court held that the father could not attack the termination of parental rights even on jurisdictional grounds. The *David B.* court stated, "Given the need for stability and certainty in child dependency matters, we do not believe that the Legislature acted arbitrarily in its restriction of the time in which juvenile court orders may be attacked for lack of notice." The court also held that Code of Civil Procedure §§ 473 and 473.5, which relate to the setting aside of default judgments in civil cases, do not apply to juvenile court dependency cases. (Since the birth father was stationed in U.S. territory at all times during the dependency proceedings, it is not clear that he suffered prejudice as a result of his military service, within the meaning of the Federal Soldiers' and Sailors' Civil Relief Act ("SSCRA"). (See 50 U.S.C. Appendix § 501, et seq.) The SSCRA was not discussed at all in the *David B.* case. The SSCRA is examined further in Chapter 10 of this book.)

The *David B.* court also held that Welfare & Institutions Code § 366.26(i) prevented the father from attacking the termination of parental rights on grounds of extrinsic fraud. But see, *In re David H.*, (1995) 33 Cal.App.4th 368, which held that "A court always has inherent equitable jurisdiction to vacate a judgment or order that was obtained through extrinsic fraud. This is no less true of an order under section 366.26 than of any other order of a court."

e) Filing of Adoption Petition in the Juvenile Court

Under Welfare & Institutions Code § 366.26(e), where the juvenile court has terminated parental rights and has made adoptive placement as the permanency plan, the prospective adoptive parents are to file the adoption petition in the juvenile court, as opposed to the superior court where such petitions are normally filed. This would appear to better facilitate the adoption, since documents regarding the child's history would not have to be transferred from court to court. In all other respects, the handling of the adoption is much like an agency adoption. Importantly, Welfare & Institutions Code § 366.26(b)(1), (e) and (j) prevent the adoption from proceeding until "after the appellate rights of the natural parents have been exhausted."

9. Petitions to Modify Dependency Court Orders

In a dependency proceeding, Welfare & Institutions Code § 388(a) allows the child (through a properly appointed guardian) or "any parent or other person having an interest in [the] child" to file a verified petition for a hearing to "change, modify, or set aside any order of court previously made or to terminate the jurisdiction of the court," based "upon grounds of change of circumstance or new evidence." However, Welfare & Institutions Code § 366.26(i) provides that an order terminating parental rights may not be modified by the juvenile court, but may only be reviewed by way of appeal.

Welfare & Institutions Code § 388(c) then states that if it appears that the best interests of the child may be promoted by the proposed change of order or termination of jurisdiction, the court shall order that a hearing on the merits be held. As stated in *In re Jasmon O.*, (1994) 8 Cal.4th 398, a Section 388 petition is the appropriate mechanism by which to seek to change or set aside any order of the juvenile court from the time the child is made a dependent child of the juvenile court, including certain kinds of orders made at a permanency planning hearing. *Jasmon O.* also holds that the petition must be liberally construed in favor of its sufficiency, and that if the petition presents any evidence that a hearing would promote the best interests of the child, the court will order the hearing, but that it is the petitioner's task to demonstrate by a preponderance of the evidence that there was new evidence or a change of circumstances showing that the requested relief is in the child's best interests.

Jasmon O. is a landmark ruling that in the context of a Section 388 hearing occurring at least 18 months after the child was put in foster care, a court may find that it is in the child's best interests to set aside an earlier order on the basis of new evidence that the child will suffer long-term, serious emotional damage if a bond with foster parents is severed. Importantly, it was a county department of social services which filed the Section 388 petition. The child's relationship with third parties such as foster parents is discussed further in Chapter 8.

In addition, in those cases where a child had been placed in long-term foster care or in a guardianship pursuant to Welfare & Institutions Code § 366.26, rather than in adoptive planning, it is possible to cause a change in the parent's rights by way of a Family Code § 7800 petition, which allows for the freeing of a child from parental custody in order to facilitate an adoption. This kind of proceeding can be pursued completely apart from Welfare & Institutions Code § 388, and is discussed in greater detail below.

10. Appeal

Welfare & Institutions Code §§ 366.26(i) and 395 provide that an order terminating parental rights is appealable. Also, as stated in Welfare & Institutions Code § 366.26(b)(1), (e) and (j), the adoption cannot proceed until "after the appellate rights of the natural parents have been exhausted." On the other hand, the mere fact that an appellant proceeds to a higher court does not mean that the appellant may have another evidentiary hearing. In *In re Zeth S.*, (2003) 31 Cal.4th 396, the California Supreme Court held that it was improper for the appellate court to look at evidence that was generated after the entry of judgment, since that was not part of the record on appeal and was never considered by the juvenile court.

In addition to the order terminating parental rights, many of the interim orders in a dependency proceeding are statutorily appealable, and those which are not may be reviewed by an appellate court by way of a petition for writ of mandate under proper circumstances. Further, any party contemplating an appeal from the termination of parental rights must comply with the specific procedures mentioned in Rules 5.585, et seq. and Rules 5.695, et seq. of the California Rules of Court, said procedures including the filing of a writ petition in certain kinds of cases.

C. Rights of Third Parties in Dependency Cases

1. Foster Parents and "De Facto Parents"

In *Sherrard v. Owens*, (6th Cir. 1981) 644 F.2d 542, the court held that foster parents and foster children do not have a constitutionally-protected interest in maintaining their family-like relationships. However, in *Brown v. County of San Joaquin*, (E.D.Cal. 1985) 601 F.Supp. 653, the court held that such a constitutional right may exist because the extended duration of the relationship (3 yrs. and 4 mos. in the *Brown* case) can bring about all the equivalent incidents of a biological family unit. It would appear that *In re Jasmon O.*, (1994) 8 Cal.4th 398, would support such a holding as well.

Rule 5.534(e) of the California Rules of Court allows "de facto parents" (which in many cases are the foster parents) to attend hearings, with or without an attorney, and to present evidence to the juvenile court. *In re B.G.*, (1974) 11 Cal.3d 679, held that a "de facto parent" is a person who, on a day-to-day basis, assumes the role of parent, seeking to fulfill both the child's physical needs and his psychological need for affection and care. In *B.G.*, a foster parent was given de facto parent status. However, the *B.G.* court only held that a de facto parent should be permitted to appear as a party in juvenile court proceedings to assert and protect their own interest in the companionship, care, custody and management of the child, and that no petition for guardianship need be filed for the purpose of being heard in the juvenile court. The *B.G.* court was also pointed out that a de facto parent is not entitled to notice in a dependency case.

More recently, the Supreme Court in *In re Kieshia E.*, (1993) 6 Cal.4th 68, held that a person who might otherwise have de facto parent status might be disqualified from such rights where there is a preponderance of evidence that that person had committed sexual and other serious physical abuse upon the child. The clear and convincing evidence standard was not used in this determination.

2. Relevancy of the Child's Bonding with the Caregiver

In *In re Jasmon O.*, (1994) 8 Cal.4th 398, the Supreme Court held that the existence of a successful relationship between a foster child and foster parent cannot be the sole basis for terminating parental rights or depriving the natural parent of custody in a dependency proceeding. However, in interpreting Welfare & Institutions Code § 396, the court also stated "When a child has been placed in foster care because of parental neglect or incapacity, after an extended period of foster care, it is within the court's discretion to decide that a child's interest in stability has come to outweigh the natural parent's interest in the care, custody and companionship of the child. ... The parent has a fundamental right to maintain the parent-child bond and to the care, custody and companionship of his or her child. However, the right is not absolute and may be abridged when it is necessary to do so to protect the welfare of the child. ... Children, too, have fundamental rights--including the fundamental right to be protected from neglect and to have a placement that is stable and permanent. Children are not simply chattels belonging to the parent, but have fundamental interests of their own that may diverge from the interests of the parent." See also Civil Code § 43.56, stating there is no cause of action by a birth parent against a foster parent for alienation of affection of a foster child.

3. Relatives and Siblings of the Child

A "relative" of the child is also allowed to be present at the hearing and to address the court pursuant to Rule 5.534(f) of the California Rules of Court. Furthermore, Rule 5.546 provides that the parties may engage in discovery, and obtain copies of police reports. However, Rule 5.552 requires that case files and court records in all "juvenile court" proceedings be accessible for inspection only by authorized persons, and in many cases access to records is denied even to foster parents.

4. Agency's "Duty to Supervise" the Foster Parents

In *County of Los Angeles v. Superior Court (Terrell R.)*, (2002) 102 Cal.App.4th 627, the court acknowledged that the social worker assigned to a particular dependency proceeding has certain duties to supervise the foster placement pursuant to code and regulations. In addition, the court held that a social services agency is vicariously liable for the conduct of social workers employed by that agency. Importantly, the *County of Los Angeles* court did not discuss whether there is a direct *respondeat superior* link between the foster parents and the agency.

III. FREEING THE CHILD FROM PARENTAL CUSTODY

A. Purposes and Public Policies Underlying Family Code § 7800

Family Code § 8606(a) states that there is no need to obtain the consent of a birth parent where the child has been freed from the custody of that parent in a proceeding brought under Family Code § 7800, et seq., which is much like the termination of parental rights in a dependency case. Also, 22 California Code of Regulations § 35101(a) states, "In those cases in which the agency is unable to accept a consent [to an independent adoption], the agency shall advise the petitioners and their attorney that legal action is necessary to free the child from parental custody and control." This section will describe the substantive and procedural aspects of a proceeding to free a child from parental custody and control under Family Code § 7800, and contrast such cases with dependency proceedings.

Family Code § 7800 states that its "purpose" is to "serve the welfare and best interest of a child by providing the stability and security of an adoptive home when those conditions are otherwise missing from the child's life." Family Code § 7801 then states that the statutes are to be "liberally construed to serve and protect the interests and welfare of the child." Based on this language, the focus is on whether the child's welfare, as opposed to the birth parents, will be served by an adoption, as opposed to a guardianship or long-term foster care.

To facilitate this goal, Family Code § 7802 provides that a proceeding may be brought "for the purpose of having a minor child declared free from the custody and control of either or both parents," while Family Code § 7803 states that such a declaration "terminates all parental rights and responsibilities with regard to the child." By virtue of Family Code § 7802 allowing for the termination of the rights of "either" parent, the statutes are often used in completing stepparent adoptions, in which only one parent's rights are terminated. (See Chapter 8.) On the other hand, Family Code § 7820 provides that only those children who are within one of the risk categories set forth in Family Code § 7800, et seq. are subject to a proceeding to be declared free from the custody and control of a parents. In other words, Family Code § 7800, et seq. was enacted to protect children who are in need of protection, not merely to adoptions.

B. Standing to Initiate a Family Code § 7800 Proceeding

1. Public and Private Agencies

Family Code § 7840(a) states that a petition to declare a child free from the custody and control of either or both parents may be filed by the CDSS, a county welfare department, a licensed private or public adoption agency, a county adoption department or a county probation department which is planning adoptive placement of the child with a licensed adoption agency. Under Family Code § 7840(b), where a governmental entity is filing the petition, the fact that the child is in foster care does not prevent the filing of the petition.

2. "Interested Person" (Prospective Adoptive Parent)

Family Code § 7841(a) states that "Any interested person may file a petition under this part for an order or judgment declaring a child free from the custody and control of either or both parents." "Interested person" is not fully defined and does not appear to be limited to governmental entities. Further, with regard to who has standing to initiate a

Family Code § 7800 case, Family Code § 7841 says nothing about custody, adoptive placements, guardianships or foster placements.

However, in 2007, the Legislature added Family Code § 7841(b), which states "interested person" includes a person who has filed a petition for an agency adoption, independent adoption or stepparent adoption, or who intends to file such an adoption petition within six months. Since standing to file the Family Code § 7800 petition may be based on the mere intent to file an adoption petition within six months, it does not appear that Family Code § 7841(b) "standing" is defeated if the adoption petition is not actually filed within six months.

Prior to 2007, in defining what constitutes an "interested person," as that term used in the predecessor to Family Code § 7841, the court in *In re Eugene W.*, (1972) 29 Cal.App.3d 623, held that an "interested person" is one who has a direct, and not merely a consequential, interest in the action, and that "a child welfare worker of the Napa County Welfare Department" was such a person. However, the court in *People ex rel. Pollock v. Bogart*, (1943) 58 Cal.App.2d 831, held that a child's grandmother who gave the "mere statement" that "the children were with her in her home and under her care and custody" was not an interested person. Under the current language of Family Code §§ 7841(b) and 8802(a)(1)(D)(ii), it appears that if the petitioner in *Bogart* had first obtained a guardianship order, she would have standing to file her petition, since she would have had standing to file her adoption petition within six months.

It would therefore appear that a private person seeking to file a Family Code § 7800 petition would first need to apply for a temporary guardianship, so as to clearly create a direct interest in the action and/or show that he or she is a prospective adoptive parent. It would also appear that a person with whom the child has been placed for adoption, either by a parent of the child by way of an independent adoption or by an adoption agency, would be an "interested person," since such a person would immediately have standing to file an adoption petition.

3. Children Who Are Not Subject to Family Code § 7800

According to Family Code § 7820, the child listed in the petition must be under 18 years old.

Additionally, Family Code § 7808 states that, with regard to children who have been adjudged a dependent child of the juvenile court under Welfare & Institutions Code § 360(c), a Family Code § 7800 proceeding may not be brought as to such a child during the period in which the minor is a dependent child of the court. Welfare & Institutions Code § 360(c) does not cover all children who are in the dependency system; it only covers certain children who are in a guardianship in the course of a dependency proceeding. It is under Welfare & Institutions Code §§ 358 and 361 that most foster children are declared to be a dependent of the juvenile court.

In any event, Family Code § 7808 provide that for children in that category, dependency proceedings may continue for the child, a consent may be signed, a relinquishment may be signed, a proceeding may be instituted to declare that a Family Code § 8606 abandonment has occurred, and a proceeding may be instituted to declare that the natural father is not a presumed father. Family Code § 7808 terms these options as the "exclusive means for the termination of parental rights" where the child is a dependent of the juvenile court pursuant to Welfare & Institutions Code § 360(c). On the other hand, Family Code § 7823(a)(2) and other statutes provide that a Family Code § 7800 proceeding may be brought for a child who has been ordered into long-term foster care.

C. Substantive Grounds to Free a Child from Parental Custody

Family Code §§ 7800, et seq. include several code sections describing certain risk categories which provide the substantive grounds for the petition. Many of those code sections presuppose that there was some level of involvement by the juvenile court in a dependency proceeding. Many do not. The code sections deal with the following types of situations:

1. Family Code § 7822 Abandonment

a) Generally

The first risk category is Family Code § 7822(a), which states that a proceeding to free a child from parental custody may be brought "where the child has been left without provision for the child's identification by the child's parent or parents or by others or has been left by both parents or the sole parent in the care and custody of another for a period of six months or by one parent in the care and custody of the other parent for a period of one year without any provision for the child's support, or without communication from the parent or parents, with the intent on the part of the parent or parents to abandon the child." Importantly, there is no provision in the statute requiring dependency proceedings to have been brought with regard to this risk category.

Based on the phrasing of the statute, the petitioner's burden of proof is to establish by clear and convincing evidence that one of the two kinds of abandonment has taken place ((1) left without provision for the child's identification or (2) left with a non-parent for six months or with one parent for one year and without support or communication), plus parental intent to abandon. (See *In re Baby Boy S.*, (1987) 194 Cal.App.3d 925.) The court in *In re Adoption of Allison C.*, (2008) 164 Cal.App.4th 1004, held that the elements of Family Code § 7822 may be satisfied even if the parent's leaving of the child and failure to support or communicate was caused his or her having been incarcerated for a crime. Also, Family Code § 7822(a) involves the failure to support the child <u>or</u> to communicate with the child. The petitioner does not have the burden to prove both, but does have the burden to prove intent to abandon.

In certain cases, a Family Code § 7822 petition is brought where the birth parent who actually placed the child for adoption is hesitant to sign the required consent to adoption. In such a case, Family Code § 7822(d) states that the court is allowed to (but not required to) find that there was an intent to abandon the child whether or not there has been a refusal to give the required consent along with a request to obtain custody of the child. One such case is *In re Timothy W.*, (1990) 223 Cal.App.3d 437, where the court stated that "when a natural mother refuses to consent to an independent adoption within a reasonable time after placing the child with prospective adoptive parents, and six months will always be a reasonable time, the court may not consider whether returning the child to the birth mother will be in the minor's best interests." In *Timothy W.*, the birth parent's first written notification of the refusal to consent (which consisted of a letter to the court) came four days short of the child becoming six months old. On the other hand, it appears that the Legislature impliedly overruled that portion of *Timothy W.* which states that a birth parent's conduct in contemplation of a proposed adoption cannot establish desertion or intent to abandon.

Where the parent has been the subject of a restraining order, that parent must show that he made a good faith attempt to comply with the court-ordered conditions for child visitation, or risk being deemed to have abandoned the child. (*In re Marriage of Jill and Victor D.* (2010) 185 Cal.App.4th 491.) On the issue of abandonment, identifying the initial cause of the family break-up is not a relevant question. (*Id.*)

Where there has been a desertion, Family Code § 7822(c) provides that if the child has been left without provision for the child's identification and the whereabouts of the parents are unknown, a petition may be filed after the 120th day following the discovery of the child and citation by publication may be commenced. The petition may not be heard until after the 180th day following the discovery of the child.

There is an additional kind of abandonment, as that term is understood in its broadest sense, where a man fails to come forward in a timely manner upon being served with notice of a paternity action or an adoption proceeding. In that instance, that man risks losing the ability to assert his parental rights. This situation is governed by Family Code §§ 7600, et seq., and is explained in detail in Chapter 3.

b) Triggering Presumption of Intent to Abandon

As to the "intent to abandon" element, Family Code § 7822(b) states, "The failure to provide identification, failure to provide support, or failure to communicate is presumptive evidence of the intent to abandon." At the very least, it would appear that this presumption is strong enough to constitute prima facie evidence sufficient to shift the burden of proof to the opposing party, meaning that such evidence would support the granting of the petition in a default proceeding.

On the other hand, the court in *In re Jacklyn F.*, (2003) 114 Cal.App.4th 747, ruled that the presumption of the intent to abandon is not triggered until the petitioner establishes that the birth parent has "left" the child. The *Jacklyn F.* court stated that, since the birth mother had contested the guardianship proceedings which resulted in her child being placed in the custody of the child's paternal grandparents, the birth mother had not "left" the child with the paternal grandparents, meaning that no presumption of intent to abandon arose by virtue of the birth mother's failure to communicate and failure to support for more than one year. (Cf., *In re Marriage of Jill and Victor D.* (2010) 185 Cal.App.4th 491.) In addition, in *In re Baby Boy S.*, (1987) 194 Cal.App.3d 925, the court held that abandonment is a question of fact, and that the birth parent's alleged intent to abandon may be negated by actions taken by the attorney acting in an actual conflict of interest.

As to the failure to support, the court in *Adoption of Coffee*, (1976) 59 Cal.App.3d 593, held that a father who is unable to comply with an order for the payment of child support cannot be adjudged in contempt for such noncompliance unless he has voluntarily created the disability for the purpose of avoiding payment. The court held that a man who was incarcerated on felony charges for robbery and burglary, and was thus unable to earn enough money to pay child support, could not be considered to be "willfully" failing to support the child. The court did not decide whether rights could be terminated based on what is now Family Code § 7825.

c) "Token Efforts" to Support or Communicate

Family Code § 7822(b) states that the court may declare the child abandoned by the parent or parents despite evidence that the parent or parents have made "token efforts to support or communicate with the child." An example of "token efforts" is *Adoption of Christopher S.*, (1987) 197 Cal.App.3d 433, where the court held that two attempts to visit and the sending of two Christmas cards did not amount to a meaningful attempt to communicate.

d) Guardian's Action to Terminate Parental Rights

According to Probate Code § 1516.5(a), the child's guardian may bring a proceeding, within the guardianship case itself, to free the child from the parents' control and custody, for example by proving that a Family Code § 7822 abandonment has occurred. The California Supreme Court held in *In re Guardianship of Ann S.*, (2009) 45 Cal.4th 1110, that Probate Code § 1516.5 is not facially unconstitutional. Also, *In re Charlotte D.*, (2009) 45 Cal.4th 1140, holds that Probate Code § 1516.5 does not violate due process or equal protection as applied to a man was qualified to assert his rights as a presumed father, as long as there is "some showing of unfitness;" and the *Ann S.* guardian had filed a Family Code § 7822 petition.

Therefore, in addition to proving the elements of Family Code § 7800, et seq., the guardian must prove under Probate Code § 1516.5(a) that one or both parents do not have the legal custody of the child, that the child has been in the guardian's physical custody for at least two years, and that the child would benefit from being adopted by the guardian. Also under Probate Code § 1516.5(d), the guardian may not bring such a proceeding if the child is a dependent of the juvenile court. If the guardian succeeds, an adoption order must still be obtained. Even so, *In re Noreen G.*, (2010) 181 Cal.App.4th 1359, holds that the court has no authority to award visitation rights to the natural parents in a Probate Code § 1516.5(a) case.

2. Family Code § 8604(b) Abandonment

a) Generally

Family Code §§ 7822 and 8604(b) provide two distinct and independent procedures by which the court may declare that an abandonment has made a birth parent's consent unnecessary to complete the adoption. Family Code § 8604(b) provides an exception to the general rule that a child having a presumed father may not be adopted without the consent of both of the birth parents. Family Code § 8604(b) states, "If one birth parent has been awarded custody by judicial order, or has custody by agreement of both parents, and the other birth parent for a period of one year willfully fails to communicate with and to pay for the care, support, and education of the child when able to do so, then the birth parent having sole custody may consent to the adoption, but only after the birth parent not having custody has been served with a copy of a citation" in the lawfully provided manner. As shown by the language of the statute, Family Code § 8604(b) only applies in the narrow situation where only one parent has legal custody of the child by court order or by agreement.

Importantly, a petition to free a child from parental custody because of the parent's Family Code § 7822 abandonment requires the petitioner to comply with all of the provisions of Family Code §§ 7800, et seq., as explained above, while a petition to dispense with a birth parent's consent pursuant to Family Code § 8604(b) does not, even though the two petitions have ultimately the same effect. In practice, both may be utilized and pled in the same petition.

b) Failure to Support and Failure to Communicate

In *Adoption of Murray*, (1978) 86 Cal.App.3d 222, the court distinguished the statutory language of the two code sections which are now Family Code §§ 7822(a) and 8604(b). Under Family Code § 8604(b), the petitioner must show evidence of both the father's willful failure to pay child support *and* the failure to communicate. However, Family Code § 7822 only requires clear and convincing evidence of one or the other. On the other hand, the Legislature has very recently enacted Family Code § 8604(c), which states that "token efforts" to support or communicate will be disregarded.

In addition, the court in *In re Jay R.*, (1983) 150 Cal.App.3d 251, held that in a Family Code § 8604(b) proceeding, the "year" in question is not limited to the one year immediately preceding the petition. Furthermore, *Adoption of Christopher S.*, (1987) 197 Cal.App.3d 433, held that the detriment standard (which is used in child custody cases involving a marital dissolution) does not apply in what would now be a Family Code § 8604(b) proceeding.

c) "Willful" Failure to Support and Communicate

Just as with Family Code § 7822(b), Family Code § 8604(c) states, "Failure of a birth parent to pay for the care, support, and education of the child for the period of one year or failure of a birth parent to communicate with the child for the period of one year is prima facie evidence that the failure was willful and without lawful excuse." However, Family Code § 8604(c) does not contain the triggering language set forth in Family Code § 7822(b), as interpreted in *In re Jacklyn F.*, (2003) 114 Cal.App.4th 747. More specifically, where the petitioner is employing Family Code § 8604(c) to dispense with the consent requirement, the petitioner need not show that the birth parent "left" the child with the petitioner.

In re Jay R., (1983) 150 Cal.App.3d 251, is an example of the Family Code § 8604(c) presumption being applied. In *Jay R.*, the court held that the petitioner only needed to show that the noncustodial parent failed to provide for and communicate with the child for a year to establish a prima facie case of willful neglect without lawful excuse, and that the burden shifted to the parent to prove he did not willfully fail to provide for or communicate with the child, or was unable to do so.

d) Procedural Requirements – Right to Counsel

Family Code § 8604 itself does not contain any procedural provisions, meaning it would appear that one need only comply with the general rules concerning serving the adoption petition (as explained in Chapter 10 and elsewhere in this book). However, in *In re Jay R.*, (1983) 150 Cal.App.3d 251, which only involved a petition filed under what is now Family Code § 8604(b), the court stated that in order to comply with due process, the service of a mere citation to appear is insufficient. The noncustodial parent must be informed of the specific factual allegations supporting the petition, by means of attaching a copy of the petition to the citation notice, and that the birth parent has the right to court-appointed counsel if unable to afford counsel.

3. Neglect or Cruel Treatment

Where a child is within this risk category, Family Code § 7823(a) requires a showing that (1) the child has been neglected or cruelly treated by either or both parents, and (2) the child has been a dependent child of the juvenile court under any subdivision of Welfare & Institutions Code § 300 and the parent or parents have been deprived of the child's custody for one year before the filing of the Family Code § 7800 petition. Due to the high cost and amount of time that would be consumed in litigating such a petition, it would appear that a petition under Family Code § 7823(b) would be economically appropriate where it appears the dependency case will not proceed to a Welfare & Institutions Code § 366.26 permanency planning hearing.

4. Depravity or Drug- or Alcohol-Induced Disability

Family Code § 7824(b) provides that a proceeding to declare a child free from parental custody may be brought where (1) the child's parent or parents "suffer a disability because of the habitual use of alcohol, or any of the controlled substances specified in" Health & Safety Code §§ 11000, et seq., or are "morally depraved," and (2) the child has been a dependent child of the juvenile court, and the parent or parents have been deprived of the child's custody continuously for one year immediately before the filing of the Family Code § 7800 petition.

Family Code § 7824(b)(1) makes an exception when the controlled substances are being used by the parent "as part of a medically prescribed plan." Also, "disability" is defined in Family Code § 7824(a) as "any physical or mental incapacity which renders the parent or parents unable to care for and control the child adequately." In other words, proof of drug addiction alone would be insufficient under this code section. The addiction must cause an inability to care for and control the child.

5. Conviction of a Felony Indicating Parental Unfitness

Family Code § 7825(a) authorizes a proceeding to be brought to declare a child free from parental custody where (1) the child's parent or parents have been "convicted of a felony," and (2) "the facts of the crime of which the parent or parents were convicted are of such a nature so as to prove the unfitness of the parent or parents to have the future custody and control of the child." This risk category does not statutorily require a dependency case to have been brought. It should be noted that there is no enumeration of felonies which will automatically warrant an order freeing the child from parental custody under this code section.

Where the conviction resulted from a verdict, Family Code § 7825(a) does not require that the evidence to be introduced in the Family Code § 7800 case had to be first introduced in the criminal trial. There is also no requirement that the judge in the Family Code § 7825(a) proceeding is barred from considering evidence that was excluded in the criminal case. If the conviction which is the factual predicate for the Family Code § 7825(a) petition was the result of a plea bargain, Family Code § 7825(a) does not require the conviction to have carried any particular prison sentence. Also, a plea of guilty or no contest to a felony charge admits to all of the essential elements of the crime charged. (*People v. Wallace*, (2004) 33 Cal.4th 738; Penal Code § 1016(3).) On the other hand, there is case law saying that a judgment of conviction resulting from a guilty plea does not have collateral estoppel effect. (*People v. Blackburn*, (1999) 72 Cal.App.4th 1520, 1528.) One should also consider the differing standards of proof – a Family Code § 7800 proceeding only requires clear and convincing evidence while criminal charges must be proven beyond a reasonable doubt.

Regarding the "unfitness of the parent element," in interpreting language similar to that used in Family Code § 7825(a), the court in *In re Case's Guardianship*, (1943) 57 Cal.App.2d 844, held that a misdeed which had occurred many years prior to the hearing is too remote to prove present parental unworthiness. That court also held that serving a prison term is not per se cause for depriving a parent of the custody of his child, and that a person who had served time in 1935 for an act involving moral turpitude might possibly be found by a court in 1942 to be a fit and proper person to have custody of the child. In addition, in *Adoption of Lenn E.*, (1986) 182 Cal.App.3d 210, the court interpreted the predecessor to Family Code § 7825 and confirmed that where the criminal case is on appeal, the conviction cannot be considered a final judgment for purposes of the application of this section.

Family Code § 7825(b) states that the mother of a child may bring a proceeding against the father of the child, where the child was conceived as a result of a rape for which the child's father was convicted, and that the father is conclusively presumed to be unfit to have custody or control of the child under such circumstances.

6. Parent's Mental or Developmental Disability or Illness

Under Family Code §§ 7826 and 7827, a petition to free a child from parental custody may be brought based on the parent's mental or developmental disability under certain circumstances. With regard to this risk category, there is no requirement of having to bring dependency proceedings. On the other hand, it would appear that the case law interpreting Welfare & Institutions Code § 300(b) and its predecessors (see above) would be pertinent, but not necessarily controlling, in interpreting Family Code §§ 7826 and 7827, as explained below.

a) Prior Judicial Declaration of Disability or Illness

Family Code § 7826(a) states that the child may be freed from parental custody where the child's "parent or parents have been declared by a court of competent jurisdiction, wherever situated, to be developmentally disabled or mentally ill." The Family Code § 7826(a) would therefore appear to rely upon the collateral estoppel effect of the prior judicial declaration. The statute does not specify how recent the prior judicial declaration must be.

b) Prior Medical Certificate of Disability or Illness

Family Code § 7826(b) provides that a Family Code § 7800 proceeding may be brought where the child's parent or parents have been certified to be developmentally disabled or mentally ill to the extent that they are not be capable of supporting or controlling the child in a proper manner. This certification must be made by the Director of Mental Health or the Director of Developmental Services, or their equivalent, if any, in the state or country in which the parent or parents reside or are hospitalized, and by the superintendent of the hospital, if any, of which the parent or parents are inmates or patients. In other words, there are cases in which Family Code § 7826(b) requires two certificates (one by a public official and one by a hospital official). The statute does not specify how recent the certificates must be.

c) Establishing Mental Disability of a Parent

Family Code § 7827(b) states that the child may be freed from parental custody where the child's "parent or parents are mentally disabled and are likely to remain so in the foreseeable future." This code section does not require a prior judicial declaration or medical certification of disability or illness, but requires the petitioner to prove the parent's mental disability by clear and convincing evidence. Family Code § 7827(a) defines "mentally disabled" to mean that the parent or parents suffer from "a mental incapacity or disorder that renders the parent or parents unable to care for and control the child adequately." This definition appears to be broader than that used in *In re Carmaleta B.*, (1978) 21 Cal.3d 482, in the context of a dependency case brought under Welfare & Institutions Code § 300(b). Family Code § 7827(e) provides that the parent is entitled to a court-appointed attorney in such cases, even where no request for an attorney is made.

This code section sets forth specific evidentiary requirements. If the parent or parents reside in California, Family Code § 7827(c) requires the petitioner to introduce the testimony of at least two experts, each of whom shall be either a licensed psychologist (with a doctoral degree in psychology and five years of postgraduate experience) or a board-certified psychiatrist (which is a licensed physician). This code section also allows the court to call witnesses such as a licensed marriage, family, and child counselor, or a licensed clinical social worker, either of whom shall have at least five years of relevant post-licensure experience, but not the adoption service provider. If the parent or parents reside in another state or in a foreign country, Family Code § 7827(d) requires at least the affidavits of two experts, each of whom shall be either a licensed and practicing psychiatrist or neurologist, or a licensed psychologist with a doctoral degree in psychology and at least five years of postgraduate experience.

d) Requirement for Reunification Services?

In *In re Victoria M.*, (1989) 207 Cal.App.3d 1317, which interpreted what is roughly the predecessor to Family Code § 7827, the court stated that before the parental rights of a "developmentally disabled parent" will be terminated, the record must establish by clear and convincing evidence that services specially designed to meet the needs of the developmentally disabled have been explored and that, despite the availability of such services, it is in the best interest of the children to be declared free for adoption. The court also stated that "if the fundamental inadequacy of the parent is a developmental disability, it must be demonstrated under any of the [statutory risk categories] that the court explored alternatives to severance, such as services offered by the state for developmentally disabled persons."

On the other hand, Family Code § 7827 was enacted after the *Victoria M.* decision, and omits any mention of reunification services. In addition, Family Code § 7827 deals with persons who are "mentally disabled" according to a very specific definition. Therefore, it is unclear whether the petitioner under Family Code § 7827 must introduce evidence that reunification services were offered but were unsuccessful. Also, it is unclear what reunification services could accomplish for an individual who is truly developmentally disabled (i.e., suffering from severe mental retardation, cerebral palsy, epilepsy or autism) or mentally disabled. In any event, as stated in *In re Anthony P.*, (2000) 84 Cal.App.4th 1112, that there is no need to comply with the Americans with Disabilities Act (42 U.S.C. § 12131 et seq.) in a Family Code § 7827 case.

7. Unsuccessful Reunification Services

a) Order Terminating Reunification Services

Family Code § 7829 appears to be a carryover from the statutory scheme that existed before the enactment of the Family Code, and before the restructuring of the dependency laws. This code section provides that a petition under Family Code § 7800 could be brought where (a) the child is a dependent of the juvenile court, and (b) the juvenile court has ruled pursuant to Welfare & Institutions Code § 361.5(b)(3), (4) or (5) that reunification services shall not be provided to the child's parent or guardian. It would appear that Family Code § 7829 would rarely be utilized, since to do so would deprive the parent of many other rights that parents have in dependency proceedings, such as the 120-day notice period for a Welfare & Institutions Code § 366.26 permanency planning hearing, the right to bring a modification petition under Welfare & Institutions Code § 388, and the right to appeal various orders in the dependency proceedings.

b) Out-of-Home Placement for One Year

Family Code § 7828(a) provides that a proceeding to declare a child free from parental custody may be brought where (1) the child has been in out-of-home placement for a one-year period under the supervision of the juvenile court, the county welfare department, or a licensed child-placing agency, and (2) the court finds that return of the child to the parent or parents would be detrimental to the child and that the parent or parents have failed during the one-year period, and are likely to fail in the future, to maintain an adequate parental relationship with the child, which includes providing both a home and care and control for the child. This is the only Family Code § 7800 risk category where the "detriment" standard applies. *In re Connie M.*, (1986) 176 Cal.App.3d 1225, held that the one-year period of foster care or "out-of-home" placement in what is now Family Code § 7828 may be shown to have transpired at any time prior to the filing of the petition, and need not be the period immediately before the petition is filed.

It would appear that the same considerations mentioned above with regard to Family Code § 7829 as to the parent's rights in a dependency proceeding would also apply if a Family Code § 7828 petition were filed. However, Family Code § 7828 could apply where one parent has relinquished parental rights to an adoption agency, and the other parent's rights for some reason have not been the subject of a dependency case. On the other hand, even if the out-of-home placement occurred as a result of one parent's valid relinquishment to an agency where the other parent could not be identified or found, Family Code § 7828(e) still requires the petitioner to prove that reasonable reunification services were provided or offered to the non-relinquishing parent but were unsuccessful, making Family Code § 7828 similar to a dependency case.

D. Procedural Aspects of a Family Code § 7800 Case

1. Generally

The proceedings under Family Code § 7800, et seq. follow a simpler pattern than do dependency proceedings under Welfare & Institutions Code § 300, et seq. For example, there are no semi-annual review hearings in a Family Code § 7800 case. Another example of is that Family Code §§ 210 and 211 provide that the rules of practice set forth in the Code of Civil Procedure and in the California Rules of Court are applicable in any proceeding under the Family Code, except for those aspects of the proceedings which are governed by specific sections of the California Rules of Court. There is no similar provision in the Welfare & Institutions Code. On the other hand, the burden of proof is essentially the same, and the resulting order is accorded essentially the same finality and appealability as a Welfare & Institutions Code § 366.26 order.

2. Filing Verified Petition in Proper County

Family Code §§ 200, 212 and 7845 state that the petition to declare the child free from parental custody shall be verified and filed in the county in which (a) the child resides or is found, or (b) the acts described in Family Code §§ 7822-7829 are alleged to have occurred. Unlike dependency proceedings, the Judicial Council has not published any standard forms to be used for a Family Code § 7800 case.

The necessity of specifically having a Family Code § 7800 petition on file is illustrated in *In re Allison H.*, (1991) 230 Cal.App.3d 154, which held that the trial court is not permitted to find *sua sponte* that the birth parent abandoned the child within the meaning of what is now Family Code § 7822, even in the context of a stepparent adoption proceeding.

3. Notice

a) Court's Notice to Social Services Agencies

Upon the filing of the petition by an "interested person," the court clerk is required by Family Code § 7850 to immediately notify the juvenile probation officer, qualified court investigator, or the county social services agency, who shall immediately investigate the circumstances facing the child and the allegations of the petition.

b) Contents of the Citation to Custodian

Family Code § 7880(a) states that upon the filing of the petition, a citation shall issue requiring any person having the custody or control of the child, or the person with whom the child is, to appear at the time and place stated in the citation. Importantly, a "citation" is not interchangeable with a "summons." Also, the Judicial Council has not published a form citation to be used for a Family Code § 7800 case, but the Ventura County Superior Court has such a form available on web site (www.ventura.courts.ca.gov/vn223.pdf).

Family Code § 7880(c) requires service of the citation to be made in the manner prescribed by law for service of civil process at least 10 days before the time stated in the citation for the appearance. Family Code § 7880(b) provides that the citation shall also require the person to appear with the child unless the child is under 10 years old, in which case appearance with the child is required only upon court order.

c) Contents of the Notice – Right to Counsel

Family Code § 7881(a) states, "Notice of the proceeding shall be given by service of a citation on the father or mother of the child, if the place of residence of the father or mother is known to the petitioner. If the place of residence of the father or mother is not known to the petitioner, then the citation shall be served on the grandparents and adult brothers, sisters, uncles, aunts, and first cousins of the child, if there are any and if their residences and relationships to the child are known to the petitioner." Family Code § 7881(b) requires the citation to the parent to provide that he or she may appear at the time and place stated in the citation, that the petition was filed for the purpose of freeing the child for placement for adoption, if that is the case, and that he or she is entitled to the rights and procedures set forth in Family Code § 7860, et seq.

One of the rights set forth in Family Code § 7860, et seq. is the right to court-appointed counsel under Family Code § 7862. Also, in *In re Jay R.*, (1983) 150 Cal.App.3d 251, the court stated that in order to comply with due process, the noncustodial parent must also be informed of the specific factual allegations supporting the petition, by means of attaching a copy of the petition to the citation notice, and that a mere citation to appear is insufficient. Although *Jay R.* only involved what would now be a

Family Code § 8604(b) petition, its logic would appear to also apply to a Family Code § 7800 proceeding.

Further as to the right to counsel, it only attaches under Family Code § 7862 if the parent "appears without counsel and is unable to afford counsel." In interpreting Family Code § 7862, the court in *In re Angela R.*, (1989) 212 Cal.App.3d 257 (citing *Lassiter v. Department of Social Services*, (1981) 452 U.S. 18), held that there is no statutory or constitutional right to court-appointed counsel for those parties who fail to appear at the hearing. Family Code § 7863 states that court-appointed counsel for an indigent birth parent is paid for by the "real parties in interest, other than the child," unless the court determines that they are unable to afford counsel, in which case counsel is paid from the county's general fund. Family Code § 7864 allows the court to grant a 30-day continuance of the hearing to allow for the appointment of counsel and to allow counsel to become acquainted with the case.

d) Locating the Parents and Serving Notice

Family Code § 7881(c) states that the citation shall be served in the manner provided by law for the service of a summons in a civil action, other than by publication. Therefore, if the whereabouts of the father (for example) are unknown, a proceeding under Family Code § 7800 cannot be brought as to him until they become known so as to allow him to be served. An exception to this rule is in Family Code § 7822(c), which provides that if the child has been left without provision for the child's identification and the whereabouts of the parents are unknown, a petition may be filed after the 120th day following the discovery of the child and citation by publication may be commenced.

In other types of cases, if the father cannot be located despite diligent inquiry, the prospective adoptive parents may proceed under Family Code §§ 7664(a), 7665 and/or 7666(b) for a judicial declaration that the natural father is not a presumed father with consent rights as provided in Family Code §§ 8604 and 8605 (see Chapter 3), or that the father has abandoned or deserted the child as described in Family Code §§ 8604 and 8606(c). Personal service of process is not statutorily required in these latter situations. In *In re Matthew S.*, (1988) 201 Cal.App.3d 315, which was a proceeding brought pursuant to former Civil Code § 232 (which essentially is now Family Code § 7800, et seq.), and wherein the basis for personal jurisdiction over the birth parent consisted of service by publication of the notice of hearing in a newspaper, the court stated that a valid service by publication did not violate due process.

If the parents can be located so as to allow for notice of the Family Code § 7800 petition, Family Code § 7881(d) requires the citations to be served at least 10 days before the time stated in the citation for the appearance.

In those instances where one parent has relinquished the child for the purpose of adoption, or has signed a consent for adoption, Family Code § 7881(c) dispenses with the need to give notice to that parent.

4. Investigation and Report by Social Services Agency

Where the petition is brought by an "interested person," Family Code § 7850 requires the juvenile probation officer, qualified court investigator or the county social services agency who was notified by the court clerk to immediately investigate the circumstances of the child and the allegations of the petition. Regardless of who files the petition, Family Code § 7851(a) requires the investigating agency to "render to the court a written report of the investigation with a recommendation to the court of the proper disposition to be made in the proceeding in the best interest of the child." Family Code § 7851(d) makes that report an admissible item of evidence (thus constituting an exception to the hearsay rule), and requires the court to consider it.

In addition to an analysis of the best interests of the child, Family Code § 7851(b) requires the report to include statements concerning (1) that the person making the report explained to the child the nature of the proceeding to end parental custody and control, (2) the child's feelings and thoughts concerning the pending proceeding, (3) the child's attitude towards the child's parent or parents and particularly whether or not the child would prefer living with his or her parent or parents, and (4) that the child was informed of the child's right to attend the hearing on the petition and the child's feelings concerning attending the hearing. Under Family Code § 7851(c) these four items are not necessary where the child's age, physical condition or emotional condition precludes meaningful responses to these four items.

5. Duty to Personally Appear at the Hearing

In *In re Angela R.*, (1989) 212 Cal.App.3d 257, it was held that the court properly entered the default of the natural parent for the failure to appear at the properly noticed hearing. In addition, the court in *Adoption of Jacob C.*, (1994) 25 Cal.App.4th 617, held that the natural parent's duty to appear is not satisfied by the mere appearance of the natural parent's attorney, and that the proceeding goes forward as an uncontested matter in such cases. The *Angela R.* court also held that for the petitioner to obtain a default, there is no need to comply with the requirements of Code of Civil Procedure §§ 585 et seq., since no responsive pleading is required on the part of the birth parents.

6. Child Abduction and the Disentitlement Doctrine

In *Adoption of Jacob C.*, (1994) 25 Cal.App.4th 617, the birth mother abducted a sibling of the child who was the subject of the proceedings; she "remained concealed and a fugitive from justice," and had been evading the service of notices to appear and felony arrest warrants. The *Jacob C.* court held that under such circumstances the mother (through her attorney) was disentitled to be heard concerning the subject child. The *Jacob C.* court stated that "a party to an action cannot, with right or reason, ask the aid and assistance of a court in hearing his demands while he stands in an attitude of contempt to legal orders and processes of the courts of this state."

Further, while the disentitlement doctrine only applies to conduct which is relevant to the proceeding at issue, the *Jacob C.* court held that the birth mother's abduction of the *sibling* was "at the very heart of" the petition to free the child from parental custody. On the other hand, "a finding of contempt is not required" for the court to apply the disentitlement doctrine. (*In re C.C.* (2003) 111 Cal.App.4th 76, 89.) And while the disentitlement doctrine is most often applied in child custody proceedings, it may be applied in other types of cases. (*TMS, Inc. v. Aihara* (1999) 71 Cal.App.4th 377, 379-380.)

7. Petitioner's Burden of Proof

Family Code § 7821 states that any finding made pursuant to Family Code § 7800, et seq. must be supported by clear and convincing evidence. As far as the kinds of evidence that should be introduced, the petitioner should proffer percipient testimony about the child, the birth parents, the caregiver(s) and the safety and stability of the child's future home, expert testimony concerning the best interests of the child and as to the particulars of the specific risk categories which are sought to be proven, medical documentation if relevant, the Family Code § 7851 report by the social services agency, and any other evidence which may be relevant.

a) No Burden to Prove "Detriment"

More specifically, with the exception of Family Code § 7828(a)(2) mentioned above, Family Code § 7807 expressly provides that Family Code §§ 3020, 3022, and 3040-3043 do not apply in a proceeding to declare a child free from parental custody. Thus, the petitioners need not prove that the placement of the child with a parent would be detrimental to the child. Family Code §§ 3020, 3022, and 3040-3043 apply in child custody disputes in marital dissolution proceedings, and provide that a child may not be placed with a non-parent unless it is proved that placement with a parent would be detrimental to the child. Family Code § 7807 also mentions the inapplicability of Family Code § 3409, which is part of the Uniform Child Custody Jurisdiction and Enforcement Act, which is discussed in Chapter 9.

One exception to this rule is Family Code § 7828, in which the statute requires the detriment standard to be applied. Another exception is provided in Family Code § 7891(a)(3), where the child at issue is at least 10 years old, as discussed below.

b) In Most Cases, No "Reunification Plan"

Unlike dependency cases, there is no indication in Family Code § 7800, et seq. that a reunification plan has to be ordered, with the possible exceptions of Family Code §§ 7827 and 7828 cases, which involve mental and developmental disabilities. However, there may be an existing reunification plan in place where the child is the subject of an ongoing dependency case.

8. Conduct of the Hearing

a) Closed Trial-like Hearing

Family Code § 214 provides that any proceeding under the Family Code shall be conducted in private in the discretion of the judge. However in *In re Jay R.*, (1983) 150 Cal.App.3d 251, the court stated that the natural parent has the right to cross-examine witnesses, which indicates that live witness testimony is a requirement, meaning that a trial-like hearing is to be conducted, at least where the petition is contested. On the other hand, there is no express provision of Family Code § 7800, et seq., requiring there to be a trial.

b) Court Shall Act in the Child's Best Interests.

Under Family Code § 7890, "the court shall consider the wishes of the child, bearing in mind the age of the child, and shall act in the best interest of the child." In order to carry out this mandate, certain logistical rules are provided, as explained below.

c) The Participation of the Child at the Hearing

Family Code § 7861 provides that "the child shall not be present in court unless the child so requests or the court so orders." In addition, Family Code § 7891(a) requires the court to conduct an in-chambers interview of a child who is at least 10 years old, unless (as stated in Family Code § 7891(c)) the child is the child is unable to attend due to illness or incapacity. The failure to interview the child could constitute reversible error. (*Neumann v. Melgar* (2004)
121 Cal.App.4th 152.) Furthermore, Family Code § 7891(b) requires the court to inform the child of the child's right to attend the hearing, but also states that counsel for the child may waive the hearing in chambers by the court.

For those children who are required to be interviewed by the court in chambers, Family Code § 7891(a) states that the child shall be heard by the court on at least the following matters: (1) the feelings and thoughts of the child concerning the "custody proceeding," (2) the feelings and thoughts of the child about the child's parent or parents, and (3) the child's preference as to custody, according to Family Code § 3042, which states that the court shall give "due weight to the wishes of the child."

As far as "testimony" from the child is concerned, the testimony is taken in chambers pursuant to Family Code § 7892(a) and (b). These provisions also allow the court to exclude the child's parents or guardians from chambers at that time, as long as the parent's attorney is present in chambers while the child is testifying, and there is clear and convincing evidence that either (1) testimony in chambers is necessary to ensure truthful testimony, (2) the child is likely to be intimidated by a formal courtroom setting, or (3) the child is afraid to testify in front of the child's parent or parents.

d) Separate Counsel for the Child?

Family Code § 7861 states that the court shall consider whether the interests of the child require the appointment of counsel. In interpreting the predecessor to Family Code § 7861, the Supreme Court in *In re Richard E.*, (1978) 21 Cal.3d 349, stated that counsel must be appointed for the child at the commencement of the proceedings absent an immediate showing upon which the court can exercise its discretion against making an appointment, and the failure to appoint counsel in such circumstances is error. However, if the court fails to appoint counsel for the child, the party aggrieved by the final order in the Family Code § 7800 case has the burden under *Richard E.* to show that the non-appointment of counsel was prejudicial, since such error is not reversible per se. Additionally, the court in *Adoption of Jacob C.*, (1994) 25 Cal.App.4th 617, held that the failure to appoint separate counsel for the child is an issue that can be raised on appeal by the birth parent, even though the separate counsel would not be representing the birth parent's interests.

The Supreme Court in *Richard E.* reasoned that a proceeding to free a child from parental custody is "directed to challenges against the parent not against the child. It is thus likely that in a particular case the court will be fully advised of matters affecting the minor's best interests, and little assistance may be expected from independent counsel for the minor in furtherance of his client's or the court's interests. However, when the court finds a child has separate interests not protected in the contest between parents and a petitioner, the court must exercise its discretion by appointing separate counsel."

e) No Specific Requirement for Written Findings

There is nothing in Family Code § 7800, et seq. which requires the court to issue findings of fact or a statement of decision. In *In re Randi D.*, (1989) 209 Cal.App.3d 624, the court held that in a proceeding to free the child from the father's custody, the trial court did not have to make detailed findings of fact to substantiate its ruling that an abandonment had occurred, since there was no request for findings or a statement of decision. However, based on the *Randi D.* opinion, it would appear that a statement of decision is required where a party makes the standard request under Code of Civil Procedure § 632.

9. Finality / Appealability of a Family Code § 7800 Order

Family Code § 7894(a) states "An order and judgment of the court declaring a child free from the custody and control of a parent or parents under this part is conclusive and binding upon the child, upon the parent or parents, and upon all other persons who have been served with citations by publication or otherwise as provided in this part." Family Code § 7894(b) then provides, "After making the order and judgment, the court has no power to set aside, change, or modify it." It would appear that these statutes would be interpreted in the same way that *David B. v. Superior Court*, (1994) 21 Cal.App.4th 1010, enforced the finality provisions of what is now Welfare & Institutions Code § 366.26(i).

Family Code § 7894(c) provides a right to appeal from the order and judgment freeing the child from parental custody. Where the case is on appeal, the case of *In re Bryce C.*, (1995) 12 Cal.4th 226, provides that Family Code § 7895 permits but does not require the appellate court to appoint counsel for the respondent birth parent. In addition, Family Code § 7893(b) states that no adoption petition may be heard until the natural parents' appellate rights have been exhausted, however this does not preclude the filing of an adoption petition.

E. Custody of Child upon Granting of Family Code § 7800 Order

1. Guardianship or Agency Custody

Under Family Code § 7893(a), if the court declares the child free from parental custody, the court shall (1) appoint a guardian for the child, or (2) refer the child to a licensed adoption agency for adoptive placement at the request of the CDSS or a licensed adoption agency, or where the court finds it is in the child's best interest to do so. Where the court places the child in agency custody, Family Code § 7893(b) makes the agency responsible for the care of the child, and gives the agency the right to exclusive custody and control over the child until a petition for adoption has been granted, and precludes the filing of a petition for guardianship without the consent of the agency.

Based on Family Code § 7893(a)(1), it would appear that the court has the authority to convert an existing temporary guardianship (which had been instituted to perfect the petitioner's "interested person" status under Family Code § 7841) to a permanent guardianship so as to facilitate an independent adoption. Where an agency's involvement in the adoption case appears appropriate, the petitioner could request that the child be placed in (or remain in) agency custody under Family Code § 7893(a)(2), assuming the agency consents.

2. Filing of the Adoption Petition Following the Order

Family Code § 7893(b)(3) states that no petition for adoption may be heard until the natural parents' appellate rights have been exhausted. Importantly, Family Code § 7893(b)(3) only precludes the hearing of the adoption petition, and not the filing of the adoption petition, meaning that the petition could be filed as soon as the petitioners have standing to file the adoption petition. For example, the prospective adoptive parents may file a petition for independent adoption under Family Code § 8802(a)(1)(D) if they have been the child's guardians for the requisite amount of time, or they may file an agency adoption petition under Family Code § 8704(b) if the court referred the child to an agency, who placed the child with the prospective adoptive parents for purposes of adoption.

IV. OTHER GROUNDS FOR DISPENSING WITH NEED FOR CONSENT

A. Desertion

Family Code § 8606(c) states that the birth parent's consent to the adoption is not necessary "where the birth parent has deserted the child without provision for identification of the child." As to what constitutes a "desertion," there is no definition in the Family Code. Penal Code § 271 makes it a crime for a parent to desert his or her child with the intent to abandon, but there is no statute defining "desertion" in the criminal context. There is also judicial interpretation of what constitutes a "desertion" within the meaning of Penal Code § 271 or Family Code § 8606(c). The definitions in Black's Law Dictionary and Webster's New Collegiate Dictionary indicate that "desertion" would involve a decision to forego and abandon all parental rights and duties. Also, Family Code § 8606(c) requires the petitioner to prove there was a failure to provide for identification of the child.

By the separate inclusion of "desertion" in Family Code § 8606(c), it would appear that the singular act of desertion, even without evidence of a six-month abandonment as described in Family Code § 7822 or a one-year abandonment as stated in Family Code § 8604, would constitute grounds to dispense with the parent's consent to the adoption. There is also nothing in the code as to where or how the desertion must occur, or how long the desertion must last, in order to constitute grounds for dispensing with the deserting parent's consent to the adoption.

B. Voluntary Surrender of the Child

Family Code § 8606(b), which is another statute which dispenses with the need for the birth parent's consent, requires evidence of the voluntary "surrender" of the child "in a judicial proceeding in another jurisdiction." There is no statute like Family Code § 8606(b) dealing with a "surrender" that occurred in California. In many states, such as Tennessee, an in-court consent to an adoption is treated as a "surrender" (Tenn. Code Ann. § 36-1-111), and one would have to resort to the law of that "other jurisdiction" to determine whether a "surrender" has occurred.

In California, Health & Safety Code § 1255.7 and Penal Code § 271.5 deal with the voluntary surrender of physical custody of the surrendering party's child to an employee on duty at a public or private hospital emergency room. This is not a "judicial proceeding" as described in Family Code § 8606(b). Penal Code § 271.5 and Health & Safety Code § 1255.7 involve children who are 72 hours old or younger. Also, Penal Code § 271.5 provides for immunity from criminal prosecution in certain instances where there has been a valid surrender. The statutes also provide that the hospital personnel have a duty to immediately render all necessary medical care to the child, and to contact the local social services agency, who is to have custody of the child. Therefore, a "surrender" in California is completed without a "judicial proceeding."

Welfare & Institutions Code § 300(g) allows for the termination of the rights of a parent who has voluntarily surrendered physical custody of the child to a health care facility pursuant to Health & Safety Code § 1255.7 if "the child has not been reclaimed within the 14-day period" specified in Health & Safety Code § 1255.7(e). As stated above, only a governmental agency may seek to terminate rights pursuant to Welfare & Institutions Code § 300(g).

SUBSTANTIVE RIGHTS OF THE ADOPTIVE PARENT 7

In this chapter:

In 1990 in the Ukraine, Oksana Baiul became an orphan at age 13. She was taken in as a foster child by Galina Zmievskaya, a prominent figure-skating coach, but who lived in a crowded three-room apartment. At age 17 at the 1994 Olympics, Ms. Baiul won a gold medal in ladies' singles.

I. CARETAKING RIGHTS OF FOSTER AND ADOPTIVE PARENTS

A. The Foster Parent's Rights and Authority

County social services agencies are generally authorized to place dependent children in licensed foster homes for the purpose of caring for the child, while Health & Safety Code § 1501, et seq. and the dependency laws permit county social services to delegate these placement functions to licensed private foster care agencies. These county agencies and licensed private agencies have the authority to investigate applicants, their families, their homes and their vehicles, and to certify such applicants as qualified foster parents, who then open up their homes and provide for the actual care of foster children. As explained in this chapter, the intent of the state and federal foster care laws is to provide a safe environment for the child in a way that most closely resembles a family home, while still allowing for supervision by the agency and the juvenile court.

Since an individual providing such care takes the role of "parent" in the eyes of many such foster children, and since that individual is the responsible adult who is with the child more than any other person, it is necessary to give that adult a certain degree of parental authority. For example, if the child wanted to join a youth baseball league, the foster parent could sign the necessary applications and waivers on behalf of the child. Health & Safety Code § 1530.6 states that, subject to CDSS regulations and the orders of the juvenile court, the foster parent has authority to give consent on behalf of the child, except in matters pertaining to marriage, entry into the armed forces, and extraordinary medical and dental treatment (e.g., medical treatment beyond mere immunizations, physical examinations, and X-rays). As another example, Vehicle Code § 17701 provides that a foster parent may sign the child's application for a driver's license.

1. Right to Parental Training by the Agency

Very briefly, according to Health & Safety Code §§ 1521.5 and 1529.1, and Welfare & Institutions Code § 903.7, county agencies and licensed private agencies are to issue foster parent certifications to individuals only after providing them training as to how to care for children who have come from a broken home. The training informs the prospective foster parents about how the neglect that the children experience in their home may have impacted them psychologically, physically and developmentally, the emotional impact of the ordeal that the child experiences in the detention process (from being taken from their home, to the housing at the temporary care facility away from the parents, to the transfer to the foster home, etc.), the logistics of the visitation schedule between the child and the birth parent, and many other aspects of the foster care process. The training also informs the prospective foster parents about the kinds of resources that the agency will provide to them as they care for children with special needs and the authority and rights they have with respect to raising the child.

2. Right to Payment for Services

Under Welfare & Institutions Code §§ 11401 and 11460, and 42 U.S.C. § 670, foster care providers are to be paid a "per child per month" rate in return for their care and supervision of the child placed with them, as long as the child qualifies under the provisions of the Aid to Families with Dependent Children-Foster Care program, which is true in the large majority of cases. Typically, the payments average approximately $500 per month per child, and are calculated according to various schedules. Under 8 U.S.C. §§ 1613 and 1632, these payments cannot be denied based on the national origin of the child.

As to tax issues, 26 U.S.C. § 131 provides that these payments for the foster care of the child do not constitute "income." In addition, the foster parent is entitled under 26 U.S.C. §§ 32 and 152 to claim the foster child as a "dependent" for purposes of claiming an exemption on the federal income tax return.

3. Right to Receive a "Health and Education Summary"

Welfare & Institutions Code § 16010(c) states that not later than 30 days after the initial foster care placement of the child, and within 48 hours of each subsequent foster care placement, the child protective services agency shall provide the caretaker with the child's current health and education summary. Welfare & Institutions Code § 16010(a) states that the health and education summary shall include information concerning "the names and addresses of the child's health, dental, and education providers, the child's grade level performance, the child's school record, assurances that the child's placement in foster care takes into account proximity to the school in which the child is enrolled at the time of placement, a record of the child's immunizations and allergies, the child's known medical problems, the child's current medications, past health problems and hospitalizations, a record of the child's relevant mental health history, the child's known mental health condition and medications, and any other relevant mental health, dental, health, and education information concerning the child determined to be appropriate by the Director of Social Services."

Importantly, the foster parent is not statutorily entitled to access to the medical records themselves, unlike the rights of a prospective adoptive parent. Also, issues may arise as to the extent of the information provided regarding the child's "known medical problems," "current medications" and "past health problems," in light of the privacy rights of the birth parents. On the other hand, the birth parent's privacy rights may be superseded by the State's compelling interest in safeguarding the child's health care rights and the foster parent's authority under Health & Safety Code § 1530.6 to consent to immunizations.

4. Right to Maintain Discipline in the Home

Welfare & Institutions Code § 16001.9(a)(2) and (12) state that the foster child may not be subjected to corporal punishment or locked in a room. However, the foster parent has the authority to administer certain lesser kinds of discipline, such as time-outs (requiring the child to sit in a corner of an unlocked room quietly for a certain period of time), withholding of television privileges, withholding of dessert, etc. It must be remembered that an unfortunately high percentage of foster children have a history of being subjected to cruel and abusive treatment.

5. Right to Privacy and Security

As set forth in Health & Safety Code § 1536, no state or local agency shall disclose the names, addresses, or other identifying information of foster parents. The statute states that this privacy right is enforceable under the Information Practices Act of 1977 (Civil Code § 1798, et seq.). It also states that the intent behind Health & Safety Code § 1536 is to encourage the recruitment of foster parents, to protect their personal privacy, and to preserve the security and confidentiality of the placements in foster homes. Where a birth parent has a history of violence, many times the child may be put in a "confidential placement," wherein the birth parents are not informed of the foster parents' names or addresses.

6. Respite Care

Generally, according to 42 U.S.C. § 629A(a)(1)(D) and 629B(a)(5)(A), the state's plan for providing child welfare services must include a provision for respite care to be made available to foster parents and foster children. In essence, one purpose of respite care is to give the foster parents temporary relief from the stress of providing foster care, in light of the difficulties which may be encountered in nurturing an abused or neglected child.

7. Right to Family and Medical Leave from Employment

Briefly, under 29 U.S.C. § 2612(a)(1)(B), an employee who for more than 12 months has been with a company that employs at least 50 people is entitled to a total of 12 workweeks of unpaid leave during any 12-month period for the placement of a child with the employee for adoption or foster care. Similar provisions are set forth at Government Code § 12945.2. Also, Labor Code § 233 allows a foster parent to use accrued sick leave to attend to a foster child's illness. There are various conditions to such family and medical leave, and the statutes should be consulted directly.

8. Medical Issues

Under 42 U.S.C. §§ 603 and 1396, and Welfare & Institutions Code § 14132, the foster child is entitled to certain specifically-described health care benefits under Medi-Cal. Also, 42 U.S.C. § 603 states that the foster child is to remain eligible for Medi-Cal after the adoption.

Health & Safety Code § 1530.6 gives foster parents the authority to give consent to nonextraordinary medical care such as immunizations, physical examinations and X-rays. There is no case law interpreting Health & Safety Code § 1530.6. Also, Education Code § 56055(a)(1) states that the foster parent may consent to nonemergency medical services for the child, mental health treatment services, and occupational or physical therapy services.

In order to be prepared in the event that extraordinary medical care is needed, such as emergency surgery, the foster parents and foster care agency should make prior arrangements for a 24-hour hotline in which the foster parents may telephone the agency or the county to obtain the needed consent for medical treatment. As to those persons who are relatives of the child and who have custody of child in long term foster care, Welfare & Institutions Code § 366.27 provides that the court may give such individuals the right to consent to all medical care.

9. Right to Make Educational Decisions

Education Code § 48200 is the compulsory school attendance law that applies to every child between ages of 6 and 18. Furthermore, under Education Code §§ 48204(a) and 48852, the agency placing the foster child must notify the local school district of the placement. Welfare & Institutions Code § 16001.9(a)(13) then states that foster children have the right "to attend school and participate in extracurricular, cultural, and personal enrichment activities."

On the other hand, Education Code § 56055 provides that, except where limited by court order, a foster parent shall have the rights related to the foster child's education that a parent would have under federal law (specifically 20 U.S.C. § 1400, et seq., and 34 C.F.R. § 300.1, et seq.). In addition, Education Code § 56055(a)(1) states that "The foster parent may represent the foster child for the duration of the foster parent-foster child relationship in matters relating to identification, assessment, instructional planning and development, educational placement, reviewing and revising an individualized education program, if necessary, and in all other matters relating to the provision of a free appropriate public education of the child. . . . The foster parent may sign any consent relating to individualized education program purposes."

a) Religious Schools

Under Welfare & Institutions Code § 16001.9(a)(22), foster children have the right "to have fair and equal access to all available services, placement, care, treatment, and benefits, and to not be subjected to discrimination or harassment on the basis of actual or perceived race, ethnic group identification, ancestry, national origin, color, religion, sex, sexual orientation, gender identity, mental or physical disability, or HIV status." Further, Welfare & Institutions Code § 16001.9(a)(10) gives foster children the right to participate in the "religious activities" of their choice. Education Code §§ 48222 and 48854 recognize the foster child's right to attend private school. It thus appears that a foster child may choose to attend a private religious school.

However, the California Constitution (at Art. IX, § 8) states, "No public money shall ever be appropriated for the support of any sectarian or denominational school, or any school not under the exclusive control of the officers of the public schools; nor shall any sectarian or denominational doctrine be taught, or instruction thereon be permitted, directly or indirectly, in any of the common schools of this State." This provision would not appear to negate Education Code § 51511, which states that references to religion and religious literature, art or music shall not be excluded from the schools, as long as they are not used in the teaching of religion.

If the foster parents cannot afford the private school's tuition, Education Code § 56157(a) states that foster children are to be first considered for public school, but that if those programs are not appropriate, the foster child shall be given the opportunity to attend a "nonpublic, nonsectarian school," which is to be made available under Education

Code §§ 56365 and 56366. The definition at Education Code § 56034 of a "nonpublic, nonsectarian school" does not specify what is meant by "nonsectarian." According to Section 3001(w) of Title 5 of the California Code of Regulations, " 'Nonsectarian' means a private, nonpublic school or agency that is not owned, operated, controlled by, or formally affiliated with a religious group or sect, whatever might be the actual character of the education program or the primary purpose of the facility and whose articles of incorporation and/or by-laws stipulate that the assets of such agency or corporation will not inure to the benefit of a religious group."

b) Homeschooling

In *Jonathan L. v. Superior Court*, (2008) 165 Cal.App.4th 1074, the court held that a child who had been declared a dependent of the juvenile court did not have an absolute right to be homeschooled by his birth parent. The family in *Jonathan L.* had a history of dependency court proceedings involving charges of physical abuse, neglect, and failure to prevent sexual abuse. After the two youngest children were declared dependent due to the abuse and neglect of their siblings, their attorney sought an order that they be sent to school, rather than educated at home by their mother, so that they would be in regular contact with individuals having a statutory duty to report abuse and neglect. (See Penal Code §§ 11165(a)(1) & (3), and 11166.) The dependency court denied the motion. The children's attorney then sought a writ of mandate.

The *Jonathan L.* court acknowledged that the U.S. Supreme Court has held that parents possess a constitutional right to direct the education of their children. In *Wisconsin v. Yoder*, (1972) 406 U.S. 205, which dealt with a fact pattern very much like a homeschooling situation, the U.S. Supreme Court held that a state cannot compel a parent with sincere religious beliefs to cause his or her child to attend public school rather than receive private religious schooling. (See also *Pierce v. Society of the Sisters*, (1925) 268 U.S. 510.) In *Peterson v. Minidoka County Sch. Dist.*, (9th Cir. 1997) 118 F.3d 1351, the court held that the Free Exercise of Religion Clause guarantees that a parent may homeschool his children, and that this right superseded an Idaho statute requiring compulsory attendance in a public, private or parochial school. Notably, *Yoder* may apply to California's foster care and school systems through Education Code § 56055(a)(1), which gives the foster parent the same federally-guaranteed rights concerning the education of the foster child that a natural parent would have. (*In re Shinn*, (1961) 195 Cal.App.2d 683, which preceded the 2001 enactment of Education Code § 56055, held that homeschooling is not a valid alternative to school attendance merely because the child is of superior intelligence.)

However, *Jonathan L.* also holds that California law permits a dependency court to issue reasonable orders for the care of a dependent child, including orders limiting the right of the parents to make educational decisions for the child. The court concluded that an order requiring a dependent child to attend school outside the home in order to protect that child's safety is not an unconstitutional violation of the parents' right to direct the education of their children, since such an order passed strict scrutiny. The *Jonathan L.* court also expressly stated that the "constitutionality of any other restriction on home schooling, including a prohibition on home schooling in its entirety, is not before us in this case." There is no other case, statute or regulation directly addressing whether a foster child may be homeschooled. It does not appear that *Jonathan L.* completely forecloses on the right to homeschool a foster child, especially if that is the most beneficial educational placement for a traumatized child.

In *Cassady v. Signorelli*, (1996) 49 Cal.App.4th 55, the court acknowledged that "a parent might normally have the right to provide home schooling," but it also held that a child could be ordered to attend public school where the homeschooling parent is found to be inadequate for the task. As far as the foster child's Welfare & Institutions Code § 16001.9(a)(13) right to "attend school," this provision is not narrow enough to exclude homeschooling, nor specific enough to deprive the child of the right to be homeschooled. As to the "religion" aspect of *Peterson* and *Hooks*, it is well-established that the receipt of benefits under a government program (such as the receipt of benefits by the foster child and the foster parent) cannot be conditioned upon giving up constitutionally-protected rights. See, *Binet-Montessori, Inc. v. San Francisco Unif. Sch. Dist.*, (1979) 98 Cal.App.3d 991.

10. Insurance Issues

a) Liability for Harm to the Child

According to Health & Safety Code § 1527, et seq., the State Foster Family Home and Small Family Home Insurance Fund has been established for the purpose of paying, on behalf of foster family homes and small family homes, the claims of foster children, their parents, guardians, or guardians ad litem resulting from occurrences peculiar to the foster-care relationship and the provision of foster-care services. The fund would appear to cover injuries the child might suffer in the foster home, but provides a $300,000 cap on recovery. In *Rodriguez v. Superior Court*, (2003) 108 Cal.App.4th 301, the court reiterated that under Health & Safety Code § 1527.3(a), the Fund does not cover injuries arising out of "a dishonest, fraudulent, criminal, or intentional act." *Rodriguez* also applied the Health & Safety Code § 1527.6(d) rule that presentation of a claim to the Fund is a precondition to filing suit against a foster parent.

b) Liability for Damage Caused by the Child

Under Insurance Code § 676.7(a), an insurer may not deny an application for insurance, or cancel insurance, solely because the applicant or policyholder is engaged in foster home activities in a licensed foster home. In addition, Insurance Code § 676.7(b) provides that insurance coverage with respect to a foster child shall be the same as that provided for a natural child. However, Insurance Code § 676.7(b) also states that unless specifically provided in the policy, there is no coverage expressly provided in the policy for bodily injury arising out of the operation or use of any motor vehicle, aircraft, or watercraft owned or operated by, or rented or loaned to, a foster parent. It appears this statute would provide that if the foster parent was operating a vehicle which was involved in an auto accident in which the foster child was injured, the foster child cannot collect from the foster parent's insurance policy.

As for indemnity by the county, Government Code § 23004.4 states that a county may provide insurance coverage for foster parents against any third-party liability for injuries or damages resulting from the acts or omissions of a child placed with the foster parent by the county. As to those children who are placed by private agencies, the foster parent and the agency are of course authorized to enter into an agreement as to indemnity, and decide between themselves how to allocate the risk of loss caused by the child.

B. The Foster Child's Rights

The foster child's rights under Welfare & Institutions Code § 16001.9(a) are,

(1) to live in a safe, healthy, and comfortable home,

(2) to be free from abuse or corporal punishment,

(3) to receive adequate and healthy food and clothing,

(4) to receive medical, dental, vision, and mental health services,

(5) to be free of the administration of medication or chemical substances, unless authorized by a physician,

(6) to contact family members, unless prohibited by court order, and social workers, attorneys, foster youth advocates and supporters, court appointed special advocates and probation officers,

(7) to visit and contact siblings, unless prohibited by court order,

(8) to confidentially contact the CDSS or the State Foster Care Ombudsperson,

(9) to make and receive confidential telephone calls and send and receive unopened mail, unless prohibited by court order,

(10) to attend religious services and activities of his or her choice,

(11) to maintain a bank account and manage personal income, consistent with the child's age and developmental level, unless prohibited by the case plan,

(12) to not be locked in any room, building, or facility premises, unless placed in a community treatment facility,

(13) to attend school and participate in extracurricular, cultural, and personal enrichment activities, consistent with the child's age and developmental level,

(14) to work and develop job skills at an age-appropriate level that is consistent with state law,

(15) to have social contacts with people outside of the foster care system, such as teachers, church members, mentors, and friends,

(16) to attend Independent Living Program classes and activities if he or she meets age requirements,

(17) to attend court hearings and speak to the judge,

(18) to have storage space for private use,

(19) to review his or her own case plan if he or she is over 12 years of age and to receive information about his or her out-of-home placement and case plan, including being told of changes to the plan,

(20) to be free from unreasonable searches of personal belongings, and

(21) to confidentiality of all juvenile court records consistent with existing law.

Some of these statutorily guaranteed rights of the foster child would seem to add to the foster parent's authority. For example, in light of the child's right to emergency medical services, if the foster care agency or governmental social services agency was not available to provide authority for medical care, the foster parent would be the logical individual to authorize all necessary emergency medical treatment for the child.

On the other hand, other statutory rights guaranteed to foster children appear to diminish the foster parent's authority. For example, the child's right "to have storage space for private use" and to be "free from unreasonable searches of personal belongings" would appear to detract from the foster parent's right to know what is in the house. (Furthermore, Welfare & Institutions Code § 16001.9(a)(18) and (20) would appear to raise Fourth Amendment issues as to who has authority to consent to a warrantless search by the police.)

C. The Prospective Adoptive Parent's Right –

1. – to Form Bonds with the Child during Placement

In *Adoption of Baby Girl B*., (1999) 74 Cal.App.4th 43, which involved an independent adoption, the court held that a prospective adoptive parent with whom a child has been placed for adoption has a liberty interest in continued custody, meaning that a prospective adoptive parent has a constitutional right to notice and "a full hearing" before the adoptive placement can be terminated, at least in the absence of urgent or emergency circumstances. This liberty interest is the substantive right which is entitled to be protected by procedural safeguards.

2. – to Medical Information on Child and Birth Parents

As to agency adoptions, Family Code § 8706(a) states, "An agency may not place a child for adoption unless a written report on the child's medical background and, if available, the medical background of the child's biological parents so far as ascertainable, has been submitted to the prospective adoptive parents and they have acknowledged in writing the receipt of the report." Family Code § 8706(b) provides that the report as to the child's background shall contain all current medical reports on the child, psychological evaluations, and scholastic information, as well as all known information regarding the child's developmental history and family life, as well as all other "known diagnostic information." Family Code § 8608(a) and related CDSS regulations require the agency to ask the birth parents questions that are "designed to elicit information on any illness, disease, or defect of a genetic or hereditary nature."

Family Code § 8706(c) states that "the biological parents may provide a blood sample." On the other hand, there is nothing in this statute that *requires* them to provide a blood sample, nor that makes the adoption contingent upon the obtaining of a blood sample, nor that gives the adoptive parents the right to obtain a blood sample from the birth parents. As to the confidentiality of the birth parent's blood sample, please refer to Chapter 12

As discussed in Chapter 3, Family Code § 8608 and 22 California Code of Regulations § 35095(b) give the prospective adoptive parents the right to be informed of the medical histories of the child and the birth parents. In addition, Family Code § 8801.3(c)(4) gives the adoptive parents the right to be informed of the basic health and social history of the birth parents. As set forth in Chapter 10, the prospective adoptive parents have the right to withdraw the petition if the birth parents and/or the agency representatives fail to comply with their duty to disclose.

Michael J. v. Los Angeles County Dept. of Adoptions, (1988) 201 Cal.App.3d 859, suggests that a county agency must expend resources "to competently investigate the total medical condition of an obviously blemished child," unless there is a disclosure to the prospective adoptive parents of the reasons for not knowing the child's true medical condition. It is not clear that this duty to conduct a medical investigation applies to private adoption agencies, nor is it clear that this duty extends to governmental adoption agencies of smaller counties that do not have public hospitals. However, it would appear that *Michael J.* holds that where there are facts about the child's medical condition that an agency could discover with a routine physical examination, the failure to conduct the examination and disclose such facts would constitute grounds for a damages award.

3. – to Authorize Medical Care for the Child

Family Code § 8607 expressly contemplates that the prospective adoptive parents who receive the child pursuant to the signing of the AD-22 form will have the right to authorize medical care for the child. In addition, the language of most adoptive placement agreements (see for example the AD 924 form) states that the prospective adoptive parents have the agreed duty to obtain medical care for the child when necessary. This obviously gives the prospective adoptive parents the corresponding right to authorize medical care for the child when necessary. Of course, if the prospective adoptive parents intend to take the child to an out-of-county medical facility to obtain that health care, consent to travel out-of-county needs to be arranged.

D. The New Adoptive Parent's Parental Rights

1. Scope of Parental Control

Parental rights are recognized in principle as being constitutionally protected, but the specific rights protected by the constitution are the subject of case-by-case analysis. On the other hand, there are certain parental rights that are recognized by statute, including the following:

a) Location of Residence

A "custodial parent" has the right to change the residence of the child, subject to the power of the court to restrain a removal that would prejudice the rights or welfare of the child. (Family Code § 7501(a).) The statute does not distinguish between a custodial parent's natural child or adopted child. If there is no third party having visitation rights and there is no post-adoption contact agreement in effect, the adoptive parents are free to take to the child anywhere in the world. If there is a third party having rights with respect to the child, then the adoptive parents should be prepared to justify the move. The issues arising in an interstate "move away case" are dealt with in Chapter 9 of this book.

As for an international "move away case," the courts have also held, "except for those of considerable means, any relocation to another continent is likely to represent a de facto termination of the non-moving parent's rights to visitation and the child's rights to maintain a relationship with that parent. Thus, when a relocation would have this practical effect, before allowing the move-away a trial court should require the moving parent to satisfy the burden of showing the termination of those rights would be in the best interests of the child." (*In re Marriage of Condon* (1998) 62 Cal.App.4th 533, 547.) On the other hand, *Condon* also held that where a modification of a child custody/visitation arrangement is involved, the party opposing the planned migration has the burden, pursuant to *In re Marriage of Burgess*, (1996) 13 Cal.4th 25, to "prove" or "show" that the children will suffer no "detriment" by the requested order.

b) Educational Decisions

California's education statutes give a public school student's parent the right to be notified about many different things, and the right to decide whether to consent to certain matters. (See, Education Code § 56056.) In addition, Education Code § 56055 provides that even a foster parent has authority to make certain decisions concerning the education of the foster child. (See also 34 C.F.R. § 300.20 and 20 U.S.C. § 1400.) It should also be noted that a parent is statutorily responsible for the actions of the child related to damage or theft of school property. (See, Education Code § 48904.) None of these statutes differentiate between the student's natural parent or adoptive parent.

c) Medical Decisions

A parent has the right to be consulted about the rendition of medical care to his or her child. Also, Health & Safety Code § 1530.6 provides that a foster parent has decision-making authority to consent, on behalf of the child, to medical and dental treatment that is not considered "extraordinary." The parent's consent rights are limited in certain circumstances by the child's right of privacy. (See *Planned Parenthood of Southeastern Pennsylvania v. Casey*, (1992) 505 U.S. 833.) These statutes and cases do not appear to differentiate between the person's natural or adopted children.

d) Right to Enter into Contracts on Child's Behalf

A parent may contract on behalf of his or her child. See, *Hohe v. San Diego Unif. Sch. Dist.*, (1990) 224 Cal.App.3d 1559, 1565, where the court held that a written release of liability signed by a father on his child's behalf was valid and enforceable. In addition, *Doyle v. Giulucci*, (1965) 62 Cal.2d 606, upheld an agreement signed by the parent to arbitrate the child's medical malpractice claim. See also, *Bolanos v. Khalatian*, (1991) 231 Cal.App.3d 1586 [mother's agreement to arbitrate claims against obstetrician held to be binding on child]; and *Herbert v. Superior Court*, (1985) 169 Cal.App.3d 718 [father's agreement to arbitrate was held to be binding on his children in a subsequent wrongful death action arising from the father's death].

e) Disciplining the Child

The second paragraph of Welfare & Institutions Code § 300(j) states that the Legislature does not intend to unnecessarily disrupt the family, inappropriately intrude into family life, prohibit the use of reasonable methods of parental discipline, or prescribe a particular method of parenting. In addition, according to Welfare & Institutions Code § 300(a), the definition of "serious physical harm" to a child, which normally allows a social services agency to detain the child and commence dependency proceedings against the parents, expressly excludes "reasonable and age-appropriate spanking to the buttocks where there is no evidence of serious physical injury." Moreover, Health & Safety Code § 1531.5 provides that no one shall be denied the right to be a foster parent on the grounds that he or she engaged in non-abusive corporal punishment of his or her own child. (However, Welfare & Institutions Code § 16001.9 prohibits foster parents from using corporal punishment on a foster child.)

2. Benefits Based on Legal Recognition of New Family

a) Workers' Compensation Death Benefits

Labor Code §§ 4701 and 4702 provides that when a worker dies because of a work-related injury, the employer must pay to the worker's "dependents" a death benefit and an amount sufficient to cover reasonable burial expenses. Labor Code § 4703.5 specifically states that the death benefits are payable to "totally dependent minor children." The court in *State Compensation Ins. Fund v. WCAB*, (1993) 19 Cal.App.4th 1645, held that this phrase "include[s] all minor dependent members of a decedent's household, including grandchildren."

In practical terms, without documentation of a parent-child relationship between the claimant and the deceased worker, such as a birth certificate or an adoption order, the child would have to present competent evidence proving that he or she was actually "dependent" upon the worker. The "dependent" element of the statute is a factual question that one would expect the employer's workers compensation insurance carrier to contest in such a case. Importantly, in *Granell v. Industrial Accident Commission*, (1944) 25 Cal.2d 209, the Supreme Court held that a woman who married the worker after the injury and before the worker's death was not a "dependent" within the meaning of what is now Labor Code § 4701.

b) Income Tax Matters

Federal tax law allows taxpayers to claim an exemption for certain kinds of dependents, such as the taxpayer's children. Under 26 U.S.C. § 152(b)(2), the definition of "dependent" includes a legally adopted child of the taxpayer (and a child who is a member of the taxpayer's household, if placed with him or her by an authorized placement agency for legal adoption by such taxpayer), or a foster child of the taxpayer (if such child satisfies the requirements of 26 U.S.C. § 152(a)(9) with respect to the taxpayer). California tax law is very similar. (See Revenue & Taxation Code § 17056.)

c) Property Tax Questions

Revenue & Taxation Code § 62(m) and (n) state that a "change in ownership" that would allow a reassessment of the value of land for property tax purposes (see Cal. Const., Art. XIIIA [Proposition 13]), does not include a transfer of title of the child's residence to the child from that child's parent or guardian. Under Revenue & Taxation Code § 62(n), the exempt transfer could be by way of "will, devise or inheritance," and could be to an adult child. Unlike the workers' compensation statutes, there does not appear to be any such exemption for a transfer to a mere "dependent" child with whom the transferor did not have a legally recognized parent-child relationship.

d) Insurance and Employee Benefit Issues

After the adoption, state law gives the child "family member" status for purposes of coverage under the adoptive parents' health insurance plans. (See Government Code § 22754, Insurance Code §§ 10121, 10198.7, 10708, and Health & Safety Code § 1357.06, et seq.) Also, the express terms of many major employee benefit plans refer to adopted children as beneficiaries. (*Rovira v. AT&T*, (S.D.N.Y. 1993) 817 F.Supp. 1062.)

Where the health plan is governed by the Employment Retirement Income Security Act ("ERISA"), as most are, the adopted child appears to be entitled to be treated as a "family member" of the adoptive parents. However, while the definition of "relative" in ERISA includes "lineal descendants" (see 29 U.S.C. § 1002(15)), it makes no express reference to adopted children. If the language of the health plan employs ERISA definitions, one could argue that an adopted child is indeed a "lineal descendant" under the laws of intestate succession, which is true in California, all other states and most nations.

As for automobile insurance, the standard liability policy defines "family member" as including an adopted child. Also, California law requires automobile liability insurance policies to provide coverage where the insured vehicle is being operated by an individual with the insured person's permission. (Insurance Code § 11580.1(b).) This permissive user law applies without regard to whether there is a family relationship between the named insured and the driver.

However, auto insurance usually does not provide liability coverage for bodily injury claims made by a "relative" of the named insured. Thus, if the prospective adoptive parent negligently caused an accident while driving the child to court for the hearing on the adoption petition, the child could make a bodily injury claim against the prospective adoptive parent's policy; but not if the accident occurred after the order is issued.

3. Duration of Parental Control

Under Family Code § 7505, the authority of a parent ceases on the occurrence of any of the following events: (a) the appointment, by a court, of a guardian of the person of the child, (b) the marriage of the child, or (c) the child attaining the age of majority.

4. Termination of Prior Parental and Visitation Rights

Although *Sharon S. v. Superior Court*, (2003) 31 Cal.4th 417, held that the parties may agree to waive the Family Code § 8617 termination of the birth parent's rights in the adoption, the parties "presumably" intend the prior parental relationship to cease. This termination of rights has several ramifications. Specifically as to visitation, Family Code § 3102(c) states that, except in the instance of a stepparent or grandparent adoption, any visitation rights that were granted prior to the adoption are automatically terminated by the adoption order. (Visitation rights are discussed more fully in Chapter 8.) As to other parental rights the natural parent had, those are likewise terminated in a general sense by Family Code § 8617.

However, in contrast to these rules recognizing the severance of the prior parental ties, the court in *People v. Mora*, (1996) 51 Cal.App.4th 1349, held that a man could be convicted for violating Penal Code § 273.5, which states it is a felony to commit an injurious battery upon the "mother or father of his or her child," even if the parental rights of both that man and the victim had been statutorily terminated prior to the alleged battery. An injurious battery is normally a misdemeanor under Penal Code § 243(a) where such family relationships are not at issue.

II. THE CHILD'S EARNINGS AND PROPERTY

A. Parents' Entitlement to the Child's Services and Earnings

Under Family Code § 7500(a) and (b), the minor child's mother and "presumed" father (see Chapter 3 of this book) are equally entitled to the child's services and earnings, and if one such parent is dead, is unable or refuses to take custody, or has abandoned the child, the other parent is entitled to the child's services and earnings. An exception to the rule is set forth at Family Code § 7500(c), which deals with the minor child's services or earnings related to the types of contracts described in Family Code § 6750, which covers artistic or creative services, the sale of certain kinds of intellectual property, sports contracts and services as an "extra" or background performer. (In these situations, it is common for the parties to agree to have all of the child's earnings paid into a trust account.) As to logistics, Family Code § 7503 requires the minor's employer to pay the minor's earnings to the minor, until the minor's parent or guardian entitled to the earnings gives the employer notice that the parent or guardian claims the earnings.

B. No Parental Control over the Child's "Property"

Under Family Code § 7502, the parent, as such, has no legal control over the property of the child. However, this statute does not preclude a parent from exercising control over property in the capacity of a trustee, or as a guardian of the estate of the child. (This practice guide will not cover guardianships of the estate, which is adequately covered in other practice guides.)

III. "SPECIAL NEEDS" CHILD – ADOPTION ASSISTANCE PROGRAM

In order to encourage the adoption of those minors who have come to be known as "special needs" children, the California Legislature has established the Adoption Assistance Program ("AAP"), which is codified at Welfare & Institutions Code §§ 16115, et seq. The AAP allows the adoptive parents to receive continuing financial aid for the child, even after the adoption is finalized. Welfare & Institutions Code § 16120 also states that a child is eligible for AAP benefits if all seven of the specified conditions are met. As set forth in Welfare & Institutions Code § 16120(c), one of those conditions is that AAP benefits are only available where the adoption was commenced as an agency adoption. The conditions are as follows:

(a) Adoptive placement of the child without financial assistance is unlikely because (1) of membership in a sibling group that should remain intact, or by virtue of race, ethnicity, color, language, age of three years or older, or parental background of a medical or behavioral nature that can be determined to adversely affect the development of the child, or (2) the child has a mental, physical, emotional, or medical disability, including even a Family Code § 4512(a) developmental disability, that has been certified by a licensed professional competent to make an assessment and operating within the scope of his or her profession.

(b) The need for adoption subsidy is evidenced by an unsuccessful search for an adoptive home to take the child without financial assistance, as documented in the case file of the prospective adoptive child. However, this requirement shall be waived when it would be against the best interest of the child because of the existence of significant emotional ties with prospective adoptive parents while in the care of these persons as a foster child.

(c) The child is the subject of an agency adoption, and was either (1) under the supervision of a county welfare department as the subject of a legal guardianship or juvenile court dependency, (2) relinquished for adoption to a licensed California private or public adoption agency, or the department, and would have otherwise been at risk of dependency as certified by the responsible public child welfare agency, or (3) committed to the department under Family Code §§ 8805 or 8918 (which deal with the denial of a prior adoption petition).

(d) The child is under 18 years of age, or under 21 years of age and has a mental or physical handicap that warrants the continuation of assistance.

(e) The adoptive family is responsible for the child pursuant to the terms of an adoptive placement agreement or a final decree of adoption and has signed an adoption assistance agreement.

(f) The adoptive family is legally responsible for the support of the child and the child is receiving support from the adoptive parent.

(g) The department or the county responsible for determining the child's AAP eligibility status and for providing financial aid, and the prospective adoptive parent, prior to or at the time the adoption decree is issued by the court, have signed an adoption assistance agreement that stipulates the need for, and the amount of, AAP benefits.

Welfare & Institutions Code § 16120(h) goes on to state that a child is eligible for AAP benefits if the child previously received such benefits with respect to a prior adoption and the child is again available for adoption because the prior adoption was dissolved and the parental rights of the adoptive parents were terminated or because the child's adoptive parents died. (See also Family Code § 8525.)

Details regarding the amounts of the AAP payments, for both recurring expenses as well as the non-recurring expenses incurred during the adoption litigation, are set forth in Welfare & Institutions Code §§ 16115, et seq. and at 22 California Code of Regulations §§ 35325, et seq. In short, the amounts presently range from approximately $300 to $400 per month per child. In addition, post-adoption counseling services may be made available for the child.

As far as federal tax law is concerned, 26 U.S.C. § 137(a), (b) and (c) exclude from the taxpayer's gross income any payments the taxpayer receives from his or her employer under a qualified adoption assistance program. While 26 U.S.C. § 131 states that "foster care payments" are not considered to be income, it is not clear that the AAP qualifies for this gross income exclusion. But see 26 U.S.C. § 23 and 42 U.S.C. §§ 602, 603 and 622.

IV. THE ADOPTIVE PARENT'S RIGHT TO ANNUL THE ADOPTION

Under Family Code § 9100(a), the court may set aside an adoption that was completed in California if the adoptive parents prove that the child "shows evidence of a developmental disability or mental illness as a result of conditions existing before the adoption to an extent that the child cannot be relinquished to an adoption agency on the grounds that the child is considered unadoptable, and of which conditions the adoptive parents or parent had no knowledge or notice before the entry of the order of adoption." The court may not set aside an adoption that was not completed in California. (*In re Adoption of M.S.* (2010) 181 Cal.App.4th 50 [no jurisdiction to annul a Ukrainian adoption by a California couple even though a private California agency helped complete the intercountry adoption].) Family Code § 9100(a) requires the petition to set aside the adoption to be filed "with the court that granted the adoption petition."

In *Department of Social Welfare v. Superior Court*, (1969) 1 Cal.3d 1, the Supreme Court allowed such an action to proceed on grounds that consisted of the alleged "feeblemindedness of the child." The court also upheld the operation of the statutory language on the ground that code sections were "remedial provisions" for which a "liberal construction" "will tend to encourage adoptions in the first instance and thus will promote the welfare of children available for adoption." This book will not attempt to answer the moral questions surrounding the exercise of that right, but will simply discuss what the present status of California law is on this subject.

A. Conduct of the Proceedings and the Burden of Proof

The Supreme Court also held in *Department of Social Welfare v. Superior Court*, (1969) 1 Cal.3d 1, that the trial court has broad discretion to decide whether to grant the relief sought by the petitioners. It also interpreted the provisions that are now codified at Family Code § 9100(c), which requires the CDSS to file a full report with the court within 60 days after the receiving notice from the court clerk, and held that the court is to consider the marital status of the adopting parents, the welfare of the child, the extent, nature, duration and prognosis as to the disability of the child, the degree of dependency, the length of time of the adoption, the bonds of affection or attachment, and should the decree be set aside as to the petitioning parent only, the sources of support for the child which may be available thereafter to the nonpetitioning parent.

Interestingly, Family Code § 9100(a) does not require the petitioner to prove that the adoption agency knew or should have known of the child's latent condition. This aspect of the law was pointed out in *Adoption of Kay C.*, (1991) 228 Cal.App.3d 741, which held that the predecessor to Family Code § 9100(a) required neither fraud, mistake nor undue influence as grounds to set aside a decree of adoption. In this respect, a Family Code § 9100(a) action is much more expansive than a natural parent's action to set aside the adoption due to the lack of notice, lack of consent or the existence of constructive fraud in the relinquishment.

In *Kay C.*, the adoptive parents had not been given one of the therapist's reports which spoke of doubt about the success of an adoption, nor were the adoptive parents told of the social worker's doubts that an adoption would be successful. After the adoption, the adoptive parents discovered that the child was "psychotic" and had "exhibited a lot of paranoid/delusional thinking and some thought disorder." Apparently, the county knew to some degree that the child had psychological disorders, but failed to fully disclose this knowledge to the adoptive parents prior to the issuance of the adoption order. As a result of the psychological problems, the child became so incorrigible that she had to be put in residential placement at a group home for emotionally disturbed children. The adoptive parents had also participated in family therapy and made efforts at reunification, but all to no avail.

B. The Child's Rights

The court in *Adoption of Kay C.*, (1991) 228 Cal.App.3d 741, held that the adoption could be set aside even over the objection of the child, since the child has no fundamental right or liberty interest in her relationship with her adoptive parents, apparently because the statutes giving rise to the adopted child's rights define the contours of those rights, which include the adoptive parents' right to rescind the adoption in certain circumstances. The court also held that the statute does not violate due process or equal protection. Likewise, in *Department of Social Welfare v. Superior Court*, (1969) 1 Cal.3d 1, the court held that such a petition could proceed on behalf of one adoptive parent over the objection of the other adoptive parent.

Under Family Code § 9101(a), if the court grants the petition to set aside the adoption, the court must direct the district attorney, the county counsel, or the county welfare department to take appropriate action under the Welfare & Institutions Code. Family Code § 9101(b) places the responsibility for the child's support on the county where the adoption was originally issued, meaning that the child will more than likely enter the foster care system. While the set aside petition is pending, the court is permitted under Family Code § 9101(a) to make any order relative to the care, custody, or confinement of the child that the court sees fit.

C. Statute of Limitations

Under Family Code § 9100(b), a petition to set aside the adoption order must be filed with the superior court "within five years after the entry of the order." Based on the fact that the annulment statute deals with latent developmental conditions in the child, it does not appear that the "discovery" rule that is applicable to other statutes of limitations would apply here.

V. CLAIM FOR NEGLIGENCE, FRAUD OR NONDISCLOSURE

A. Fraud and Concealment Claims

1. Agency's Duty to Disclose

In *Michael J. v. Los Angeles County Dept. of Adoptions*, (1988) 201 Cal.App.3d 859, the court held that the adopting parents may sue a county adoption agency for damages for fraud for failing to disclose that it knew or had reason to know of a medical condition of the child that made it unlikely that the child would be adopted, even in light of the Government Code §§ 818.8 and 822.2 immunities that protect governmental entities from damages suits. It held that those statutes dealt with immunity in the context of "commercial transactions," which did not include the adoption process. *Michael J.* also holds that the county agency must make a good faith full disclosure of material facts as to existing or past conditions of the child's health.

The facts in *Michael J.* were that from the time the child was born, he had a large "port wine stain on his upper torso and face." The county agency made written disclosures to the adoptive parents about the port wine stain, informed them that the stain would not fade away, and stated that the child was classified as "hard to place." However, the adoptive parents adopted the child anyway. Ten years after the adoption, the child began to suffer from seizures, and was diagnosed as suffering from Sturge-Weber Syndrome, a congenital degenerative nerve disorder. In the case, an expert submitted a declaration stating that the development of medical science was advanced enough at the time of the adoption that it should have been known that the port wine stain was an indicator of the presence of Sturge-Weber Syndrome. Importantly, the case came to the appellate court upon the grant of a summary judgment motion, meaning that the court was not permitted to weigh the conflicting expert testimony on these medical questions in determining whether there was a triable issue of material fact.

2. Proving "Reasonable Reliance"

As for establishing the elements of fraud, the plaintiff must prove that he or she reasonably relied on the defendant's representations or nondisclosures. On this point, the *Michael J.* court held that the "reliance" element was satisfied. It partially distinguished the case of *Richard P. v. Vista Del Mar Child Care Service*, (1980) 106 Cal.App.3d 860, holding that the adoptive parents in *Richard P.* did not properly plead "reliance," since their independent investigation of the child's medical condition established a disregard of the defendant's representations in that respect. However, in *Mi-*

chael J., the adoptive parents took the child to an independent pediatrician several times before the adoption, which would likewise appear to negate the "reliance" element. There was also no actual evidence in *Michael J.* that the county agency actually knew, prior to the adoption, that the child had Sturge-Weber Syndrome, or knew that large birthmarks were an indicator of Sturge-Weber Syndrome. On the other hand, the non-disclosure in *Michael J.* was further evidenced by the county's "doctor's refusal to make a prognosis," and the county's failure to disclose that doctor's refusal, making it easier to prove the adoptive parents' reliance on the false state of facts put forward by the county.

3. Statute of Limitations

The lawsuit in *Michael J. v. Los Angeles County Dept. of Adoptions*, (1988) 201 Cal.App.3d 859, which sought damages for fraud, was filed more than ten years after the adoption order was issued, but less than three years after the fraud was discovered. The statute of limitations for a fraud claim is Code of Civil Procedure § 338(d), which allows suit to be brought within three years after discovery of the fraud. Also, the Family Code § 9100(b) five-year rule, by its own terms, only deals with an action to set aside an adoption, and not a damages cause of action. This appears to be why *Michael J.* does not discuss the statute of limitations.

B. Negligence Causes of Action against Agencies

1. Governmental Immunity

The court in *Michael J. v. Los Angeles County Dept. of Adoptions*, (1988) 201 Cal.App.3d 859, held that the Government Code immunities did protect county adoption agencies from suit by the adopting parents for damages for *negligence*. The *Michael J.* court agreed with *Richard P. v. Vista Del Mar Child Care Service*, (1980) 106 Cal.App.3d 860, to the extent that *Richard P.* held, for public policy reasons, that there is no cause of action for an adoptive parent for negligence or breach of warranty against an adoption agency.

Both courts agreed that "an adoption agency cannot be made the guarantor of an infant's future good health and should not be liable for mere negligence in providing information regarding the health of a prospective adoptee," since natural parents have no such guarantee upon the birth of the child. In addition, there are dozens of other statutory and judicially-created immunities that may apply, and a full explanation of those immunities is beyond the scope of this adoption law book.

2. Possible Liability of Private Agencies

Where a private agency has impaired a constitutional right belonging to a prospective adoptive parent, *Scott v. Family Ministries*, (1976) 65 Cal.App.3d 492, *Tyler v. Children's Home Society*, (1994) 29 Cal.App.4th 511, and other cases treat private adoption agencies as if they were public entities. On the other hand, at present, there is no case stating whether or not the immunities of the California Government Code extend to private adoption agencies in an action for compensatory money damages. In other words, it is unclear whether a private agency could be sued for negligence, strict liability or breach of contract. On the other hand, Family Code § 8638 specifically allows a person to seek damages against "adoption facilitators," who are only involved in independent adoptions, but there is no such specific provision directed against adoption agencies.

C. Attorney Malpractice

There is nothing in the adoption statutes or case law which diminishes or expands the attorney's duties to his or her clients. However, there is also nothing in the statutes which makes the attorney for the birth parent or for the prospective adoption parents responsible for the conduct of persons outside the attorney's control, or responsible to a non-client.

As to the issue of causation, the typical contested adoption proceeding, more so than most other types of cases, will usually involve a wide variety of parties and other affected persons, all of whom have widely divergent interests. Therefore, in light of this high number of "variables" in the case, an error or omission by the attorney may not be deemed to be a substantial factor in the causation of the precise harm which the aggrieved party suffered.

VI. FEDERALLY ENFORCEABLE CIVIL RIGHTS

Very briefly, pursuant to 42 U.S.C. § 1983, a person may recover damages where there has been (1) government action (2) under color of law (3) which caused (4) a deprivation of federally protected rights, and (5) pecuniary damages. See *Carey v. Piphus*, (1978) 435 U.S. 247. As explained in Chapter 5, *Scott v. Family Ministries*, (1976) 65 Cal.App.3d 492, holds that a private agency may be deemed a government entity for purposes of the Establishment of Religion Clause. On the other hand, the issue of whether the conduct of a private agency may give rise to a federal civil rights claim is a question of federal law, and it is unclear if *Scott* would apply to a 42 U.S.C. § 1983 claim against a private agency. As for a civil rights claim against the CDSS, a state agency may not be sued on a 42 U.S.C. § 1983 cause of action (*Will v. Michigan Dept. of State Police*, (1989) 491 U.S. 58), but a local agency can be. (*Owen v. City of Independence, Mo.* (1980) 445 U.S. 622.) As for "color of law," conduct that is undertaken ostensibly pursuant to the California statutes or the CDSS regulations would satisfy this element.

As for identifying the federally protected right at issue, one may look to federal statutes or the U.S. Constitution. The U.S. Supreme Court has also held that even apart from Section 1983, a damages action may be based solely on a violation of constitutional rights. See, *Bivens v. Six Unknown Named Agents of the Federal Bureau of Narcotics*, (1971) 403 U.S. 388. As for statutes, the U.S. Supreme Court held in *Wilder v. Virginia Hosp. Assoc.*, (1990) 496 U.S. 498, that in order to bring a Section 1983 action pursuant to a violation of the United States Code, the plaintiff must show that (1) Congress enacted the provision for the benefit of individuals such as the plaintiff, (2) the right assertedly protected by the statute is not so vague and amorphous that its enforcement would strain judicial competence, and (3) the statute must unambiguously impose a binding obligation on the States.

The practitioner must also be aware that there are many different immunities that may be asserted as a defense. Federal civil rights litigation is extremely complicated, and a full exposition of this subject is well beyond the scope of this adoption law book.

A. Enforcement of Rights Arising from the Constitution

The courts have recognized that the Due Process Clause protects the "liberty interest" in family unity and privacy. See, *Moore v. City of East Cleveland*, (1977) 431 U.S. 494, where the court held that an extended non-nuclear family unit could not be penalized by a housing ordinance, and *In re Jasmon O.*, (1994) 8 Cal.4th 398, which upheld the rights of the prospective adoptive parents in the context of dependency proceedings. In *In re David B.*, (1979) 91 Cal.App.3d 184, the court held that "a parent's interest in the care, custody and companionship of a child is a 'liberty' to be ranked among the most basic of civil rights."

Courts have also recognized that children have a fundamental, independent right to belong to a family unit. See *Smith v. City of Fontana*, (9th Cir. 1987) 818 F.2d 1411, and *Duchesne v. Sugarman*, (2d Cir. 1977) 566 F.2d 817, which held that the right to maintain the family relationship involves the "interest of the parent in the companionship, care, custody and management of his or her children, and of the children in not being dislocated from the emotional attachments that derive from the intimacy of daily association with the parent."

However, in *Smith v. Organization of Foster Families*, (1977) 431 U.S. 816, the court held that while "no one would seriously dispute that a deeply loving and interdependent relationship between an adult and a child in his or her care may exist even in the absence of blood relationship," there is no recognized liberty interest in the continuation of a foster family unit as such. Likewise, the court in *Adoption of Kay C.*, (1991) 228 Cal.App.3d 741, recognized that "the status created by adoption has far greater implication than that established by the foster care arrangement." *Kay C.* also held that the adopted child's liberty interest in the continuation of the family unit only extended as far as the statutes and the "contractual arrangements" which allowed for the creation of that family unit. In *Kay C.*, the court held that the child did not have a liberty interest in the continuation of adoptive status where the adoptive parents were seeking to have the adoption annulled pursuant to a statutory procedure which existed at all relevant times.

B. Discrimination Statutes

Discrimination on the basis of race, color, or national origin is strictly prohibited under 42 U.S.C. § 1996b, which is directed at "persons" or "governments" that are "involved in adoption." Under 42 U.S.C. § 1996b(1)(A), an adoption agency may not "deny to any individual the opportunity to become an adoptive or a foster parent, on the basis of the race, color, or national origin of the individual, or of the child, involved." According to 42 U.S.C. § 1996b(1)(B), an adoption agency may not "delay or deny the placement of a child for adoption or into foster care, on the basis of the race, color, or national origin of the adoptive or foster parent, or the child, involved." The express language of 42 U.S.C. § 1996b(2) then makes such a violation actionable pursuant to 42 U.S.C. § 2000d et seq. There is one exception: 42 U.S.C. § 1996b(3) expressly state that its provisions are not applicable in cases subject to the Indian Child Welfare Act (25 U.S.C. § 1901 et seq.), which is explained in Chapter 9 of this book.

C. The Adoption Assistance and Child Welfare Act

1. The General Nature of the AACWA Funding Program

The Adoption Assistance and Child Welfare Act ("AACWA") is designed to promote the adoption of children in foster care systems. The AACWA is dispersed in various parts of the U.S. Code, such as 42 U.S.C. §§ 620-628, 670-679a, 996b, 1613, 1632 and 1320a-2. One AACWA provision is 42 U.S.C. § 673B, wherein incentives are provided for foster child adoptions. In addition, 42 U.S.C. § 602 provides that a state must comply with AACWA in order to qualify for Medi-Cal grants.

Briefly, the AACWA is a federal grant program in which the State of California participates (see Welfare & Institutions Code §§ 10601.2, 11155.5 and 16177; *Cynthia D. v. Superior Court* (1993) 5 Cal.4th 242, 246; *In re Christina A.* (2001) 91 Cal.App.4th 1153), and receives hundreds of thousands of federal tax dollars per year in exchange for its agreement to follow a "plan" for its foster care program that conforms to certain federally-enacted criteria. In Welfare & Institutions Code § 16131, the California Legislature stated its intent "to conform state statutes to recently enacted federal legislation, the Adoption and Safe Families Act of 1997 (Public Law 105-89) [see 42 U.S.C. §§ 671 and 674, and related statutes] and to reinvest any incentive payments received through implementation of the federal act into the child welfare system in order to provide increased postadoption social services, as needed, to families who have adopted children from the public foster care system."

2. The AACWA's Requirements for the State Plan

The AACWA expresses Congress's intent to provide federal funding to states on the condition that those states conform their child welfare procedures to certain standards. For example, in order for a state to be eligible for grants under the AACWA, the state plan "shall," under 42 U.S.C. § 671(a)(16), provide for the development of a case plan and a case review system for each foster child. "Case review system" is defined at 42 U.S.C. § 675(5) as "a procedure for assuring" (among other things) that, (a) each foster child is placed in an appropriate family-like setting that is consistent with the best interests of the child (42 U.S.C. § 675(5)(A)); (b) the status of each child is reviewed no less than once every six months in order to determine such things as the projected likely date by which the child may be placed for adoption or legal guardianship should reunification efforts fail (see 42 U.S.C. § 675(5)(B)); (c) procedural safeguards will be applied to assure each foster child that a permanency hearing will be held "no later than 12 months after the date the child is considered to have entered foster care" (i.e., the date of the first judicial finding that the child was subjected to child abuse or neglect), which hearing shall determine the permanency plan for the child that includes whether and when (if applicable) the child will be returned to the parent, or placed for adoption or guardianship, unless it is in the child's best interests not to (42 U.S.C. § 675(5)(C); and

45 C.F.R. § 1355.20 [defining "permanency hearing"]); and (d) in the case of a child who has been in foster care under the responsibility of the State for 15 of the most recent 22 months, the State shall petition to terminate the parental rights of the child's parents unless it is in the child's best interests not to; and, concurrently, to identify, recruit, process, and approve a qualified family for an adoption (see 42 U.S.C. § 675(5)(E)).

Participating States are required under 42 U.S.C. § 622(b)(10)(B)(ii) and (iii) to "operate" a case review system as defined in 42 U.S.C. § 675(5) for each foster child, and a service program designed to help children be placed for adoption or guardianship, and to be returned to the natural parents only where safe and appropriate. In addition to a "case review system," 42 U.S.C. § 671(a)(16) requires that "case plans" be formulated for each child. The phrase "case plan" is defined at 42 U.S.C. § 675(1)(E) as a written document, which includes, among other things, "In the case of a child with respect to whom the permanency plan is adoption or placement in another permanent home, documentation of the steps the agency is taking to find an adoptive family or other permanent living arrangement for the child, to place the child with an adoptive family, a fit and willing relative, a legal guardian, or in another planned permanent living arrangement, and to finalize the adoption or legal guardianship. At a minimum, such documentation shall include child specific recruitment efforts such as the use of State, regional, and national adoption exchanges including electronic exchange systems."

3. Obtaining Federal Approval of the State Plan

Under 45 C.F.R. § 1356.20(c), states must undergo a detailed six-step process in order to receive federal approval of the state plan. Under 45 C.F.R. § 1356.20(d)(1), all matters affecting the state plan, such as state statutes, rules, regulations, interpretations, and court decisions, must be submitted to the authorized representative of the U.S. Secretary of Health and Human Services to determine if they meet federal requirements and policies. Also, according to 45 C.F.R. § 1356.71(a)(3), states are only subject to review of their plans once every three years. However, 45 C.F.R. § 1356.20(f) provides that once a state plan has been approved, it must remain in effect as state law, until amendments are required by Congress or the Secretary. In fact, 45 C.F.R. § 1356.20(e)(7) provides that if the state plan is amended, the amendments are treated as the submission of a new state plan for consideration by the Secretary.

4. The Child's Cause of Action under the AACWA

The courts have held that the AACWA (particularly 42 U.S.C. §§ 622(b)(10)(B), 671(a)(16) and 675, are enforceable by way of private right of action under 42 U.S.C. § 1983. See, *Brian A. ex rel. Brooks v. Sundquist*, 149 F.Supp.2d 941, 949 (M.D.Tenn. 2000); *Marisol A. by Forbes v. Giuliani*, 929 F.Supp. 662, 683 (S.D.N.Y. 1996), *aff'd*, 126 F.3d 372 (2d Cir. 1997); *Jeanine B. by Blondis v. Thompson*, 877 F.Supp. 1268, 1283-1285 (E.D.Wis. 1995). These courts held that the AACWA was enacted by Congress for the intended benefit of the foster children, and that the children therefore had enforceable rights arising by virtue of the state's agreement to accept the federal grants. The recent Congressional amendments to the AACWA (i.e., 42 U.S.C. § 1320A-2) essentially mandate this result. On the other hand, the Congressional amendments preserve, yet isolate, the holding of *Suter v. Artist M.*, (1992) 503 U.S. 347, which held that there is no private right of action for an alleged violation of 42 U.S.C. § 671(a)(15).

As an example of a possible violation, in *Renee J. v. Superior Court*, (2002) 96 Cal.App.4th 1450, the California Legislature's amendments to Welfare & Institutions Code § 361.5(b)(10), which govern reunification with birth parents, were held to operate retroactively, even though the statutes did not say they operated retroactively. However, the *Renee J.* court interpreted the amendments as being retroactive, but did not first receive the necessary federal approval for this change in California's plan of state foster care laws.

FAMILY RELATIVES AND OTHER THIRD PARTIES 8

In this chapter:

William Jefferson Blythe, III was born three months after his father died. He was raised by his grandparents for four years while his mother was in nursing school. When she returned, she married Roger Clinton, who adopted the young man a few years later. Young William later became President, and signed the Adoption Assistance and Child Welfare Act ("AACWA") into law.

I. STEPPARENT ADOPTIONS AND DOMESTIC PARTNER ADOPTIONS

According to Family Code § 8548, a "stepparent adoption" is "an adoption of a child by a stepparent where one birth parent retains custody and control of the child." Stepparent adoptions are provided for in Family Code §§ 9000, et seq. These statutes allow a stepparent adoption to be completed by the spouse of the custodial parent, or by the domestic partner of the custodial parent, as explained below.

In *Adoption of Christopher S.*, (1987) 197 Cal.App.3d 433, the court held that since the child must already be in the custody of one of the parents, the child is not being completely placed with nonparents in a stepparent adoption. Therefore, custody is not directly at issue, and there is no need to prove that depriving the noncustodial parent of rights will be detrimental to the child. The *Christopher S.* court also held that a presumed father must consent to the adoption, or a court must rule that his consent is unnecessary, and that the intended stepparent adoption is in the best interests of the child.

A. Major Issues Presented in Most Stepparent Adoptions

1. Legally Recognized Relationship to Custodial Parent

Family Code § 9000(a) states that a stepparent desiring to adopt a child of the stepparent's spouse may for that purpose file a petition in the county in which the petitioner resides. As for a stepparent desiring to adopt the child of the stepparent's domestic partner, Family Code § 9000(b) states the same rule. There is no other provision for a "stepparent adoption," meaning that the petitioning stepparent must have one of two specific kinds of relationships with the custodial parent. (See also Family Code § 8548.)

a) Spousal Relationship

In *Adoption of Bird*, (1960) 183 Cal.App.2d 140, the court held that the stepparent seeking to adopt the child must be the lawful spouse of the child's existing parent, and not a mere unmarried cohabitant. As stated in *Elden v. Sheldon*, (1988) 46 Cal.3d 267, California has abolished the concept of "common law marriage," but still "recognizes common law marriages entered into in states in which such marriages are valid."

b) Domestic Partnership Relationship

Under Family Code § 297, domestic partnerships are legally recognized, and Family Code § 9000(b) states that an adult may file a petition to adopt the child of his or her domestic partner. Based on the location of Family Code § 9000(b) among the stepparent adoption statutes, and based on Family Code § 9000(g), it would appear that all of the procedures for a stepparent adoption are the same regardless of sexual orientation.

Family Code § 297 defines "domestic partners" as "two adults who have chosen to share one another's lives in an intimate and committed relationship of mutual caring," and who (1) have a common residence, (2) agree to be jointly responsible for each other's basic living expenses incurred during the domestic partnership, (3) are not married or a member of another domestic partnership, (4) are not related by blood in a way that would prevent them from being married to each other in this state, (5) are at least 18 years of age, (6) are either of the same sex or at least one of whom is over the age of 62, (7) are both capable of consenting to the domestic partnership, (8) have not previously filed a Declaration of Domestic Partnership as with any other person with the Secretary of State that has not been terminated, and (9) have together filed a Declaration of Domestic Partnership with the Secretary of State.

2. The Consent of the Non-Custodial Parent

a) Whether There Is a Need for Consent

Family Code § 9006(b) states that "if a birth parent has refused to give the required consent, the adoption petition shall be dismissed." On the other hand, there is always a question in any adoption as to whether a "birth parent's" consent is "required." To answer this question, one must determine whether that birth parent has consent rights under Family Code §§ 8604-8605 and the Uniform Parentage Act (see Chapter 3), and/or whether there are grounds to dispense with that birth parent's consent pursuant to Family Code §§ 7800, et seq. or 8606 (see Chapter 6). Family Code § 9003(d) provides that a birth parent who is a minor has the right to sign a consent for the adoption of the birth parent's child and the consent is not subject to revocation by reason of the minority.

b) The Manner of Taking Consent

Family Code § 9003(a) provides that in a stepparent adoption, the consent of either or both birth parents shall be signed in the presence of a county clerk, probation officer, qualified court investigator, or county welfare department staff member of any county of this state. After that, that government employee shall immediately file the consent with the clerk of the court, and notify the probation officer or the county welfare department. Under Family Code § 9003(b), if the noncustodial parent is outside this state at the time of signing the consent, the consent may be signed before a notary.

c) The Right to Give Consent

According to Family Code § 9003(c), the consent, when reciting that the person giving it is entitled to sole custody of the child and when acknowledged before the county clerk, probation officer, qualified court investigator, or county welfare department staff member, is prima facie evidence of the right of the person signing the consent to the sole custody of the child and of that person's sole right to consent. It appears that the phrase "entitled to sole custody of the child" refers to the consenting birth parent's right vis-à-vis third parties, but not as against the custodial parent. The stepparent adoption consent forms on the CDSS web site do not have this language.

d) Required Notice Regarding Inheritance Rights

Family Code § 9004 states that in a stepparent adoption, the form prescribed by the CDSS for the consent of the birth parent shall state: "If you and your child lived together at any time as parent and child, the adoption of your child by a stepparent does not affect the child's right to inherit your property or the property of other blood relatives." This is discussed further in Chapter 1. The CDSS forms do contain this language.

If there is difficulty in obtaining, or in dispensing with the need for, the consent of the non-custodial parent, that person might be persuaded to give consent through the device of a post-adoption contact agreement pursuant to Family Code §§ 8616.5 and 9000(f), which are discussed in more detail below. On the other hand, the existence of a post-adoption contact agreement does not change the status of the consenting parent's intestate inheritance rights, or absence thereof, as the case may be.

e) Withdrawal of Non-Custodial Parent's Consent

Under Family Code § 9005(a), the birth parent's consent to the stepparent adoption may not be withdrawn except with court approval, upon written request by that birth parent. When the written request is received by the court, Family Code § 9005(b) requires the court clerk to set the matter for hearing and give at least 10 days notice to the prospective adoptive parent, the birth parent or parents, and the probation officer, qualified court investigator or county welfare department. The probation officer, court investigator or county welfare department must then (under Family Code § 9005(c)) file a full report with the court before the hearing, and appear at the hearing to represent the child's interests. The hearing is held in chambers with a court reporter under Family Code § 9005(d), wherein the parties may appear in person or by counsel.

Also according to Family Code § 9005(d), if the court finds that withdrawal of the consent to adoption is reasonable in view of all the circumstances and that withdrawal of the consent is in the child's best interest, the court shall approve the withdrawal of the consent. Otherwise the court shall withhold its approval. Consideration of the child's best interest shall include, but is not limited to, an assessment of the child's age, the extent of bonding with the prospective adoptive parent, the extent of bonding or the potential to bond with the birth parent, and the ability of the birth parent to provide adequate and proper care and guidance to the child.

Family Code § 9005(d) also provides that if the court approves the withdrawal of consent, the adoption proceeding shall be dismissed. Regardless of the court's decision, the court's order is appealable under Family Code § 9005(e) "in the same manner as an order of the juvenile court declaring a person to be a ward of the juvenile court."

Based on the language of Family Code § 9005, it would appear that this procedure for "withdrawal" of consent is limited to stepparent adoption proceedings. In addition, it does not appear that the provisions of Family Code § 8814.5 (see Chapter 3), allowing for a "revocation" of consent within 30 days, would apply in a stepparent adoption case. Family Code § 8814.5 is in the chapter of the Family Code entitled "independent adoptions," and only covers consents taken pursuant to Family Code §§ 8801.3 and 8814, both of which assume that the child was or is or will be in an adoptive placement. In a stepparent adoption, there is no "placement" because the child remains with the custodial parent at all times.

3. Age of the Adopting Stepparent

Family Code § 8601(a) and (b) state that the adopting parent must be at least 10 years older than the child, except as allowed by court order. However, Family Code § 8601(b) states that if the court is satisfied that the adoption is in the best interests of the parties and is in the public interest, the court may approve the adoption without reference to the parties' ages.

4. Child's Best Interests and Investigation of the Parties

As with any adoption, the child's best interests are of paramount concern. In order to properly ascertain the child's best interests, Family Code § 9001(a) requires the probation officer, qualified court investigator, or county welfare department to investigate each case of stepparent adoption. The statute also provides that a court may not make an order of adoption until after that agency has filed its report and recommendation and they have been considered by the court.

5. Consent of the Child Over 12 Years Old

In all adoptions, Family Code § 8602 requires the child's consent, if the child is over 12 years old. If a child under 12 years old refuses to consent to the adoption, that should be taken into account when evaluating whether the adoption is in the child's best interests. There is no legal requirement for the consent of any sibling or step-sibling.

6. Matters Normally Not at Issue in Stepparent Adoptions

a) No Home Study

Family Code § 9001(b) states that unless ordered by the court, no home study is required of the petitioner's home in a stepparent adoption. The agency conducting the investigation or any interested person may request the court to order a home study or the court may order a home study on its own motion. Family Code § 9001(c) defines "home study" as a physical investigation of the premises where the child is residing.

b) No Need for Placement or Guardianship

As explained above, since the child is already in the legal and physical custody of the spouse or domestic partner of the person seeking to adopt, the child is not "placed" for adoption. The petitioner typically already lives with the child, with the custodial parent's consent. Also, the only requirement for standing to file the petition is to be the custodial parent's spouse or domestic partner. Therefore, there is no need for an adoptive placement or a guardianship.

B. Second Parent Adoptions

1. Statutory Context for Second Parent Adoptions

In *Sharon S. v. Superior Court*, (2003) 31 Cal.4th 417, the California Supreme Court held that the parties may petition for an independent adoption in order to effectuate a "second parent adoption," i.e., where the birth parent has waived his or her right under Family Code § 8617 to have his or her parental relationship terminated by the adoption. In other words, the prospective "second parent" literally petitions to adopt a child that is in the custodial parent's actual custody.

However, second parent adoptions do not proceed as a stepparent adoption pursuant to Family Code § 9000, et seq., meaning that the petitioner need not show that he or she is the spouse or domestic partner of the custodial birth parent. *Sharon S.* literally involved a petition for an independent adoption under Family Code § 8800, et seq., and explained the jurisdictional aspects of second parent adoptions generally.

2. Interstate Enforcement of Second Parent Adoptions

As explained in Chapter 9, an adoption decree is in fact a judgment which, pursuant to the Full Faith and Credit clause of Article IV of the U.S. Constitution, is entitled to be judicially recognized in all 50 states, as long as the court that issued the adoption decree had jurisdiction to do so. As stated in *Sharon S. v. Superior Court*, (2003) 31

Cal.4th 417, the California Legislature has impliedly given its courts the jurisdiction to approve a second parent adoption. On the other hand, there is no published decision in California analyzing the notion of a second parent adoption in the context of the Full Faith and Credit clause.

In *Russell v. Bridgens*, (Neb. 2002) 647 N.W.2d 56, the Nebraska Supreme Court was faced with this question arising from a Pennsylvania adoption. Nebraska law expressly disapproves of second parent adoptions, while Pennsylvania allows them. In *Russell*, a second parent adoption was completed in Pennsylvania, and some time later, a controversy arose in which enforcement of that adoption was required in Nebraska. *Russell* held that the Full Faith and Credit clause required the Nebraska courts to recognize the second parent adoption.

3. Joint Parent Adoptions

The court in *Nancy S. v. Michele G.*, (1991) 228 Cal.App.3d 831, stated, "We see nothing in these provisions that would preclude a child from being jointly adopted by someone of the same sex as the natural parent." However, *Nancy S.* was not an adoption case. On the other hand, the California Supreme Court's opinion in *Sharon S. v. Superior Court*, (2003) 31 Cal.4th 417, appears to incorporate this statement from *Nancy S.* as the law of the state. The *Sharon S./Nancy S.* rule would therefore permit two unrelated individuals to complete an independent adoption or an agency adoption of a child that is in the custody of another. One should note that the majority opinion in *Sharon S.* does not appear to make any express reference to sexual orientation, meaning that an unmarried heterosexual couple would seem to have the same rights.

C. Issues Concerning Child Support Obligations

As explained in Chapter 1, an adoption ordinarily terminates all of the birth parent's rights and duties concerning the child, including continuing child support obligations. On the other hand, in *Tiffany & Co. v. Spreckels*, (1927) 202 Cal. 778, the Supreme Court upheld a mother's agreement to renounce her claim to custody of her children in exchange for the father's agreement to accept responsibility for the payment of the mother's child support debt. However, *Tiffany* is the minority rule (cf. *Stambaugh v. Child Support Admin.*, (Md.App. 1991) 591 A.2d 501), and such an agreement might actually violate Penal Code § 181, as interpreted in *People v. Daniel*, (1987) 195 Cal.App.3d 623, and as explained in Chapter 3.

II. RIGHTS OF GRANDPARENTS, OTHER RELATIVES, THIRD PARTIES

A. Grandparents and Other Relatives

1. Adoption Rights

As stated in *Mullins v. State of Oregon*, (9th Cir. 1995) 57 F.3d 789, the mere fact of a biological link between grandparent and grandchild does not give rise to a constitutional right to adopt the child. However, there is no statutory prohibition against a grandparent adopting his or her grandchild, and thereby assuming the legal status of that child's parent. Moreover, Family Code § 8802(a)(1)(A) expressly allows a grandparent of the child to file a petition for independent adoption, even in the absence of a guardianship or a formal placement of the child. Furthermore, as explained in Chapter 2 and in *Adoption of Michelle T.*, (1975) 44 Cal.App.3d 699, age alone does not disqualify one from adopting a child.

2. Visitation Rights

a) Generally

There are occasions when an adoption petition is filed concerning a child for which there already exists an order granting visitation rights. Pursuant to Family Code §§ 3102-3104 and 3429(a), the petitioner may be required to inform the court if anyone claims visitation rights. On the other hand, Family Code § 3102(c) provides that a visitation order is not available if the child has been adopted by a person other than a stepparent or grandparent of the child, and that any visitation rights granted before the adoption terminate automatically if the child is adopted by a person other than a stepparent or grandparent of the child. But the court in *Fenn v. Sherriff*, (2003) 109 Cal.App.4th 1466, held that the converse is also true -- if the child is adopted by a stepparent, the visitation rights remain intact (although the statutes do not expressly say so). The same would appear to hold true where the adoption is by a grandparent.

It should also be noted that in *Miller v. California*, (9th Cir. 2004) 355 F.3d 1172, the court held that noncustodial grandparents do not have a "substantive due process" right to visit their grandchildren, where the grandchildren are dependents of the juvenile court, and both the children's mother and the child protective services agency agreed that visitation with the grandparents should cease. The court also held that the grandparents' status under California law as "de facto" parents of their grandchildren did not create a liberty interest entitling the grandparents to visitation with the grandchildren, who had been removed from their natural parents due to neglect.

b) Post-Adoption Visitation Proceedings

Notwithstanding Family Code § 3102(c), Family Code § 3104 provides for a separate procedure whereby a court may grant visitation rights, in limited situations, to a grandparent even after the adoption has taken place, regardless of the kind of adoption that was ordered. However, Family Code § 3104(a) allows the court to grant a grandparent's petition for visitation rights only if the court (1) finds that there is a preexisting relationship between the grandparent and the grandchild that has engendered a bond such that visitation is in the best interest of the child, and (2) balances the interest of the child in having visitation with the grandparent against the right of the parents to exercise their parental authority. Accordingly, *Huffman v. Grob*, (1985) 172 Cal.App.3d 1153, holds that a grandparent who was not a de facto parent prior to the adoption has no right to seek visitation rights after the entry of the adoption order.

Procedurally, Family Code § 3104(c) requires personal service of the petition on each parent, and Family Code § 3104(g) and (j) preclude the entry of an order conflicting with the custody or visitation rights of a birth parent or adoptive parent who was not made a party. If the adoptive parents are "married," Family Code § 3104(b) precludes the filing of a grandparental visitation petition unless (1) the parents are currently living separately and apart on a permanent or indefinite basis, (2) one of the parents has been absent for more than one month without the other spouse knowing the whereabouts of the absent spouse, (3) one of the parents joins in the petition with the grandparents, or (4) the child is not residing with either parent. The last sentence of Family Code § 3104(b) states that if a change of circumstances occurs such that none of these four situations exist, the parent or parents may move the court to terminate grandparental visitation and the court shall grant the termination. In *Lopez v. Martinez*, (2000) 85 Cal.App.4th 279, the court held that an intervening stepparent adoption was such a change of circumstance, thus requiring dismissal of the Family Code § 3104 petition for grandparental visitation.

c) Seeking Post-Adoption Visitation Rights

Substantively, Family Code § 3104(e) sets forth a rebuttable presumption that grandparental visitation is not in the child's best interest if the natural or adoptive parents agree that the grandparent should not be granted visitation rights. Likewise, Family Code § 3104(f) sets forth a rebuttable presumption that grandparental visitation is not in the child's best interest if the parent who has been awarded sole legal and physical custody of the child in another proceeding, or with whom the child resides if there is currently no operative custody order, objects to visitation by the grandparent.

The court in *Lopez v. Martinez*, (2000) 85 Cal.App.4th 279, addressed substantive issues to a certain extent, and treated the U.S. Supreme Court's decision in *Troxel v. Granville*, (2000) 530 U.S. 57, which analyzed a Washington statute covering grandparental visitation rights, as if *Troxel* were binding precedent. In *Troxel*, a plurality of the U.S. Supreme Court affirmed the Washington state supreme court's decision that Washington's grandparental visitation statute infringed on the parents' fundamental due process right to rear their children, since the U.S. Constitution permits a state to interfere with this right only to prevent harm or potential harm to the child. While Justice O'Connor noted in *Troxel* that all 50 states have statutes providing for grandparental visitation in some form, she declined to "define ... the precise scope of the parental due process right in the visitation context." The *Lopez* court's recognition of the *Troxel* plurality's view of the strength of the parents' rights is now a matter of binding precedent in California. On the other hand, *Lopez* ruled that California's visitation statutes are not nearly as "breathtakingly broad" as those enacted in Washington.

d) Post-Adoption Visitation Orders

If the court grants the grandparental visitation petition, Family Code § 3104(i) allows the court to (1) allocate the percentage of grandparental visitation between the parents for purposes of the calculation of child support, and (2) order a parent or grandparent to pay to the other, an amount for the child's or grandchild's "support," which includes transportation costs and basic expenses relating to such things as medical expenses and day care costs. In addition, the court decides to grant the grandparental visitation petition does not create a basis for or against a change of residence of the child, but shall, pursuant to Family Code § 3104(h), be one of the factors for the court to consider in ordering a change of residence.

3. No Right to Notice of the Adoption Proceeding

In *Adoption of Berman*, (1975) 44 Cal.App.3d 687, the court specifically held that there is no constitutional or statutory requirement to give a grandparent notice of a stepparent adoption proceeding where the minor is in the care and control of a natural parent and a stepparent. The *Berman* court also held that a person's status as a de facto parent does not give rise to any requirement that that person be given notice of the adoption proceedings. Likewise, in *Sweeney v. Bowles*, (1961) 188 Cal.App.2d 196, the court held that notice of adoption proceedings need not be given to relatives. *Berman* also held that "while the kindly and courteous thing would be to give the grandparents such notice, the grandparents would still have no standing to object to the adoption, nor to attack the order of adoption when made."

4. Enforceable Visitation Rights Includes Right to Notice

In *Reeves v. Bailey*, (1975) 53 Cal.App.3d 1019, the court held that where a grandparent already has court-ordered visitation rights, that grandparent is entitled to notice of the adoption proceeding, and that where there is no attempt to inform that grandparent of the adoption proceeding, the adoption may be attacked on the basis of extrinsic fraud. The "extrinsic fraud" doctrine is explained more fully in Chapter 10.

Also, *Reeves* held that an adoption does not automatically terminate previously granted visitation rights, although this ruling may have been legislatively superseded by the enactment of Family Code § 3102(c), which is explained above. Furthermore, *Lopez v. Martinez*, (2000) 85 Cal.App.4th 279, construed *Reeves* narrowly, and stated that a grandparent's mere petition to seek visitation rights must be dismissed once a third party's adoption petition is granted. On the other hand, *Lopez* did not address the issue of whether a grandparent must be notified of the adoption proceeding. Also, if a grandparent's rights in a pending visitation order are deemed to be a vested interest, the termination of that interest by operation of Family Code § 3102(c) might require the grandparent to be notified of the adoption as a matter of procedural due process.

5. Intervention in Pending Adoption Proceedings

As discussed in further detail in Chapter 10, the superior court may permit a grandparent to intervene in pending adoption proceedings. In *Adoption of Lenn E.*, (1986) 182 Cal.App.3d 210, the superior court did allow such intervention. In that case, which involved an adoption petition by the child's paternal grandparents following the child's father's murder of the child's mother, the child's maternal grandparents were allowed to introduce expert psychiatric testimony concerning the best interests of the child, and were allowed to argue against the adoption. Since the maternal grandparents were allowed to intervene in the superior court proceedings, the appellate court held that they also had standing to appeal from the superior court's granting of the adoption petition. One should note that the *Lenn E.* court characterized the matter as one dealing with permissive intervention, and not a "right" to intervene. The *Lenn E.* court also did not examine whether the maternal grandparents had an "interest" that they were seeking to protect by means of the intervention.

B. Guardians

As explained in previous chapters, the adoption statutes require the court to be informed if there is a guardianship in place. However, *In re Santos' Estate*, (1921) 185 Cal. 127, holds that the consent even of a lawfully appointed guardian is not necessary to the adoption. *Santos* reasons that while a guardian of the person of a minor is charged with a high duty and serious responsibility in the care of his ward, the statutes should not be construed to exclude a child in the custody of a guardian from the advantages of an adoption. *Santos* also holds that since the adoptive parents acquire superior rights to the custody of the child, the reasons for the existence of a guardianship of the person of the child cease, and the continuation thereof is no longer appropriate.

As stated in Chapter 1, Probate Code § 1600(b) provides that a guardianship automatically terminates upon the adoption of the child. However, *Santos* also states that even after the adoption, a "guardianship of the estate" of the child (as opposed to a "guardianship of the person") may remain in existence in the court's discretion.

C. Same Sex Partners

As explained in Chapter 3, Family Code § 7540 provides that a child born while the mother is married is conclusively presumed to be the child of the mother's "husband." Also, *In re M.C.*, (2011) 195 Cal.App.4th 197, held that the birth mother's same-sex spouse (The two women married each other at a time when marriage was legal in California.) was deemed to be a "presumed mother" pursuant to Family Code § 7611(a). As such, the same-sex spouse would be entitled to notice of the adoption proceeding.

There is no case law addressing whether a child born while the domestic partner of the birth mother is "presumed mother." Therefore, it would appear that the non-birthing domestic partner would have to prove that he or she acquired legally recognized "presumed" parental status pursuant to Family Code § 7611(d) by having received the child into his or her home and holding the child out as his or her own.

Prior to the enactment of the domestic partner laws, but while the Uniform Parentage Act was in force, the court in *Nancy S. v. Michele G.*, (1991) 228 Cal.App.3d 831, held that a gay partner with no biological connection to the child is not a "parent," but may be deemed to be a de facto parent. However, as discussed in Chapter 6, de facto parent status merely gives an individual the right to be heard in a dependency proceeding, which would otherwise be closed to the public. Accordingly, *Nancy S.* holds that mere status as a de facto parent does not confer standing to seek custody or visitation over the objection of the child's natural parent.

On the other hand, in *In re Hirenia C.*, (1993) 18 Cal.App.4th 504, a non-parent gay partner of the child's foster parent/prospective adoptive parent was allowed to seek visitation rights as to a child who had been the subject of dependency proceedings, and whose parents' rights were terminated. (There is an indication in the case that both partners were foster parents.) One should note that the child in *Hirenia C.* was actually adopted by the child's prospective adoptive parent during the pendency of the appeal, in spite of the statutory stay of all proceedings upon the perfecting of the appeal. However, the appellate court in *Hirenia C.* remanded the case back to the juvenile court for the purpose of deciding the visitation rights question.

III. OPEN ADOPTIONS – POSTADOPTION CONTACT AGREEMENTS

A. What Is a Postadoption Contact Agreement?

Under Family Code §§ 8616.5, 8714(c), 8714.5(d), 8802(a)(3), 8912(e) and 9000(f), California law expressly allows the parties to enter into an enforceable agreement to remain in contact after the adoption. (See also Rule 5.400 of the California Rules of Court.) The postadoption contact agreement was previously called a "kinship agreement," and the law governing such agreements was formerly codified at Family Code § 8714.7. The "contact after adoption" agreement can be a useful tool to help prospective adoptive parents, birth parents and third parties agree to a "settlement" of their disputes in an adoption proceeding. Further, the courts in *In re Kimberly S.*, (1999) 71 Cal.App.4th 405, and *In re Noreen G.*, (2010) 181 Cal.App.4th 1359, held that postadoption contact agreements are not limited to children in the dependency system. The California statutes allow them in every type of adoption.

In addition, Family Code § 8616.5(b)(1) expressly states that nothing in any of the "adoption laws of this state" shall be construed to prevent the adopting parent or parents, the birth relatives, including the birth parent or parents, and the child from voluntarily entering into a written agreement to permit continuing contact between the birth relatives, including the birth parent or parents, and the child.

B. Parties to the Postadoption Contact Agreement

Family Code § 8616.5(a) mentions that it is the Legislature's intent that the child's birth parents and birth relatives be permitted to enter into a postadoption contact agreement where the child may benefit from such direct or indirect contact, and the agreement is voluntarily entered into by all parties, including the adoptive parents. Family Code § 8616.5(b)(1) and (d) state that the child is also a party to the agreement.

C. Permissible and Required Terms in the Agreement

According to Family Code § 8616.5(b)(2), the terms of a postadoption contact agreement shall be limited to, but need not include, (A) provisions for visitation between the child and a birth parent or parents and other birth relatives, including siblings, and the child's tribe (where the Indian Child Welfare Act applies -- see Chapter 9 of this book), (B) provisions for future contact between a birth parent or parents or other birth relatives, including siblings, or both, and the child or an adoptive parent, or both, and the child Indian tribe, and/or (C) provisions for the sharing of information about the child in the future. However, a postadoption contact agreement is limited under Family Code § 8616.5(b)(3) to the sharing of information about the child, unless the child has an existing relationship with the birth relative. On the other hand, the court is now authorized by the 2004 amendments to Family Code § 8616.5(c), at the time it grants the adoption petition, to also grant "postadoption privileges" when an agreement for those privileges has been entered into between the parties. It is unclear what "postadoption privileges" are.

Family Code § 8616.5(e) requires the postadoption contact agreement to contain the following warnings in bold type: (1) that after the adoption petition has been granted by the court, the adoption cannot be set aside due to the failure of an adopting parent, a birth parent, a birth relative, or the child to follow the terms of this agreement or a later change to this agreement, (2) that a disagreement between the parties or litigation brought to enforce or modify the agreement shall not affect the validity of the adoption and shall not serve as a basis for orders affecting the custody of the child, and (3) that a court will not act on a petition to change or enforce this agreement unless the petitioner has participated, or attempted to participate, in good faith in mediation or other appropriate dispute resolution proceedings to resolve the dispute. The subject of remedies for the breach of the agreement is discussed below.

D. Creating and Judicially Approving the Agreement

1. Entering Into the Agreement in the Adoption Case

In re Kimberly S., (1999) 71 Cal.App.4th 405, holds that any party can initiate the discussion of whether to enter into a postadoption contact agreement. When the parties arrive at an agreement, Family Code § 8616.5 contemplates that the postadoption contact agreement is to be put in writing and signed by the parties. Also, the Judicial Council has published standard postadoption contact agreement forms for this purpose.

As for those children who are at least 12 years old, Family Code § 8616.5(d) states that the child's written consent to the terms and conditions of the postadoption contact agreement and any subsequent modifications of the agreement is a necessary condition to the granting of privileges regarding visitation, contact, or sharing of information about the child, unless the court finds by a preponderance of the evidence that the agreement, as written, is in the best interests of the child. Family Code § 8616.5(d) also states that any child who has been the subject of a Welfare & Institutions Code § 300 dependency proceeding shall be represented by an attorney for purposes of consent to the postadoption contact agreement.

Family Code § 8616.5(b)(1) contemplates that the postadoption contact agreement is not enforceable unless the court finds, at the time the adoption petition is granted, that the agreement was entered into voluntarily and that it is in the best interests of the child. The Judicial Council forms provide language for the court to express its approval of the agreement. In order to allow the court to make an informed decision, Family Code § 8715(c) provides that where a petition for adoption has been filed with a postadoption contact agreement, the agency's report shall address whether the postadoption contact agreement has been entered into voluntarily, and whether it is in the best interests of the child.

Family Code § 8616.5(b)(1) contemplates that the agreement has to be in written form and be judicially approved before it can constitute an enforceable postadoption contact agreement. The Judicial Council has published standard forms for this purpose. When these requirements are satisfied, Family Code § 8616.5(f) provides that enforcement of the postadoption contact agreement shall be under the continuing jurisdiction of the court granting the adoption petition.

2. Modifying or Terminating the Agreement

Family Code § 8616.5(h)(1) provides that a postadoption contact agreement may be modified or terminated only if all parties, including the child if the child is at least 12 years old at the time of the requested termination or modification, have signed a modified postadoption contact agreement and the agreement is filed with the court that granted the adoption petition.

Family Code § 8616.5(h)(2) states that the only other way that the agreement may be modified or terminated is if the court finds (A) the termination or modification is necessary to serve the child's best interests, (B) there has been a substantial change of circumstances since the original agreement was executed and approved by the court, and (C) the party seeking the termination or modification has participated, or attempted to participate, in good faith in mediation or other appropriate dispute resolution proceedings prior to seeking court action.

E. Move-Away Rights

There is no case law on the issue of whether the adoptive parents who have signed a postadoption contact agreement may move out of California with the adopted minor child. On the other hand, there is nothing in Family Code § 8616.5 that prevents the adoptive parents from taking the adopted minor child out of state, and the adoptive parents are expressly allowed by Family Code § 7501(a) to change the child's residence, subject to the power of the court to restrain a removal that would prejudice the child's rights or welfare. (See also Chapter 7 of this book concerning the adoptive parents' rights.) Also, if the postadoption contact agreement provides for "visitation," all the provisions of the Uniform Child Custody Jurisdiction and Enforcement Act would apply in a move-away case.

Family Code § 8616.5(b)(2) states that a postadoption contact agreement "shall be limited to" (A) visitation, (B) future contact, and/or (C) the sharing of information about the child in the future. Unless the court's order or the agreement itself contains some contrary specification as to how, when and where the visitations, the future contact, and/or the sharing of information are to take place, it does not appear that the adoptive parents' mere moving out-of-state with the adopted minor child would constitute a violation of the court order, the statutes or the agreement. In other words, the visitations for example do not have to take place in California.

F. Enforcing the Postadoption Contact Agreement

1. Necessity for Mediation before Court Action

Family Code § 8616.5(e)(3), (f) and (h)(2)(C) state that the court may not order compliance with, modification of or termination of the postadoption contact agreement absent a finding that the party seeking the enforcement participated, or attempted to participate, in good faith in mediation or other appropriate dispute resolution proceedings regarding the conflict, prior to the filing of the enforcement action.

2. Rule that Court Action be in the Child's Best Interests

Family Code § 8616.5(f) states that the court may not order compliance with the postadoption contact agreement absent a finding that enforcement is in the best interests of the child. As stated above, this is also true with regard to a contested modification and termination of the postadoption contact agreement.

3. Conduct of the Proceedings

Family Code § 8616.5(f) allows the court to rule on the enforcement petition based solely on documentary evidence or offers of proof; the court may, but is not required to, hear testimony or conduct an evidentiary hearing before deciding the enforcement petition. Further, Family Code § 8616.5(f) and (h)(2) provide that the court shall not order further investigation or evaluation by any public or private agency or individual absent a finding by clear and convincing evidence that the best interests of the child may be protected or advanced only by such inquiry and that the inquiry will not disturb the stability of the child's home to the detriment of the child.

4. Remedies in the Proceedings

Family Code § 8616.5(e)(1) and (k) expressly prohibit the court from setting aside a decree of adoption, rescinding a relinquishment, or modifying an order to terminate parental rights or any other prior court order because of the failure of a birth parent, adoptive parent, birth relative, or the child to comply with any or all of the original terms of, or subsequent modifications to, the postadoption contact agreement. It would appear that a court would not be permitted to create a "fraudulent promise" exception to Family Code § 8616.5(e)(1) and (k), since a "fraudulent promise" claim necessarily requires evidence of a breach of that promise, and the statute expressly excludes such a breach from forming the basis of setting aside the adoption. In addition, although *In re Kimberly S.*, (1999) 71 Cal.App.4th 405, holds that the agreement is incorporated into the terms of the adoption, it does not appear that the holding of *Kimberly S.* would give rise to any grounds to set aside an adoption.

Family Code § 8616.5(g) also prohibits the awarding of monetary damages in an action to enforce the agreement. It therefore appears that the most that can be substantively awarded in an enforcement proceeding is an order for specific performance, modification or termination of the agreement. Also, the prevailing party in an enforcement proceeding is entitled to recover the "costs and fees of litigation."

INTERSTATE ADOPTIONS AND JURISDICTION 9

In this chapter:

CHAPTER 9 – INTERSTATE ADOPTIONS AND JURISDICTION

- Giving Notice to Parent or Indian Custodian, and the Tribe
  - Ascertaining Whether the Child is an Indian Child
  - Ascertaining Which Tribe is the Indian Child's Tribe
  - Addressing the Notice
- The ICWA's Changes to California Adoption Law
  - Consent to or Relinquishment for the Adoption
    - Consent Form Must Be Signed Before a Judge with Jurisdiction
    - Consent Cannot Be Made Within 10 Days of Child's Birth
    - Consent Is Revocable Up to Time of Granting Adoption Petition
    - Two-Year Limitation for Setting Aside Adoption
  - Placement for Purposes of Adoption
    - Placement Must Be Near Indian Child's Home
    - Preferential Status for "Indian Families"
    - Preferential Status for Indian Foster Home
    - Order of Preferential Status Set by the Tribe
    - Documenting the Placement Decision
  - Remedial Services and Rehabilitative Programs for the Parent
  - "Detriment Rule" Applies to the Termination of Parental Rights

Terrence Stephen McQueen was born in Indiana. Within months, his father abandoned him, and his mother took him to Missouri to live for several years with his great-uncle, who treated him well and "like a son." His mother remarried, and then took the boy to live in Indiana with his new step-father, who beat him. The boy ran away first to live on the streets and then to be with his great-uncle. He returned to his mother in California, where she was living with a third husband, who also beat the boy, prompting the boy to be sent back to the great-uncle.

I. THE FULL FAITH AND CREDIT CLAUSE OF THE U.S. CONSTITUTION

A. Diversity of the Laws of the States and Territories

The Full Faith and Credit Clause (Article IV, Section 1 of the U.S. Constitution) requires that both federal and state courts give binding effect to the judicial acts of all other states. In *Estate of Hart*, (1984) 165 Cal.App.3d 392, the court held that adoption decrees from other states are constitutionally entitled to full faith and credit. For that reason, the courts must give effect to adoptions which are completed under pursuant to laws that may be very different from those existing in California. Just as with any other field of law, the adoption laws of the 50 states and the U.S. territories are widely divergent.

There are various aspects of adoption law which are directly controlled by the U.S. Constitution, such as the jurisdictional need for a valid consent or permissible grounds to dispense with consent. Adoptions are also governed by various uniform acts, such as the Uniform Parentage Act, which is discussed in Chapter 3. However, while all 50 states and all U.S. territories and districts have statutes allowing for the adoption of children, a few states do not permit independent adoptions at all, such as in Connecticut, where all adoptions must proceed by way of an agency adoption. (See Conn. Gen'l Stat.Ann. § 45a-724 and 45a-733.)

1. Residency of Adoptive Parents as a Prerequisite

As explained in Chapter 10 and later in this chapter, there are some instances in which a non-resident of California may file an adoption petition in California. In contrast, Georgia law (Ga.Dom.Rel. Code § 19-8-3) requires the adoptive parents to be 25 years old and "bona fide" residents of the state for at least six months before filing the adoption petition, while Minnesota law (Minn.Stat.Ann. § 259-22) sets forth a one-year residency requirement for the petitioner. Interestingly, the U.S. Supreme Court has almost always upheld statutes that simply make "residency" a requirement (see *McCarthy v. Philadelphia Civil Service Comm'n*, (1976) 424 U.S. 645), but have often held that statutes that make a distinction based on the length of residency violate equal protection. See, *Zobel v. Williams*, (1982) 457 U.S. 55.

Residency requirements do not appear to exist in Alabama (Ala.Code § 26-10A-5), Kansas (Kan.Stat.Ann. §§ 59-2113 and 59-2132), or Maine (Me.Rev.Stat.Ann. § 1121). In the District of Columbia, D.C. Code Ann. § 16-302 states that the prospective adoptive parent need not be a resident as long as the child was relinquished to an agency licensed in D.C. or to the Mayor of Washington (i.e., the equivalent of a state social services agency).

Texas law (Tex.Fam.Code § 16.01) provides that the child to be adopted must reside in the forum state. While it appears that this statute may conflict with the Interstate Compact for the Placement of Children (see below), the validity of the Texas statute would be an issue of statutory interpretation for the Texas courts. It would also appear that the federal Parental Kidnapping Prevention Act would not override this statute, since the PKPA first looks to whether the state court may exercise jurisdiction pursuant to its own state laws, as explained below.

2. Whether Notice to the "Unknown Father" is Required

In *Matter of Karen A.B.*, (Del. 1986) 513 A.2d 770, it was held that an unknown father simply does not satisfy the requirements of the Uniform Parentage Act and therefore has no right to notice of the adoption proceedings. The Delaware court reasoned, much like the *Kelsey S.* court, that the unknown father simply had not done anything in the way of exercising parental rights. The same conclusion was reached in *In re S.J.B.*, (Ark. 1988) 745 S.W.2d 606. There would seem to be a similar result under California Family Code § 7666(b). Virginia came to the opposite conclusion, holding that the unknown father at least needs to have notice by publication, in order to be made aware that there are parental rights to be exercised and protected. *Augusta Co. Dept. of Soc. Serv. v. Unnamed Mother*, (Va. App. 1986) 348 S.E.2d 26.

3. Whether the Uniform Parentage Act is "Uniform"

The Uniform Parentage Act is the law in the District of Columbia, and D.C. Code § 16-909 is similar to parts of California's Family Code § 7611. On the other hand, the language of Calif. Family Code §§ 7611(d) and 7664(b) is not found anywhere in the statutes of the District of Columbia. Further, although the District of Columbia courts follow the parental rights decisions of the U.S. Supreme Court, they have expressly rejected the holding of *Adoption of Kelsey S.*, (1992) 1 Cal.4th 816. (See *In re Baby Boy C.*, (D.C. 1993) 630 A.2d 670, 678, fn.24.)

4. Time and Manner of Taking Consent

In Alabama, consent may be given before birth. See, Alab. Code § 26-10A-13. On the other hand, in Delaware, the birth father's consent may be given before birth, while the birth mother must wait until after the child is born. Del. Code Ann. Title 13, § 1106(e). There is yet a third rule in Arizona, where both mother and father must wait until the child is 72 hours old before a consent form may be signed. (Ariz.R.S.A. § 8-107.) In Colorado, the consent is required to be signed in the presence of a judge. (Colo.Rev.Stat. § 19-4-101, et seq.)

5. Notice to Consenting Birth Parents

California law states that there is no need to serve notice on a person who has already consented to the adoption (however for practical reasons it may be wise to serve notice anyway). On the other hand, New York law (*Matter of Sarah K.*, (N.Y. 1985) 496 N.Y.S.2d 384, 487 N.E.2d 241) requires service of notice even on persons who consented to the adoption, unless the consent form contains a waiver of notice.

6. Revocability of Consent

In Texas, a birth parent's consent to the adoption is revocable at any time before the adoption petition is granted (Texas Family Code § 162.011), which is a broader right of revocation than California allows, as set forth in Chapter 3 of this book. On the other hand, North Carolina only provides for a seven day revocation period (N.C.Stat.Ann. § 48-3-608), and in Massachusetts, there is no revocability, at least where the statutorily prescribed forms are used. See, Mass.Ann. Laws, Ch. 210, § 2.

7. Grounds to Dispense with a Birth Parent's Consent

Under Iowa law (Iowa Code Ann. § 600A-8), parental rights can be terminated based on that parent's abduction of the child. Interestingly, no such provision exists in California Family Code §§ 7800, et seq., nor in Welfare & Institutions Code § 300. In addition, unlike California law (as explained in Chapter 6), Colorado provides that long-term incarceration alone (i.e., imprisonment without parole for at least six months) is a sufficient basis to proceed with an adoption without the imprisoned parent's consent. Colo.Rev.Stat. § 19-3-604.

In Texas, parental consent to an adoption is not required for a child who is "born alive as the result of an abortion." Texas Family Code § 161.006. The statute defines "abortion" as merely the expulsion of the fetus with the intent to kill, and not the actual killing. There is no case law stating whether this Texas statute is constitutional.

8. The Court's Involvement in the Adoption

Tennessee requires that all "surrenders," i.e., consents to adoption, be made in the presence of a judge. (See Tenn.Code Ann. § 36-1-111.) Also, unlike California law, Colorado allows the court to place a child for adoption (Colo.Rev.Stat. § 19-5-104(2)), and in Maine it is the court which investigates the prospective adoptive parents. See, Maine Rev.Stat.Ann. § 1125.

9. Limitations Period for Collateral Attack on Adoption

California's Family Code § 9102, gives an interested party one year to attack a California adoption, or three years if the adoption resulted from fraud. However, the statute of limitations is much shorter in other states. Under Louisiana law (La. Children's Code Art. §§ 1262 and 1263), the statute of limitations for a collateral attack is only six months from the discovery of the grounds for the attack.

B. Conflicts of Laws Doctrines

California follows the "governmental interests" approach to conflicts of laws issues, wherein the court inquires as to which state has the greater interest in seeing that its laws are applied to a particular issue. See *Zimmerman v. Allstate Ins. Co.*, (1986) 179 Cal.App.3d 840, 844-845. Therefore, if the *MM* case were pending in California today, and the California court had subject matter jurisdiction, and the birth parent had waited until after the expiration of the 30-day Family Code § 8814.5 period to attempt to revoke consent, the California court would have to inquire as to whether California or New York had a greater governmental interest in seeing its laws applied to the facts.

Different states apply different "conflicts of laws" doctrines. For example, in *In re Adoption of MM*, (Wyo. 1982) 652 P.2d 974, the child's "home state" appeared to be

New York, and there did not appear to be any objection to jurisdiction in Wyoming. The birth parents signed the consent forms in New York, where revocation of consent is allowed. After the adoption proceeding was commenced in Wyoming, where revocation of consent is not allowed, the birth parent sought to revoke her consent. The Wyoming Supreme Court held that, according to the "law of the forum state" principle taken from the Restatement of Conflict of Laws, the birth mother would not be allowed to revoke her consent.

Besides these doctrines, many states apply the law of the state of the child's residence, where there is a conflict with the law of the forum state. See for example, *In re Adoption of Baby Boy S.*, (Kan.App. 1996) 912 P.2d 761; *In re Jarrett*, (N.Y.App.Div. 1996) 637 N.Y.S.2d 912; *In re Adoption of Baby Boy W.*, (Utah App. 1995) 904 P.2d 1113; and *In re Adoption of Baby Boy Hylland/Ohnemus*, (Or.App. 1994) 867 P.2d 551. These states held that the law of the residence of the birth father did not apply.

C. Application of the Full Faith and Credit Clause

1. Necessity of a Prior Judicial Proceeding

Milliken v. Meyer, (1940) 311 U.S. 457, holds that a final judgment of one state's court must be given full faith and credit by another state's court, regardless of the logic or consistency of the decision, or the validity of the legal principles upon which the judgment is based. An example of an application of this rule is *George M. v. Superior Court*, (1988) 201 Cal.App.3d 755, where it was held that even though the lower court found that the petitioner was merely a "natural father" as described in the Uniform Parentage Act, and not a "presumed father," the petitioner had the right to object to the proposed adoption in California in light of an Arizona judgment declaring that child was his "legitimate" child.

In *Estate of Hart*, (1984) 165 Cal.App.3d 392, the court further stated that upon a claim that a foreign judgment is not entitled to full faith and credit, the permissible scope of inquiry is limited to a determination of whether the original court had jurisdiction in the case, since the differing public policies or laws of the enforcing state cannot contravene the full faith and credit clause, and since California must, regardless of policy objections, recognize the judgment of another state as res judicata. *Estate of Hart* held that in probate proceedings in California, the status of adoption (or non-adoption) is determined by the laws of the state where the adoption was allegedly effectuated. In addition, full faith and credit statutes have also been enacted in California (see Code of Civil Procedure § 1913(a) and Family Code § 3453), and at the federal level (see 28 U.S.C. § 1738).

Although the Full Faith and Credit Clause contains language requiring the courts to give due regard to the "public Acts" of the several states, *Estate of Hart* interprets the Full Faith and Credit Clause to say that only the *judicial* acts and proceedings of one state are binding on the others. Thus, for example, if the prospective adoptive parents resided in another state and were given an unfavorable assessment by an investigating agency there, the Full Faith and Credit clause would not *require* a California court to give binding effect to that home study report.

2. Jurisdictional Questions

In *May v. Anderson*, (1953) 345 U.S. 528, the Supreme Court held that the Full Faith and Credit Clause does not apply where the judgment or order sought to be enforced was issued by a court having no personal jurisdiction over the parties. Likewise, *Estate of Hart*, (1984) 165 Cal.App.3d 392, appears to allow a California court to reexamine whether the sister state court had "fundamental jurisdiction."

On the other hand, *Estate of Hart* followed the "general rule" (citing *Durfee v. Duke* (1963) 375 U.S. 106), which is that "a judgment is entitled to full faith and credit--even as to questions of jurisdiction--when the second court's inquiry discloses that those questions have been fully and fairly litigated and finally decided in the court which rendered the original judgment." The court in *Estate of Hart* allowed the Oklahoma court's express determination on the issue of jurisdiction to operate as res judicata, especially because the underlying litigation had proceeded all the way to the Oklahoma Supreme Court. On the other hand, in *Estate of Hampton*, (1942) 55 Cal.App.2d 543, the court held that a Kansas adoption decree could be challenged on due process grounds because the natural mother had never received notice of the adoption. It appears that there was no express determination of jurisdiction in *Hampton* in the Kansas courts, unlike what had occurred in *Hart*.

3. *In Personam* v. *In Rem* Jurisdiction

May v. Anderson, (1953) 345 U.S. 528, which involved a parent's custody rights, holds that in order to qualify for full faith and credit treatment under the Constitution, where a court issues an *in personam* order, it must have personal jurisdiction over the party who is subject to the order. For example, a court acts *in personam* against a parent when it cuts off that parent's child custody rights. While California case law describes an adoption as an *in rem* proceeding, as explained in Chapter 1, if a birth parent's rights are cut off in the course of an adoption, even as a result of that parent having failed to come forward when served with the petition, the proceeding does possess *in personam* characteristics. As to persons or entities to whom no notice is required (see *In re Radovich's Estate*, (1957) 48 Cal.2d 116 [which involved a taxing agency]), the adoption is *in rem*, unlike the situation in *May*, and thus must be accorded full faith and credit under the Constitution as to that person or entity.

The impact of the *May* decision is mitigated by Congress's enactment of the Parental Kidnapping Prevention Act (28 U.S.C. § 1738A), which was passed pursuant to Congress's express authority under Article IV, Section 1 of the U.S. Constitution to pass laws concerning the full faith and credit effect that the states must give to judgments of other states. The PKPA, which is explained in detail below, does not require the court issuing the child custody decree to have personal jurisdiction over the affected birth parent, as long as that court has complied with the provisions of the PKPA. If that occurs, then as a matter of federal law, the courts of all other states must abide by that custody decree, without regard to issues of personal jurisdiction. The only "personal jurisdiction" requirement is that the birth parent be given "reasonable notice and opportunity to be heard," pursuant to 28 U.S.C. § 1738A(e).

4. "Continuing Jurisdiction" and Full Faith and Credit

The U.S. Supreme Court held in *New York ex rel. Halvey v. Halvey*, (1947) 330 U.S. 610, that as to a modifiable child custody order, the Full Faith and Credit Clause generally does not prevent a court of a different state to re-visit custody issues in a subsequent proceeding. Since an adoption does not generally allow for continuing jurisdiction (except for possibly where there is a postadoption contact agreement or visitation orders), it would appear that *Halvey* would not be entirely applicable to a completed adoption. On the other hand, where a party in California is attempting to complete an adoption of a child who is the subject of custody or visitation orders in another state, *Halvey* would be relevant. In addition, such a case would be governed directly by the Uniform Child Custody Jurisdiction and Enforcement Act and the Federal Parental Kidnapping Prevention Act, as explained below.

II. SUBJECT MATTER JURISDICTION

A court must have jurisdiction over the subject matter of the proceeding before it may issue a binding adoption order. In a purely uncontested adoption, such as one in which there is no issue as to paternity or the termination of parental rights, the court's jurisdiction to issue an adoption order is governed by Family Code § 9210. However, in practice, such issues do arise.

Where they do, a court order relating to "child custody" must comply with both the jurisdictional laws of the forum state (in California, the Uniform Child Custody Jurisdiction and Enforcement Act (Family Code § 3400, et seq.)), and the jurisdictional provisions of the federal Parental Kidnapping Prevention Act (28 U.S.C. § 1738A), in order to be entitled to nationwide enforceability. California's jurisdictional statutes were provided by the Uniform Child Custody Jurisdiction Act ("UCCJA"), which had been enacted in all 50 states. However, in 1999, the California Legislature replaced the UCCJA with the almost identical Uniform Child Custody Jurisdiction and Enforcement Act ("UCCJEA"). All other states now also use the UCCJEA. Vermont adopted the UCCJEA on July 1, 2011, and was the last state to do so. One difference between the UCCJA and UCCJEA is that "adoptions" are expressly excluded from UCCJEA coverage (see California Family Code § 3403), while the UCCJA had covered adoption proceedings. On the other hand, some courts have held that the interpretations of the UCCJA constitute persuasive authority in interpreting the UCCJEA. (*In re Marriage of Sareen* (2007) 153 Cal.App.4th 371; but see *In re Marriage of Nurie* (2009) 176 Cal.App.4th 478.) Other states, like Wisconsin, Massachusetts and the District of Columbia, have recently enacted *forms* of the UCCJEA, but they did not expressly exclude "adoptions" from UCCJEA coverage. Therefore, as is the case with many "uniform" acts, the UCCJEA is not 100% "uniform" nationwide.

The UCCJEA and the UCCJA both set forth a four-part jurisdictional analysis. They both consist of essentially identical provisions in their four-part analyses, with minor exceptions in the procedural rules and minor changes in what constitutes a "convenient forum." As explained herein, the jurisdictional provisions apply to "child custody proceedings." Also, the court in *In re Gloria F.*, (1989) 212 Cal.App.3d 576, held that the laws now codified in the UCCJEA are the exclusive means of determining subject matter jurisdiction in California custody cases. *Gloria F.* further held that the jurisdictional language contained in the Interstate Compact for the Placement of Children (Family Code § 7901) was subservient to what is now codified in the UCCJEA. Moreover, as explained in this chapter, the Federal Parental Kidnapping Prevention Act ("PKPA"), which uses a jurisdictional framework that is similar to the UCCJEA, has pre-emptive jurisdictional ramifications. The same type of jurisdictional analysis is used in California "adoption" cases pursuant to Family Code § 9210.

A. Purposes of the Jurisdictional Statutes

In *Kumar v. Superior Court*, (1982) 32 Cal.3d 689, which was decided when California still used the UCCJA, the Supreme Court recited that the UCCJA's purposes included preventing jurisdictional competition, promoting interstate cooperation, litigating child custody disputes in the most suitable forum, discouraging continuing conflict over custody, deterring abductions, avoiding relitigation of another state's custody decisions, and promoting interstate exchange of information and cooperation. In addition, *People v. Beach*, (1987) 194 Cal.App.3d 955, held that the UCCJA seeks to promote the best interest of the child by giving greater stability to custody decrees through limiting jurisdiction to decide custody matters and enabling courts to arrive at a fully informed judgment which transcends state lines and considers all claimants, residents and nonresidents, on an equal basis and from the standpoint of the welfare of the child.

Interestingly, when the California Legislature replaced the UCCJA with the UCCJEA, former Family Code § 3401 (which set forth the legislative purposes of the UCCJA) was repealed but was not replaced with any code section setting forth the legislative purposes of the UCCJEA. Although California's version of the UCCJEA does not expressly provide a "legislative purposes" section, the ideals recited in *Kumar* and *Beach* would appear to be served by the UCCJEA, since its language is largely identical to the UCCJA.

The PKPA has jurisdictional ramifications, but its main purpose is that of determining whether full faith and credit is to be accorded to a given child custody decree. The PKPA applies to all states, since it is federal law. However, as will be explained herein, the PKPA does not apply until (1) "such court has jurisdiction under the law of such State," (2) one of five other conditions have been met, and (3) "reasonable notice and opportunity to be heard" has been given to interested parties. In California, the first federally-imposed prong is answered by Family Code § 9210 and/or the UCCJEA. The second prong entails a complex analysis that is very similar to the legal methodology set forth in the UCCJEA, as outlined herein. It appears the third prong could be established by providing minimal due process.

B. Jurisdiction over the Adoption – Family Code § 9210

According to Family Code § 9210(a), a California court has jurisdiction to conduct an adoption proceeding if one of five conditions are met. However, Family Code § 9210(b) sets forth a comity provision that requires the California court to abstain from taking jurisdiction where another state's court has properly taken jurisdiction. In addition, Family Code § 9210(c) contains jurisdictional provisions governing situations where another state's court has already issued a decree bearing on the proposed adoption. There is still no case law interpreting this statute, however the jurisdictional scheme can be explained as follows:

1. Alternative Jurisdictional Grounds for the Adoption

a) California is Child's Home State

The first of the five alternative jurisdictional conditions of Family Code § 9210(a) is met if, immediately before the adoption proceeding commenced, the minor lived in California with a parent, a guardian, a prospective adoptive parent, or another person acting as parent, for at least six consecutive months, excluding periods of temporary absence, or, in the case of a minor under six months of age, lived in this state with any of those individuals from soon after birth and there is substantial evidence available in California concerning the minor's present or future care. (See Family Code § 9210(a)(1).) This provision is very similar to the "home state" jurisdictional rule of the UCCJEA (Family Code § 3421(a)(1)), which is discussed later in this chapter.

b) California is Adoptive Parent's Home State

Secondly, Family Code § 9210(a)(2) allows a California court to take jurisdiction if, immediately before the proceeding commences, the prospective adoptive parent lived in California for at least six consecutive months, excluding periods of temporary absence, and there is available in this state substantial evidence concerning the minor's present or future care. Importantly, the statute only requires residency of one of the adoptive parents, but that residency must be for "six consecutive months." As explained below, the UCCJEA does not directly utilize a "residency of the adoptive parent" basis for jurisdiction.

c) Child is Placed by a California Agency

Family Code § 9210(a)(3) permits the California courts to exercise jurisdiction if (A) the child to be adopted was placed by an agency, (B) that agency is located in California, (C) the child and his or her parents, or the child and the prospective adoptive parent, have a significant connection with California, and (D) there is substantial evidence available in California concerning the child's present or future care. This provision would allow a California court to complete the adoption in certain instances even if neither the child nor the adoptive parent resided in California.

d) Physical Presence Plus Emergency to the Child

Under Family Code § 9210(a)(4), a California court may exercise jurisdiction if the minor and the prospective adoptive parent are physically present in California and the minor has been abandoned or it is necessary in an emergency to protect the minor because the minor has been subjected to or threatened with mistreatment or abuse or is otherwise neglected. As explained below, a proceeding for the termination of parental rights is covered by the UCCJEA, meaning the UCCJEA and Family Code § 9210(a)(4) would have to be satisfied in such a case.

e) Jurisdictional Vacuum

According Family Code § 9210(a)(5), jurisdiction is proper in California if it appears that no other state would have jurisdiction under requirements similar to Family Code § 9210(a)(1) through (4), or another state has declined to exercise jurisdiction on the ground that California is the more appropriate forum to hear a petition for adoption of the minor, and substantial evidence is available in California concerning the child's present or future care.

2. Exclusive Jurisdiction

a) Proceedings Pending in Another State

If at the time the adoption petition is filed there is another adoption or custody proceeding concerning the same child pending in another state, and that court is exercising jurisdiction substantially in conformity with Family Code § 9210, the California court is prohibited by Family Code § 9210(b) from taking jurisdiction over the adoption case, unless the other state's court issues a stay of its proceedings (for example, if California is a more appropriate forum).

b) Prior Custody Decree Issued in Other State

Family Code § 9210(c) provides that if a court of another state has issued a decree or order concerning the custody of a minor who may be the subject of an adoption proceeding in California, the California court may not exercise jurisdiction over an adoption proceeding regarding that child, unless (1) the requirements for modifying an order of another state's court are met, the other state's court has no jurisdiction over an adoption proceeding substantially in conformity with Family Code § 9210(a)(1) to (4), or the other state's court has declined to assume jurisdiction over the adoption, and (2) the California court otherwise would have jurisdiction over the adoption proceeding.

C. The Uniform Child Custody Jurisdiction and Enforcement Act

According to Family Code § 3406, a child custody decree complying with the UCCJEA is binding on all persons who have been served, and all persons who have made a general appearance and have had an opportunity to be heard. In addition, as explained below, compliance with the UCCJEA allows a court not only to have subject matter jurisdiction to bind all such persons, but the exclusive authority under Family Code § 3422(a) to do so regardless of the actions of the courts of other states. Conversely, if a court of another state issues a child custody order that does not substantially comply with UCCJEA principles, it need not be enforced by a California court. (*In re Marriage of Nurie* (2009) 176 Cal.App.4th 478.)

1. Cases Which Are Expressly Governed by the UCCJEA

a) "Child Custody Proceeding"

Family Code § 3421(a) gives a California court jurisdiction to make an "initial child custody determination" under certain prescribed situations. Family Code § 3402(c) states that the phrase "child custody determination" includes a judgment, decree, or other order of a court providing for the legal custody, physical custody, or visitation as to a child, and also includes a permanent, temporary, initial and modification order. In *In re Gloria F.*, (1989) 212 Cal.App.3d 576, the court held that the removal of a child from parental custody in a dependency proceeding fell within this definition. *Gloria F.* also held that the predecessor provision of the UCCJA applied even though no "jurisdictional conflict" existed with any other state.

The Family Code § 3402(d) definition of "child custody proceeding" includes a proceeding for dissolution of marriage, legal separation of the parties, neglect, abuse, dependency, guardianship, paternity, termination of parental rights, and protection from domestic violence, "in which the issue may appear." The Family Code § 3402(d) definition expressly excludes a proceeding involving juvenile delinquency, contractual emancipation, or visitation order enforcement under Family Code § 3441. According to Family Code § 3402(b), the word "child" means one who has not reached 18 years old. Also, Family Code § 3402(c) expressly states that proceedings relating solely to child support are not covered by the UCCJEA.

b) Adoption Cases?

Presently, California Family Code § 3403, which uses the original language of the UCCJEA, provides that the UCCJEA "does not govern an adoption proceeding or a proceeding pertaining to the authorization of emergency medical care for a child." As of May 1, 2011, there was no published California case law interpreting Family Code § 3403. Also, as mentioned above, not all UCCJEA states have enacted this provision in their states' laws.

Formerly, in interpreting the UCCJA, most states had followed the rule expressed in *Souza v. Superior Court*, (1987) 193 Cal.App.3d 1304, which held that the UCCJA covers adoptions, since an adoption proceeding terminates parental custody rights and is clearly a custody-determining proceeding of the most drastic kind. Importantly, *Souza* held that adoption cases are governed by the PKPA, which has not been significantly amended since *Souza* was decided. See also, *Adoption of Zachariah K.*, (1992) 6 Cal.App.4th 1025, which held that a petition to withdraw consent to an independent adoption was a "proceeding affecting custody," and therefore covered by the UCCJA. On the other side, one state holds that since the word "adoption" is not found in the UCCJA, the UCCJA does not apply to adoptions. See *In re Johnson*, (Ind.App. 1981) 415 N.E.2d 108.

One must note that most of the issues expressly described in the Family Code § 3402(d) definition of "child custody proceeding" could be involved in a contested adoption proceeding, and any proceeding "in which such issue may appear" is expressly covered by the UCCJEA. In other words, a contested adoption proceeding could involve an issue dealing with "neglect," "abuse," "dependency," "guardianship," "paternity," "termination of parental rights," or "protection from domestic violence," as stated in Family Code § 3402(d). Importantly, there is no provision in the Parental Kidnapping Prevention Act that is similar to Family Code § 3403. In addition, the vast majority of state courts which have interpreted the PKPA appear to hold that the federal act applies to adoption proceedings, according to the reasoning of the *Souza* decision.

c) Definition of "State"

The UCCJEA covers child custody determinations made almost anywhere. First, Family Code § 3402(o) defines "state" as a U.S. state, the District of Columbia, Puerto Rico, the U.S. Virgin Islands, or any U.S. territory or insular possession. As for foreign countries, Family Code § 3405(a) provides that they shall be treated as if they were a state of the United States for the purpose of applying the UCCJEA, and Family Code § 3405(b) states that a foreign country's child custody determination made under factual circumstances in substantial conformity with the UCCJEA must be recognized and enforced pursuant to Family Code § 3441. (See *In re Jorge G.* (2008) 164 Cal.App.4th 125.) However, Family Code § 3405(c) provides that the decree of a foreign country need not be regarded "if the child custody law of a foreign country violates fundamental principles of human rights."

As for Native American tribes, Family Code § 3404(b) provides that a tribe shall be treated as if it were a state of the United States for the purpose of applying the UCCJEA, and Family Code § 3404(c) provides that a child custody determination made by a tribe under factual circumstances in substantial conformity with the UCCJEA must be recognized and enforced under Family Code § 3441. Family Code § 3402(p) defines "tribe" as an Indian tribe or band, or Alaskan Native village, that is recognized by federal law or formally acknowledged by a state. On the other hand, Family Code § 3404(a) provides that a child custody proceeding that pertains to an "Indian child" is not subject to the UCCJEA to the extent that it is governed by the Indian Child Welfare Act (25 U.S.C. §§ 1901, et seq.), which is explained later in this chapter.

2. Bases for California's Initial UCCJEA Jurisdiction

a) Four Independent Jurisdictional Triggers

As explained immediately below, California's version of the UCCJEA provides that a California court has jurisdiction to make an initial child custody determination in any one of four different situations. Once a California court properly takes jurisdiction, the UCCJEA's and UCCJA's exclusivity provisions require all other states to decline to exercise jurisdiction as to the particular child, with certain exceptions. However, it is possible for that jurisdiction to "erode" due to the migration of the parties and the child to other states, as explained below.

According to Family Code § 3421(a), a California court has jurisdiction to make an "initial child custody determination" only if at least one of four situations exist, as described below. Family Code § 3421(b) states that the four-part analysis constitutes "the exclusive jurisdictional basis for making a child custody determination by a court of this state." Family Code § 3402(h) defines "initial child custody determination" as "the first child custody determination concerning a particular child," and not necessarily a determination as to a sibling or other relative of the child. As to all four categories, Family Code § 3421(c) provides that physical presence of, or personal jurisdiction over, a party or a child is neither necessary, nor sufficient, to make a custody determination.

(1) California is the Child's "Home State"

The first alternative basis for jurisdiction is Family Code § 3421(a)(1), which allows a California court to make an initial child custody determination if (A) California is the home state of the child on the date of the commencement of the proceeding, or (B) was the home state of the child within six months before the commencement of the proceeding and the child is absent from this state but a parent or person acting as a parent continues to live in this state.

(a) What is a "Home State"?

Family Code § 3402(g) defines "home state" as the state in which a child lived with a parent or a person acting as a parent for at least six consecutive months immediately before the commencement of a child custody proceeding, and as to those children less than six months old, the state in which the child lived from birth with such persons. Also, Family Code § 3402(g) states that a period of the child's temporary absence from these persons is part of the period.

In *In re Marriage of Nurie*, (2009) 176 Cal.App.4th 478, which involved a child who spent the first five months of his life in California and was then taken to Pakistan where he stayed until after he turned six months old, the court held that California was the child's "home state." The court reasoned that as of the date the child became six months old, both parents had intended for the child to return to California shortly thereafter, meaning that the child's time in Pakistan was deemed to be a "temporary absence." The court also held that a person can have more than one legally-recognized residence at the same time for UCCJEA purposes.

(b) Residence of a "Person Acting as a Parent"

"Person acting as a parent" is defined by Family Code § 3402(m) as a person other than a parent who (1) has physical custody of the child or has had physical custody for a period of six consecutive months, including any temporary absence, within one year immediately before the commencement of a child custody proceeding, and (2) has been awarded legal custody by a court or claims a right to legal custody under the law of California. Based on the extremely broad definition of "person" in Family Code § 3402(*l*), it would appear that physical custody of the child by a public or private agency could lead to "home state" jurisdiction. "Physical custody" is defined under Family Code § 3402(n) as the physical care and supervision of the child.

Rogers v. Platt, (1988) 199 Cal.App.3d 1204, interprets the "home state" provisions of the PKPA, which are very similar to those in the UCCJEA, and held that a "bald claim to custody, without any legal basis, cannot meet the statutory requirement of a person acting as a parent." The court said that the PKPA does not explain what was intended to be encompassed within the phrase "claims a right to custody," but held that "the claim must at least be a colorable one," otherwise an outright kidnapper making self-serving declarations could qualify as a person acting as a parent. The California *Rogers v. Platt* decision further explained that a "colorable claim" means "a claim that is advanced in good faith on some plausible legal theory," and that it "must be asserted in good faith and must be legally tenable under the theory advanced."

In *Adoption of Zachariah K.*, (1992) 6 Cal.App.4th 1025, the court interpreted both the UCCJA and the PKPA, and made reference to *Rogers v. Platt*, and held that, "Where the birth parent has formally consented to adoption and legal guardianship in the pre-adoptive parents' pending adoption and where, as here, the pre-adoptive parents obtain a court appointment of guardianship, [the prospective adoptive parents have] at least a colorable claim to custody of the minor child." The *Zachariah K.* court held that an Oregon court had jurisdiction over an adoption proceeding filed in Oregon by an Oregon couple who had brought a child from California to Oregon only two days after his birth.

The California *Rogers v. Platt* decision also states that a colorable claim to the right to custody may arise by virtue of a parental relationship or other close familial relationship which gives rise to a right to custody pursuant to law, or by means of a lawful relinquishment, or by the action of a state agency or an order of a court with jurisdiction to confer the right to custody upon a person. The California *Rogers v. Platt* decision ultimately held that the right to temporary physical "custody" upon the completion of an AD-22 form did not confer a sufficient "colorable" right to custody upon the prospective adoptive parents who desired to adopt the child in the District of Columbia. (An AD-22 form only allows a health care facility to release the child to a non-parent, as explained in Chapter 4 of this book.) *Rogers v. Platt* therefore did not have occasion to discuss whether a formal placement of the child, which did occur in *Zachariah K.*, would confer a sufficient colorable claim of right.

(c) Residence of the Child

In interpreting the term "lived from birth," the federal court in *Rogers v. Platt*, (D.D.C. 1986) 641 F.Supp. 381, held that it is irrelevant whether the child was living in a hospital or a more traditional home, given the almost completely dependent nature of an infant. (The federal *Rogers* decision involved a child who was only three months old.) The court also held that since the child had lived for two days in a California hospital, the child could not have lived from birth in the District of Columbia. A similar holding was made in *Zachariah K.*, where an infant was placed for adoption in Oregon with an Oregon couple just days after being born in California.

In re Gloria F., (1989) 212 Cal.App.3d 576, dealt with a situation where a California juvenile court properly took initial jurisdiction of the child under the UCCJA in the context of dependency proceedings, and the court approved of the foster placement of the child with a relative in Michigan, where the child later resided for more than six months. The *Gloria F.* court held that in such a situation the minor is not considered to have "moved away" from California. Instead, as the *Gloria F.* court reasoned, "given the structure of California's dependency statutes," (see Welfare & Institutions Code § 300, et seq.) "the state of California has assumed the normal parental control." The court also held that in dependency proceedings, "a special custodial relationship is created between the court and the subject minor." Thus, one could say that it was actually the juvenile court which was the "person acting as a parent" in *Gloria F.*, and that the relative/foster parent in Michigan was not a "person acting as a parent," even though the Michigan relative/foster parent was charged with the duty to physically care for and supervise the child. Also, *Gloria F.* illustrates the rule of Family Code § 3421(c), which is that the child's physical location is not determinative of jurisdiction.

(d) Home State/Temporary Emergency Jurisdiction

It is possible for California to become the child's home state under circumstances where a California court has issued a child custody order pursuant to its temporary emergency jurisdiction over the child under Family Code § 3424, as explained below. It is unclear whether the six-month rule of Family Code § 3402(g) and (m) would apply in such a case.

(2) "Significant Connections" to California

Family Code § 3421(a)(2) allows a California court to make an initial child custody determination if there is either no "home state" or the child's home state has declined to exercise jurisdiction pursuant to grounds stated in Family Code §§ 3427 (dealing with inconvenient forum) or 3428 (covering "unjustifiable conduct" of a party), and both of the following are true: (A) The child and the child's parent or person acting as a parent have a significant connection with California other than mere physical presence, and (B) substantial evidence is available in California concerning the child's care, protection, training, and personal relationships.

Rogers v. Platt, (1988) 199 Cal.App.3d 1204, applied 28 U.S.C. § 1738A(c)(2)(B), which is similar to Family Code § 3421(a)(2), and held that California had jurisdiction where the birth mother (from California) sought the return of her infant child from a District of Columbia couple with whom the birth mother had originally given temporary physical custody. The court stated that the significant connection to California was that the child's mother lived in California and that the child was born in California. In addition to what was stated in the California *Rogers v. Platt* case, other facts relevant to the "significant connection" rule would include the location of the infant child's health care providers and medical records, which are relevant to "the child's present or future care" (see 28 U.S.C. § 1738A(c)(2)(B)(ii) and Family Code § 3421(a)(2)(B)), if an emergency medical decision needed to be made for the child.

Adoption of Zachariah K., (1992) 6 Cal.App.4th 1025, which interprets both the PKPA and the UCCJA, holds that the mere fact that one state has a significant connection to the child does not exclude another state from having a significant connection to the child. Thus, a court could hold that it is in the best interests of the child for decisions concerning the child's custody be decided by the court in the state wherein the prospective adoptive parents with whom the child has been placed are located, rather than the state wherein the contesting birth parent is located.

Other courts have held that the use of "residency of the birth parent" as a factor in the best interests of the child analysis actually violates the Interstate Compact for the Placement of Children (which is explained later in this chapter), since such criteria hinders the interstate placement of children, in which all of the states have agreed to cooperate. *Adoptive Parents v. Biological Parents*, (S.C. 1994) 446 S.E.2d 404. In other words, in many situations it is in the child's best interests to accord the child his or her substantive rights arising under the ICPC.

(3) California is "More Appropriate Forum"

Under Family Code § 3421(a)(3), a California court may make an initial child custody determination if the courts of all states having jurisdiction under Family Code § 3421(a)(1) [home state] or (2) [significant connections and no home state] have declined to exercise jurisdiction on the ground that a California court is the more appropriate forum to determine the custody of the child under Family Code §§ 3427 or 3428. Family Code § 3427 deals with the classic doctrine of forum non conveniens, while Family Code § 3428 involves attempts to confer jurisdiction based on the "unjustifiable conduct" of a party, both of which are explained below.

(4) "Vacuum" Jurisdiction

Family Code § 3421(a)(4) allows a California court to make an initial child custody determination if no court of any other state would have jurisdiction under the criteria specified in Family Code § 3421(a)(1), (2) or (3). In other words, if there is technically a vacuum of jurisdiction, a California court is permitted by the UCCJEA (as well as the UCCJA and the federal Parental Kidnapping Prevention Act as explained below) to take jurisdiction for the purpose of entering an order that is to be given full faith and credit nationwide.

b) When Does UCCJEA Exclusivity Attach?

Where the court has complied with the provisions of the UCCJEA, and has made a "child custody determination," Family Code § 3422(a) gives that court the exclusive authority to conduct further custody proceedings concerning that child regardless of the actions of the parties or the courts other states. Family Code § 3426 generally prohibits a California court from acting where a proceeding has been "commenced" in another state's court, and vice versa according to the laws of all other states. Family Code § 3402(e) states that "commencement" means the filing of the first pleading.

In *Adoption of Zachariah K.*, (1992) 6 Cal.App.4th 1025, the court held that a guardianship order that was issued by an Oregon court concerning a two-month old child born in California was sufficient to vest Oregon with exclusive jurisdiction to conduct all subsequent proceedings concerning custody of that child. After the Oregon guardianship was ordered, the birth mother attempted to bring a California proceeding for the purpose of seeking to withdraw her consent to the adoption under the laws of California then in existence, but she did nothing in the Oregon courts. The California appellate court held that the Oregon court's subsequent adoption order was final, and that the California court had no jurisdiction to approve the withdrawal of consent.

In *People v. Beach*, (1987) 194 Cal.App.3d 955, a husband moved to San Diego, California in 1977, brought the child of the marriage to live with him in December 1979, and in January 1980 commenced a marital dissolution proceeding in the California courts. The court held that the standard custody order which is pre-printed on the back of the Judicial Council form dissolution summons (see Family Code §§ 3060-3064), and which was properly served 10 days before the first order to show cause hearing in the California court, was sufficient to trigger the exclusivity provisions of the UCCJA. The wife thereafter took the child out-of-state for two days before the order to show cause hearing, and the court held that the pre-printed custody order was considered to be sufficient evidence of a court order to support a conviction of stealing a child from a custodial parent in violation of a custody order (as provided by Penal Code § 278.5(a)). The *People v. Beach* court also held that the wife's attempt to later commence similar child custody litigation in New Mexico was deemed to have no jurisdictional effect.

Beach also speaks of the court's "inherent" (i.e., non-statutory) jurisdiction to determine whether it has jurisdiction. Included in this inherent jurisdiction is the power to issue all orders necessary to preserve the status quo so as to allow the court to ultimately provide complete relief to the parties and act in the best interests of the child. This inherent jurisdiction could form the basis for satisfying the first prong of the federal Parental Kidnapping Prevention Act exclusivity rule, as explained below.

c) Interstate Communication between Courts

Family Code § 3410(a) provides that a California court may communicate directly with a court in another state concerning a proceeding arising under the UCCJEA. Such interstate judicial communication would be appropriate for example where it is necessary for a court to take "temporary emergency jurisdiction," as explained later in this chapter, or in analyzing the factors set forth in Family Code § 3427(b) regarding which state is the most convenient forum. Similar language is provided in the UCCJA, meaning that all courts nationwide are permitted to communicate as to child custody matters. Indeed, in *Adoption of Zachariah K.*, (1992) 6 Cal.App.4th 1025, it was held that the California court abused its discretion by not communicating with the court in the other state.

In addition, the language of Family Code § 3410(a) does not require the communication to be in writing, nor does it limit the right to communicate only to trial courts. In other words, it is conceivable that the judge in the other state could be put on "speaker phone" during oral argument in an appellate court in California. Furthermore, the language of Family Code § 3410 does not place any limits on what the judges in the different states may discuss.

Under Family Code § 3410(b), the court may, but is not required to, allow the parties to participate in the communication. If the parties are not able to participate in the communication, they must be given the opportunity to present facts and legal arguments before a decision on jurisdiction is made. Furthermore, under Family Code § 3410(d), a record must be made of the inter-court communication, and the parties must be informed promptly of the communication and granted access to the "record," which may consist of information provided in a tangible medium or stored in an electronic form. It would appear that an audio recording, or a printout of a string of e-mails, would suffice under the rule.

An exception to the rule concerning access to the record of inter-court communication is set forth in Family Code § 3410(c), which allows courts to communicate with each other concerning schedules, calendars, court records, and similar non-substantive matters, without informing the parties, and without making a record of such communication.

d) Court-Approved Stipulations

In *S.M. v. E.P.*, (2010) 184 Cal.App.4th 1249, child custody proceedings were pending in California and Iowa at the same time. The parties then entered into a stipulation to dismiss the California case, and that stipulation was approved by the Iowa court. The California court in *S.M. v. E.P.* then held that that stipulation brought about a mooting of the California child custody proceedings, and thus dismissed that aspect of the California appeal without prejudice. Since it was a stipulation for a dismissal, it did not constitute "stipulated jurisdiction," which the UCCJEA does not allow. (*In re Marriage of Nurie* (2009) 176 Cal.App.4th 478.)

3. Exclusive Continuing UCCJEA Jurisdiction

As explained in Chapter 1, an order granting an adoption petition is a final order and courts generally do not have continuing jurisdiction to modify an adoption order. However, certain child custody orders are modifiable, such as post-adoption contact and visitation orders, and courts generally do have continuing jurisdiction to modify such orders where needed. In *Adoption of Zachariah K.*, (1992) 6 Cal.App.4th 1025, the court held that even where it appears there is concurrent jurisdiction, only one state should exercise jurisdiction. Therefore, such continuing jurisdiction is deemed to be exclusive, and this exclusivity is enforced by rules which have been enacted nationwide in the form of the UCCJEA or the UCCJA, as well as by the federal PKPA as explained below. Thus, where a child who is subject to a child custody order issued by another state is sought to be adopted in California, or vice versa, one must determine if there is jurisdiction to do so pursuant to the UCCJEA, or UCCJA where applicable.

a) Mandatory Recognition of Out-of-State Orders

Family Code § 3443(a) provides that the California courts shall recognize and enforce a child custody determination of a court of another state if the latter court exercised jurisdiction in substantial conformity with the UCCJEA, or the determination was made under factual circumstances meeting the jurisdictional standards of the UCCJEA (which are likewise contained in the UCCJA) and the determination has not been modified in accordance with the UCCJEA. In order to recognize and enforce a valid out-of-state child custody order, Family Code § 3443(b) allows the California court to utilize any remedy available under the UCCJEA and other laws of California, in cumulative fashion, to enforce that child custody determination.

b) Mandatory Stay due to Out-of-State Proceeding

Family Code § 3426(a) provides that, except with regard to temporary emergency jurisdiction as explained below, a California court may not exercise jurisdiction if, at the time of the commencement of the proceeding, another proceeding concerning the custody of the child has been commenced in a court of a different state having jurisdiction substantially in conformity with the UCCJEA (as with the provisions of the UCCJA), unless the proceeding has been terminated or is stayed by the court of the other state because a court of California is a more convenient forum. If the court determines that a child custody proceeding has been validly commenced in a court in another state, Family Code § 3426(b) requires the California court to order a stay of its proceedings and communicate with the court of the other state. In addition, Family Code § 3426(b) requires the California court to dismiss its proceeding if the out-of-state court which is validly exercising jurisdiction does not determine that a California court is a more appropriate forum.

c) Jurisdiction to Modify a Custody Determination

Where a California court has already issued a child custody order, Family Code § 3422(a) provides that, with the exception of when a court must take "temporary emergency jurisdiction," California has exclusive continuing jurisdiction over child custody questions if the California court made the child custody determination consistent with Family Code § 3421 [the four-part analysis mentioned above] or Family Code § 3423 [forum non conveniens jurisdiction as explained below], until either (1) a California court determines that neither the child, nor the child and one parent, nor the child and a person acting as a parent have a significant connection with this state and that substantial evidence is no longer available in this state concerning the child's care, protection, training, and personal relationships, or (2) a California court or a court of another state determines that the child, the child's parents, and any person acting as a parent do not presently reside in California.

As to the modification of child custody orders issued by other states, Family Code § 3423 provides that, with the exception of when a court must take temporary emergency jurisdiction, a California court may not modify a child custody determination made by a court of another state unless a California court has jurisdiction to make an initial determination pursuant to Family Code § 3421(a)(1) or (2), and either (a) the court of the other state determines it no longer has exclusive, continuing jurisdiction under Family Code § 3422 or that a California court would be a more convenient forum under Family Code § 3427 [dealing with forum non conveniens], or (b) a California court or a court of the other state determines that the child, the child's parents, and any person acting as a parent do not presently reside in the other state.

In *Kumar v. Superior Court*, (1982) 32 Cal.3d 689, the Supreme Court interpreted a similar provision in the UCCJA and held that all petitions for modification of child custody decrees must generally be addressed to the state of original rendition unless that state has lost jurisdiction under the Act's standards. Normally, so long as one parent still lives in the original state, jurisdiction continues in that state. Only when the child and all parties have moved away is deference to that state's continuing jurisdiction no longer required.

In *In re Marriage of Fox*, (1986) 180 Cal.App.3d 862, the court said that where a parent files a petition in a California court for custody, but an out-of-state decree vests custody in the other parent, the California court must first determine whether substantial evidence exists demonstrating that that decree is enforceable under what was then the UCCJA. However, in *Souza v. Superior Court*, (1987) 193 Cal.App.3d 1304, the court held that where a court of another state has prima facie jurisdiction to modify its decree, and proceedings are pending there to specifically determine whether that court still has jurisdiction, the only orderly procedure avoiding a conflict of state rulings is to require the contestant to challenge the other court's assumption of jurisdiction by direct attack in that proceeding. If she does not do so, it becomes a final ruling and is entitled to full faith and credit like any other state court judgment. *Souza* holds that "normal principles of res judicata apply to the determination of subject matter jurisdiction."

In addition, Family Code § 3426(c) provides that in a proceeding to modify a child custody determination, the California court shall determine whether a proceeding to enforce the determination has been commenced in another state. If so, the California court may do any of the following: (1) stay the California proceeding for modification pending the entry of an order of the other state's court enforcing, staying, denying, or dismissing the proceeding for enforcement, (2) enjoin the parties from continuing with the proceeding for enforcement, and/or (3) proceed with the modification under conditions it considers appropriate.

d) "Erosion" of Continuing Jurisdiction

As to child custody orders issued by California courts, Family Code § 3422(a) essentially provides that California may lose exclusive continuing jurisdiction over the child where the parties have moved to another state or have lost all significant connection to California. Family Code § 3422(b) then provides that a California court that has made a child custody determination but has lost exclusive continuing jurisdiction may modify its orders only if it regains Family Code § 3421 jurisdiction to make an initial determination.

As to child custody orders issued in other states, Family Code § 3423 provides that, with the exception of when a court must take temporary emergency jurisdiction as described below, a California court may not modify a child custody determination made by a court of another state unless a California court would have jurisdiction to make an initial determination under Family Code § 3421(a)(1) or (2), and either (a) the court of the other state determines it no longer has exclusive, continuing jurisdiction under Family Code § 3422 or that a California court would be a more convenient forum under Family Code § 3427 [dealing with forum non conveniens], or (b) a California court or a court of the other state determines that the child, the child's parents, and any person acting as a parent do not presently reside in the other state.

In *Souza v. Superior Court*, (1987) 193 Cal.App.3d 1304, the court cited the legislative history behind the Act and stated that for example when the mother moves away with the children to another state, and the father remains in the original state, and allows the mother to keep the children for several years without asserting his custody rights and without visitation, "modification jurisdiction" in the original state ceases. However, in *In re Gloria F.*, (1989) 212 Cal.App.3d 576, which involved a California dependency proceeding in which the juvenile court placed the child with a relative/foster parent in Michigan, and the birth parents and all other parties had gone to Michigan as well, it was held that California retained continuing jurisdiction. On the other hand, *Gloria F.* held that the juvenile court had the authority to conduct proceedings and communicate with the Michigan court for the purpose of determining whether California was still a convenient forum, and was not compelled by the Interstate Compact on the Placement of Children [now codified at Family Code § 7901] to do otherwise.

e) Temporary Emergency Jurisdiction

Family Code § 3424(a) states that a California court may take temporary emergency jurisdiction if the child (i) is present in this state and (ii) has been abandoned or it is necessary in an emergency to protect the child because the child, or a sibling or parent of the child, is subjected to, or threatened with, mistreatment or abuse. Family Code § 3402(a) defines "abandoned" merely as "left without provision for reasonable and necessary care or supervision." *People v. Beach*, (1987) 194 Cal.App.3d 955, held that a threatened abduction of the child represents an emergency type situation since it threatens the welfare of the child and the court's ability to make a meaningful determination of jurisdiction, and since a threatened abduction represents a threatened mistreatment. Notably, there was no physical evidence in *Beach* of an actual threat of bodily harm to the child.

In interpreting Family Code § 3424(a), the court in *In re Jorge G.*, (2008) 164 Cal.App.4th 125, stated that an order assuming emergency jurisdiction under the UCCJEA has time limitations. It must specify a period that the court considers adequate to allow the person seeking an order to obtain an order from the state having jurisdiction. It remains in effect until an order is obtained from the other state within the period specified or the period expires. Even though emergency jurisdiction ordinarily is intended to be short term and limited, the juvenile court may continue to exercise its authority as long as the risk of harm creating the emergency is ongoing. Aside from the necessity of protecting a child from immediate harm, presence of the child in the state is the only prerequisite' to taking action. The finding of an emergency is to be made only after an evidentiary hearing, although the juvenile court can detain the child before that hearing. And emergency jurisdiction continues over the minor after the determination of the existence of an emergency because of the emergency presented by the abuse of the child, and the impossibility of returning him immediately to his parents.

If there is no previous enforceable child custody determination and if there is no child custody proceeding has been commenced in a state having jurisdiction, Family

Code § 3424(b) provides that a child custody determination made pursuant to the California court's temporary emergency jurisdiction remains in effect until an order is obtained from another state having jurisdiction under the UCCJEA or UCCJA. If no child custody proceeding has been commenced in a state having jurisdiction under the UCCJEA or UCCJA, the California court's child custody order made pursuant to temporary emergency jurisdiction becomes a final determination if it so provides, and California becomes the child's home state.

If there is a previous enforceable child custody determination or a child custody proceeding has been commenced in another state with jurisdiction, Family Code § 3424(c) provides that a California court order issued pursuant to temporary emergency jurisdiction must specify in the order a period of time that the court considers adequate to allow the person seeking the California order to obtain an enforceable order from the other state as well. The California order remains in effect either until an order is obtained from the other state within the specified period, or until the period expires.

Family Code § 3424(d) requires the courts to communicate. The statute addresses both situations, i.e., when a California court is asked to take temporary emergency jurisdiction where there is also a proceeding or order in another state, and when a California child custody proceeding or order is pending and that California court is informed that another state is taking temporary emergency jurisdiction over the child. The purpose of the interstate judicial communication is to attempt to resolve the emergency, protect the safety of the parties and the child, and determine a period for the duration of the temporary order.

4. Declining Jurisdiction – Forum Non Conveniens

Even if a California court has jurisdiction to make a child custody order, the court is authorized by Family Code § 3427(a) to decline to exercise its jurisdiction at any time if it determines that it is an inconvenient forum under the circumstances and that a court of another state is a more appropriate forum. The laws of all other states have a similar provision, and if a court in another state has determined that it was an inconvenient forum, California could take jurisdiction pursuant to Family Code § 3421(a)(2) or (3).

The issue of inconvenient forum may be raised upon motion of a party, the court's own motion, or request of another court. In addition, Family Code § 3427(d) even allows the California courts to decline to exercise its jurisdiction if the child custody determination is incidental to a dissolution of marriage action or other proceeding while still retaining jurisdiction over the marital dissolution or other proceeding.

If the California court does determine that it is an inconvenient forum and that a court of another state is a more appropriate forum, Family Code § 3427(c) requires the California court to order a stay of its proceedings upon condition that a child custody proceeding be promptly commenced in another designated state, and any other condition that it considers just and proper.

To determine whether California is an inconvenient forum, Family Code § 3427(b) requires the court to consider whether it is appropriate for a court of another state to exercise jurisdiction and allows the parties to submit information concerning (1) whether domestic violence has occurred and is likely to continue in the future and which state could best protect the parties and the child, (2) the length of time the child has resided outside California, (3) the distance between the California court and the court in the state that would assume jurisdiction, (4) the degree of financial hardship to the parties in litigating in one forum over the other, (5) any agreement of the parties as to which state should assume jurisdiction, (6) the nature and location of the evidence required to resolve the pending litigation, including testimony of the child, (7) the ability of the court of each state to decide the issue expeditiously and the procedures necessary to present the evidence, and (8) the familiarity of the court of each state with the facts and issues in the pending litigation.

Family Code § 3427(e) sets forth a provision for costs and fees. It provides that if California is clearly an inappropriate forum for the proceeding, the California court may require the party who commenced the California proceeding to pay attorney's fees, necessary travel and other expenses for the parties and witnesses, in addition to the costs of the proceeding in this state. Payment is to be made to the clerk of the court for remittance to the proper party.

5. Declining Jurisdiction – "Unjustifiable Conduct"

Family Code § 3428(a) provides that, except with regard to taking temporary emergency jurisdiction, if a California court has jurisdiction because a person seeking to invoke jurisdiction has engaged in unjustifiable conduct, the court shall decline to exercise its jurisdiction unless one of the following are true: (1) the parents and all persons acting as parents have acquiesced in the exercise of jurisdiction, (2) a court of the state otherwise having jurisdiction under the UCCJEA or UCCJA determines that California is a more appropriate forum under Family Code § 3427, or (3) no court of any other state would have jurisdiction under the UCCJEA or UCCJA. *In re Marriage of Nurie*, (2009) 176 Cal.App.4th 478, held that Family Code § 3428(a) "requires a court to decline jurisdiction only when the court's jurisdiction is invoked as a result of unclean hands, not when one of the party's hands get dirty after jurisdiction has been properly asserted."

The statute appears to cover cases involving child abduction for the purpose of forum-shopping, which is essentially what occurred in *People v. Beach*, (1987) 194 Cal.App.3d 955, though the court did not expressly state that the mother's taking of the child from California to New Mexico, with the assistance of the child's grandfather, triggered the "unjustifiable conduct" rule. However, the *Beach* court did cite *Wilborn v. Superior Court*, (1959) 51 Cal.2d 828, which explains that whatever right a parent has in the absence of a custody order to invade another's custody of the child may not be delegated to an agent, even if that agent is a relative.

However, Family Code § 3428(d) provides that a court shall not consider as a factor weighing against the petitioner any taking of the child, or retention of the child after a visit or other temporary relinquishment of physical custody, from the person who has legal custody, if there is evidence that the taking or retention of the child was a result of domestic violence against the petitioner, as defined in Family Code § 6211 (which speaks of abuse against a child or against a spouse, or against someone merely involved in a "dating or engagement relationship.")

If the California court declines to exercise its jurisdiction because of a party's unjustifiable conduct, Family Code § 3428(b) allows the court to fashion an appropriate remedy to ensure the safety of the child and prevent a repetition of the unjustifiable conduct, including staying the proceeding until a child custody proceeding is commenced in a court having jurisdiction under the UCCJEA or UCCJA, as the case may be.

Family Code § 3428(c) includes a costs provision. It states that if a court dismisses a petition or stays a proceeding because it declines jurisdiction due to a party's unjustifiable conduct, it shall assess against the party seeking to invoke its jurisdiction necessary and reasonable expenses including costs, communication expenses, attorney's fees, investigative fees, expenses for witnesses, travel expenses, and child care during the course of the proceedings, unless the party from whom fees are sought establishes that the assessment would be clearly improper. The court may not assess fees, costs, or expenses against the CDSS unless authorized by law other than the UCCJEA.

D. Procedural Considerations as to California Jurisdiction

1. Necessity for Notice and an Opportunity to be Heard

Family Code § 3425(a) provides that before a child custody determination is made, notice and an opportunity to be heard must be given to all persons entitled to notice under California law as in child custody proceedings between California residents, plus any parent whose parental rights have not been terminated, and any person having physical custody of the child. Where notice and opportunity to be heard have not been provided, the person seeking to enforce the child custody order is not entitled to utilize the enforcement provisions of the UCCJEA. *Cole v. Superior Court*, (1985) 173 Cal.App.3d 265, holds that the jurisdictional determination is an important preliminary decision, and should be made after a full and fair evidentiary hearing.

As to joinder of parties, Family Code § 3425(c) states that the obligation to join a party and the right to intervene as a party in a child custody proceeding under the UCCJEA are governed by California law as in child custody proceedings between residents of this state. Such law is mentioned in Chapters 3, 4, 5 and 7, and elsewhere in this book.

2. Service of Process on Out-of-State Domiciliaries

Family Code § 3408(a) states, "Notice required for the exercise of jurisdiction when a person is outside this state may be given in a manner prescribed by the law of this state for service of process or by the law of the state in which the service is made." As a matter of practice, the person serving notice should comply with both sets of laws. The statute also says, "Notice must be given in a manner reasonably calculated to give actual notice but may be by publication if other means are not effective." To obtain leave of court to serve by publication, the person serving notice should provide evidence showing that other means are not effective.

Code of Civil Procedure § 415.40 allows service on "a person outside this state" (which is a broader category than "residents" of other states) by first-class mail, postage prepaid, return receipt requested, and states that service is complete 10 days after the mailing. Where the person is in a foreign country, one must comply with the applicable treaty governing service of process. For example, service of process on an individual in Mexico must comply with the Inter-American Convention on Letters Rogatory (see *Kreimerman v. Casa Veerkamp, S.A.*, (9th Cir. 1994) 22 F.3d 634), and one must comply with the Hague Service Convention to effectuate service on individuals located in various other countries (see *Kott v. Superior Court*, (1996) 45 Cal.App.4th 1126).

Importantly, Family Code § 3408(c) states, "Notice is not required for the exercise of jurisdiction with respect to a person who submits to the jurisdiction of the court." It is not clear how the courts would interpret this rule, i.e., whether "submitting to jurisdiction" would include an unrepresented person's mere physical presence in court or sending of a letter to the judge asking that some particular thing be done.

3. Duty to Immediately Provide Information to the Court

Under Family Code § 3429(a), each party, in his or her first pleading or in an attached affidavit, shall give information, if reasonably ascertainable, under oath as to the child's present address or whereabouts, the places where the child has lived during the last five years, and the names and present addresses of the persons with whom the child has lived during that period. However, where there are allegations of domestic violence or child abuse, any confidential addresses of the child and of the party alleging violence or abuse may not be disclosed.

The pleading or affidavit must also state whether the party: (1) has participated in any capacity in any other proceeding concerning the custody of or visitation with the child, (2) knows of any proceeding that could affect the current proceeding, including enforcement proceedings, domestic violence proceedings, protective orders, termination of parental rights, and adoptions and, (3) knows the names and addresses of any person not a party to the proceeding who has physical custody of the child or claims rights of legal custody or physical custody of or visitation with the child and if so the names and addresses of those persons. Where there is a proceeding that is pending or that has been completed, Family Code § 3429(a) requires the petitioner to identify the court, the case number, nature of the proceeding and the date of the child custody determination, if any. The Judicial Council publishes a standard form UCCJEA declaration which asks for the specifically required information. In addition, Family Code §§ 3445 and 3446 allow any party to register an out-of-state custody order in California, and provides a procedure where that order may be brought to the attention of the court for the purposes of enforcement.

Family Code § 3426(b) requires the court to examine the court documents and the information the parties' supplied in the UCCJEA declaration. Family Code § 3429(d) then provides that each party has a continuing duty to inform the court of any proceeding in this or any other state that could affect the current proceeding. Family Code § 3429(b) states that if this information is not provided, the court may order a stay of the proceedings until the required information is furnished. Likewise, Family Code §

3429(c) states that if the UCCJEA declaration described above answers any of the questions described in Family Code § 3429(a)(1) through (3) in the affirmative, the declarant shall give additional information under oath as required by the court. The court may examine the parties under oath as to details of the information furnished and other matters pertinent to the court's jurisdiction, as well as to the disposition of the case.

In interpreting similar provisions in the UCCJA, the court in *People v. Beach*, (1987) 194 Cal.App.3d 955, held that the declaration is not statutorily required to cover all of the jurisdictional grounds and that there is no requirement that the declaration to be used as the sole basis for the jurisdictional determination. The *Beach* court also held that an interim custody order is not void merely because the petitioner has made some allegations showing that there are grounds for jurisdiction in a state other than California.

4. Immunity from General Purpose Jurisdiction

Family Code § 3409(a) and (c) provides that a party to a child custody proceeding is not subject to personal jurisdiction in this state for another proceeding or purpose solely by reason of having participated, or of having been physically present for the purpose of participating, in the proceeding. On the other hand, Family Code § 3409(b) states that such a person is not immune from service of process in this state, nor immune from service of process allowable under the laws of other states.

5. Interstate Cooperation in Marshalling Evidence

a) Securing the In-Court Appearance of Parties

As to parties who are California residents, Family Code § 3430(a) provides that in a California child custody proceeding, the court may order a party to the proceeding who is in California to appear before the court in person with or without the child, and may order any person who is in California and who has physical custody or control of the child to appear in person with the child. In addition, Family Code § 3430(c) provides that the court may enter any orders necessary to ensure the safety of the child and of any person ordered to appear.

As to individuals who are not California residents, Family Code § 3430(b) states that if the court desires the presence of a party who is outside California, the court may order that the notice given pursuant to Family Code § 3408 [which describes the manner of serving process] include a statement directing the party to appear in person with or without the child and informing the party that failure to appear may result in a decision adverse to the party. Family Code § 3430(d) then provides that the court may require another party to pay the out-of-state party's reasonable and necessary expenses.

b) Depositions of Out-of-State Residents

Family Code § 3411(a) provides that, in addition to other procedures, a party to a child custody proceeding may offer testimony of witnesses who are located in another state, including the testimony of the parties and of the child. This may be accomplished by deposition or other means allowable in California for testimony taken in another state (which normally entails an out-of-state commission pursuant to Code of Civil Procedure § 2026.010). In addition, under Family Code § 3411(b), a California court may permit an individual residing in another state to be deposed or to testify by telephone, audiovisual means, or other electronic means before a designated court or at another location in that state, and the courts of the two states are to cooperate in designating an appropriate location for the deposition or testimony.

c) Documentary Evidence

The rules of evidence do not bar the introduction of a hard copy of a document merely because it was created outside of California. In addition, Family Code § 3411(c) says that documentary evidence transmitted from another state to a California court by technological means that do not produce an original writing may not be excluded from evidence on an objection based on the means of transmission. Of course, these rules do not superseded other rules governing documentary evidence.

d) Court's Cooperation in Interstate Proceeding

Family Code § 3412(b) allows, but does not require, a California court to accede to various kinds of requests made by courts of other states. These requests are outlined in Family Code § 3412(a) and include requests to, (1) hold an evidentiary hearing, (2) order a person to produce or give evidence pursuant to procedures of the other state, (3) order that an evaluation be made with respect to the custody of a child involved in a pending proceeding, (4) forward to the other court a certified copy of the transcript of the record of the hearing in the California court, the evidence otherwise presented, and any evaluation prepared in compliance with the request, and (5) order a party to a child custody proceeding or any person having physical custody of the child to appear in the proceeding with or without the child. The first sentence of Family Code § 3412(a) allows the court of the other state to do likewise upon the request of a California court.

In addition, Family Code § 3412(d) requires the California courts to preserve the pleadings, orders, decrees, records of hearings, evaluations, and other pertinent records with respect to a child custody proceeding until the child is 18 years old, and upon appropriate request by a court or law enforcement official of another state, the court shall forward a certified copy of those records. This would therefore be an exception to the general rule of confidentiality of such records, as explained in Chapter 12 of this book.

6. Calendar Preference for UCCJEA Issues

According to Family Code § 3407, if a question of existence or exercise of jurisdiction under this part is raised in a child custody proceeding, the question, upon request of a party, must be given priority on the calendar and handled expeditiously.

7. Appellate Procedure

Family Code § 3454 and Code of Civil Procedure § 904.1(a)(10) allow an aggrieved party to take an immediate appeal from "a final order under this chapter [i.e., the "general provisions" of the UCCJEA] in accordance with expedited appellate procedures in other civil cases." The UCCJEA, as codified in California, contains four "chapters," and it is not clear why Family Code § 3454 speaks only in terms of "this chapter." The statute also provides that a stay of the order cannot be imposed on appeal unless it is a "temporary emergency order."

As for the scope of appellate review, *Adoption of Zachariah K.*, (1992) 6 Cal.App.4th 1025, interpreted the UCCJA, and stated that "a reviewing court is not bound by the trial court's findings and may independently reweigh the jurisdictional facts. Subject matter jurisdiction either exists or does not exist at the time the action is commenced." This is a departure from the appellate court's customary deference to a trial court's factual findings that are based on substantial evidence.

E. The U.S. Parental Kidnapping Prevention Act

1. Nationally Exclusive Jurisdiction under the PKPA

The PKPA was enacted in 1980 and is set forth at 28 U.S.C. § 1738A. It provides at 28 U.S.C. § 1738A(a) that the appropriate authorities of every State generally must enforce, according to its terms, any "custody determination" or "visitation determination" made consistently with the PKPA by a court of another State. Also, under 28 U.S.C. § 1738A(d), the initial PKPA court is entitled to exclusive continuing jurisdiction over the child. As for proceedings which are pending, 28 U.S.C. § 1738A(g) provides that a court in one state shall not exercise jurisdiction in any custody or visitation proceeding commenced during the pendency of a custody or visitation proceeding in a court in another State which is exercising jurisdiction consistently with the PKPA.

In order for a court to act consistently with the PKPA, it must comply with a three-prong rule, which is essentially that (a) the state court must have jurisdiction under its own state laws, (b) it must meet one of five specifically stated conditions (which are very similar to the UCCJEA), and (c) all interested persons must be given "reasonable notice and opportunity to be heard." This rule is explained further below. There is no U.S. Supreme Court case law substantively interpreting any of the three prongs.

In *Thompson v. Thompson*, (1988) 484 U.S. 174, the U.S. Supreme Court held that once a state exercises jurisdiction consistently with the PKPA, no other state may exercise concurrent jurisdiction over the custody dispute, even if such a state would have been empowered to take jurisdiction in the first instance, and all states must accord full faith and credit to the first state's ensuing custody decree. The California Supreme Court has held that the PKPA preempts state law on the issue of jurisdiction by a state to render a valid custody decree. (See *People v. Superior Court (Smolin)* (1986) 41 Cal.3d 758, *rev'd on different grounds*, *California v. Superior Court* (1987) 482 U.S. 400.) The court in *Adoption of Zachariah K.*, (1992) 6 Cal.App.4th 1025, took pre-emption a step further and held that whether a California court may find jurisdiction under the UCCJA depends upon whether the other state had jurisdiction to make its orders under the PKPA. The U.S. Supreme Court decision in *Smolin* also held the PKPA creates a uniform federal rule governing custody determinations to which state courts must adhere.

2. What Cases and Orders Are Subject to the PKPA?

The PKPA identifies "custody determinations" and "visitation determinations" as being the judicial acts which are enforceable nationwide under 28 U.S.C. § 1738A(a). "Custody determination" is defined at 28 U.S.C. § 1738A(b)(3) as "a judgment, decree, or other order of a court providing for the custody of a child, and includes permanent and temporary orders, and initial orders and modifications." Under 28 U.S.C. § 1738A(b)(9), "visitation determination" is defined as "a judgment, decree, or other order of a court providing for the visitation of a child and includes permanent and temporary orders and initial orders and modifications." In addition, the court in *Rogers v. Platt*, (1988) 199 Cal.App.3d 1204, held that the issuance of a writ of habeas corpus for the child constituted an order which triggered PKPA exclusivity. (Habeas corpus is discussed in Chapter 10.)

Unlike the UCCJEA, there is no provision in the PKPA which excludes adoptions from its coverage. Thus, it appears that the statement from *Souza v. Superior Court*, (1987) 193 Cal.App.3d 1304, that an adoption case is a custody proceeding, would be the governing rule, meaning that adoptions are subject to the PKPA. Nevertheless, it should be noted that the word "custody" is not defined by the PKPA.

3. Definition of "State"

The PKPA defines "State" at 28 U.S.C. § 1738A(b)(8) as "a State of the United States, the District of Columbia, the Commonwealth of Puerto Rico, or a territory or possession of the United States." Thus, while the PKPA covers the entire nation, it does not have the global scope that is contemplated by the UCCJEA, as explained above.

4. Three-Prong Analysis to Determine PKPA Compliance

According to 28 U.S.C. § 1738A(c) and (e), the PKPA is satisfied if the court which issued the child custody or visitation determination has jurisdiction under the laws of its State, and one of five specifically stated conditions are met (as explained below), and all interested persons are given "reasonable notice and opportunity to be heard."

a) Jurisdiction under the Laws of the Forum State

As to first prong (28 U.S.C. § 1738A(c)(1)), which is "jurisdiction under the laws of the forum state," this element would be satisfied as to a California adoption by compliance with Family Code § 9210 and/or the UCCJEA. The same would be true for an adoption completed in a state having enacted the UCCJEA and/or a law similar to Family Code § 9210, where the adoption is being enforced in California for some reason. Compliance with the UCCJA would satisfy the first prong as to orders issued in those states still using the UCCJA. In addition, as stated in *People v. Beach*, (1987) 194 Cal.App.3d 955, the laws of the forum state might include judicial decisions speaking of the court's inherent jurisdiction to decide whether it has subject matter jurisdiction over a particular child custody matter.

While the UCCJEA states that adoptions are excluded from its coverage, the termination of parental rights which may occur concurrently with the adoption is expressly included in the UCCJEA at Family Code § 3402(d). In addition, if there were an attack on a California adoption in another state by a person whose parental rights were terminated by a California court which was properly exercising jurisdiction under the UCCJEA, that person's attack on the termination of parental rights would be dismissed pursuant to the PKPA, and the attack purely on the adoption could be dismissed for lack of standing.

b) Satisfaction of One of Five PKPA Conditions

The second prong (28 U.S.C. § 1738A(c)(2)) is the satisfaction of one of five conditions, which are somewhat similar to the UCCJEA's four-part analysis, and which are explained below:

(1) Home State

According to 28 U.S.C. § 1738A(c)(2)(A), the second prong is met if the State which issued the child custody order (i) is the home State of the child on the date of the commencement of the proceeding, or (ii) had been the child's home State within six months before the date of the commencement of the proceeding and the child is absent from such State because of his removal or retention by a contestant or for other reasons, and a contestant continues to live in such State. In interpreting this provision, the courts have applied essentially the same reasoning used to determine whether there is a "home state" under the UCCJEA and the UCCJA.

Statutorily, "home State" is defined at 28 U.S.C. § 1738A(b)(4) as follows: "the State in which, immediately preceding the time involved, the child lived with his parents, a parent, or a person acting as parent, for at least six consecutive months, and in the case of a child less than six months old, the State in which the child lived from birth with any of such persons. Periods of temporary absence of any of such persons are counted as part of the six-month or other period."

"Person acting as parent" is then defined at 28 U.S.C. § 1738A(b)(6) as "a person, other than a parent, who has physical custody of a child and who has either been awarded custody by a court or claims a right to custody." According to 28 U.S.C. § 1738A(b)(1), "child" means a person under the age of eighteen. "Physical custody" is defined by 28 U.S.C. § 1738A(b)(7) as "actual possession and control of a child." These terms are explained earlier in this chapter with regard to the UCCJEA's use of these phrases.

(2) Significant Connection – Best Interests

Under 28 U.S.C. § 1738A(c)(2)(B), the second prong for PKPA compliance is met if (i) it appears that no state would have had "home state" jurisdiction as explained above, and (ii) it is in the best interest of the child that a court of the State which issued the order assume jurisdiction because the child and at least one contestant have a significant connection with that State other than their mere physical presence there, and there is available in that state substantial evidence concerning the child's present or future care, protection, training, and personal relationships. The word "contestant" is defined at 28 U.S.C. § 1738A(b)(2) as "a person, including a parent or grandparent, who claims a right to custody or visitation of a child." In interpreting this provision, the courts apply essentially the same reasoning used to determine whether there are "significant connections" with a state under the UCCJEA and the UCCJA.

(3) Emergency – Abandonment or Threat of Abuse

According to 28 U.S.C. § 1738A(c)(2)(C), the second prong is met if the child is physically present in the state which issued the order and (i) the child has been abandoned, or (ii) it is necessary in an emergency to protect the child because the child, a sibling, or parent of the child has been subjected to or threatened with mistreatment or abuse." This is very similar to the "temporary emergency jurisdiction" rules set forth in the UCCJEA, as explained above.

(4) Vacuum or More Appropriate Forum

According to 28 U.S.C. § 1738A(c)(2)(D), the second prong is met if (i) it appears that no State would have been able to satisfy any of the other four PKPA conditions or another state declined to exercise jurisdiction on the ground that the state whose jurisdiction is in issue is the more appropriate forum to determine the custody or visitation of the child, and (ii) it is in the best interest of the child that such court assume jurisdiction. This section appears to be the conjunction of the two UCCJEA jurisdictional grounds set forth at Family Code § 3421(a)(3) and (4), which are explained above.

(5) Continuing Jurisdiction and Residence

According to 28 U.S.C. § 1738A(c)(2)(E), the second prong is met if the court which issued the order had continuing jurisdiction pursuant to 28 U.S.C. § 1738A(d), which is explained below. Under 28 U.S.C. § 1738A(d), the jurisdiction of a state court which has made a child custody or visitation determination consistently with the PKPA continues as long as the jurisdictional requirements under its own laws continue to be met (as for example where California is still a "convenient forum" under the UCCJEA) and that state remains the residence of the child or of any contestant.

c) Reasonable Notice / Opportunity to Be Heard

The third prong for nationwide enforceability of a child custody order pursuant to 28 U.S.C. § 1738A(a) is that under 28 U.S.C. § 1738A(e), "Before a child custody or visitation determination is made, reasonable notice and opportunity to be heard shall be given to the contestants, any parent whose parental rights have not been previously terminated and any person who has physical custody of a child." The PKPA does not define what is "reasonable."

As for child custody determinations that are made after an interested party has been merely served by publication, it would appear that such notice would be deemed "reasonable" only if there was strict compliance with the due diligence requirements of Code of Civil Procedure § 415.50 prior to a court-approved service by publication.

5. Article IV Full Faith and Credit v. the PKPA

Generally, the Full Faith and Credit Clause of Article IV, Section 1 of the U.S. Constitution requires that both federal and state courts give binding effect to the judicial acts of all other states. The Constitution's Full Faith and Credit Clause does not entail a three-prong analysis nor does it have five alternative jurisdictional conditions, as does the PKPA. However, Congress clearly had legislative authority to enact the PKPA in light of the Constitution's express grant of legislative power in Article IV, Section 1 itself.

Therefore, it is possible that a child custody order could be nationally enforceable pursuant to the PKPA, even if the parent contesting the order did not have minimum contacts with the forum state wherein the order was issued, as would otherwise appear to be required under the Full Faith and Credit Clause. (See *May v. Anderson*, (1953) 345 U.S. 528; *International Shoe Co. v. Washington* (1945) 326 U.S. 310, 316.) On the flip side, it is also possible that an initial child custody determination could be non-compliant with the PKPA while still being entitled to full faith and credit under the U.S. Constitution and the doctrines of res judicata and collateral estoppel. For these reasons, the PKPA adds to the Constitution's Full Faith and Credit Clause, and vice versa, with regard to the kinds of custody orders which are entitled to nationwide enforceability.

6. PKPA Jurisdiction to Modify Another State's Order

According to 28 U.S.C. § 1738A(f), a court of one state may modify another state court's determination of the custody of a particular child if (1) it has jurisdiction to make such a child custody determination; and (2) the initial court no longer has jurisdiction, or it has declined to exercise jurisdiction to modify such determination. At 28 U.S.C. § 1738A(h) the converse is also stated, in that a court of one state may not modify a visitation determination made by a court of another state unless the court of the other state no longer has jurisdiction to modify such determination or has declined to exercise jurisdiction to modify such determination. The terms "modification" and "modify" are described by 28 U.S.C. § 1738A(b)(5) as referring to a "custody or visitation determination which modifies, replaces, supersedes, or otherwise is made subsequent to, a prior custody or visitation determination concerning the same child, whether made by the same court or not."

7. No Private Federal Cause of Action under the PKPA

In *Thompson v. Thompson*, (1988) 484 U.S. 174, the U.S. Supreme Court held that the PKPA does not create a cause of action in federal court to determine which of two conflicting state custody decrees is valid. Therefore, where there are conflicting state custody decrees, it would appear that the remedy is to petition the court which issued the inappropriate decree to vacate its order, and to pursue appellate remedies after that if the inappropriate decree is not vacated. Unless there is an obvious defect in jurisdiction, disobedience of an order is not a viable option, even if the order rests on substantively inappropriate grounds. In *Walker v. City of Birmingham*, (1967) 388 U.S. 307, the U.S. Supreme Court held that disobedience of an injunction that violated the constitutional guarantee of free speech was punishable by contempt sanctions, even including incarceration.

III. THE INTERSTATE COMPACT ON THE PLACEMENT OF CHILDREN

All 50 states and the District of Columbia have ratified the Interstate Compact on the Placement of Children ("ICPC") through state legislative enactment. The 10 articles of the ICPC provide a system whereby the entity placing the child from one state (referred to as the "sending agency" in the "sending state") may communicate and cooperate with the authorities located in the state wherein the child is being placed (referred to as the "receiving state").

Family Code § 7907 provides that if there has been compliance with the ICPC, no provision of California law restricting out-of-state placement of children for adoption shall apply. The actual compact is codified in California at Family Code § 7901, and the Legislature has enacted additional statutes related to the ICPC at Family Code §§ 7900-7912. Also, Family Code § 7901, Art. 7, expressly gives the "compact administrator" or "general coordinator" (which in California is the Director of the CDSS) "power to promulgate rules and regulations to carry out more effectively the terms and provisions of this compact."

A. Purposes of the ICPC

Family Code § 7901, Art. 1, states that the overriding purpose and policy is that all 50 states and the District of Columbia "cooperate with each other in the interstate placement of children." Additional purposes are provided in Article 1 such that the interstate cooperation shall result in, (a) each child receiving the maximum opportunity to be placed in a suitable environment and with persons or institutions having appropriate qualifications and facilities to provide a necessary and desirable degree and type of care, (b) the appropriate authorities in the receiving state having full opportunity to ascertain the circumstances of the proposed placement so as to promote full compliance with applicable requirements for the protection of the child, (c) the proper authorities of the sending state obtaining the most complete information on the basis on which to evaluate a projected placement before it is made, and (d) promoting appropriate jurisdictional arrangements for the care of children.

B. General Operation of the ICPC

1. Conduct Prohibited Under the ICPC

a) General Rule

Family Code § 7901, Art. 3, subsec. (a), states, "No sending agency shall send, bring, or cause to be sent or brought into any other party state any child for placement in foster care or as a preliminary to a possible adoption unless the sending agency shall comply with each and every requirement set forth in this article and with the applicable laws of the receiving state governing the placement of children therein."

The court in *In re Eli F.*, (1989) 212 Cal.App.3d 228, held that the ICPC applies to the juvenile court in a dependency case where an out-of-state placement with a relative is contemplated. However, in *Tara S. v. Superior Court*, (1993) 13 Cal.App.4th 1834, the court held that the ICPC does not apply in dependency proceedings when a California juvenile court sends the child to a parent in another state, even if that parent was subject to a prior court order depriving him of custody rights.

b) Definition of "Sending Agency"

Family Code § 7901, Art. 2, subsec. (b), defines "sending agency" as "a party state, or officer or employee thereof; subdivision of a party state, or officer or employee thereof; a court of a party state; a person, corporation, association, charitable agency, or other entity which sends, brings, or causes to be sent or brought any child to another party state."

Although not defined, a "party state" would appear to mean one of the 50 states or the District of Columbia, since all have enacted the ICPC. Since this is merely an "interstate" compact, it does not appear that the ICPC applies to a purely intercountry adoption, wherein only one U.S. state is involved. It would also appear that a "subdivision of a party state" would include a county, and an officer thereof would include a director of a county social services agency. Where the child is in the custody of the juvenile court in the course of dependency proceedings, the decision in *In re Eli F.*, (1989) 212 Cal.App.3d 228, holds that it is the juvenile court which is the sending agency.

Interestingly, the ICPC definition of "sending agency" includes a "person" who causes a child to be "sent" to another state. Importantly, the ICPC definition of "sending agency" does not include the words "place" or "placement." Just as importantly, there is nothing in this ICPC definition that allows the substitution of one entity for another in the role of "sending agency," nor is there any provision allowing for more than one sending agency.

c) Definition of "Child"

Family Code § 7901, Art. 2, subsec. (a), defines "child" merely as "a person who, by reason of minority, is legally subject to parental, guardianship, or similar control." Based on this definition of "child," it does not appear that the ICPC covers the situation in which a pregnant woman comes to the receiving state for the purpose of giving birth to the child to be adopted. A fetus is not a "minor," and cannot be the subject of a guardianship.

The ICPC is ambiguous as to the criteria for determining if the child comes within the jurisdiction of the "sending state" or the "receiving state" in the first place, meaning the ICPC might impermissibly intrude into the PKPA and UCCJEA. The ICPC does not use the word "residence" or "domicile" or "birth," nor any form thereof, in referring to the child. Instead, the ICPC definition of "sending agency" refers broadly to "any child." On the other hand, if a court in the receiving state, which would presumably be the state where the adoption would be completed, had PKPA jurisdiction over the child, it would also have jurisdiction to determine if there was an ICPC violation as to that child.

d) Definition of "Receiving State"

Family Code § 7901, Art. 2, subsec. (c), defines "receiving state" as "the state to which a child is sent, brought, or caused to be sent or brought, whether by public authorities or private persons or agencies, and whether for placement with state or local public authorities or for placement with private agencies or persons." This definition of "receiving state" does not appear to require that state's agencies to actually or constructively "receive" the child. Therefore, a state could become a receiving state upon the child's mere arrival in that state.

e) Definition of "Placement"

Family Code § 7901, Art. 2, subsec. (d), defines "placement" as "the arrangement for the care of a child in a family free or boarding home or in a child-caring agency or institution but does not include any institution caring for the mentally ill, mentally defective or epileptic or any institution primarily educational in character, and any hospital or other medical facility." Since the ICPC definition of "placement" includes "the arrangement for the care of a child in a family," adoptive placements would clearly be covered by the definition. Also, this definition does not require the signing of a placement agreement or any document. However, according to Family Code § 7901, Art. 3, subsec. (a), as explained later in this chapter, an ICPC violation would exist in California if there were no placement agreement.

Family Code § 7907.5(a) states that the ICPC does not apply to the adoptive placement with a California resident in California of a child who was born in California. However, Family Code § 7907.5(b) states that the ICPC shall apply if the adoptive placement is with a non-California resident (apparently if that person's home is in another U.S. state), even if the child was born in California and regardless of where the adoption petition is filed.

Where an Indian child is being moved, Family Code § 7907.3 states that the ICPC shall not apply to any placement, sending, or bringing of an Indian child into another state pursuant to a transfer of jurisdiction to a tribal court under the Indian Child Welfare Act. It does not appear that Family Code § 7907.3 applies to all movement of an Indian child across state lines.

2. Requirements for Compliance with the ICPC

a) Sending Agency's Notice of Intent

Family Code § 7901, Art. 3, subsec. (b), provides that before sending, bringing, or causing any child to be sent or brought into a receiving state for placement in foster care or as a preliminary to a possible adoption, the sending agency must furnish the appropriate public authorities in the receiving state with written notice of the intention to send, bring, or place the child in the receiving state. The notice must contain (1) The child's name, birthdate and birthplace, (2) the identity and address or addresses of the parents or legal guardian, (3) the name and address of the person, agency, or institution to or with which the sending agency proposes to send, bring, or place the child, and (4) a full statement of the reasons for the proposed action and evidence of the authority pursuant to which the placement is proposed to be made.

In California, the CDSS has published Form ICPC-100A, entitled Interstate Compact Placement Request, to allow for easy compliance with Family Code § 7901, Art. 3, subsec. (b). The ICPC-100A Form provides instructions both to the individual seeking to comply with the ICPC, the sending agency and the receiving state. The ICPC-100B Form is simply the document which allows the sending agency to be informed of the final status of the case.

b) Receiving State's Notice of Acceptance of Child

Family Code § 7901, Art. 3, subsec. (d), provides that the child shall not be sent, brought, or caused to be sent or brought into the receiving state until the appropriate public authorities in the receiving state shall notify the sending agency, in writing, to the effect that the proposed placement does not appear to be contrary to the child's interests.

Where the placement to another state is a "priority placement," and the receiving state's public officials are slow in processing the ICPC notifications, an individual may seek relief from a California court, which may, pursuant to California Rule of Court 5.616(b) and (f), request "assistance" from a court in the receiving state in expediting the interstate placement. For these purposes, the California Judicial Council has published Standard Form JV-565 by which a California judge may "urge" the authorities in the receiving state to "communicate directly with" the California judge in an effort to expedite the interstate placement. Form JV-567 is also used in connection with these purposes.

In addition, where it is permitted in the particular state at issue, one could seek a writ of mandate from the court in the receiving state. Writs of mandate in California are discussed generally in Chapter 5 of this book, however one would have to consult with an attorney licensed in the other state concerning whether such a procedure exists in the receiving state, and the procedures related thereto. In any event, it would appear that a person would have to exhaust his or her remedies under California Rule of Court 5.616 before petitioning for a writ of mandate.

c) Receiving State's Right to Information

Family Code § 7901, Art. 3, subsec. (c), provides that any public officer or agency in a receiving state which is in receipt of the sending agency's written notification may request of the sending agency, or any other appropriate officer or agency of or in the sending agency's state, and shall be entitled to receive therefrom, supporting or additional information as it may deem necessary under the circumstances to carry out the purpose and policy of the Compact.

d) California's Duties as the "Receiving State"

Under Family Code § 7901.1(a), within 60 days of receipt of a request from another state to conduct a study of a home environment for purposes of assessing the safety and suitability of placing a child in the home, a county child welfare agency shall, directly or by contract, (1) conduct and complete the study, and (2) return a report to the requesting state on the results of the study and the extent to which placement in the home would meet the child's needs. Family Code § 7901.1(b) gives the agency an additional 15 days to complete the study under certain circumstances. Under Family Code § 7901.1(c), the agency is not required to complete the parts of the home study involving the education and training of the prospective foster or adoptive parents within the 60/75 day period.

e) California's Duties as the "Sending State"

Where the report mentioned immediately above is provided to a California agency by another state, an Indian tribe, or a private agency under contract with another state, for the purpose of "sending" a California child, Family Code § 7901.1(d) requires the California agency to treat that report as meeting any requirements imposed by California for the completion of a home study before placing a child in the home, unless, within 14 days after receipt of the report, the California agency determines, based on grounds that are specific to the content of the report, that making a decision in reliance on the report would be contrary to the welfare of the child.

3. Situations Expressly Excluded from the ICPC

a) Relative, Stepparent or Guardian Sending or Bringing the Child

Family Code § 7901, Art. 8, subsec. (a), provides that the ICPC does not apply to the sending or bringing of a child into a receiving state by his or her parent, stepparent, grandparent, adult brother or sister, adult uncle or aunt, or his or her guardian and leaving the child with any such relative or nonagency guardian in the receiving state.

There is nothing in this section setting forth the timing requirements for the transportation of the child, or for the setting up of the guardianship. Therefore, it is clearly permissible for the child's relative (with the consent of the parent) to bring the child into another state, stay with the child long enough for the prospective adoptive parent to have letters of guardianship issued (which can be accomplished on an ex parte basis in many states including California), and then leave the child with the duly appointed guardian.

b) Sending or Bringing the Child Pursuant to Another Compact

Family Code § 7901, Art. 8, subsec. (b), provides that the ICPC does not apply to any placement, sending or bringing of a child into a receiving state pursuant to any other interstate compact to which both the state from which the child is sent or brought and the receiving state are party, or to any other agreement between said states which has the force of law.

It appears that the only other compact ratified in California concerning children would be the Interstate Compact on Juveniles (see Welfare & Institutions Code § 1300, et seq.), which deals with delinquents and wards of the court. Therefore, if the child is brought across state lines for purposes relating to juvenile delinquency proceedings, his or her eventual "placement in foster care or as a preliminary to a possible adoption" would not have to comply with the ICPC, as long as the Interstate Compact on Juveniles has been ratified by all involved states, and has been satisfied by the parties.

4. Penalties for Non-Compliance with the ICPC

Family Code § 7901, Art. 4, states, "The sending, bringing, or causing to be sent or brought into any receiving state of a child in violation of the terms of this compact shall constitute a violation of the laws respecting the placement of children of both the state in which the sending agency is located or from which it sends or brings the child and of the receiving state. A violation may be punished or subjected to penalty in either jurisdiction in accordance with its laws." In interpreting this language, *In re Eli F.*, (1989) 212 Cal.App.3d 228, states "the Compact prescribes no particular remedy for the violation of its terms, and does not explicitly state the placement of a child in contravention of the terms of the Compact is remediable."

The *Eli F.* court held that juvenile court's placement order in a dependency proceeding, which put a foster child with an out-of-state relative, and which was not in compliance with the ICPC, required reversal. On the other hand, it is not clear whether an ICPC violation would deprive a court of "jurisdiction" to issue an adoption order, or that it would void an adoptive placement. Therefore, it is not clear that a adoption could be voided due to an ICPC violation.

Family Code § 7901, Art. 4, also states, "any violation shall constitute full and sufficient grounds for the suspension or revocation of any license, permit, or other legal authorization held by the sending agency which empowers or allows it to place, or care for children." Based on this language, it would appear that the decision to revoke the license is still a discretionary decision, and that an ICPC violation alone would not automatically void a license as a matter of law.

C. General Questions about the ICPC

1. Is ICPC Compliance Necessary for Jurisdiction?

a) The Sending Agency's ICPC "Jurisdiction"

Family Code § 7901, Art. 5, subsec. (a), states, "The sending agency shall retain jurisdiction over the child sufficient to determine all matters in relation to the custody, supervision, care, treatment, and disposition of the child which it would have had if the child had remained in the sending agency's state, until the child is adopted, reaches majority, becomes self-supporting, or is discharged with the concurrence of the appropriate authority in the receiving state." Article 5(a) also provides that the sending agency's jurisdiction shall include the power to effect or cause the return of the child or its transfer to another location and custody pursuant to law, and that the sending agency shall continue to have financial responsibility for support and maintenance of the child during the period of the placement.

Article 5(c) allows a private charitable adoption agency in the receiving state to perform services, discharge financial responsibility for the support and maintenance of the child, or act as an agent for a private charitable adoption agency of the sending state. Article 5(b) provides the statutory authority for entering into agreements for these purposes.

b) The ICPC Definition of "Jurisdiction"

It does not appear that the language of the ICPC which speaks of "jurisdiction" is sufficient to trump the UCCJEA's provisions setting forth the "exclusive means of determining jurisdiction," based on the reasoning of *In re Gloria F.*, (1989) 212 Cal.App.3d 576. Further, the court in *Adoption of Zachariah K.*, (1992) 6 Cal.App.4th 1025, clearly held that the PKPA preempts the ICPC. *Zachariah K.* also noted that, in the context of an independent adoption wherein the birth parent (and not the court) would technically be the "sending agency," it would not make sense to say that the birth parent/sending agency had "jurisdiction" as that word is commonly understood. Apparently based on this case law, the Legislature enacted Family Code § 7908.5, which states that the word "jurisdiction" as used in California's version of the ICPC means "legal responsibility for the child."

2. Does the ICPC Apply to Adoptions?

Family Code § 7901, Art. 3, subsec. (a) clearly contemplates that the ICPC applies to adoptive placements. As to agency adoptions, even though adoption agencies are covered by the ICPC, the agency adoption statutes (Family Code §§ 8700-8736) do not mention the ICPC at all. Therefore, it is unclear whether a relinquishing parent could seek to set aside the relinquishment or a subsequent adoption based on the agency's noncompliance with the ICPC.

As to independent adoptions, while Family Code § 8801.3(d) requires that the placement agreement in an independent adoption must "meet the requirements of the

Interstate Compact on the Placement of Children" (see Chapter 4), it does not appear that the ICPC actually imposes any substantive requirements on an independent adoption. There is no California case voiding an adoption based on noncompliance with the ICPC or with Family Code § 8801.3(d). In any event, by using a guardianship, the placement may fall within the exception in Family Code § 7901, Art. 8, subsec. (a), for placements between relatives, stepparents and/or guardians.

Family Code § 7910 states that "approval of an interstate placement of a child for adoption shall not be granted by the compact administrator" where there has been a kidnapping or where the prospective adoptive parents were not personally selected by the birth parent for purposes of placement. However, there is nothing in the adoption statutes requiring the compact administrator's approval before an adoption can be finalized by the court. Furthermore, the court in *Adoption of Zachariah K.*, (1992) 6 Cal.App.4th 1025, held that "it is not clear whether the ICPC applies to independent adoptions between private parties." Similar holdings were issued in *Adoption of Child by I.T.*, (N.J.App. 1978) 397 A.2d 341; and *Adoption of Baby Boy M.G.*, (N.Y.App. 1987) 515 N.Y.S.2d 198, where the courts held that even though there was absolutely no compliance with the ICPC, the orders granting the petitions for independent adoption would be affirmed since the adoptive parents complied with all other aspects of the adoption laws and the adoptions were in the best interests of the children. Moreover, the court in *In re Adoption of MM*, (Wyo. 1982) 652 P.2d 974, went so far as to say, "There is no provision in the adoption laws requiring compliance with the [ICPC] before a decree of adoption can be sought or entered. We just simply cannot find nexus between the circumstances here and the compact. There is no legislative intent present which makes the compact pari materia with the statutory law of adoption. Such intent is necessary. It is our view that the compact is applicable only to those engaged in the governmental or private service of placing children for care."

As set forth in Chapters 2, 3 and 4 of this book, adoption service providers and social services agencies are involved in various aspects of independent adoptions, such as the taking of the consent, assisting the birth parent in the assessment of the adoptive parents, and providing a report to the court. If the adoption is to be completed in another state, one would obviously have to comply with the laws of that state as to these functions. Suffice it to say here that the laws of many states require ICPC compliance and interstate cooperation in the taking of consents, the providing of counseling and several other aspects of independent adoptions.

3. Is the ICPC Constitutional?

If the ICPC were truly held to be a "compact," rather than merely a set of uniform laws, it is unclear that the ICPC would pass constitutional scrutiny. Article I, Section 10 of the Constitution clearly forbids states from entering into treaties with one another, and specifically prohibits "any Agreement or Compact" between states. However, the U.S. Supreme Court has generally held that only those compacts which affect the political balance of the federal system or which encroach on a power delegated to the federal government violate the Constitution. (*U.S. Steel Corp. v. Multistate Tax Comm'n* (1978) 434 U.S. 452.)

There is no case stating whether the ICPC satisfies the *U.S. Steel* rule. However, with regard to the political balance of the federal system, *Adoption of Zachariah K.*, (1992) 6 Cal.App.4th 1025, holds that the PKPA (28 U.S.C. § 1738A) pre-empts the ICPC's jurisdictional language. As to the validity of the ICPC's license revocation provisions governing private adoption agencies (see Family Code § 7901, Art. IV), a significant question would arise as to whether such provisions are superseded by the constitutional prohibition on treaties, agreements and compacts between states, or whether such provisions constitute an impermissible burden on interstate commerce (although it is questionable whether the placement of a child constitutes "commerce" under any definition of the word). But see, *Birth Hope Adoption Agency, Inc. v. Arizona Health Care Cost Containment System*, (9th Cir. 2000) 218 F.3d 1040, which invalidated (on Commerce Clause grounds) an Arizona statute which required persons from outside of Arizona who were seeking to adopt an Arizona child to reimburse the state for its payment of prenatal care expenses.

In any event, depending on the circumstances of the constitutional challenge, the severability clause set forth at Family Code § 7901, Art. 10, would appear to "save" the ICPC from the particular offending provision. For example, if an adoption agency claims that it is unconstitutional for the State to revoke its license based on non-compliance with a "Compact with another state," the court could simply strike the license revocation provision set forth in Family Code § 7901, Art. 4, and save the rest of California's version of the ICPC.

IV. THE INDIAN CHILD WELFARE ACT

The Indian Child Welfare Act (25 U.S.C. §§ 1901, et seq., "ICWA") was enacted in 1978, and generally governs the adoption of, the termination of parental rights over, and foster placement of children of Native American heritage. Since the ICWA repeatedly refers to such a child as "Indian," this book will also do so in order to minimize ambiguity in the explanations of the statutes. No disrespect toward any tribe or individual is intended.

The ICWA provides for tribal jurisdiction as well as for transfer to state courts in appropriate cases. The Act also provides for tribal intervention into, and notice of, pending state court proceedings where the custody of an Indian child is at issue. Most importantly, according to 25 U.S.C. § 1911(d), full faith and credit must be given to tribal court custody decisions, and 25 U.S.C. §§ 1911(a) and 1914 give the tribe exclusive jurisdiction over custody proceedings where the Indian child resides or is domiciled on a reservation. The ICWA gives statutory preference for placement of Indian children with Indian families or other members of the tribe.

A. Congressional Purposes and Policies Underlying the ICWA

According to 25 U.S.C. § 1902, it is the policy of the United States "to protect the best interests of Indian children and to promote the stability and security of Indian tribes and families by the establishment of minimum Federal standards for the removal of Indian children from their families and the placement of such children in foster or adoptive homes which will reflect the unique values of Indian culture, and by providing for assistance to Indian tribes in the operation of child and family service programs."

Congress also stated at 25 U.S.C. § 1901(3) that there is no resource that is more vital to the continued existence and integrity of Indian tribes than their children, and that the United States has a direct interest, as trustee, in protecting Indian children who are members of or are eligible for membership in an Indian tribe. As stated at 25 U.S.C. § 1901(4), Congress found that an alarmingly high percentage of Indian families are broken up by the removal, often unwarranted, of their children from them by nontribal public and private agencies and that an alarmingly high percentage of such children are placed in non-Indian foster and adoptive homes and institutions. It is based on these Congressional findings that the ICWA was enacted. Also, while it appears that the ICWA is a race-based statute, 42 U.S.C. § 1996b(3) provides that the rules against racial discrimination in adoptive or foster placement do not apply to children subject to the ICWA. The constitutional challenges to ICWA enforcement are explained below.

It also appears that the ICWA supersedes federal law with regard to "outgoing" adoptions under the Hague Convention on Intercountry Adoptions. Under 42 U.S.C. § 14953(b), the federal statutes which implement the Hague Convention "not be construed to affect the application of the Indian Child Welfare Act of 1978." On the other hand, it would appear that the appropriate tribe could consent to an intercountry adoption of an Indian child.

B. Jurisdictional Aspects of the ICWA

1. Exclusive Tribal Jurisdiction re "Indian" Custody Case

Under 25 U.S.C. § 1911(a), an Indian tribe has exclusive jurisdiction over any child custody proceeding involving an Indian child who is a ward of a tribal court, or who resides or is domiciled within the reservation of such tribe, except where such jurisdiction is otherwise vested in the State by existing Federal law (such as the Parental Kidnapping Prevention Act, as explained above). The statutory language does not differentiate between completed proceedings and pending proceedings.

2. Definitions of Relevant Terms

a) "Indian," "Indian Tribe" and "Indian Child"

One of the most significant issues arising from the ICWA is whether the child who is the subject of the proceedings is an "Indian." If not, then none of the provisions of the ICWA are applicable. If the child is an "Indian," then the adoption is governed primarily by the ICWA.

(1) Statutory Definitions

The word "Indian" is defined at 25 U.S.C. § 1903(3) as any person who is a member of an Indian tribe, or who is an Alaska Native and a member of a regional corporation as defined in 43 U.S.C. § 1606. The phrase "Indian tribe" is defined at 25

U.S.C. § 1903(8) as any Indian tribe, band, nation, or other organized group or community of Indians recognized as eligible for the services provided to Indians by the Secretary of Interior because of their status as Indians, including any Alaska Native village as defined in 43 U.S.C. § 1602(c). In applying the 25 U.S.C. § 1903(8) definition of "Indian tribe," the court in *In re Wanomi P.*, (1989) 216 Cal.App.3d 156, held that the ICWA does not apply to children whose affiliation is solely with a Canadian tribe.

"Indian child" is defined at 25 U.S.C. § 1903(4) as any unmarried person who is under age eighteen and is either (a) a member of an Indian tribe or (b) is eligible for membership in an Indian tribe and is the biological child of a member of an Indian tribe.

(2) The "Existing Indian Family" Doctrine

Courts of various states have developed the "existing Indian family" doctrine in declining to apply the ICWA to situations where an Indian child is not being removed from an existing Indian family, since the underlying policies of the ICWA are not affected when the child is removed from a setting which is other than an Indian family. Various states follow varying formulations of the existing Indian family doctrine, such that the phrase "Indian family" is defined broadly or narrowly depending on what state's jurisprudence applies.

In *In re Bridget R.*, (1986) 41 Cal.App.4th 1483, the court expressly recognized the validity of the existing Indian family doctrine in order to preserve the ICWA's constitutionality. *Bridget R.* held that "under the Fifth, Tenth and Fourteenth Amendments to the United States Constitution, [the] ICWA does not and cannot apply to invalidate a voluntary termination of parental rights respecting an Indian child who is not domiciled on a reservation, unless the child's biological parent, or parents, are not only of American Indian descent, but also maintain a significant social, cultural or political relationship with their tribe."

The court in *In re Alexandria Y.*, (1996) 45 Cal.App.4th 1483, agreed with the *Bridget R.* court's conclusion that the existing Indian family doctrine is necessary to avoid serious constitutional flaws in the ICWA. However, *Alexandria Y.* disagreed that the doctrine cannot come into play unless the child and both his parents lack a significant relationship with Indian life. *Alexandria Y.* also held that whether there is an existing Indian family is dependent on the unique facts of each situation.

In interpreting *Alexandria Y.*, *Bridget R.* and the statutes, the court in *In re Santos Y.*, (2001) 92 Cal.App.4th 1274, held that the ICWA cannot constitutionally allow a juvenile court to order that a child, whose parents' rights were terminated, be placed in a pre-adoptive home on an Indian reservation, where the child's only connection to the tribe was the maternal grandparent's one-quarter genetic contribution. Importantly, *Santos Y.* dealt with placement, not jurisdiction.

(3) Failure to Respond to Notice

As explained in more detail below, the ICWA requires that if there is a possibility that the child is an "Indian child," notice must be served on the tribe and/or the Bureau of Indian Affairs of the U.S. Department of the Interior. In *In re Levi U.*, (2000) 78 Cal.App.4th 191, the court held that when no response is received from the tribes after proper inquiry and notice, this is tantamount to a determination that the minor is not an "Indian child" within the meaning of the ICWA. Under such circumstances, neither the court nor the social services agency has any further duties under the ICWA.

b) The Meaning of "Domiciled" on a "Reservation"

As mentioned above, 25 U.S.C. § 1911(a) gives the Indian tribe exclusive jurisdiction over child custody proceedings involving an Indian child who resides or is domiciled within the reservation of such tribe. Furthermore, 25 U.S.C. § 1911(a) does not contain any provision allowing the tribe to decline to exercise jurisdiction. Therefore, the jurisdictional rules are dependent upon whether the Indian child resides or is domiciled within the tribe's reservation.

Under 25 U.S.C. § 1903(10), "reservation" means Indian country as defined in 18 U.S.C. § 1151 and any lands, not covered under such section, title to which is either held by the United States in trust for the benefit of any Indian tribe or individual or held by any Indian tribe or individual subject to a restriction by the United States against alienation. Although the definition of "reservation" is quite broad, one must note that under 25 U.S.C. § 1911, the relevant question is whether the child is residing or domiciled within "the tribe's reservation," and not merely the property of an individual Native American.

In *Mississippi Band of Choctaw Indians v. Holyfield*, (1989) 490 U.S. 30, the U.S. Supreme Court recognized that the ICWA itself does not define "domicile," but held that the term has a different meaning than "residence." In *Holyfield*, both birth parents were enrolled members of the Choctaw tribe of Mississippi and resided on the tribe's reservation, but the twin children were born in a hospital in Gulfport, Mississippi. The *Holyfield* court held that under the "federal" definition of domicile, the twins' domicile was determined by reference to the domicile of the parent. It further held that the children were "domiciled" on the reservation even though they had never been to the reservation, and even though the hospital was 200 miles from the reservation, and even though the birth parents both signed the adoption consent forms before a judge of the Mississippi state courts. The *Holyfield* court "reasoned" that a rule of domicile that would permit individual Indian parents to defeat the ICWA's jurisdictional scheme is inconsistent with what Congress intended. Accordingly, the U.S. Supreme Court actually held that the tribe's rights under the ICWA superseded the parents' fundamental rights arising under the U.S. Constitution to make decisions concerning the care and custody of the children, where the children would be born, and the best possible family setting for the raising of their children.

c) "Child Custody Proceeding"

Under 25 U.S.C. § 1903(1) the phrase "child custody proceeding" includes (i) foster care placements, (ii) any action resulting in the termination of the parent-child relationship, (iii) "preadoptive placement," meaning the temporary placement of an Indian child in a foster home or institution after the termination of parental rights, but prior to or in lieu of adoptive placement, and (iv) adoptive placement.

d) "Parent"

The 25 U.S.C. § 1903(9) definition of "parent" includes any biological parent or parents of an Indian child or any Indian person who has lawfully adopted an Indian child, including adoptions under tribal law or custom, but expressly excludes the unwed father where paternity has not been acknowledged or established. It is not clear whether the provisions of the Uniform Parentage Act are to be used in determining if paternity has been "acknowledged or established." It is also not clear which court "establishes" paternity – whether in the State court or the tribal court. On the other hand, one could argue that if the child is an Indian child, then the jurisdiction of any matter affecting child custody, such as paternity, would be determined by the formula prescribed under the ICWA, as set forth below. In any event, as stated in *In re Daniel M.*, (2003) 110 Cal.App.4th 703, an alleged father who does not meet the 25 U.S.C. § 1903(9) definition of "parent" has no standing to claim that an ICWA violation occurred.

e) "Indian Child's Tribe"

The phrase "Indian child's tribe" is defined by 25 U.S.C. § 1903(5) as (a) the Indian tribe in which an Indian child is a member or eligible for membership or (b) in the case of an Indian child who is a member of or eligible for membership in more than one tribe, the Indian tribe with which the Indian child has the more significant contacts.

f) "Indian Custodian"

According to 25 U.S.C. § 1903(6) the phrase "Indian custodian" is defined as any Indian person who has legal custody of an Indian child under tribal law or custom or under State law or to whom temporary physical care, custody, and control has been transferred by the parent of such child.

3. Full Faith and Credit to Tribal Custody Decrees

Under 25 U.S.C. § 1911(d), the United States, every State, every territory or possession of the United States, and every Indian tribe shall give full faith and credit to the public acts, records, and judicial proceedings of any Indian tribe applicable to Indian child custody proceedings to the same extent that such entities give full faith and credit to the public acts, records, and judicial proceedings of any other entity.

4. Court's Duty to Offer to Transfer Jurisdiction to Tribe

According to 25 U.S.C. § 1911(b), in any state court proceeding for a foster care placement of, or termination of parental rights to, an Indian child not domiciled or residing within the reservation of the Indian child's tribe, the court, in the absence of good cause to the contrary, shall transfer such proceeding to the jurisdiction of the tribe, absent objection by either parent, upon the petition of either parent or the Indian custodian or the Indian child's tribe. However, such transfer is subject to declination by the tribal court of such tribe.

There is a split of authority as to whether the notice provisions of the ICWA are jurisdictional. The court in *In re Nikki R.*, (2003) 106 Cal.App.4th 844, held that the provisions of 25 U.S.C. § 1912(a) requiring notice to the Indian tribe where there is "a suggestion of Indian ancestry" are jurisdictional. Furthermore, the *Nikki R.* court held that the ICWA notice provisions related to the court's subject matter jurisdiction, meaning that the issue of the failure to provide notice to the tribe could be raised by any party at any time, even on appeal by a party who did have notice and even where the issue was not raised in the trial court.

On the other hand, *In re Antoinette S.*, (2002) 104 Cal.App.4th 1401, holds that the ICWA's notice provisions are not jurisdictional. It reasoned that such a holding would strip a court of all authority over the dependent child in its care, and require immediate return of the child to parents who have demonstrated, at least temporarily, that they are unfit or unwilling to care for the child. It also cited other ICWA provisions tending to show that the notice provisions are not jurisdictional.

5. Tribal Right to Intervene in State Court Custody Cases

Under 25 U.S.C. § 1911(c), in any State court proceeding for the foster care placement of, or termination of parental rights to, an Indian child, the Indian custodian of the child and the Indian child's tribe shall have a right to intervene at any point in the proceeding. Presumably, the right to intervene is exercised for the purpose of ascertaining whether the tribe should demand immediate transfer of the case to it pursuant to 25 U.S.C. § 1911(a) or (b).

6. Tribal Petition to Invalidate State Court Orders

25 U.S.C. § 1914 states that, where there has been a foster care placement or a termination of parental rights concerning an Indian child, a petition may be filed by the child, the child's parent or Indian custodian or the child's tribe to invalidate such action under 25 U.S.C. §§ 1911, 1912 or 1913. The case law bears out that the petition is filed with the state court, who would thus have to determine if the proceeding complied with the ICWA. Also significantly, there is no statute of limitations or "best interests of the child" element set forth in 25 U.S.C. § 1914. However, it is the petitioner who has the burden of proving that an "Indian child" is involved and that the state court proceedings violated 25 U.S.C. §§ 1911, 1912 or 1913, as explained herein.

C. Giving Notice to Parent or Indian Custodian, and the Tribe

Under 25 U.S.C. § 1912(a), in any involuntary proceeding in a State court, where the court knows or has reason to know that an Indian child is involved, the party seeking the foster care placement of, or termination of parental rights to, an Indian child shall notify the parent or Indian custodian and the Indian child's tribe, by registered mail with return receipt requested, of the pending proceedings and of their right of intervention. The practical and logistical means of complying with the mandate are as follows:

1. Ascertaining Whether the Child is an Indian Child

The CDSS and the California Judicial Council have published several standard forms to be used in the event the child to be adopted is possibly an Indian child. It is in the prospective adoptive parent's interest to provide full disclosure of facts, at the soonest possible time, concerning possible Indian heritage. The state court is forced to depend upon the parties and the applicable private agency and/or social services agencies to provide the information about the child's ancestry, and to serve the necessary notices. Thus, it is up to the parties and the applicable private agency and/or social services agency to do everything possible to increase the enforceability of whatever decree is being sought.

Furthermore, if it appears to the tribe that the proceedings are being conducted in the Indian child's best interests, in that the tribe is being notified of the proceedings with all due diligence, it is very possible that the Indian tribe would decline to exercise jurisdiction pursuant to 25 U.S.C. § 1911(b), and allow the state court to complete the adoption. On the other hand, if there has been no effort to notify the tribe, the tribe very well may exercise its right to file a 25 U.S.C. § 1914 petition to invalidate the adoption.

2. Ascertaining Which Tribe is the Indian Child's Tribe

The ICWA also provides at 25 U.S.C. § 1912(a) that if the identity or location of the parent or Indian custodian and the tribe cannot be determined, such notice shall be given to the Secretary of the Interior in like manner, who shall have fifteen days after receipt to provide the requisite notice to the parent or Indian custodian and the tribe. No foster care placement or termination of parental rights proceeding shall be held until at least ten days after receipt of notice by the parent or Indian custodian and the tribe or the Secretary. However, the parent or the Indian custodian or the tribe shall, upon request, be granted up to twenty additional days to prepare for such proceeding. Based on the language of 25 U.S.C. § 1912(a), it would appear that the state court could proceed without the participation of the parent or the Indian custodian or the tribe if the requisite notices have been given and there has no response within the statutory time.

3. Addressing the Notice

The U.S. Bureau of Indian Affairs web site (http://www.bia.gov) has links to lists of designated tribal agents for service of notice. These lists are also published in the Federal Register, the most recent being at 76 Fed.Reg. 30438 (May 25, 2011). The U.S. Secretary of the Interior's address is 1849 C Street, N.W., Washington, DC 20240.

D. The ICWA's Changes to California Adoption Law

1. Consent to or Relinquishment for the Adoption

a) Consent Form Must Be Signed Before a Judge with Jurisdiction

Effective in 2007, California's adoption statutes were amended to comport with the provision of the ICWA. In particular, according to 25 U.S.C. § 1913(a), where any parent voluntarily consents to a termination of parental rights as to an Indian child, such consent shall not be valid unless executed in writing and recorded before a judge of a court of competent jurisdiction and accompanied by the presiding judge's certificate that the terms and consequences of the consent were fully explained in detail and were fully understood by the parent or Indian custodian. The court shall also certify that either the parent or Indian custodian fully understood the explanation in English or that it was interpreted into a language that the parent or Indian custodian understood. Since this code section deals with "any voluntary proceeding for termination of parental rights," it would appear that 25 U.S.C. § 1913(a) deals not only with the taking of a consent to an independent adoption, but to the relinquishment of the child to an adoption agency as well.

b) Consent Cannot Be Made Within 10 Days of Child's Birth

Under 25 U.S.C. § 1913(a), any consent given prior to, or within ten days after, the birth of the Indian child shall not be valid. It appears that California law normally allows the consent to be given from the moment of the child's birth.

c) Consent Is Revocable Up to Time of Granting Adoption Petition

Pursuant to 25 U.S.C. § 1913(c), in any voluntary proceeding for termination of parental rights to, or adoptive placement of, an Indian child, the consent of the parent may be withdrawn for any reason at any time prior to the entry of a final decree of termination or adoption, as the case may be, and the child shall be returned to the parent. Since this code section deals with "any voluntary proceeding for termination of parental rights," it would appear that 25 U.S.C. § 1913(c) supersedes California law with regard to the irrevocability of a relinquishment (see Chapter 5 of this book), and with regard to the 30-day revocation rule for consents to independent adoptions (see Chapter 3 of this book).

d) Two-Year Limitation for Setting Aside Adoption

Under 25 U.S.C. § 1913(d), after the entry of a final decree of adoption of an Indian child in any State court, the parent may withdraw consent thereto upon the grounds that consent was obtained through fraud or duress, and may petition the court to vacate such decree, and return the child to the parent. No adoption which has been effective for at least two years may be invalidated under the provisions of this subsection unless otherwise permitted under State law.

As set forth in Chapter 10 of this book, the Family Code § 9102(b) statute of limitations for a collateral attack based on fraud is three years. There is no California or federal case law interpreting 25 U.S.C. § 1913(d), although it is generally held that a state may grant more rights to individuals than are provided under federal law.

Where the adoption has been set aside, 25 U.S.C. § 1916(a), custody of the child may be returned to the biological parent or prior Indian custodian unless there is a showing that return of custody is not in the child's best interests. Interestingly, 25

U.S.C. § 1916(a) contemplates that the adoptive parents and the biological parents may simply agree to rescind the adoption.

2. Placement for Purposes of Adoption

a) Placement Must Be Near Indian Child's Home

Under 25 U.S.C. § 1915(b), any Indian child accepted for foster care or preadoptive placement shall be placed in the least restrictive setting which most approximates a family and in which his special needs, if any, may be met. The child shall also be placed "within reasonable proximity to his or her home, taking into account any special needs of the child." According to 25 U.S.C. § 1915(d), the standards to be applied in meeting these preference requirements shall be the prevailing social and cultural standards of the Indian community in which the parent or extended family resides or with which the parent or extended family members maintain social and cultural ties.

b) Preferential Status for "Indian Families"

Under 25 U.S.C. § 1915(a), in any adoptive placement of an Indian child under State law, a preference shall be given, in the absence of good cause to the contrary, to a placement with (1) a member of the child's extended family; (2) other members of the Indian child's tribe; or (3) other Indian families. At 25 U.S.C. § 1903(2), "extended family member" is "defined by the law or custom of the Indian child's tribe or, in the absence of such law or custom, shall be a person who has reached the age of eighteen and who is the Indian child's grandparent, aunt or uncle, brother or sister, brother-in-law or sister-in-law, niece or nephew, first or second cousin, or stepparent. Therefore, the ICWA provides preferential placement status to a much wider range of individuals than is provided under California law.

c) Preferential Status for Indian Foster Home

According to 25 U.S.C. § 1915(b), in any foster care or preadoptive placement, a preference shall be given, in the absence of good cause to the contrary, to a placement with (i) a member of the Indian child's extended family, (ii) a foster home licensed, approved, or specified by the Indian child's tribe, (iii) an Indian foster home licensed or approved by an authorized non-Indian licensing authority, or (iv) an institution for children approved by an Indian tribe or operated by an Indian organization which has a program suitable to meet the Indian child's needs. The 25 U.S.C. § 1903(7) definition of "Indian organization" includes "any group, association, partnership, corporation, or other legal entity owned or controlled by Indians, or a majority of whose members are Indians."

d) Order of Preferential Status Set by the Tribe

Under 25 U.S.C. § 1915(c), the Indian child's tribe may establish the order for preferential placement status by resolution, and the agency or court effecting the placement shall follow such order so long as the placement is the least restrictive setting appropriate to the particular needs of the child. Where appropriate, the preference of the Indian child or parent shall be considered, however where a consenting parent evidences a desire for anonymity, the court or agency shall give weight to such desire in applying the preferences.

e) Documenting the Placement Decision

According to 25 U.S.C. § 1915(e), a record of each placement, under State law, of an Indian child shall be maintained by the State in which the placement was made, evidencing the efforts to comply with the order of preference specified in this section. Such record shall be made available at any time upon the request of the Secretary or the Indian child's tribe.

3. Remedial Services and Rehabilitative Programs for the Parent

Under 25 U.S.C. § 1912(d), any party seeking to effect a foster care placement of, or termination of parental rights to, an Indian child under State law shall satisfy the court that active efforts have been made to provide remedial services and rehabilitative programs designed to prevent the breakup of the Indian family and that these efforts have proved unsuccessful. It would appear that these requirements are roughly the equivalent of the reunification services that are provided in dependency proceedings.

Therefore, even if one were proceeding under Family Code § 7822 to free an Indian child from parental custody due to an abandonment, the ICWA would appear to require the court to provide reunification services. However, 25 U.S.C. § 1912(d) only requires "active efforts ... to provide remedial services and rehabilitative programs," meaning that the actual provision of such remedial services and rehabilitative programs is not statutorily required in all cases. Therefore, as long as all of the required notices have been served, the Family Code § 7822 proceeding could be completed in the absence of the parent, and without an actual order requiring remedial services and rehabilitative programs.

4. "Detriment Rule" Applies to the Termination of Parental Rights

25 U.S.C. § 1912(f) provides that no termination of parental rights may be ordered in "such proceeding" (apparently meaning a foster placement or a termination of parental rights based on the language of the previous subsection) in the absence of a determination, supported by evidence beyond a reasonable doubt, including testimony of qualified expert witnesses, that the continued custody of the child by the parent or Indian custodian is likely to result in serious emotional or physical damage to the child. Consequently, while the detriment rule is normally not applicable in a Family Code § 7800 proceeding to free the child from parental custody, federal law mandates that one must satisfy this rule with "evidence beyond a reasonable doubt" where an Indian child is involved.

OTHER PROCEDURAL MATTERS 10

In this chapter:

After the adoption agency finally called Al Roker and his wife Alice with the good news that they would be able to adopt five-month old Courtney, they had exactly four days to completely outfit a nursery.

I. VENUE SELECTION, PREPARING THE PETITION, FILING, SERVING

A. State Court

Adoption petitions are filed in state court, unless the child is subject to certain provisions of the Indian Child Welfare Act, as explained in Chapter 9. If the adoption is to be completed in California, Family Code § 200 provides that the petition is to be filed in the superior court. As for petitions for the adoption of children who were part of the dependency system, as explained in Chapter 6, such petitions are filed and heard in the juvenile court pursuant to Rule 5.730(c) of the California Rules of Court.

As far as which state's court is the proper venue, that question is answered by Family Code § 9210, the Uniform Child Custody Jurisdiction and Enforcement Act and the Parental Kidnapping Prevention Act, which are explained in Chapter 9. In addition, all of the state statutes across the country that authorize the commencement of an adoption proceeding contemplate that the proceeding is brought in state court. There are no federal statutes authorizing the filing of an adoption petition in federal court.

There is no federal diversity jurisdiction in an adoption case, even if there was an interstate dispute regarding paternity or termination of parental rights. In *Ankenbrandt v. Richards*, (1992) 504 U.S. 689, the U.S. Supreme Court generally held that there is a "domestic relations" exception to the constitutional and statutory provisions for federal court jurisdiction over disputes between citizens of different states. Also, in *Congleton v. Holy Cross Child Placement Agency, Inc.*, (5th Cir. 1990) 919 F.2d 1077, a federal appellate court held that a birth mother could not bring a federal suit against a child placement agency for placing her infant boy for adoption because her request to have the court invalidate the relinquishment was of necessity so intertwined with her parental rights and the custodial status of the child that her claims could not be fairly separated from the "federal" issues.

B. Counties Wherein the Adoption Petition May Be Filed

Family Code § 9211 generally provides that an adoption petition may be filed in the county in which (a) a petitioner lives, (b) the minor lives, or (c) an office of an agency that placed the minor is located. Interestingly, Family Code § 9211(c) technically allows the petition to be filed in a county wherein neither the petitioner nor the minor live, and in which the specific private agency's adoption worker is not stationed, as long as that agency has "an" office in that county. On the other hand, the laws governing specific kinds of adoptions also have specific venue requirements, and if the adoption proceeding will also entail a parentage action or a petition to terminate parental rights, the specific venue provisions governing those proceedings must also be satisfied.

1. Petition for Agency Adoption

As set forth in Family Code § 8714(a), an agency adoption petition may be filed in the county wherein the adopting parent "resides," or in the county wherein the relinquishing birth parent resided when the relinquishment was signed if the prospective adoptive parents reside out-of state. Family Code § 8714(a) also states that, where the child's parents' rights were terminated in a dependency case, the agency adoption petition may be filed either in the county wherein the petitioner resides, or in the county where the child was freed for adoption. As for the adoption of a child who was in the dependency system, the petition is filed and heard in the juvenile court which conducted the dependency case. (Cal. Rules of Court, Rule 5.730(c).)

Therefore, it is possible for a non-California resident to file an agency adoption petition in California, regardless of how the child came into the custody of the agency. It should be noted that Family Code § 8704(b) requires the prospective adoptive parents to have received placement of the child for purposes of adoption before a petition can be filed, meaning that compliance with the Interstate Compact for the Placement of Children will have had to be completed in such a case. In addition, Family Code §§ 8704(b) and 8714(a) do not prevent non-California residents from filing an adoption petition concerning a California child in their own state and pursuant to their own state's laws.

2. Petition for Independent Adoption

Family Code § 8802(a)(1) states that a petition for an independent adoption may be filed in the county wherein the adopting parent "resides," or in the county wherein the birth parent resided when he or she signed the placement agreement if the prospective adoptive parents reside out-of state, or in the county wherein the birth parent resides at the time of filing the petition. Again, it is possible for a non-California resident to file a petition for an independent adoption in California, and there is nothing in California's laws on independent adoptions preventing non- residents from filing an adoption petition concerning a California child in their own state under their own state's laws.

3. Petition for Intercountry Adoption

Family Code § 8912(a) provides that a petition for an intercountry adoption is filed in the county wherein the adopting parent "resides." With regard to foreign-born children who are already residing in California, it would appear that the adoption proceedings could be framed in terms of an agency adoption, an independent adoption or a stepparent adoption, depending upon the facts. As explained in Chapter 11, international adoptions are usually completed in the foreign country where the child resides, and those adoptions are to be legally recognized in California either by treaty or through the doctrine of comity. California intercountry adoptions are usually undertaken in those cases where the foreign court will only grant a guardianship or other non-adoptive custody order, or where the U.S. Government requires a "readoption."

4. Petition for Stepparent Adoption

Family Code § 9000(a) provides that a petition for a stepparent adoption is filed in the county wherein the adopting parent "resides." Presumably, this is the same county in which the child resides, since the adopting stepparent is required to be the spouse or domestic partner of the custodial parent.

5. Petition re Parentage or Termination of Right

Family Code § 7845 states that a proceeding to free a child from parental custody must be brought in the county in which (a) the minor resides or is found, or (b) any of the alleged acts occurred. Likewise, as to proceedings under the Uniform Parentage Act, Family Code § 7620 states that a paternity (or maternity) proceeding may be brought in the county in which the minor resides or is found.

In most cases, the child resides with the prospective adoptive parents at the time the adoption petition is filed, meaning that the Family Code § 7845 would permit the venue for the proceedings to free the child from parental custody to be in the same county as the adoption petition. In addition, with respect to the adoption of a child who was the subject of dependency proceedings, it is also possible to file an adoption petition in the juvenile court wherein the dependency proceedings were pending, as explained in Chapter 6 of this book. In those rare cases where two different counties are involved, it would be possible to file a motion to consolidate or to coordinate the proceedings of the different county superior courts.

6. Determining "Residency"

As explained above, "residency" is a factor in determining where, or if, an adoption petition can be filed in California, regardless of what type of adoption is involved. Family Code § 9210(a), which governs jurisdictional issues in an uncontested adoption case, states generally that the California courts have jurisdiction over the adoption if the child or the prospective adoptive parents "lived" in California for at least six consecutive months, or (under certain circumstances) the placing agency is "located" in California. Residency is also significant in determining jurisdiction under the UCCJEA, as explained in Chapter 9. The California Family Code does not define "lived," "reside" or "residence," nor does any California statute give a general definition of these terms. (For further explanation of the concept of "residency," see *Smith v. Smith*, (1955) 45 Cal.2d 235, *Mississippi Band of Choctaw Indians v. Holyfield*, (1989) 490 U.S. 30, *Pennoyer v. Neff*, (1877) 95 U.S. 714, and *Black's Law Dict.*, 5th Ed., p.1176.)

C. Preparing and Filing the Petition

Family Code §§ 200 and 212 state that all petitions under the Family Code, which includes adoption petitions, must be verified. In addition, the Judicial Council has provided standard forms to cover whatever sort of adoption is being sought, and in many cases the petition is required to use those forms. Fully answering the questions on the forms should constitute compliance with the disclosure requirements for the petition itself, which are described in more detail in the previous chapters of this book. Further, all of the standard forms remind the petitioner of the requirements to attach copies of related papers, such as letters of guardianship, orders terminating parental rights, postadoption contact agreements, and so on, to the adoption petition, as explained in previous chapters of this book.

D. Serving the Adoption Petition

1. Parties to Be Served

California's adoption statutes do not expressly state who must be served with the petition. Those provisions are set forth in the Uniform Parentage Act, and the "list" of persons who are "required" to be served with the petition depends upon whether the child has a presumed father or not. The requirement for serving parties with the adoption petition arises by virtue of constitutional law. *Lehr v. Robertson*, (1983) 463 U.S. 248, generally provides that a person who has the right to withhold consent to the adoption has the constitutional right to receive formal notice of the adoption proceedings.

As for notifying the birth father, under Family Code § 7660, if the child's mother relinquishes for or consents to, or proposes to relinquish for or consent to, the adoption of a child having a presumed father (which is explained in Chapter 3 of this book), the father shall be given notice of the adoption proceedings, unless the father's relationship to the child has been previously terminated or determined by a court not to exist or the father has voluntarily relinquished for or consented to the adoption of the child. Even if the child does not have a presumed father, there are other instances explained in Chapter 3 which require the child'a alleged father to be given notice of the adoption proceeding. (See for example *Adoption of Kelsey S.*, (1992) 1 Cal.4th 816.)

As to notifying the birth mother, Family Code § 7661 states that if a father relinquishes for or consents to, or proposes to relinquish for or consent to, the adoption of the child, the mother shall be given notice of the adoption proceeding, unless her relationship to the child has been previously terminated by a court or the mother has voluntarily relinquished for or consented to the adoption of the child. Family Code §§ 7660 and 7662 provide similar provisions where the mother's rights have been dispensed with, and it is the father who must be notified.

Regarding grandparents and other relatives, as explained in Chapter 8, *Reeves v. Bailey*, (1975) 53 Cal.App.3d 1019, holds that where a grandparent already has court-ordered visitation rights, that grandparent is entitled to notice of the adoption proceeding. The same would appear to apply to other relatives and other persons who have obtained court-ordered visitation rights. Otherwise, these individuals have no right to notice.

2. Notifying State and County Social Services Agencies

Family Code § 8808 provides that, at the same time a petition for an independent adoption is filed with the court, the petitioners shall file a copy of the petition with the district office of the CDSS or with the delegated county adoption agency responsible for the investigation of the adoption, together with the names, addresses, and telephone numbers of all parties to be interviewed. The practitioner should assume that the CDSS must be so notified.

3. Notifying Child's Attorney in the Dependency Case

With regard to the adoption of children who were involved in the dependency system, Rule 5.730(b) of the California Rules of Court requires the petitioners to serve a copy of the petition on the attorney that had been representing the child in the dependency proceeding.

4. Manner of Service

In addition to personal service, the case of *David B. v. Superior Court*, (1994) 21 Cal.App.4th 1010, states that under certain circumstances the birth parents may be notified of the proceedings "by publication," pursuant to a court order allowing service by publication as authorized by Code of Civil Procedure § 415.50. That statute provides that the court may allow a party to be served with process by means of publishing the court papers in a newspaper of general circulation in California for four consecutive weeks. The statute also states that an application for an order directing service by publication requires detailed proof that diligent but unsuccessful efforts were made to locate the party to be served. See *Watts v. Crawford*, (1995) 10 Cal.4th 743, 749, fn.5; *Olvera v. Olvera*, (1991) 232 Cal.App.3d 32; *Slusher v. Durr*, (1977) 69 Cal.App.3d 747, 755-756; and *Sanford v. Smith*, (1970) 11 Cal.App.3d 991, 1001.

Code of Civil Procedure § 415.20 gives litigants the right to effectuate "substituted service" of process by having someone go to the party's office or home, hand the court papers to an adult who is apparently in charge there, and thereafter mail an additional copy of the papers to that address. In addition, Code of Civil Procedure § 415.40 gives litigants the right to serve process on persons residing outside of California simply by sending the summons by first class certified mail, return receipt requested. However, service by the latter two methods is not deemed complete until 10 days after the mailing.

Under the Soldiers' and Sailors' Civil Relief Act ("SSCRA"), codified at 50 U.S.C. Appendix § 501, et seq., a serviceman is allowed to attack a final judgment under 50 U.S.C. App. § 523, where it is shown that the serviceman suffered prejudice due to his military service, and that he or she has a meritorious defense. The SSCRA also contains a provision at 50 U.S.C. App. § 525 staying statutes of limitations. There does not appear to be a provision in the SSCRA allowing a subsequent federal court action where the serviceman was able to, but failed to, assert the SSCRA in the prior state court case.

E. Voluntary Withdrawal of the Adoption Petition

1. Agency Adoptions

As set forth in Family Code § 8719, if the petitioners move to withdraw the adoption petition or to dismiss the proceeding, the court clerk shall immediately notify the CDSS at Sacramento of the action. Since the child is in the continuing legal custody of the agency throughout the proceedings, there is no need to make a custody order. In addition, if there is no longer an agency adoption proceeding pending, it would appear that the agency's full discretion to make placement decisions (see Chapter 5) is restored.

2. Independent Adoptions

Family Code § 8804(a) states that whenever the petitioners move to withdraw the adoption petition or dismiss the proceeding, the court clerk shall immediately notify the CDSS at Sacramento. At that point, the CDSS or the delegated county adoption agency shall file a full report with the court recommending a suitable plan for the child, and shall appear before the court for the purpose of representing the child. Family Code § 8804(b) then states that the court may retain jurisdiction over the child for the purposes of making any order for the child's custody that the court deems to be in the child's best interests. Under Family Code § 8804(c), if the birth parent who was not involved in placing the child for adoption has refused to give the required consent, or a birth parent lawfully revokes consent, the court shall order the child restored to the care and custody of the birth parent or parents. Therefore, where the birth parent still retains parental rights, the court has essentially no discretion, and would appear to be allowed to retain custody of the child only if there are grounds to commence a dependency proceeding under Welfare & Institutions Code § 300.

3. Intercountry Adoptions

Family Code § 8916 allows the petitioner to move to withdraw the adoption petition or to dismiss the proceeding. Since the status of the child is affected by a complex set of rules set forth in the federal immigration regulations and the laws of the foreign country, questions concerning the care and custody of the child will be addressed in Chapter 11 on intercountry adoptions.

4. Stepparent Adoptions

Family Code § 9006(a) provides that if the petitioner moves to withdraw the adoption petition or to dismiss the proceeding, the court clerk shall immediately notify the probation officer, qualified court investigator, or county welfare department of the action. In a stepparent adoption, the child has been in the custody of a custodial parent at all relevant times, meaning that there is ordinarily no need for a social services agency to be involved in the care and custody of the child.

II. CONDUCT OF THE ADOPTION CASE AND ENTRY OF FINAL ORDER

A. A "Non-Adversarial" Proceeding?

As stated in *In re Jay R.*, (1983) 150 Cal.App.3d 251, an adoption proceeding is not generally considered an adversarial proceeding. However when a petitioner alleges facts that would tend to controvert an interested party's claim of right, that party is entitled to contest the allegations, disprove the contents of any reports submitted, and be heard on the issue of the best interests of the child. In these contested adoption cases, Family Code §§ 210 and 211 provide that the rules of evidence and of civil procedure, as well as specifically directed rules of practice as set forth in the California Rules of Court, are to be followed.

B. "Private" and Closed Proceedings

Adoption proceedings are not held in "open" court. Family Code §§ 214 and 8611 state that the proceedings are conducted by way of a "private trial," meaning that the court may exclude from the courtroom all individuals except the court officers, the parties, their counsel and their witnesses. In addition, as set forth in Chapter 12, the court records are sealed and confidential pursuant to Family Code §§ 9200, et seq.

C. "Trial-Like Hearing"

1. Determining If There Is a Contested Hearing

a) Contest between Adoptive Parents and Agency

As set forth in Family Code §§ 8715(a), 8807(a) and 8914, in every type of adoption except for a stepparent adoption, the applicable agency is required to submit a full report of the facts of the case to the court. (As stated in Chapter 8 of this book, there is usually no home study performed in a stepparent adoption because the child is already in the custody of the spouse or domestic partner of the petitioner.) Under Family Code §§ 8717, 8821 and 8915, a copy of the report or findings, regardless of what the findings are, must be given to the petitioner or to the petitioner's attorney.

If the report is unfavorable to the petitioners (for example because the agency finds that the home of the petitioners is not suitable for the child or that the required agency consents are not available and there is a recommendation to deny the petition), Family Code §§ 8720(a), 8822(a) and 8917(a) require the court clerk, upon receipt of the report, to immediately refer it to the court for review. The court is then required by Family Code §§ 8720(b), 8822(b) and 8917(b) to set a date for a hearing of the petition and to give reasonable notice by mail of the hearing to the agency and the petitioners. While Family Code §§ 8720(b) and 8822(b) require that the court's notice of the hearing be served on the birth parents if necessary, there is no such parallel provision in Family Code § 8917(b) for intercountry adoptions. Also, the case of *Adoption of Baby Girl B.*, (1999) 74 Cal.App.4th 43, requires that the trial court allow the prospective adoptive parents to have the issues decided in a contested hearing, if one becomes necessary from their standpoint because of the filing of an adverse agency report.

Where it is the prospective adoptive parent that desires the hearing, *Adoption of Baby Girl B.* also provides that the requirement of a hearing on the adoption issues is not satisfied by a later hearing on a Code of Civil Procedure § 473(b) motion to vacate the prior denial of the adoption petition, since the sole issue on such a motion is whether its previous order had been made due to "mistake, inadvertence, surprise, or excusable neglect." *Baby Girl B.* holds that the petitioner is statutorily entitled to an evidentiary hearing on whether the adoption would promote the child's interests.

b) Contest by Non-Parties

The court in *Adoption of Lenn E.*, (1986) 182 Cal.App.3d 210, was concerned with an order allowing a grandparent to intervene in the adoption proceeding. The *Lenn E.* court recognized that the code contains no provisions for formal opposition to an adoption petition. However, the court held that the rules of standing have been liberally construed where a party, such as a grandparent, has an interest in the proceeding.

Although a formal motion for leave to intervene is authorized (see Code of Civil Procedure § 387(a)), *Lenn E.*held that it is not required and the application for leave to intervene may be made informally or ex parte and authorized by an ex parte order. An order granting leave to intervene may be reviewed only on appeal from the final judgment, and is reversible only if there has been an abuse of discretion.

c) Contest between Adoptive and Birth Parents

The birth parents and other interested parties are also entitled to a contested hearing, such as where there is a question about parental rights, or whether the required consents were obtained in the required manner, or whether consent was revoked, or whether the adoption is in the best interests of the child. The circumstances for such a contested hearing are widely varied.

2. The Agency's Representation of the Child

As set forth in Family Code §§ 8720(c), 8822(c) and 8917(c), it is the agency which represents the child before the court. There is no such parallel provision in the stepparent adoption statutes, since the child already has a custodial parent and no agency is involved.

3. Pre-Trial Proceedings

In *In re Backhaus' Adoption*, (1962) 209 Cal.App.2d 13, the court held that the summary judgment procedure set forth in Code of Civil Procedure § 437c does not apply to adoption proceedings. In *Backhaus*, the social services agency sought a judgment in the adoption proceedings without a trial on the grounds that a jurisdictional defect allegedly existed. In contrast to *Backhaus*, the court in *Arnold v. Howell*, (1950) 98 Cal.App.2d 202, held that a party may demur to the pleadings in an action to set aside an adoption. However, since an adoption petition and a complaint to set aside an adoption pose a different set of issues, it does not appear that *Arnold* would allow a demurrer to an adoption petition.

In light of the general language of Family Code §§ 210 and 211, it would appear that other procedural mechanisms are also available, such as depositions and discovery. In other words, the author of an adverse home study report could be deposed.

4. Entitlement to a Non-Jury "Trial"

In *Adoption of Baby Girl B.*, (1999) 74 Cal.App.4th 43, the court held that the petitioner is statutorily entitled to an evidentiary hearing, and that the failure to afford one constitutes reversible error per se. In interpreting the adoption statutes, the *Baby Girl B.* court stated that the hearing on the adoption petition is to be a trial-like hearing, in which the decision is based on the testimony of live witnesses, rather than a motion-like procedure which only uses declarations. The *Baby Girl B.* court also held that the adoption statutes simply do not allow the trial court to dispense with a hearing, even if the child is in danger, since under certain circumstances the agency may immediately remove the child from a caretaker's custody (see Chapters 5 and 6 of this book), but still must at least afford a post-deprivation hearing.

In addition, the case is decided by way of a bench trial, since there is no right to jury trial mentioned for an adoption proceeding either in the adoption statutes or in the jury trial provisions of Article I, Section 16, of the California Constitution. Furthermore, the court in *Arnold v. Howell*, (1950) 98 Cal.App.2d 202, held that an adoption decree is issued by "a court of equity."

5. Mandatory Appearance of the Parties at the Hearing

a) The Prospective Adoptive Parents and the Child

As set forth in Family Code §§ 8718, 8823, 8913 and 9007, and Rule 5.730(c) of the California Rules of Court, the prospective adoptive parents and the child proposed to be adopted must appear before the court, regardless of what kind of adoption is at issue. An exception to this rule is provided in Family Code § 8613 for certain military and governmental personnel and persons working abroad for various relief organizations, and their spouses who are also located out-of-state.

Under Family Code § 8613(a) and (b), an attorney who provides a notarized statement documenting his or her representation of the petitioner or an individual with a power of attorney from the petitioner may appear on behalf the prospective adoptive parent if there is satisfactory evidence that it is impossible or impracticable to appear in court because he or she is (i) enlisted in the military service, or auxiliary thereof, of the United States, or of any of its allies, or (ii) engaged in service on behalf of any governmental entity of the United States, or (iii) engaged in service in the American Red Cross, or in any other recognized charitable or religious organization. Where the prospective adoptive parent is permitted to appear by counsel, or otherwise, Family Code § 8613(c) gives the court the authority to have the prospective adoptive parent examined by way of deposition.

According to Family Code § 8613(f), where neither prospective adoptive parent is required to appear before the court, the child proposed to be adopted need not appear. If in this situation the child's consent to the adoption is necessary, the child may provide it through counsel. In addition, under Family Code § 8613(g), where none of the parties appears, the court may not make an order of adoption until after the social services agency's report has been filed with the court pursuant to Family Code §§ 8715, 8807, 8914, or 9001. It should be noted that Family Code § 8613 does not alter the rules of evidence, meaning that the absence of a particular party at the hearing could make it more difficult for the petitioners to meet their burden of proof.

b) The Agency's Representative

As set forth in Family Code §§ 8720(c), 8822(c) and 8917(c), a representative of the agency shall appear in independent, agency and intercountry adoption cases. There is no such parallel provision in the stepparent adoption statutes.

6. Taking Testimony from the Parties

Under Family Code § 8612(a), the court shall examine all persons appearing before it, and the examination of each person shall be conducted separately but within the physical presence of every other person unless the court, in its discretion, orders otherwise.

With regard to taking testimony from the child, Family Code § 3042(a) states that if a child is of sufficient age and capacity to reason so as to form an intelligent preference as to custody, the court shall consider and give due weight to the wishes of the child in making an order granting or modifying custody. Furthermore, Family Code § 3042(b) states that, in addition to the requirements of Evidence Code § 765, which concerns controlling witness interrogation and protecting witnesses under 14 years old, the court shall protect the best interests of the child, and in so doing, may preclude the calling of the child as a witness where the best interests of the child so dictates and may provide alternative means of obtaining information regarding the child's preferences.

7. Evidentiary Rules Governing Social Services Reports

In *Adoption of Baby Girl B.*, (1999) 74 Cal.App.4th 43, the court pointed out that while there is no requirement that the agency report be sworn, the specific statutes that provide for the admissibility of an agency report in a juvenile dependency proceeding (see Welfare & Institutions Code §§ 281, 355(b) and 358(b)) do not have a counterpart in the adoption statutes. It also pointed out that while the agency report might be arguably admissible under the Evidence Code § 1280 official records exception to the hearsay rule, matters in the report that are not based on the author's personal observation are not admissible. The *Baby Girl B.* court thus concluded that the agency will normally need to call witnesses to prove the facts mentioned in its report.

The *Baby Girl B.* court also ruled that the agency may not file mere declarations in support of its report, and that the petitioner is not permitted to file any further pleadings or declarations in opposition to an adverse report, meaning that the court's decision on the agency's recommendations are to be made following a trial-like hearing. On the other hand, where the evidentiary foundation for the written report is satisfied, allowing it to be admitted into evidence, *San Diego County Dept. of Pub. Welfare v. Superior Court*, (1972) 7 Cal.3d 1, requires the court to accord "due weight" to the agency's expertise as expressed in the report. However, the agency's recommendation is not binding on the court.

In an adoption case in *juvenile court following a dependency proceeding*, Rule 5.730(d) of the California Rules of Court states that the record shall reflect that the court has read and considered the assessment submitted by the applicable social services agency and the report by the child's advocate. Rule 5.730(e) of the California Rules of Court allows any party to call the preparer of the agency's assessment for examination.

8. Consolidation or Coordination of Multiple Proceedings

In *San Diego County Dept. of Pub. Welfare v. Superior Court*, (1972) 7 Cal.3d 1, the court held that when petitions for guardianship and adoption of the same child are pending in separate departments of the same court, the proceedings upon the two petitions are to be consolidated for hearing before one judge. Where proceedings are pending in two different counties, Code of Civil Procedure § 404, et seq. and California Rules of Court 3.520, et seq. permit an interested party to submit a petition to the Judicial Council to have the matters "coordinated," and/or to have one forum selected for the trial of all of the pending matters.

In *In re Berth*, (1947) 79 Cal.App.2d 221, the trial court was faced with two adoption petitions which were competing for the same child. The trials were scheduled for the same day. The trial court denied the petition that was the subject of the first trial, although it stated that the petitioners were "very good people who have taken excellent care of the child." The trial court then granted the petition that was the subject of the second trial. The appellate court affirmed, impliedly holding that a trial court may determine the best interests of the child by looking past the evidence submitted in support of the petition, and consider "evidence" that is yet to be heard in the subsequent trial of a competing adoption petition. However, in keeping with the decision in *Adoption of Baby Girl B.*, (1999) 74 Cal.App.4th 43, which holds that the petitioner has a statutory right to a trial-like hearing and to confront the evidence in opposition to the petition, it would appear that the better practice is to reserve the decision until after all evidence concerning both petitions has been received.

9. The Accounting Report

Family Code § 8610 provides that certain accountings must be filed with the court during the adoption proceedings, apparently to ensure compliance with Penal Code §§ 181 and 273, which prohibit the giving of money for a parental consent to an adoption. There is an exception under Family Code § 8610(c), i.e., that the need for an accounting does not apply to stepparent adoptions.

Under Family Code § 8610(a) and (b), on or before the date set for the hearing on the adoption petition, the petitioners must file with the court a full, itemized and detailed accounting report, signed under penalty of perjury, which identifies all disbursements of money or anything of value made or agreed to be made by them or on their behalf in connection with the birth of the child, the placement of the child with the petitioners, any medical or hospital care received by the child's birth mother or by the child in connection with the child's birth, and any other expenses of either birth parent, or the adoption.

In addition, Family Code § 8610(b) requires the accounting report to show the services relating to the adoption or to the placement of the child for adoption that were received by the petitioners, by either birth parent, by the child, or by any other person for whom payment was made by or on behalf of the petitioners. The report shall also include the dates of each payment, the names and addresses of each attorney, physician and surgeon, hospital, licensed adoption agency, or other person or organization who received any funds of the petitioners in connection with the adoption or the placement of the child with them, or participated in any way in the handling of those funds, either directly or indirectly. Family Code § 8630 specifically states that the fees paid to an adoption facilitator must be reported to the court.

10. Additional Procedures for Specific Types of Adoptions

In an agency adoption, Family Code § 8715(d) permits the CDSS to submit a report to the court, in addition to the report submitted by the private agency. Moreover, if the child was the subject of dependency proceedings, Family Code § 8715(b) provides that the report shall state whether the dependency proceedings have concluded.

In an intercountry adoption, a "readoption" is permitted under Family Code § 8919. The concept of readoption will be discussed further in Chapter 11 of this book.

D. The Order

1. Granting of the Petition

Family Code § 8612(c) states that if the court is satisfied that the interest of the child will be promoted by the adoption, it may make and enter an order of adoption of the child by the prospective adoptive parent or parents. This rule applies to all adoptions.

As to a child who was in the dependency system, Welfare & Institutions Code § 366.3(a) states that if a juvenile court orders a permanency plan of adoption or legal guardianship, it shall retain jurisdiction over the minor until the minor is adopted or the legal guardianship is established; it shall review the status of the minor every six months to ensure that the adoption or guardianship is completed as expeditiously as possible; and it shall terminate its own jurisdiction over the minor when the adoption of the minor has been granted.

2. Denial of the Petition

The converse of Family Code § 8612(c) is that if the court makes the factual finding that the adoption is not in the child's best interests, it may deny the petition. At that point, if there is someone present with enforceable parental rights, that person is then given custody of the child. In addition, the statutes mentioned above with regard to withdrawal of an agency adoption or intercountry adoption petition also state that the court may place the child in agency custody where there is a denial of the petition.

In an independent adoption, Family Code § 8805 states that if the court dismisses the petition or sustains the agency's recommendation to deny the petition and have the child removed from the petitioner's home, and the court chooses not return the child to the birth parents, the court shall commit the child to the care of the CDSS or delegated county adoption agency, whichever made the recommendation, for the CDSS or agency to arrange adoptive placement or to make a suitable plan.

Furthermore, the petitioners whose petition is denied have no say in the placement of the child. In *In re Adoption of Schroetter*, (1968) 261 Cal.App.2d 365, the trial court committed the child to the Los Angeles County Bureau of Adoptions after denying the adoption petition. The appellate court then held that the prospective adoptive parents' physical (not legal) custody of the child was only as an incident to the proposed adoption, and once that objective was denied, they had no further claim to custody of the child, and could not object to a placement with the agency.

III. APPEALS AND WRITS

A. The Right to "Appeal"

The courts in *In re Eli F.*, (1989) 212 Cal.App.3d 228, and *People v. Keener*, (1961) 55 Cal.2d 714, held that the right to appeal is conferred only by statute. Under Code of Civil Procedure §§ 902 and 904.1(a)(1) and (10), an "aggrieved party" may file an appeal from a final judgment (however designated) and from those orders identified in the Family Code wherein a right to appeal has been provided. A final adoption order, whether it is a grant or a denial of the petition, would usually constitute a final adjudication of all issues between the parties to the adoption. Also, appeals from orders issued by the superior court are heard by the state appellate court. Under 28 U.S.C. § 1291, which delineates the jurisdiction of the federal appellate courts, such as the Ninth Circuit, grant no power over any California state court's judgments or orders.

The statutes that specifically confer a right to appeal from certain orders in adoption cases include Family Code §§ 7669 and 9005(e), which provide for the right to appeal from an order requiring or dispensing with the need to obtain the birth parent's consent for the adoption of a child. In addition, Family Code § 3454 states that an appeal may be taken from a final order in a proceeding concerning enforcement of rights under the UCCJEA. Family Code § 8820(a) provides for a right of "appeal" where the agency refuses to participate in taking the birth parent's consent to the adoption, although the statute appears to deal with a petition to the superior court to force the agency to take the birth parent's consent.

In dependency proceedings, there are many provisions of the Welfare and Institutions Code providing appellate rights during various stages of the juvenile court proceeding. Likewise, Family Code § 7894 allows an appeal from an order and judgment of the court declaring a child free from the custody and control of a parent or parents.

According to Rule 8.104(a) of the California Rules of Court, the last day to file a notice of appeal is generally 60 days from the service of written notice of the entry of the judgment or appealable order, or 180 days from the entry of the judgment or order where there has been no service of written notice. The Rules of Court provide for specific ways for these deadlines to be extended for specific periods. However, the California courts have consistently held that the deadlines are jurisdictional, and that motions for extensions of time to appeal, other than what is provided in the Rules of Court, will not be granted.

Where the aggrieved party has perfected appellate jurisdiction by timely filing a notice of appeal from a final judgment or appealable order, and has complied with all rules concerning the record on appeal and the filing of appellate briefs, the appellate court is generally required to decide the case in a written opinion "with reasons stated." (Cal. Const., Art. VI, § 14.) As a practical matter, the appellate court must do so within 90 days after the completion of oral argument. (Cal. Const., Art. VI, § 19.) However, there are exceptions to the 90-day rule.

B. Petitions for Interlocutory Writs

Where there is no "right to an appeal," a party aggrieved by a non-appealable order may file a petition for a writ from the appellate court directing the superior court to take certain action (mandate) or refrain from taking certain action (prohibition). The lower court is actually the respondent on such a petition.

There is no "right" to appellate review by way of writ. While an "appeal" must be decided on the merits, a writ petition may be summarily denied with no reason given for the ruling. One such instance where the writ petition was granted was *San Diego County Dept. of Pub. Welfare v. Superior Court*, (1972) 7 Cal.3d 1, where the Supreme Court stated that extraordinary relief may be granted in an adoption or guardianship matter in order that the child involved can be placed in a permanent and stable environment as soon as possible, and where normal appellate procedures are inadequate to provide speedy and complete relief.

C. The Writ of Supersedeas

If an appeal has been perfected, a party to the appeal may immediately ask the appellate court to issue a writ of supersedeas commanding the parties or the superior court to preserve the status quo such that the appellate court may be able to provide an appropriate remedy upon disposition of the appeal. A writ of supersedeas is issued by the appellate court while the appeal is pending, and is not itself a decision on the merits. Also, since an appellate stay may only be imposed where an actual notice of appeal has been filed, the court in *In re Berth*, (1947) 79 Cal.App.2d 221, held there is no such thing as a stay in contemplation of an appeal.

In *Adoption of Baby Girl B.*, (1999) 74 Cal.App.4th 43, the court wholly agreed with the prospective adoptive parent on the substantive issues in the case and issued the requested reversal. However, the *Baby Girl B.* court stated that the appellant "won the appellate battle only to lose the adoptive war," because the child had been in the agency's custody during the entire 1½ years of appellate proceedings. The *Baby Girl B.* court stated that since the appeal did not automatically stay the order removing the child from the appellant's custody, the appellant should have asked for a stay from the trial court and/or sought a writ of supersedeas pursuant to Code of Civil Procedure § 923. As such, the court on remand would have had grounds to find that it was not in the child's best interests to grant the adoption and thus sever the bonds with the new caregivers. Since the appellant in *Baby Girl B.* failed to seek a supersedeas writ or a stay from the trial court, it was probable that the child bonded with the new caregivers who were acting at the agency's behest.

D. The Consequences of a Party's Failure to Timely Appeal

In *Coughlin v. Coughlin*, (1954) 129 Cal.App.2d 294, and *In re Guardianship of Coughlin*, (1954) 129 Cal.App.2d 290, which concerned the same operative facts and the same courts, the appellate court held that where a person has filed a motion to vacate an adoption order, successfully or unsuccessfully, he or she becomes a party to the adoption proceeding, and if there is no appeal from the denial of the post-adoption motion, the order becomes final and res judicata. As shown in the cases reprinted below, there are certain instances where a party may wage a collateral attack on the adoption order despite the res judicata effect of the prior case.

E. "Law of the Case" Doctrine vis-à-vis Intervening Legislation

Generally, where an appellant obtains a reversal of a judgment or order, along with a remand to the trial court for further proceedings, the appellate court's written decision is thereafter constitutes the law of the case for all purposes. As stated in *Citizens for Open Access to Sand and Tide, Inc. v. Seadrift Assoc.*, (1998) 60 Cal.App.4th 1053, and *Clemente v. State*, (1985) 40 Cal.3d 202, where an appellate court sets forth a principle of law necessary to the decision, that principle becomes law of the case and must be adhered to in all subsequent proceedings, including appeals, so as to provide for judicial economy and the finality of court rulings.

But what happens when the Legislature enacts a relevant new statute immediately after the appeal is decided? In *Renee J. v. Superior Court*, (2002) 96 Cal.App.4th 1450, a juvenile court initially ordered that the birth mother was not entitled to reunification services based on Welfare & Institutions Code § 361.5(b)(10) as it existed in 2000. The birth mother appealed to the Court of Appeal, which reversed based on its own interpretation of the statute, however the social services agency successfully petitioned to the California Supreme Court, which held on August 16, 2001 that the juvenile court's ruling and original interpretation of the statute were correct. (*Renee J. v. Superior Court*, (2001) 26 Cal.4th 735.) The Supreme Court then remanded the case back to the juvenile court to complete the dependency proceedings. However, the California Legislature then passed Assembly Bill No. 1695, which substantially changed the statute, and the bill was signed into law on October 10, 2001 as an "urgency measure," causing the law to become effective immediately, but not retroactively. Around the same time, the question of reunification was again at issue in the juvenile court, which ultimately held, after the signing of Assembly Bill No. 1695, that the California Supreme Court's decision was law of the case and that the new statute did not control.

The birth mother filed another writ petition. The 2002 *Renee J.* decision pointed out that Assembly Bill No. 1695 was intended by the Legislature to be a "clarification" of the meaning of the pre-existing Welfare & Institutions Code § 361.5(b)(10), even though there was no statutory language declaring that Assembly Bill No. 1695 was retroactive. The appellate court's 2002 *Renee J.* decision then stated that Assembly Bill No. 1695 should have been applied in the most recent juvenile court proceedings, since the bill "properly overrode the effect of the Supreme Court's decision, which would otherwise have been law of the case." Curiously, although it was held that Assembly Bill No. 1695 was merely a "clarification" of pre-existing law, the appellate court's 2002 *Renee J.* decision stated that Assembly Bill No. 1695 constituted an "intervening or contemporaneous change in the law," which is an exception to the law of the case doctrine. The California Supreme Court denied review, thereby allowing the appellate court's 2002 decision in *Renee J.* to become binding precedent throughout the State of California.

Every year, the Legislature amends the laws affecting adoptions. However, unlike the reunification rulings at issue in *Renee J.*, the granting of an adoption petition and the subsequent unsuccessful exhaustion of appellate remedies results in a final order which has res judicata and collateral estoppel effect, as explained above and in *Coughlin v. Coughlin*, (1954) 129 Cal.App.2d 294, and *In re Guardianship of Coughlin*, (1954) 129 Cal.App.2d 290. Furthermore, there is no "change in the law" exception to the doctrines of res judicata and collateral estoppel. (See *Producers Dairy Delivery Co. v. Sentry Ins. Co.*, (1986) 41 Cal.3d 903; *Slater v. Blackwood*, (1975) 15 Cal.3d 791; *Busick v. WCAB*, (1972) 7 Cal.3d 967.) Therefore, a change in the law that occurs after the exhaustion of appellate remedies would not overcome the res judicata and collateral estoppel effect of the adoption decree, and it would not appear that the point of view expressed in the appellate court's 2002 *Renee J.* decision would vitiate the res judicata and collateral estoppel effect of a final order granting an adoption, since the doctrine of law of the case necessarily contemplates the existence of ongoing proceedings.

IV. DIRECT AND COLLATERAL ATTACKS ON THE ADOPTION DECREE

In *People v. Beach*, (1987) 194 Cal.App.3d 955, the court stated that a direct attack is a proceeding instituted for the specific purpose of vacating, reversing or otherwise attacking the judgment or order, and that a collateral attack is indirect, and is made not in a proceeding brought for the specific purpose of attacking the judgment or order, but in some other proceeding having a different purpose. An appeal, a writ petition to an appellate court, or a post-adoption motion (whether for new trial or to set aside the order based on extrinsic fraud) would qualify as a direct attack. In addition, a petition filed in a separate suit to set aside the adoption and secure custody of the child would be a direct attack. All other attacks on the adoption order (such as a defense in a wrongful death suit that the plaintiff is not the heir of the decedent) would be deemed a "collateral" attack. As explained below, the significance of differentiating between direct and collateral attacks relates primarily to whether the person bringing the attack has standing to do so.

A. Direct Post-Adoption Attacks in the Trial Court

1. Motion to Set Aside Adoption due to Extrinsic Fraud

In *In re David H.*, (1995) 33 Cal.App.4th 368, the court held that "A court always has inherent equitable jurisdiction to vacate a judgment or order that was obtained through extrinsic fraud." In *Arnold v. Howell*, (1950) 98 Cal.App.2d 202, also held that a judgment of a court of equity may be set aside for extrinsic fraud.

Importantly, *Arnold* implies that "extrinsic fraud" is not the only grounds by which a court may set aside an adoption. The court held that consent is a jurisdictional prerequisite to the adoption, and that where the consent was obtained by fraud, duress or undue influence, no true consent actually exists.

a) Extrinsic v. Intrinsic Fraud

In defining "extrinsic fraud," *Arnold* states, "The fraud which will justify the setting aside of a final judgment by a court of equity must be of such character as prevents a trial of the issues presented to the court for determination," or where it "deprives the unsuccessful party of an opportunity to present his case to the court." *Arnold* also held, "A consent which is required before a court can act, and which is based upon misrepresentation or given by a person who is unable to comprehend its meaning, prevents a fair and full hearing of the issues which the court is required to determine." *Arnold* held that a misrepresentation to the birth parent as to the status of his parental rights following the adoption would constitute extrinsic fraud.

The *David H.* court noted that intrinsic fraud consists for example of a witness telling a lie in court where the opposing party has the right of cross-examination, while extrinsic fraud is a dishonest act or statement occurring outside the courtroom causing the aggrieved party to do or not do something of consequence. In *County of Orange v. Superior Court*, (2007) 155 Cal.App.4th 1253, the court held that allegations of the birth mother's statement to the alleged birth father that he was the biological father, even though the two were not in a "mutually exclusive" relationship, did not satisfy the requirements for pleading any kind of fraud. *In re William K.*, (2008) 161 Cal.App.4th 1, held that the false signing of a paternity declaration was only intrinsic fraud.

b) Statute of Limitations

According to Family Code § 9102(a), an action or proceeding of any kind to vacate, set aside, or otherwise nullify an order of adoption on any ground, except fraud, shall be commenced within one year after entry of the order. Family Code § 9102(b) then states that an action or proceeding of any kind to vacate, set aside, or nullify an order of adoption, based on fraud, shall be commenced within three years after entry of the order. The "discovery rule" applicable to most statute of limitations does not apply to either subsection of Family Code § 9102. (*In re Adoption of B.C., Jr.*, (2011) 195 Cal.App.4th 913.) In interpreting the predecessor of this statute, *Walter v. August*, (1960) 186 Cal.App.2d 395, held that the Legislature intended to preclude any attack whatsoever on a decree of adoption after the statutory period has lapsed.

In *Walter*, it was undisputed that the natural parents were not properly notified and that there were no valid grounds to dispense with their consent to the adoption. However, the court held that even if the natural parents' due process rights were violated, the jurisdictional defect in the adoption was cured by the natural parents' failure to comply with the statute of limitations. It also held that that adoption was not "void" but rather "voidable" upon the timely request of the nonconsenting natural parents.

In civil litigation, a statute of limitations is "tolled" or "stayed" during the time in which the party could not have discovered the grounds for the complaint or petition, or where the opposing party is estopped to assert a statute of limitations defense. See, *Norgart v. Upjohn*, (1999) 21 Cal.4th 383. However, there is no case law stating that this jurisprudence would apply in an action to set aside an adoption, since the best interests of the child would militate against tearing the child away from the bonds that have formed in his or her adoptive home.

2. Petition for Habeas Corpus for Lack of Jurisdiction

"Habeas corpus" is Latin for "you have the body." The writ of habeas corpus is a device used in a variety of contexts for the purpose of having an individual released from the responding party's custody. The writ is commonly used to address judicial error of constitutional or jurisdictional dimension. In *Adoption of Alexander S.*, (1988) 44 Cal.3d 857, the California Supreme Court held that habeas corpus may be used in an adoption case where the superior court lacked jurisdiction to grant the adoption.

Alexander S. holds that habeas corpus may be available in six different subcategories of child custody cases, which are those cases brought (1) to enforce an existing right to physical custody established by prior order, (2) to determine physical custody in the first instance where no previous custody order has issued, such as where habeas corpus is not brought as a collateral attack, (3) to modify a modifiable order such as a custody provision in a divorce decree, (4) to protect a child from imminent danger, (5) where a natural parent lacking physical custody is seeking a writ of habeas corpus where his or her consent to an adoption was required but not obtained, and (6) to collaterally attack a prior order where the court issuing the prior order lacked jurisdiction to issue it.

An example of the fifth category is *In re Timothy W.*, (1990) 223 Cal.App.3d 437, where the court granted a writ of habeas corpus in a proceeding wherein the birth mother claimed she never consented to the adoption. However, in *In re Meranda P.*, (1997) 56 Cal.App.4th 1143, the court held that the *Alexander S.* rule prohibited a birth parent from seeking habeas corpus from a final non-modifiable order issued in a juvenile dependency proceeding. On the other hand, *In re O.S.*, (2002) 102 Cal.App.4th 1402, holds that where the birth parent files a timely appeal pursuant to Welfare & Institutions Code § 366.26(i) and 395, a claim of ineffective assistance of counsel may be pursued concurrently by way of writ of habeas corpus.

The *Alexander S.* court expressly stated that habeas corpus may not be used to collaterally attack a final nonmodifiable judgment in an adoption-related action where the trial court had jurisdiction to render the final judgment. In *Alexander S.*, the intermediate appellate court treated a belated appeal from her unsuccessful request to withdraw consent as a petition for writ of habeas corpus, but made no reference to jurisdictional deficiencies, upon which the Supreme Court held that such an action was not authorized in that case.

As for *Timothy W.*, habeas corpus was appropriate since the birth mother never consented and there were no grounds to dispense with her consent. Consent is a jurisdictional issue, as explained in Chapter 3. Other jurisdictional issues may arise from questions surrounding compliance with Family Code § 9210, the Uniform Child Custody Jurisdiction and Enforcement Act and the Indian Child Welfare Act, all of which are explained in Chapter 9.

3. Code of Civil Procedure Section 473 Motion?

Various courts have described *In re Yoder*, (1926) 199 Cal. 699, as holding that the provisions of Code of Civil Procedure § 473, which allow a court within six months to set aside an order or a judgment merely on the grounds that it was obtained as a result of the mistake, inadvertence, surprise or excusable neglect of a party, could be utilized to vacate an adoption. (*In re Duarte's Adoption*, (1964) 229 Cal.App.2d 775.) However, the *Yoder* case was actually a resolution of an issue of appellate procedure, and did not actually decide whether or not a particular adoption would be vacated or not. In addition, there is no other published California decision wherein an adoption was set aside pursuant to Code of Civil Procedure § 473 alone, and all of the cases mentioning *Yoder* relied on some provision of law which more specifically addressed the rights of the parties to the adoption. See for example, *Adoption of Kay C.*, (1991) 228 Cal.App.3d 741, wherein the adoptive parents were permitted to have the adoption vacated pursuant to the predecessor of Family Code § 9100(a).

Yoder cited *Bell v. Krauss*, (1926) 169 Cal. 387, which held that a father who was not notified of the adoption proceeding could move to set it aside. However, as applied today, such a claim is better characterized as a constitutional challenge pursuant to *Armstrong v. Manzo*, (1965) 380 U.S. 545, as explained in Chapter 3. *Yoder* also mentioned *In re McGrew*, (1926) 169 Cal. 387, in which a man who was deemed to be the father of the child by virtue of having received the child into his home and holding her out as his own child (which today would qualify him as a presumed father under Family Code § 7611(d)) did not receive notice of the adoption proceeding. Again, under the present law, such a man would be constitutionally and statutorily entitled to notice, making the Code of Civil Procedure § 473 claim of lesser importance.

In contrast to the *Yoder* case, *David B. v. Superior Court*, (1994) 21 Cal.App.4th 1010, specifically held that Code of Civil Procedure §§ 473 and 473.5 do not apply to a juvenile court dependency case. While several cases apply Code of Civil Procedure § 473 in the context of a guardianship, it must be remembered that guardianships are under the continuing jurisdiction and supervision of the court, and do not involve a final judgment or order, unlike an adoption. Also, since the best interests of the child are the paramount consideration in any adoption-related case (as explained in Chapter 2), the mistake, inadvertence, surprise or excusable neglect forming the basis of the Code of Civil Procedure § 473 motion would be superseded by the child's interests.

B. Collateral Attacks

1. Standing to Wage the Collateral Attack

In *Hubbard v. Superior Court*, (1961) 189 Cal.App.2d 741, the court held that an adoption could not be collaterally attacked in probate proceedings by individuals who were not parties to the adoption, even if the collateral attack was based on evidence that the adoptive parent fraudulently misrepresented to the California court that she was a California resident, and failed to disclose to the California court that she was suffering from cancer and that a Connecticut court had earlier ordered that her two previous children be removed from her care and custody. The parties waging the collateral attack simply had no standing to assert the issues, no matter how factually and legally compelling they were.

In *Walter v. August*, (1960) 186 Cal.App.2d 395, the court held that the lack of consent by the natural parents would, at most, render the adoption decree subject to attack by them, but the adoption decree would not be void in the sense that it could be treated as a nullity, or even attacked directly, by anyone else except the child himself. The *Walter* court also held that the natural parents had no standing to complain that the child's grandmother had not been given notice of the proceeding, even if the grandmother was entitled to such notice.

Therefore, it appears that a collateral attack could only be made by an individual who was harmed in some way by the deficiency in the adoption proceedings. Even then, if that individual was a party to the proceedings and had actual notice of the deficiency, the failure to appeal from the ruling would bring about a res judicata effect that would bar the collateral attack. (See *Coughlin v. Coughlin*, (1954) 129 Cal.App.2d 294, and *In re Guardianship of Coughlin*, (1954) 129 Cal.App.2d 290.) For these reasons, it would appear that an individual bringing a collateral attack would have to establish an injurious jurisdictional deficiency coupled with a lack of notice. In fact, the California Supreme Court held in *In re Radovich's Estate* (1957) 48 Cal.2d 116, that even a governmental agency would lack standing to mount a collateral attack on a prior order of a probate court declaring that a person became one of the decedent's heirs by virtue of an equitable adoption, even if the prior order is based on an erroneous interpretation of the law.

2. Attacks against Decrees from Other Jurisdictions

As explained in Chapter 9, adoption decrees from other states are entitled to full faith and credit. In *Estate of Hart*, (1984) 165 Cal.App.3d 392, the court held that an Oklahoma adoption decree was constitutionally entitled to full faith and credit in a California probate proceeding. In *Young v. Reno*, (9th Cir. 1997) 114 F.3d 879, an adoption decree from Hong Kong was required to be recognized for purposes of immigration proceedings concerning a birth sibling. However, as also explained in Chapter 9, full faith and credit does not apply where jurisdiction for the underlying decree is lacking.

As to modifiable decrees, in *New York ex rel. Halvey v. Halvey*, (1947) 330 U.S. 610, the U.S. Supreme Court held that the Full Faith & Credit Clause generally does not prevent a court in one state from re-visiting a different state's rulings that would be modifiable by the original court. However, the California Supreme Court specifically held in *Adoption of Alexander S.*, (1988) 44 Cal.3d 857, that an adoption is not a modifiable decree. On the other hand, Family Code § 8714.7 expressly states that a postadoption contact agreement is modifiable.

INTERCOUNTRY ADOPTIONS 11

In this chapter:

Involvement of the Foreign Government in the Case
Status of the Child if Adoption Cannot be Completed
Readoption in California

"They're as much my blood as I am theirs. And they are brothers and sisters. One came from Ethiopia, one from Vietnam, one from Cambodia, and one was born in Namibia. And they are brothers and sisters, and they have fun and they squabble and they fight, just like any other family. And it makes me so proud." – Brad Pitt

I. INTRODUCTION

Family Code § 8527 defines an "intercountry adoption" as an adoption of a foreign-born child who is to be brought to the United States. International adoptions became popular in 1975 with Congress' sweeping amendments to the immigration statutes signed into law by President Gerald Ford (who is considered to be adopted), giving preferential immigrant status to adoptees.

Most intercountry adoptions are finalized in the foreign country. Intercountry adoptions thus differ from other types of adoptions in that, in most cases, the child is not yet physically in the home of the adoptive parents at the time the adoption order is issued. In addition, it is essential to secure the services of an attorney who is licensed by the foreign jurisdiction, along with those professionals who are qualified (under state law and federal law) to complete the home study in California. Since there are literally hundreds of nations, this book cannot examine the adoption laws of all of them, nor of any particular nation other than the United States.

For intercountry adoptions that are completed in the U.S., Family Code §§ 8900, et seq. now deal with how an intercountry adoptions are to be handled for children who are to be brought to California (i.e., "incoming" cases), and those who are intended for emigration to other countries (i.e., "outgoing" cases). As explained in Chapter 10, Family Code § 8714(a) allows a foreign national to adopt a child in the custody of a California agency, and then bring the child to the foreign national's country for emigration.

Since intercountry adoptions involve interaction between nations, and have become increasingly common, a treaty called the "Convention on Protection of Children and Co-Operation In Respect Of Intercountry Adoption" was created on May 29, 1993 in The Hague, Netherlands. In this book, it will be referred to simply as the "Hague Convention on Intercountry Adoption," or the "Hague Convention," or the "Treaty." The Treaty is also known as "Convention No. 33." Over 80 other nations are parties to the Hague Convention. On October 6, 2000, the U.S. ratified the Treaty (42 U.S.C. §§ 14901, et seq.), and enacted implementing regulations in 2008. Most nations – including the U.S. – have also ratified a treaty called the Convention on the Civil Aspects of International Child Abduction. (See *Abbott v. Abbott*, 130 S.Ct. 1983 (2010).)

An intercountry adoption contemplates that a non-citizen, non-resident child will be brought into the United States for permanent residence. Therefore, a visa must be obtained for the child through applications and petitions to U.S. Citizenship and Immigration Services (the "USCIS") and the U.S. State Department. The U.S. Government does not issue adoption decrees. The obtaining of a visa is also the first step in securing U.S. citizenship for the child.

Regarding the adoption of children with foreign birth parents, under the 14th Amendment of the U.S. Constitution, all persons born or naturalized in the United States are U.S. citizens. If, therefore, a pregnant woman who is not a U.S. citizen comes to the U.S. to have her baby, the child is a U.S. citizen, and no visa is needed for the child. Therefore, the adoption of such a child would not be an "intercountry adoption." Also, 8 U.S.C. § 1401(f) provides that a person of unknown parentage found in the U.S. while under five years old is a citizen and a "national" of the U.S., until it is shown, before the child becomes 21 years old, that he or she was not born in the United States. Therefore, again, the adoption of such a child with unknown parents would not be considered an "intercountry adoption."

Conversely, there are instances where a child of a U.S. citizen is deemed to be a U.S. citizen even if born in a foreign country. If proof exists that the child is a U.S. citizen, there is no need to obtain a visa, even if the child were in the custody of an adoption agency in a foreign country. It is unclear whether the Hague Convention would govern the rare case of a U.S. citizen going to a foreign country to adopt another U.S. citizen, or whether that would be considered an "intercountry adoption."

II. THE DOMESTIC ENFORCEABILITY OF FOREIGN ADOPTIONS

A. Enforceability under the Hague Convention

Article 23 of the Hague Convention states,

> "(1) An adoption certified by the competent authority of the State [i.e., country] of the adoption as having been made in accordance with the Convention shall be recognised by operation of law in the other Contracting States. The certificate shall specify when and by whom the agreements

under Article 17, sub-paragraph c) [which are entered into between the central authorities of the two countries at issue], were given.

(2) Each Contracting State shall, at the time of signature, ratification, acceptance, approval or accession, notify the depositary of the Convention of the identity and the functions of the authority or the authorities which, in that State, are competent to make the certification. It shall also notify the depositary of any modification in the designation of these authorities."

At Article 24, the Treaty states, "The recognition of an adoption may be refused in a Contracting State only if the adoption is manifestly contrary to its public policy, taking into account the best interests of the child." There is no published federal or California case ever declaring that an adoption was "manifestly contrary" to public policy.

Under 42 U.S.C. § 14931(b), a final adoption in another Convention country, certified by the U.S. Secretary of State pursuant to 42 U.S.C. §§ 14931(a) or 14932(c), shall be recognized as a final valid adoption for purposes of all Federal, State, and local laws of the United States. Adoption decrees from other Treaty nations are also formally recognized pursuant to California Family Code § 8925. If appended to the adoption decree, the Secretary of State's certificate under 42 U.S.C. § 14931(a) shall be treated by Federal and State agencies, courts, and other public and private persons and entities as conclusive evidence of the facts certified therein and shall constitute the certification required by 8 U.S.C. § 1154(d)(2).

Additionally, pursuant to 42 U.S.C. § 14954, a final adoption concluded between two other Convention countries that meet the requirements of Article 23 of the Convention and that became final before the date of entry into force of the Convention for the United States shall be recognized thereafter in the United States and given full effect. Such recognition shall include the specific effects described in Article 26 of the Convention.

B. Statutes Recognizing Non-Hague Custody Orders

Federal statute provides for formal recognition of pre-Treaty adoption decrees from other Treaty nations. (See 42 U.S.C. § 14951.) Also, the Uniform Child Custody Jurisdiction and Enforcement Act ("UCCJEA") provides (at Family Code § 3405(a) in California) that a foreign country is to be treated as if it were a U.S. state. Family Code § 3405(b) and (c) then provides that a foreign country's child custody determination which is made under factual circumstances in substantial conformity with the UCCJEA must be recognized and enforced, unless that country's child custody laws "violate fundamental principles of human rights." (There is no "human rights" counterpart either in the Federal Parental Kidnapping Prevention Act ("PKPA") or in the Interstate Compact for the Placement of Children ("ICPC").) There is no published California case ever declaring that any particular country is in this category.

Although the UCCJEA (as enacted in most states, including California) does not apply to "adoptions" (Family Code § 3403), it would apply to a foreign country's termination of the birth parents' rights or the ordering of a guardianship, pursuant to Family Code § 3402(d). Therefore, for UCCJEA purposes, if the child is to be brought to the U.S. in order to complete the adoption, the foreign country's orders concerning the birth parents' rights and/or a guardianship would be valid if, for example, that foreign country were the child's "home state." Since an adoption terminates a guardianship, the adoption proceeding could then be brought in the California courts once California becomes the child's new UCCJEA "home state" or if the foreign court ceded jurisdiction to California, as explained in Chapter 9.

C. Doctrine of International Comity with Non-Hague Countries

As for children who are not from a Hague country, there is a judicially-imposed full faith and credit doctrine that arises by virtue of the comity relationship that the courts encourage with foreign countries. At the time this book was written, several populous nations, including Japan, the Koreas, Argentina, Russia and several former Soviet republics, many of the Balkan nations, most African nations and almost all Islamic countries still had not ratified the Treaty, according to the U.S. State Department. Nevertheless, tens of thousands of international adoptions involving children from these non-Hague countries have been completed in just the last 15 years.

Prior to U.S. ratification of the Hague Convention, the California Supreme Court held in *In re Stephanie M.*, (1994) 7 Cal.4th 295, that as a matter of comity, the courts of this state *may* enforce the judgment of a foreign nation. (The Full Faith & Credit Clause [U.S. Const., Art. IV] only applies to judicial acts undertaken within the U.S.) Thus, an adoption that was completed in a non-Hague country may still be entitled to domestic enforceability. (Since the doctrine of comity is only discretionary, it may be wise to complete a readoption where the child is from a non-Hague country. Readoptions are discussed near the end of this chapter.)

Citing *Hilton v. Guyot*, (1895) 159 U.S. 113, the *Stephanie M.* court held that pursuant to the doctrine of comity, an American court will recognize the judgment of a foreign nation's court if (1) the foreign court had proper jurisdiction and (2) enforcement does not prejudice the rights of U.S. citizens or violate domestic public policy. *Stephanie M.* also holds that extension or denial of comity is discretionary and is reviewed for abuse of discretion. In applying the doctrine of comity, it was held in *Young v. Reno*, (9th Cir. 1997) 114 F.3d 879, which was decided prior to U.S. ratification of the Hague Convention, that an adoption that was completed in Hong Kong was enforceable in the U.S., and that that foreign adoption severed the legal relationship between an adopted child and her natural parents and siblings.

D. The Nature of the Adoption as Defined by Foreign Law

1. Adoptions Completed in a Hague Country

Article 26 of the Hague Convention provides,

"(1) The recognition of an adoption includes recognition of –

a) the legal parent-child relationship between the child and his or her adoptive parents;

b) parental responsibility of the adoptive parents for the child;

> c) the termination of a pre-existing legal relationship between the child and his or her mother and father, if the adoption has this effect in the Contracting State [i.e., country] where it was made.
>
> (2) In the case of an adoption having the effect of terminating a pre-existing legal parent-child relationship, the child shall enjoy in the receiving State, and in any other Contracting State where the adoption is recognised, rights equivalent to those resulting from adoptions having this effect in each such State.
>
> (3) The preceding paragraphs shall not prejudice the application of any provision more favourable for the child, in force in the Contracting State which recognises the adoption."

As for post-adoption contact between the child and the birth parents, there is no provision in the Hague Convention either allowing it or prohibiting it. However, it may be that the adoption law of the foreign nation allows for post-adoption contact agreements, or automatically allows for post-adoption contact between the child and the birth parents. The law of the foreign country must be researched on this question, since Article 26(2) of the Treaty obligates the California court to enforce this aspect of the child's "rights" arising from the foreign adoption.

2. Foreign Law in the Context of a Non-Hague Adoption

Estate of O'Dea, (1973) 29 Cal.App.3d 759, which was decided before the Hague Treaty was ratified, held that the status of adoption or non-adoption as established in Canada must be recognized in California under principles of either comity or "full faith and credit."

The California court in *O'Dea* held that the laws of Canada allowed an adoption that was decreed by a Canadian court to be annulled by a "private legislative act" in the province of Alberta, and that the California courts were required to abide by this legislative annulment. The *O'Dea* court in California exhaustively studied Canadian law and held that the provincial legislature did have authority to enact this "private legislation" specifically directed at one person. The *O'Dea* court in California then enforced the Canadian private legislative act and held that the individual was no longer an adopted person, but rather was entitled to share in the estate of the deceased birth parent. There is no case stating whether or not a court would enforce an adoption that was declared by a foreign legislature.

The *O'Dea* court also held California will refuse to recognize, and will allow collateral attacks on, adoptions in foreign jurisdictions if the same were obtained without notice and opportunity to be heard. On the other hand, there are no such procedural due process rights in the context of a true legislative act. (*Arnel Development Co. v. City of Costa Mesa*, (1980) 28 Cal.3d 511.) However, the court held that the private statute enacted by the Alberta Legislative Assembly voiding the adoption was not repugnant to such a policy.

In *Kaho v. Ilchert*, (9th Cir. 1985) 765 F.2d 877, the court held that for an adoption to be valid under federal immigration law, an adoption need not conform to "Anglo-American" notions of what an adoption entails, but that the adoption need only be recognized under the law of the country where the adoption occurred. *Kaho* held that an adoption under Tongan law which did not carry with it the right of intestate succession could still be considered an "adoption" for purposes of a visa petition under 8 U.S.C. § 1101(b)(1)(E). *Kaho* also held that the lack of a statutory procedure in Tonga for the adoption of children did not mean that common law adoptions are not recognized under the foreign law. *Kaho* also ruled that since Tongan law recognized inter vivos equitable adoptions (i.e., those not formalized by a court order), that the immigration agency in the U.S. had to also recognize that such common law adoptions take place in Tonga. (As stated in Chapter 1, California law does not recognize common law adoptions.)

3. Foreign Birth Parent's Attempt to Void the Adoption

a) Generally

The Hague Treaty itself is silent on the issue of revocability. As for the foreign court's jurisdiction to vacate a Hague adoption, for example because of some alleged invalidity or defect in the birth parents' consent, there is no specific provision in the Treaty either allowing or prohibiting such jurisdiction, nor is there anything in the United States Code dealing with a foreign court's attempt to vacate an adoption. However, one must note that Article 17(c) of the Hague Convention literally requires, for each adoption, that an agreement be entered into between the central authorities of the two nations involved in the intercountry adoption. Thus, a foreign court's attempt to vacate an adoption would infringe on the contractual rights of the U.S. in connection with the enforceability of the adoption.

Further, while Article 26(2) of the Treaty protects the *child's* "rights equivalent to those resulting from adoptions" in the foreign country, a petition to vacate an adoption due to a lack of consent is brought to vindicate the *birth parent's* right to custody, since the best interests of the child are usually not examined in such a contest. As for adoptions completed in pre-Hague or non-Hague countries, the California courts have enforced "orders" by the foreign jurisdiction invalidating the adoption. See *Estate of O'Dea*, (1973) 29 Cal.App.3d 759.

As for the foreign birth parent's attempt to sue in California to vacate the foreign adoption, there appears to be no case law directly on point. However, the California Supreme Court held in *Adoption of Alexander S.*, (1988) 44 Cal.3d 857, that a natural parent lacking physical custody may bring "an original action in habeas corpus where his or her consent to an adoption was required but not obtained," and that "habeas corpus may be brought to collaterally attack a prior order where the court issuing the prior order lacked jurisdiction." True, *Alexander S.* involved adoption proceedings in California, but it does not appear that habeas corpus relief in California would be limited to California child custody decrees, since the power of the court is imposed against the person who presently has custody, as long as the child is in California or the California court has personal jurisdiction over the custodian of the child. On the other hand, applying Article 26(2) of the Hague Convention, if the foreign country does not recognize anything similar to the writ of habeas corpus in the context of adoptions, then the child should be entitled to be free from a birth parent's attempts in California to seek habeas corpus.

b) Irrevocable Consent

Many of the USCIS regulations, as well as 8 U.S.C. § 1101(b)(1)(G)(i), speak in terms of birth parents giving "irrevocable" consent to the adoption. According to 8 C.F.R. § 204.301, "irrevocable consent" means a document which indicates the place and date the document was signed by a child's legal custodian in which the legal custodian freely consents to the termination of the legal custodian's legal relationship with the child. If the irrevocable consent is signed by the child's birth mother or any legal custodian other than the birth father, the irrevocable consent must have been signed after the child's birth; *the birth father may sign an irrevocable consent before the child's birth if permitted by the law of the child's habitual residence*. If more than one individual or entity is the child's legal custodian, the consent of each legal custodian may be recorded in one document, or in an additional document, but all documents, taken together, must show that each legal custodian has given the necessary irrevocable consent.

It should also be noted that 8 C.F.R. § 204.313(d)(4)(ii) requires that the USCIS be given, in the case of a Hague adoption, a copy of the irrevocable consent(s) signed by the legal custodian(s) and any other individual or entity who must consent to the child's adoption unless, as permitted under article 16 of the Hague Convention, the law of the country of the child's habitual residence provides that their identities may not be disclosed, so long as the Central Authority of the country of the child's habitual residence certifies in its report that the required documents exist and that they establish the child's age and availability for adoption. (See also 8 U.S.C. § 1101(b)(1)(G)(i).) However, as explained in Chapter 3, California courts distinguish between the revocation of a consent and a judicial invalidation of a consent.

As for the timing of such efforts, *Estate of O'Dea* holds that under Code of Civil Procedure § 361, when a foreign statute of limitations bars a claim which arose there, an action shall not be maintained thereon against a person in this state. In other words, if a foreign jurisdiction has a six-month limit on attacking an adoption decree on the grounds of fraud, the plaintiff may not rely upon the three-year Family Code § 9102(b) rule.

(1) Concerns re Literacy

To qualify as an irrevocable consent under 8 C.F.R. § 204.301, the document must specify whether the legal custodian is able to read and understand the language in which the consent is written. If the legal custodian is not able to read or understand the language in which the document is written, then the document must be accompanied by a declaration, signed under penalty of perjury under U.S. law, by an identified individual, establishing that that person is competent to translate the language in the irrevocable consent into a language that the parent understands, and that person, on the date and at the place specified in the declaration, did in fact read and explain the consent to the legal custodian in a language (and in what language) that the legal custodian understands.

(2) "Factual Basis" for the Consent

For purposes of filing the Form I-800 petition for preferential immigration status, the petitioner is required by 8 C.F.R. § 204.313(d)(4)(iv)(B) to provide a summary of the "irrevocable consent," including "the factual basis for determining that they [the birth parents] are incapable of providing proper care for the child." In other words, the petitioner is required to state why he or she believes the birth parents felt they could not care for the child but instead consented to the adoption. The regulations do not require the consenting birth parents themselves to write out the reasons for giving the consent.

(3) "Sole Parent"

The USCIS regulations (at 8 C.F.R. § 204.301) define "sole parent" as –

- The child's mother, when the competent [foreign] authority has determined that the child's father has abandoned or deserted the child, or has disappeared from the child's life; or
- The child's father, when the competent [foreign] authority has determined that the child's mother has abandoned or deserted the child, or has disappeared from the child's life; except that
- A child's parent is not a sole parent if the child has acquired another parent within the meaning of federal law.

Under 8 C.F.R. § 204.313(d)(4)(iv)(B), if the irrevocable consent is signed by a "sole parent," the Form I-800 petition must summarize "the circumstances leading to the determination that the other parent abandoned or deserted the child, or disappeared from the child's life."

4. Adoptive Parent's Attempt to Annul Foreign Adoption

In *In re Adoption of M.S.*, (2010) 181 Cal.App.4th 50, the adoptive parents asserted that pursuant to Family Code § 9100, et seq., their adoption of a young girl in the Ukraine should be set aside. However, the court held that a court's authority under Family Code § 9100 to annul an adoption only applies to adoptions that were completed *in* California, even though the statute only describes adoptions completed "pursuant to the law of this state." It relied on the statutory language that the set aside petition "may be filed with the court that granted the adoption petition." It should also be noted that the *M.S.* court intentionally chose not to decide whether a California court could annul a "re-adoption" that was completed in California. As for going to the Ukraine (or whichever foreign country) to annul the adoption, one would have to research the laws of that foreign country to determine whether such efforts are permitted.

III. IMMIGRATION MATTERS CONCERNING THE FOREIGN CHILD

Article I, Section 8 of the U.S. Constitution gives Congress the authority to enact all "necessary and proper" legislation "to establish an uniform Rule of Naturalization." Further, *U.S. v. Curtiss-Wright Export Corp.*, (1936) 299 U.S. 304, held that "the power to expel undesirable aliens" is one of the inherent powers the U.S. possesses by virtue of its status as a nation. Also, *Nyquist v. Mauclet*, (1977) 432 U.S. 1, holds that the federal government has *exclusive* control over matters involving immigration and naturalization.

A. Federal Reorganization of Immigration Law and Agencies

Prior to September 11, 2001, the U.S. Immigration and Naturalization Service ("INS"), which was an agency within the U.S. Department of Justice, which is headed by the Attorney General, handled immigration matters with regard to adopted children and children to be adopted domestically. However, Congress has since restructured the federal agencies so as to entrust immigration issues to the Bureau of Citizenship and Immigration Services ("BCIS") – a new agency within the new Department of Homeland Security. (See 6 U.S.C. § 542.) The BCIS is now called U.S. Citizenship and Immigration Services (the "USCIS").

Most of the cases interpreting the federal immigration statutes and regulations involving children were decided prior to the restructuring and renaming of the agencies, and therefore dealt with the "INS." However, this practice guide will describe those cases as they would now apply to the present day USCIS. In addition, since many immigration statutes still speak in terms of the Attorney General, and not the Secretary of the Department of Homeland Security, it does not appear that Congress has completed its work of revising the statutes to reflect the organizational restructuring. As to the regulations, it would appear that, at least for the short term, the regulations enacted by the "Immigration and Naturalization Service, Department of Justice" will continue to be used by the USCIS.

B. The Child's Need for an Immigration Visa to Gain Citizenship

Under 8 U.S.C. §§ 1181 and 1182(a)(4)(C) and (a)(7)(i), no "immigrant," not even a child who is adopted or who is to be adopted, may enter the U.S. unless he or she possesses a valid immigrant visa along with a passport issued by the "country of origin." In *Munoz v. Ashcroft*, (9th Cir. 2003) 339 F.3d 950, the court held that a person who had been brought to the U.S. as an infant and who had lived here continuously since then could be deported even at age 24.

On the other hand, under 8 U.S.C. § 1431(a), an adopted child who has obtained a visa from the U.S. Government pursuant to the laws governing "orphans" or "alien relatives" or "Hague relatives" (as explained in more detail below) qualifies for U.S. citizenship. Also, where the child is lawfully admitted into the U.S. for purposes of permanent residence, the child may be eligible for automatic citizenship according to 8 U.S.C. § 1431(b), as explained below. It is therefore in the child's interests to obtain an immigrant visa, and not merely a temporary visa.

The visa, which allows entrance into the U.S., is issued by the USCIS. The passport is issued by the foreign country, and in essence gives the child permission to leave that country. In like manner, under 8 U.S.C. § 1401 et seq., the U.S. Government only issues passports to U.S. "nationals and citizens." Therefore, one must consult the foreign country's laws to determine how a passport may be obtained for the child. As stated in *U.S. ex rel. Calamia v. Redfern*, (E.D.La. 1910) 180 F. 506, a passport from a foreign government to its citizen merely constitutes written permission from that government to travel abroad, and does not affect his or her status in the U.S., in the absence of a treaty provision, and is therefore no defense to a deportation action.

While only a limited number of visas are allowed each year, Congress has established a multi-tiered system of giving preference for the issuance of visas to individuals qualifying under these categories. (See 8 U.S.C. §§ 1151 and 1153(a).) One category is reserved for individuals who qualify as an "immediate relative" of a U.S. citizen or a lawful permanent resident. (8 U.S.C. § 1151(a) and (b).) For an adopted child to qualify as an "immediate relative," the child must be either an "alien relative" who was adopted abroad (8 U.S.C. § 1101(b)(1)(E)), a child who was adopted abroad in a Hague Convention country and who is a "Hague relative" (as defined at 8 U.S.C. § 1101(b)(1)(G) and 8 C.F.R. § 204.2), or one who will be adopted in the U.S. and who is an "orphan." (8 U.S.C. § 1101(b)(1)(F) and 8 C.F.R. § 204.3).

Besides seeking "immediate relative" status, there are also children who are permitted to enter the U.S. by being classified by the BCIS as refugees under 8 U.S.C. § 1157, or by qualifying for asylum under 8 U.S.C. § 1158, or those who come from a country whose numerical immigration quota has not been filled. In addition, under 8 U.S.C. § 1182(d)(5), certain individuals may be "paroled" into the United States. This latter code section provides that an alien who appears to be technically inadmissible to the inspecting officer may, on a case-by-case basis, be given permission for temporary entry into the U.S. for urgent humanitarian reasons or significant public benefit. A grant of parole does not constitute a formal admission to the United States. It confers only temporary permission to be present, requiring parolees to leave when the justification supporting their parole ceases to exist, or to be admitted in a lawful alien status for which they are eligible. However, 8 C.F.R. § 204.3(k)(3) allows one to file an orphan petition for a child who is in parole status and who has not yet been adopted in the U.S., as explained below. Also under 8 C.F.R. § 204.3(k)(3), a child who is in the U.S. either "illegally" or as a nonimmigrant is not eligible for the benefits of an orphan petition.

IV. ADOPTING A CHILD FROM A HAGUE CONVENTION COUNTRY

A. The Basic Framework of the Hague Treaty

The Hague Convention covers adoptions between two countries who are both parties to the Treaty. Importantly, under 8 U.S.C. § 1154(d)(2), if the child is a "habitual resident" of a country outside the U.S. that is a party to the Treaty, then the only way a U.S. resident may adopt that child is to comply with the federal statutes and regulations enacted pursuant to the Treaty, which are explained below. If the child is not a "habitual resident" of a Hague country, then the proceedings may follow the more traditional methods, such as to obtain preferential immigration status for the child as an "orphan" or an "immediate relative."

The Hague Convention sets out certain internationally agreed-upon minimum standards and procedures, and officially signaled a major shift in international public opinion. As provided in Article 17 of United Nations Resolution 41/85 (December 3, 1986), the U.N. had previously stated that foster care or even institutionalized care within the child's native country is preferred over intercountry adoption. However, under Article 4(b) of the Hague Convention, the signatory nations have now agreed that adoption is a preferred alternative for children without families. As of June 1, 2012, there were 84 nations who had ratified the Treaty. (However, U.S. State Department officials stated that they were "not currently processing" adoptions from Cambodia, Guatemala, Kazakhstan, Senegal or Vietnam, all of which are Hague countries.)

The Treaty provides for formal international recognition of intercountry adoptions between member states "made in accordance with the Convention." (Where the Treaty uses the word "state," which is often, it is referring to member nations, and not U.S. states.) On the other hand, such an adoption requires compliance with a complicated set of rules and approvals by government agencies and courts in two countries, as 42 U.S.C. § 14901(b)(3) states that one of the purposes of the Intercountry Adoption Act, which is the U.S. ratification or incorporation of the Hague Convention, is "to improve the ability of the Federal Government to assist United States citizens seeking to adopt children from abroad." Also, pursuant to Article VI of the U.S. Constitution, the Hague Convention and the Intercountry Adoption Act are in fact the "supreme law of the land," which the "judges of every state" must follow, notwithstanding state law.

The Hague Convention regulates adoptions across national boundaries by providing (in Article 4) that the adoption may take place only if (1) the country of origin has established that the child is adoptable, (2) due consideration has been given to the child's adoption in its country of origin and an intercountry adoption is in the child's best interests, (3) that after counseling, the necessary consents to the adoption have been given freely, (4) the receiving country has determined that the prospective adoptive parents are eligible and suited to adopt, and (5) that the child they wish to adopt will be authorized to enter and reside permanently in that country.

To carry out these functions, Article 6 of the Hague Convention provides that every country establish a "central authority" to (a) oversee its cooperation with the central authorities of other member states, (b) implement the treaty in its country (including the accreditation of adoption agencies), and (c) provide information on the laws of its country. According to 42 U.S.C. § 14911(a), Congress has designated the U.S. State Department as the "central authority of the United States," and the Secretary of State as the "head of the central authority."

B. Eight Steps in Completing the Adoption of an Incoming Child

The federal statutes and regulations that implement the Hague Convention incorporate significant aspects of state law with regard to the home study of the petitioners. A favorable home study report is probably the most important factor in obtaining the immigration visa and the foreign country's adoption decree. Therefore, to complete the adoption, the petitioners must complete the following steps, in order:

- Choose a Hague-accredited provider to complete the home study.
- Obtain a favorable home study report from that Hague-accredited provider.
- Before adopting a child or accepting a placement, apply to the USCIS for a determination that an intercountry adoption would be appropriate. (Use Form I-800A.)
- After the USCIS makes that determination, work with the Hague-accredited provider (in the foreign country) to obtain a proposed adoptive placement (from the foreign authority).

- Before adopting the child, file a petition with the USCIS to have the child found eligible to immigrate to the U.S. based on the proposed adoption. (Use Form I-800. The USCIS issues provisional approval and then final approval of the petition.)
- In the foreign country, adopt the child, or obtain custody of the child in order to adopt the child in the United States.
- Obtain an immigration visa for the child.
- Bring the child to the United States for admission with the visa.

C. Accreditation to Provide Hague Adoption Services

According to 42 U.S.C. § 14921(a), no person may offer or provide adoption services relating to a Convention adoption in the U.S. unless that person is accredited or approved to do so (i.e., a "primary provider"); or is providing such services through or under the supervision and responsibility of an accredited agency or approved person (i.e., a "supervised provider").

1. Who Accredits / Oversees Primary Service Providers?

a) The Council on Accreditation

Under 42 U.S.C. § 14912(c), the Secretary of State carries out the functions prescribed by the Treaty with respect to the accreditation of agencies and the approval of persons to provide adoption services in the U.S. in Hague cases, and such functions may not be delegated to any other Federal agency. However, under 42 U.S.C. § 14922(a), the Secretary of State is required to designate an "accrediting entity" to carry out the function of accrediting agencies to perform services in the context of Hague adoptions. Currently, the Council on Accreditation has been so designated. Also, in order to provide services in connection with Hague adoptions, Family Code § 8900(a) requires agencies to be accredited by the Council on Accreditation, or be working under the supervision of an accredited primary provider.

The duties of the Council on Accreditation (see 42 U.S.C. § 14922(b)) are:

(1) The accreditation of agencies, and approval of persons, to provide adoption services in the United States in cases subject to the Convention;

(2) To engage in ongoing monitoring of the compliance of accredited agencies and approved persons with applicable requirements, including review of complaints against such agencies and persons in accordance with procedures established by the accrediting entity and approved by the Secretary;

(3) The taking of adverse actions (including requiring corrective action, imposing sanctions, and refusing to renew, suspending, or canceling accreditation or approval) for noncompliance with applicable requirements, and notifying the agency or person against whom adverse actions are taken of the deficiencies necessitating the adverse action; and

(4) The collection of data, maintenance of records, and reporting to the Secretary, the United States central authority, State courts, and other entities (including on persons and agencies granted or denied approval or accreditation), to the extent and in the manner that the Secretary requires.

b) Judicial Review of Accrediting Entity's Actions

Under 42 U.S.C. § 14922(c), if the "accrediting entity" (i.e., the Council on Accreditation) has taken adverse action against an agency, the following rules apply:

(1) That agency or person may re-apply for accreditation or approval (or petition for termination of the adverse action) on demonstrating to the satisfaction of the accrediting entity that the deficiencies necessitating the adverse action have been corrected;

(2) The accrediting entity's adverse action shall not be subject to administrative review; and

(3) That agency or person may petition the federal court to set aside the adverse action. The petition is to be filed in the judicial district in which the agency is located or the person resides. The court shall review the adverse action in accordance with 5 U.S.C. § 706 [which describes the judicial authority], and for purposes of such review the accrediting entity shall be considered an "agency" within the meaning of 5 U.S.C. § 701.

c) Direct Oversight by the Secretary of State

Under 42 U.S.C. § 14924(b)(1), the Secretary of State may suspend or cancel an agency's or a person's accreditation if the Secretary finds that (A) that agency or person is substantially out of compliance with applicable requirements; and (B) the accrediting entity has failed or refused, after consultation with the Secretary, to take appropriate enforcement action. If the Secretary of State suspends or cancels the accreditation of an agency or person, and that agency or person then satisfies the Secretary of State that the deficiencies that prompted the suspension or cancellation have been corrected, 42 U.S.C. § 14924(b)(2) requires that agency or person must to reapply *with the accrediting entity* for accreditation or approval.

It also appears that 42 U.S.C. § 14924(c) allow the Secretary of State to "temporarily or permanently debar an agency from accreditation or a person from approval," and that such an action by the Secretary of State may be undertaken even if the accrediting entity has not failed or refused to act. This authority may be exercised where "there has been a pattern of serious, willful, or grossly negligent failures to comply or other aggravating circumstances indicating that continued accreditation or approval would not be in the best interests of the children and families concerned." A failure to comply with the requirements for home studies (42 U.S.C. § 14923(b)(1)(A)(ii) [see below]) shall constitute a "serious failure to comply" unless it is shown by clear and convincing evidence that such noncompliance had neither the purpose nor the effect of determining the outcome of a decision or proceeding by a court or other competent authority in the U.S. or the child's country of origin." (42 U.S.C. § 14924(e)(4)) The actions of the Secretary of State are subject to review by the federal courts. (See 42 U.S.C. § 14924(d).)

Under 42 U.S.C. § 14912(b)(1)(A), the Secretary of State shall be responsible for providing the central authorities of other Convention countries with information concerning accredited agencies and approved persons, agencies and persons whose accreditation or approval has been suspended or canceled, and agencies and persons who have been temporarily or permanently debarred from accreditation or approval.

2. How to Obtain "Primary Provider" Accreditation

Under 42 U.S.C. § 14923(a)(1), the Secretary of State may enact regulations prescribing the standards and procedures to be used by accrediting entities for the accreditation of agencies and the approval of persons to provide adoption services in the U.S. in Hague cases, or to "continue" its accreditation or approval. Those regulations appear at 22 C.F.R. § 96.29, et seq., and are subject to certain "minimum requirements" imposed by 42 U.S.C. § 14923(b)(1):

a) Private Non-Profit Status

The agency is required by 42 U.S.C. § 14923(b)(1)(G) to be "a private nonprofit organization licensed to provide adoption services in at least one State." (Interestingly, 42 U.S.C. § 14923(b)(2) states that a "person" (as opposed to an agency) must operate on a for-profit basis.) For Hague agencies located in California, private non-profit status and state-*licensed* agency status is also required under California Family Code §§ 8521(b), 8533(b) and 8900(a). Therefore, it would appear that the California side of an "incoming" Hague adoption is not handled by the CDSS or any county agency. On the other hand, in the case of an "outgoing" intercountry adoption of a foster child, it would appear that federal law (42 U.S.C. § 14921(b)(1) and (2)) and California law (Family Code § 8900.5(g)) permits a county agency to perform child welfare services and investigate the "background of the child," as long as an Hague accredited agency approves the county agency's report concerning the child background.

b) Specific Requirements re Agency's Practices

(1) Adoptive Children's Medical Records

To become accredited, 42 U.S.C. § 14923(b)(1)(A)(i) requires the agency to show that it provides the adoptive parents of children in prospective Convention adoptions with copies of the medical records of the child (which, to the fullest extent practicable, shall include an English-language translation of such records) on a date which is not later than the earlier of the date that is 2 weeks before: (I) the adoption; or (II) the date on which the prospective parents travel to a foreign country to complete all procedures in such country relating to the adoption.

(2) Home Studies of Adoptive Parents

Under 42 U.S.C. § 14923(b)(1)(A)(ii), the agency must ensure that thorough background reports (home studies) on prospective adoptive parent or parents are completed in accordance with the Convention and with applicable Federal and State requirements, and transmitted to the Attorney General with respect to each Convention adoption. Each such report shall include a criminal background check and a full and complete statement of all facts relevant to the eligibility of the prospective adopting parent or parents to adopt a child under any requirements specified by the central authority of the child's country of origin under 42 U.S.C. § 14912(b)(3), including, in the case of a child emigrating to the U.S. for the purpose of adoption, the requirements of the child's country of origin applicable to adoptions taking place in such country. For purposes of this clause, the term "background report (home study)" includes any supplemental statement submitted by the agency to the Attorney General for the purpose of providing information relevant to any requirements specified by the child's country of origin.

(3) Training Program for Adoptive Parents

According to 42 U.S.C. § 14923(b)(1)(A)(iii), the agency must provide prospective adoptive parents with a training program that includes counseling and guidance for the purpose of promoting a successful intercountry adoption before such parents travel to adopt the child or the child is placed with such parents for adoption. The subject of training is discussed below.

(4) Payment for Services

The agency's personnel may only provide intercountry adoption services on a fee for service basis (see 42 U.S.C. § 14923(b)(1)(A)(iv)), and not on a contingent fee basis.

(5) Disclosure of Agency's Policies, Fees, Disruption Rates

Under 42 U.S.C. § 14923(b)(1)(A)(i), the agency must fully disclose its policies and practices, the disruption rates of its placements for intercountry adoption, and all fees charged by such agency for intercountry adoption.

c) Personnel and Financial Requirements

The agency must, pursuant to 42 U.S.C. § 14923(b)(1)(B), either directly or through arrangements with other persons, maintain a sufficient number of appropriately trained and qualified personnel, sufficient financial resources, appropriate organizational structure, and appropriate procedures to enable the agency to provide, in accordance with this chapter, all adoption services in cases subject to the Convention.

The agency is required by 42 U.S.C. § 14923(b)(1)(E) to "agree[] to have in force adequate liability insurance for professional negligence and any other insurance that the Secretary considers appropriate."

d) Qualifications of Agency Personnel

Under 42 U.S.C. § 14923(b)(1)(C), the agency must establish procedures designed to ensure that social service functions requiring the application of clinical skills and judgment are performed only by professionals with appropriate qualifications and credentials.

e) Record-Keeping

According to 42 U.S.C. § 14923(b)(1)(D), the agency is required to show that it "is capable of" (i) maintaining such records and making such reports as may be required by the Secretary, the United States central authority, and the accrediting entity that accredits the agency; (ii) cooperating with reviews, inspections, and audits; (iii) safeguarding sensitive individual information; and (iv) complying with other requirements concerning information management necessary to ensure compliance with the Convention, this chapter, and any other applicable law.

f) Measures Ensuring Compliance with Law

Under 42 U.S.C. § 14923(b)(1)(F), the agency must "establish[] adequate measures to comply (and to ensure compliance of their agents and clients) with the Convention, this chapter, and any other applicable law."

g) Three- to Five-Year Renewable Terms

According to 42 U.S.C. § 14923(b)(3), the accreditation of an agency or approval of a person for Hague cases shall be for a period of not less than 3 years and not more than 5 years, and may be renewed on a showing that the agency or person meets the requirements applicable to original accreditation or approval.

3. Temporary Registration as an Accredited Community-based Agency

A"community-based agency" may register with the Secretary of State, pursuant to 42 U.S.C. § 14923(c), for temporary accreditation for two years (if the agency has provided adoption services in fewer than 50 intercountry adoptions in the preceding calendar year) or one year (if the agency has provided adoption services in fewer than 100 intercountry adoptions in the preceding calendar year). (It appears that the requirements for securing Hague accreditation as a primary provider may be obtained by working through a temporary registration.) To secure temporary registration, the agency must –

> (A) be licensed in the State in which it is located and is a nonprofit agency;
>
> (B) have been providing adoption services in connection with intercountry adoptions [not necessarily Hague adoptions] for at least 3 years;
>
> (C) demonstrate that it will be able to provide the U.S. Government with all information related to the elements described in 42 U.S.C. § 14914(b) [regarding past adoptions] and provides such information;
>
> (D) initiate the process of becoming regularly accredited and actively take steps to become an accredited agency; and

(E) not have been involved in any "improper conduct" relating to intercountry adoptions.

4. What Services May an Accredited Provider Provide?

According to 42 U.S.C. § 14902(3), the "adoption services" that an "accredited agency" may "provide" (which "includes facilitating") are as follows:

(A) identifying a child for adoption and arranging an adoption;

(B) securing necessary consent to termination of parental rights and to adoption;

(C) performing a background study on a child or a home study on a prospective adoptive parent, and reporting on such a study;

(D) making determinations of the best interests of a child and the appropriateness of adoptive placement for the child;

(E) post-placement monitoring of a case until final adoption; and

(F) where made necessary by disruption before final adoption, assuming custody and providing child care or any other social service pending an alternative placement.

California Family Code §§ 8900.5(b) and 8902 provide a similar rule. As explained in Chapter 5, California *agencies* provide all of the above-mentioned services in a domestic adoption. "Facilitators" and "adoption service providers" (as described by *California* law) do not provide all of these services.

It does not appear that the publication of standard forms is considered an "adoption service." In addition, the U.S. Secretary of State has not published any forms regarding, for example, a questionnaire that can be used in conjunction with the completion of a home study, nor any other form that one would see in a typical adoption. For these reasons, it would appear that the accredited agency would be permitted to use the CDSS forms in connection with completing the home study and other aspects of its work, even though the CDSS is not an accredited agency.

5. Services that a "Supervised Provider" May Provide

Under 42 U.S.C. § 14921(a)(2), certain Hague adoption services may be provided by someone who is working through or under the supervision and responsibility of an accredited agency or approved person. (See also 22 C.F.R. § 96.2) "Supervised provider" is also defined by Family Code § 8900.5(n) as "any agency, person, or other nongovernmental entity that is providing any adoption service in a convention adoption under the supervision and responsibility of an accredited agency that is acting as the primary provider in the case." It does not appear that federal or California law provides any specific restrictions on what a supervised provider can do, as long as the supervised provider is working within the accredited agency's supervision and responsibility.

Further, Family Code § 8900(a) appears to imply that a supervised provider must be licensed by the CDSS to provide intercountry adoption services. Therefore, it would appear that if a California resident were seeking to complete an intercountry adoption, the home study would have to be completed by an agency that is so licensed by the CDSS, although the agency's headquarters could be located outside California.

6. Services that an "Exempt Provider" May Provide

Under 42 U.S.C. § 14921(b), the accreditation requirement does not apply to:

(1) the mere performance of a background study on a child or a home study on a prospective adoptive parent, or the preparation of any report on any such study by a social work professional or organization who is not providing any other adoption service in the case, if the background or home study is approved by an accredited agency. (However, under 22 C.F.R. § 96.13(a), an exempted provider's home study must be approved by an accredited agency or temporarily accredited agency in accordance with 22 C.F.R. § 96.47(c), and an exempted provider's child background study must be approved by an accredited agency or temporarily accredited agency in accordance with 22 C.F.R. § 96.53(b).)

(2) the provision of a child welfare service by a person who is not providing any other adoption service in the case.

(3) the provision of legal services by a person who is not providing any adoption service in the case. (Notably, there is nothing in federal law that permits an attorney to provide both legal services and adoption services in an adoption case.)

(4) and the conduct of a prospective adoptive parent on his or her own behalf in the case, to the extent not prohibited by the law of the State in which the prospective adoptive parent resides. (There is nothing in California or federal law that allows a prospective adoptive parent to complete his or her own home study.)

At 22 C.F.R. § 96.2, the Secretary of State has defined "legal services" as "services, other than those defined in this section as "adoption services," that relate to the provision of legal advice and information and to the drafting of legal instruments. Such services include, but are not limited to, drawing up contracts, powers of attorney, and other legal instruments; providing advice and counsel to adoptive parent(s) on completing DHS [Department of Homeland Security] or Central Authority forms; and providing advice and counsel to accredited agencies, temporarily accredited agencies, approved persons, or prospective adoptive parent(s) on how to comply with the Convention, the IAA [Intercountry Adoption Act], and the regulations implementing the IAA." (See also Family Code § 8900.5(j))

7. Penalties for the Unauthorized or Illegal Services

According to 42 U.S.C. § 14944, the penalties for the unauthorized provision of services in a Hague adoption case can be three-fold:

a) Civil and Criminal Penalties

Under 42 U.S.C. § 14944(a), a "civil money penalty" of no more than $50,000 for a first violation, and no more than $100,000 for each succeeding violation may be imposed against one:

(1) who violates 42 U.S.C. § 14921 (which relates to accreditation);

(2) who makes a false or fraudulent statement, or misrepresentation, with respect to a material fact, or offers, gives, solicits, or accepts inducement by way of compensation, intended to influence or affect in the United States or a foreign country (A) a decision by an accrediting entity with respect to the accreditation of an agency or approval of a person, (B) the relinquishment of parental rights or the giving of parental consent relating to the adoption of a child in a case subject to the Convention, or (C) a decision or action of any entity performing a central authority function;

(3) or who engages another person as an agent, whether in the U.S. or in a foreign country, who in the course of that agency takes any of the actions described in the above two paragraphs.

According to 42 U.S.C. § 14944(c), whoever knowingly and willfully violates 42 U.S.C. § 14944(a)(1) or (2) shall be subject to a fine of not more than $250,000, imprisonment for not more than 5 years, or both.

b) Civil Enforcement

The Attorney General is authorized by 42 U.S.C. § 14944(b) to bring a civil action in federal court to enforce the civil money penalties mentioned immediately above, in which case the court shall consider the gravity of the violation, the degree of culpability of the defendant, and any history of prior violations by the defendant. It is unclear why the court would be allowed to consider these matters unless the court had the authority to reduce or set aside the penalties.

Under 42 U.S.C. § 14954, the Hague Convention and the Federal Intercountry Adoption Act shall not be construed to create a private right of action to seek administrative or judicial relief, except to the extent expressly provided by the Act.

D. The Home Study in a Hague Adoption Case

Before one can obtain the visa, a favorable home study report must be submitted to USCIS, thereby making the home study critically important. Under 8 C.F.R. § 204.311(b), the entity performing the home study must be accredited to handle Hague cases, and must be authorized to complete adoption home studies under the law of the jurisdiction in which the home study is conducted. Also, according to 8 C.F.R. § 204.311(c), the home study must satisfy the following 16 criteria:

1. The Home Study Must Be Tailored to the Applicant

The home study must be tailored to the particular situation of the applicant and to the specific Convention country in which the applicant intends to seek a child for adoption. For example, an applicant who has previously adopted children will require different preparation than an applicant who has no adopted children. A home study may address the applicant's suitability to adopt in more than one Convention country, but if the home study does so, the home study must separately assess the applicant's suitability as to each specific Convention country.

2. Adult Members in the Household

If there are any additional adult members of the household, the home study must identify each of them by name, alien registration number (if the individual has one), and date of birth.

3. The Home Study Preparer Must Conduct Interviews.

The home study must include an interview by the preparer of any additional adult member of the household and an assessment of him or her in light of the requirements of 8 C.F.R. § 204.311.

4. Home Study Report Submission within Six Months

The home study must be no more than 6 months old at the time the home study is submitted to USCIS.

5. Full Disclosure in Home Study Report

The home study must include the home study preparer's assessment of any potential problem areas, a copy of any outside evaluation(s), and the home study preparer's recommended restrictions, if any, on the characteristics of the child to be placed in the home.

6. Home Study Preparer's Signature

The home study preparer must sign the home study report, and any updated or amended home study report, under penalty of perjury.

a) Home Study Preparer's Personal Knowledge

According to 8 C.F.R. § 204.311(f)(1), the signature signifies that the signer personally, and with the professional diligence reasonably necessary to protect the best interests of any child whom the applicant might adopt, either actually conducted or supervised the home study, including personal interview(s), the home visits, and all other aspects of the investigation needed to prepare the home study. If the signer did not personally conduct the home study, the person who actually did so must be identified.

b) Verification of the Home Study Report

Under 8 C.F.R. § 204.311(f)(2), the signature denotes that the factual statements in the home study are true and correct, to the best of the signer's knowledge, information and belief.

c) Duty to Advise of Ongoing Duty to Disclose

The signature means, according to 8 C.F.R. § 204.311(f)(3), that the home study preparer has advised the applicant of the duty of candor under 8 C.F.R. § 204.311(d), specifically including the on-going duty under paragraph (d)(2) concerning disclosure of new events or information warranting submission of an updated or amended home study.

7. Number of Interviews

Under 8 C.F.R. § 204.311(c)(7), the home study must state the number of interviews and visits, the participants, date and location of each interview and visit, and the date and location of any other contacts with the applicant and any additional adult member of the household.

8. Pre-Placement Preparation, Training and Counseling

The home study report must summarize the pre-placement preparation and training already provided to the applicant concerning the issues specified in 22 C.F.R. § 96.48(a) and (b), the plans for future preparation and training with respect to those issues, or with respect to a particular child, as specified in 22 C.F.R. § 96.48(c), and the plans for post-placement monitoring specified in 22 C.F.R. § 96.50, in the event that the child will be adopted in the United States rather than abroad. Post-placement monitoring is discussed later in this chapter.

a) Ten Hours of Preparation and Training

Under 22 C.F.R. § 96.48(a), the agency must provide the prospective adoptive parents with at least ten hours of preparation and training – independent of the home study. The training must be provided before the prospective adoptive parents travel to adopt the child or the child is placed with the prospective adoptive parents for adoption. According to 22 C.F.R. § 96.48(b)(1) - (8), the training must address the following:

(1) Conditions in the Foreign Country

The agency must address the intercountry adoption process, the general characteristics and needs of children awaiting adoption, and the in-country conditions that affect children in the Convention country from which the prospective adoptive parent(s) plan to adopt.

(2) Effects of Health Issues on Children

The prospective adoptive parents must be informed of the effects on children of malnutrition, relevant environmental toxins, maternal substance abuse, and of any other known genetic, health, emotional, and developmental risk factors associated with children from the expected country of origin.

(3) Impact of Immigration upon the Child

The training must provide information about the impact on a child of leaving familiar ties and surroundings, as appropriate to the expected age of the child.

(4) Data on Institutionalized Children

The prospective adoptive parents must be given the data on institutionalized children and the impact of institutionalization on children, including the effect on children of the length of time spent in an institution and of the type of care provided in the expected country of origin.

(5) Attachment and Emotional Disorders

Information on attachment disorders and other emotional problems that institutionalized or traumatized children and children with a history of multiple caregivers may experience, before and after their adoption, must be included in the training.

(6) Laws of the Foreign Country

The agency must give information about the laws and adoption processes of the expected country of origin, including foreseeable delays and impediments to finalization of an adoption .

(7) Long-term Implications

The prospective adoptive parents must be given information on the long-term implications for a family that has become multicultural through intercountry adoption.

(8) Explanation of Reporting Requirements

The agency must explain any reporting requirements associated with Convention adoptions, including any post-placement or post-adoption reports required by the expected country of origin.

b) Required Counseling re the Particular Child

According to 22 C.F.R. § 96.48(c), the agency must provide the prospective adoptive parents with counseling regarding (1) the child's history and cultural, racial, religious, ethnic, and linguistic background; (2) the known health risks in the specific region or country where the child resides; and (3) any other medical, social, background, birth history, educational data, developmental history, or any other data known about the particular child.

9. Referrals of the Applicant to Licensed Professionals

The home study must specify whether the home study preparer made any referrals as described in 8 C.F.R. § 204.311(g)(4), and include a copy of the report resulting from each referral, the home study preparer's assessment of the impact of the report on the suitability of the applicant to adopt, and the home study preparer's recommended restrictions, if any, on the characteristics of the child to be placed in the home. As explained in 8 C.F.R. § 204.311(g)(4), such a referral would consist of advice to see a licensed professional such as a physician, psychiatrist, clinical psychologist, clinical social worker, or professional substance abuse counselor, to deal with specific issues.

10. Results of Child Abuse and Criminal Record Checks

The home study report must include results of the checks conducted in accordance with 8 C.F.R. § 204.311(i) including that no record was found to exist, that the State or foreign country will not release information to the home study preparer or anyone in the household, or that the State or foreign country does not have a child abuse registry.

11. Responses to Background Questionnaire

The home study must include the responses, under penalty of perjury, by each person (applicants and adult members of the household) to the 8 C.F.R. § 204.311(j) questions regarding abuse and violence. Those questions relate to whether he or she has a history as an offender, whether in the United States or abroad, of substance abuse, sexual abuse, or child abuse, or family violence, even if such history did not result in an arrest or conviction. The responses must include: (1) the dates of each arrest or conviction or history of substance abuse, sexual abuse or child abuse, and/or family violence; or (2) if not resulting in an arrest, the date or time period (if occurring over an extended period of time) of each occurrence and (3) details including any mitigating circumstances about each incident.

12. Certified Copies of Documentation re Background

The home study report must include a certified copy of the documentation showing the final disposition of each incident which resulted in arrest, indictment, conviction, and/or any other judicial or administrative action for anyone subject to the home study and a written statement submitted with the home study giving details, including any mitigating circumstances about each arrest, signed, under penalty of perjury, by the person to whom the arrest relates.

13. Evaluation of Suitability vis-à-vis Criminal Record

The home study report must contain an evaluation of the suitability of the home for adoptive placement of a child in light of any applicant's or additional adult member of the household's history of abuse and/or violence as an offender, whether this history is disclosed by an applicant or any additional adult member of the household or is discovered by home study preparer, regardless of the source of the home study preparer's discovery. A single incident of sexual abuse, child abuse, or family violence will constitute a "history" of abuse and/or violence.

14. Evaluation of Suitability vis-à-vis Substance Abuse

The home study report must contain an evaluation of the suitability of the home for adoptive placement of a child in light of disclosure by an applicant, or any additional adult member of the household, of a history of substance abuse. A person has a history of substance abuse if his or her current or past use of alcohol, controlled substances, or other substances impaired or impairs his or her ability to fulfill obligations at work, school, or home, or creates other social or interpersonal problems that may adversely affect the applicant's suitability as an adoptive parent.

15. Physical, Mental, Emotional or Behavioral Issues

The home study must include a general description of the information disclosed in accordance with 8 C.F.R. § 204.311(m) concerning the physical, mental, and emotional health of the applicant and of any additional adult member of the household. The home study preparer is required by 8 C.F.R. § 204.311(m) to address the current physical, mental and emotional health of the applicant, or any additional adult member of the household, as well as any history of illness or of any mental, emotional, psychological, or behavioral instability if the home study preparer determines, in the exercise of reasonable professional judgment, that the suitability of the applicant as an adoptive parent may be affected adversely by such history.

16. Disclosures re Prior Home Studies

The home study report is required to identify the agency involved in each prior or terminated home study in accordance with 8 C.F.R. § 204.311(o), when the prior home study process began, the date the prior home study was completed, and whether the prior home study recommended for or against finding the applicant or additional adult member of the household suitable for adoption, foster care, or other custodial care of a child. If a prior home study was terminated without completion, the current home study must indicate when the prior home study began, the date of termination, and the reason for the termination.

E. Processing the Background Report

Under 42 U.S.C. § 14912(b)(4), the Secretary of State shall be responsible for ensuring the provision of a background report (home study) on prospective adoptive parent or parents (pursuant to the requirements of 42 U.S.C. § 14923(b)(1)(A)(ii)), through the central authority of each child's country of origin, to the court having jurisdiction over the adoption (or, in the case of a child emigrating to the United States for the purpose of adoption, to the competent authority in the child's country of origin with responsibility for approving the child's emigration) in adequate time to be considered prior to the granting of such adoption or approval

1. The Secretary of State's Authority

According to 42 U.S.C. § 14912(d), the Secretary of State shall monitor individual Convention adoption cases involving United States citizens; and may facilitate interactions between such citizens and officials of other Convention countries on matters relating to the Convention in any case in which an accredited agency or approved person is unwilling or unable to provide such facilitation. Under 42 U.S.C. § 14952(b), the Secretary of State may, on a case-by-case basis and consistently with the terms of the Treaty, waive applicable requirements of federal law in the interests of justice or to prevent grave physical harm to the child.

2. Prohibited Payments

Under 8 C.F.R. § 204.304(a), no "payment" (which is very broadly defined) may be made to induce or influence any decision concerning (1) the placement of a child for adoption; (2) the consent of a parent, a legal custodian, individual, or agency to the adoption of a child; (3) the relinquishment of a child to a competent authority, agency or person for the purpose of adoption; or (4) the performance by the child's parent or parents of any act that makes the child a Convention adoptee.

3. Payments that May be Made in a Hague Case

Under 8 C.F.R. § 204.304(b), payments may be made for the reasonable costs of:

(1) The services of an adoption service provider in connection with an adoption;

(2) Expenses incurred in locating a child for adoption;

(3) Medical, hospital, nursing, pharmaceutical, travel, or other similar expenses incurred by a mother or her child in connection with the birth or any illness of the child;

(4) Counseling services for a parent or a child for a reasonable time before and after the child's placement for adoption;

(5) Expenses, in an amount commensurate with the living standards in the country of the child's habitual residence, for the care of the birth mother while pregnant and immediately following the birth of the child;

(6) Expenses incurred in obtaining the home study;

(7) Expenses incurred in obtaining the reports on the child as described in 8 C.F.R. § 204.313(d)(3) and (4);

(8) Legal services, court costs, and travel or other administrative expenses connected with an adoption, including any legal services performed for a parent who consents to the adoption of a child or relinquishes the child to an agency; and

(9) Any other service the payment for which the officer finds, on the basis of the facts of the case, was reasonably necessary.

F. Form I-800A: USCIS Advance Processing for Hague Adoption

1. Overview of the Process

Once the home study is completed, it is submitted to USCIS with the Form I–800A application. Under 8 C.F.R. § 204.1(a)(5), a U.S. citizen seeking to have USCIS accord immediate relative status to a child under 8 U.S.C. § 1101(b)(1)(G) on the basis of a Hague adoption must (i) file a Form I–800A (Application to Determine Suitability as Adoptive Parents for a Convention Adoptee); and (ii) after the USCIS approves the Form I–800A, file a Form I–800 (Petition to Classify Convention Adoptee as Immediate Relative).

It appears that the primary purpose of the Form I-800A application is to prequalify the prospective adoptive parents for an intercountry adoption. The screening of the specific child is performed after the Form I-800 petition is filed. Therefore, the Form I-800A application does not ask for the name of the child (i.e., the "beneficiary"); it only asks what foreign country is involved in the proposed adoption.

2. Who May File the Form I-800A Application?

Under 8 C.F.R. § 204.307(a), the following persons may file a Form I-800A Hague advanced processing application:

(1) An unmarried U.S. citizen who is at least 24 years old and who is habitually resident in the U.S., as determined under 8 CFR 204.303(a); or

(2) A married U.S. citizen, who is habitually resident in the United States, as determined under 8 CFR 204.303(a), and whose spouse will also adopt any child adopted by the citizen based on the approval of a Form I-800A; and

(3) The citizen's spouse must also be either a U.S. citizen, a non-citizen U.S. national, or an alien who, if living in the United States, holds a lawful status under U.S. immigration law. If an alien spouse is present in a lawful status other than the status of an alien lawfully admitted for permanent residence, such status will be a factor evaluated in determining if the family's situation is sufficiently stable to support a finding that the applicant is suitable as the adoptive parent of a Convention adoptee.

According to 8 C.F.R. § 204.303(a), a U.S. citizen is deemed to be "habitually resident" in the U.S. for purposes of a Hague adoption if that individual,

(1) has his or her domicile in the U.S., even if living temporarily abroad; or

(2) is not domiciled in the U.S. but establishes by a preponderance of the evidence that:

(i) the citizen will have established a domicile in the U.S. on or before the date of the child's admission to the U.S. for permanent residence as a Convention adoptee; or

(ii) the citizen indicates on the Form I-800 that the citizen intends to bring the child to the U.S. after adopting the child abroad, and before the child's 18th birthday, at which time the child will be eligible for, and will apply for, naturalization. This option is not available if the child will be adopted in the United States.

3. Who Is Barred from Filing a Form I-800A Application?

According to 8 C.F.R. § 204.307(c)(1), a Form I-800A Hague advanced processing application may not be filed by an applicant who: (i) filed a prior Form I-800A that USCIS denied under 8 CFR 204.309(a); (ii) filed a prior Form I-600A under 8 CFR 204.3 that USCIS denied under 8 CFR 204.3(h)(4); (iii) filed a prior Form I-800 that USCIS denied under 8 CFR 204.309(b)(3); or (iv) filed a prior Form I-600 under 8 CFR 204.3 that USCIS denied under 8 CFR 204.3(i). Under 8 C.F.R. § 204.307(c)(2), the prohibition ends one year after the decision denying the prior Form I-800A, I-600A, I-800 or I-600 became administratively final. However, 8 C.F.R. § 204.307(c)(3) states that the facts underlying the prior denial of a Form I-800A, I-800, I-600A, or I-600 are relevant to the adjudication of any subsequently filed Form I-800A or Form I-800, even though it is filed after the expiration of this one year bar.

4. Who May Assist the Applicant with the Form I-800A?

According to 8 C.F.R. § 204.302(a), a U.S. citizen who is seeking to file a Form I–800A or Form I–800 may use the services of any individual or entity authorized to provide services in connection with adoption, except that the U.S. citizen must use the services of an accredited agency, temporarily accredited agency, approved person, supervised provider public domestic authority or exempted provider. However, 8 C.F.R. §

204.302(b) states that an adoption service provider is not permitted to engage in the unauthorized practice of law.

5. Where and How Is the Application Filed?

Pursuant to 8 C.F.R. § 204.308, the application is filed with the office identified in the instructions to the Form I-800A application. Those instructions now state that the application is sent by mail or courier to the "Dallas Lockbox Facility."

6. What Must Accompany the Form I-800A Application?

a) Filing Fee and Biometrics Information

The filing fee must accompany the application according to 8 C.F.R. § 204.310(a)(3)(i) and (ii). As of the time of writing this book, the filing fee is $720 plus a fingerprint (aka "biometrics") fee of $85 for each applicant and every other adult living in the applicant's household. Under 8 C.F.R. § 204.310(b), the USCIS will arrange for the collection of biometrics from the applicant and each additional adult member of the household.

b) Favorable and Valid Home Study Report

Under 8 U.S.C. § 1154(d)(1), as well as 8 C.F.R. §§ 204.3(c)(2) and 204.310(a)(3)(viii), the applicant must file a home study that meets the requirements of 8 CFR § 204.311 (i.e., the 16 criteria explained above) and that bears the home study preparer's original signature.

If the home study is not included with the Form I–800A, the director of the office that has jurisdiction to adjudicate the Form I–800A will make a written request for evidence, directing the applicant to submit the home study. If the applicant fails to do so within the period specified in the request for evidence, the director of the office that has jurisdiction to adjudicate the application will deny it. According to 8 C.F.R. § 204.310(a)(3)(viii), denial of the application for failure to submit a home study is not subject to appeal, but the applicant may file a new I–800A, accompanied by a new filing fee.

c) Proof of U.S. Citizenship and/or Residency

Under 8 C.F.R. §§ 204.1(g)(1) and 204.310(a)(3)(iii), the application must be accompanied by one of the following:

- a birth certificate establishing the petitioner's birth in the United States;
- an unexpired U.S. passport issued initially to a petitioner over the age of 18 years as a U.S. citizen;
- an unexpired U.S. passport issued initially to the petitioner under the age of 18 years as a U.S. citizen;
- a statement executed by a U.S. consular officer certifying the petitioner to be a U.S. citizen and the bearer of a currently valid U.S. passport;
- the petitioner's Certificate of Naturalization or Certificate of Citizenship;

- a Form FS-240 (issued by the U.S. State Department) relating to the petitioner and documenting his or her birth abroad as a U.S. citizen; or
- the petitioner's Form I-551 (permanent resident card) or other proof given by the USCIS as evidence of lawful permanent residence.

If such "primary evidence" of U.S. citizenship or permanent residency, 8 C.F.R. § 204.1(g)(2) allows "secondary evidence" to be submitted, which may include –

- a baptismal certificate with the seal of the church, showing the date and place of birth in the U.S. and the date of baptism;
- affidavits sworn to by persons who were living at the time and who have personal knowledge of the event to which they attest (the affidavits must contain the affiant's full name and address, date and place of birth, relationship to the parties, if any, and complete details concerning how the affiant acquired knowledge of the events described);
- early school records (preferably from the first school) showing the date of admission to the school, the child's date and place of birth, and the name(s) and place(s) of birth of the parent(s);
- census records showing the petitioner's name, place of birth, and date of birth or age; or
- a U.S. citizen petitioner who is a member of the U.S. Armed Forces and who is serving outside the U.S. may submit a statement from the appropriate authority of the Armed Forces (attesting to the fact that the personnel records of the Armed Forces show that the petitioner was born in the U.S. on a certain date), if it is determined that it would cause unusual delay or hardship to obtain documentary proof of birth in the United States.

However, under 8 C.F.R. § 204.1(f)(1), the petitioner must submit primary evidence, if it is available. These regulations also state that secondary evidence will be scrutinized by the USCIS much more closely than primary evidence.

According to 8 C.F.R. § 204.1(f)(2), the petitioner must submit original documents or legible, true copies of original documents, however the USCIS may require the submission of original documents when deemed necessary. Documents submitted with the petition will not be returned to the petitioner, except when originals are requested by the USCIS, in which case they will be returned to the petitioner after a decision on the petition has been rendered, unless their validity or authenticity is in question. When an interview is required, all original documents must be presented for examination at the interview.

d) Documents re Marriage(s) and/or Age

According to 8 C.F.R. § 204.310(a)(3)(iv), the application must be accompanied by a copy of the current marriage certificate, unless the applicant is not married.

Under 8 C.F.R. § 204.310(a)(3)(v), if the applicant was married previously, the application must be accompanied by a copy of a death certificate or divorce or dissolution decree to establish the legal termination of all previous marriages, regardless of current marital status.

If the applicant is not married, 8 C.F.R. § 204.310(a)(3)(vi) requires him or her to produce documentation showing that he or she is at least 24 years old.

If the applicant's marital status changes after the application is filed, the applicant must, pursuant to 8 C.F.R. § 204.310(c), file an amended Form I–800A and amended home study report to reflect the change in marital status.

e) Description of State Law Preadoption Requirements, If Required

The application must set forth, pursuant to 8 C.F.R. § 204.310(a)(3)(vii), a description of the preadoption requirements, if any, of the State of the child's proposed residence in cases where it is *known* that any child the applicant may adopt *will* be adopted in the U.S., and of the steps that have already been taken or that are planned to comply with these requirements. The written description must include a citation to the State statutes and regulations establishing the requirements. Any preadoption requirements which cannot be met at the time the Form I–800A is filed because of the operation of State law must be noted and explained when it is filed.

As stated above, most intercountry adoptions in incoming cases are completed in the foreign country. In certain cases, the foreign country may only order a guardianship (in which case the adoption must be completed in the U.S.) or, depending on what country the child is from, the U.S. Government may require a re-adoption (as it had before the Hague Convention was ratified). In those instances, the state's preadoption requirements must be explained.

7. Factors Requiring Denial of Form I-800A Application

According to 8 C.F.R. § 204.309(a), the USCIS officer must deny a Form I-800A if:

a) Non-Disclosure of Criminal History

The application must be denied if the applicant or any additional adult member of the household failed to disclose to the home study preparer or to USCIS, or concealed or misrepresented, any fact(s) about the applicant or any additional member of the household concerning the arrest, conviction, or history of substance abuse, sexual abuse, child abuse, and/or family violence, or any other criminal history as an offender; the fact that an arrest or conviction or other criminal history has been expunged, sealed, pardoned, or the subject of any other amelioration does not relieve the applicant or additional adult member of the household of the obligation to disclose the arrest, conviction or other criminal history.

b) Failure to Cooperate in Checking Child Abuse Registries

The Form I-800A application will be denied if the applicant, or any additional adult member of the household, failed to cooperate in having available child abuse registries checked in accordance with 8 C.F.R. § 204.311.

c) Failure to Disclose All Prior Home Studies

The application must be denied if the applicant, or any additional adult member of the household, failed to disclose, as required by 8 C.F.R. § 204.311, each and every prior adoption home study, whether completed or not, including those that did not favorably recommend for adoption or custodial care, the person(s) to whom the prior home study related.

d) Transmitting Home Study to the USCIS

No application will be granted if the applicant is barred by 8 C.F.R. § 204.307(c) from filing the Form I-800A, as explained below.

8. Adjudication of the Form I-800A Application

a) Granting of the Application

Under 8 C.F.R. § 204.312(a), the Form I–800A will be approved if the USCIS officer finds, based on the evidence of record, that the applicant is eligible under 8 C.F.R. § 204.307(a) and the USCIS officer is satisfied that the applicant is suitable as the adoptive parent of a child from the specified Convention country. According to 8 C.F.R. § 204.312(b), in determining suitability to adopt, the USCIS officer will give considerable weight to the home study, but is not bound by it. Even if the home study is favorable, the USCIS officer must deny the Form I–800A if, on the basis of the evidence of record, the officer finds, for a specific and articulable reason, that the applicant has failed to establish that he or she is suitable as the adoptive parent of a child from the Convention country.

The USCIS officer may, under 8 C.F.R. § 204.312(b), consult the accredited agency or temporarily accredited agency that approved the home study, the home study preparer, the applicant, the relevant State or local child welfare agency, or any appropriate licensed professional, as needed to clarify issues as to whether the applicant is suitable as the adoptive parent of a Convention adoptee. If this consultation yields evidence that is adverse to the applicant, the USCIS officer may rely on the evidence only after complying with the terms of 8 C.F.R. § 103.2(b)(16) relating to the applicant's right to review and rebut adverse information.

b) Duration of a Form I-800A Notice of Approval

Under 8 C.F.R. § 204.312(d), if USCIS approves the Form I–800A, it will so notify the applicant and the Department of State in writing. The notice of approval will specify its expiration date. According to 8 C.F.R. § 204.312(e), that expiration date will be 15 months after the date on which USCIS received the FBI response to the biometrics information (i.e., fingerprinting). *Importantly, the home study is still only valid for six months.*

According to 8 C.F.R. § 204.312(e)(2), the approval is automatically revoked if (A) the marriage of the applicant terminates, (B) an unmarried applicant marries, or (C) either spouse files a written withdrawal of his or her signature on the Form I–800A. This revocation is without prejudice to the filing of a new Form I–800A.

c) Denial of a Form I-800A Application

Under 8 C.F.R. § 204.312(c), the following rules are to be followed in connection with the denial of a Form I–800A application:

> (1) The USCIS officer will deny the Form I–800A if the officer finds that the applicant has failed to establish that the applicant is "eligible" or suitable as the adoptive parent of a child from that particular Hague country.
>
> (2) Before denying a Form I–800A, the USCIS officer will comply with 8 C.F.R. § 103.2(b)(16), if required to do so under that provision, and may issue a request for evidence or a notice of intent to deny under 8 C.F.R. § 103.2(b)(8).
>
> (3) A denial will be in writing, giving the reason for the denial and notifying the applicant of the right to appeal, if any, as provided in 8 C.F.R. § 204.314.
>
> (4) It is for the Central Authority of the other Hague country to determine how its own adoption requirements, as disclosed in the home study under 8 C.F.R. § 204.311(q), should be applied in a given case. For this reason, the fact that the applicant may be ineligible to adopt in the other Convention country under those requirements, will not warrant the denial of a Form I–800A, if USCIS finds that the applicant has otherwise established eligibility and suitability as the adoptive parent of a Convention adoptee.

Under 8 C.F.R. § 204.314(a)(1)(i), the denial of a Form I-800A application is administratively appealable. However, 8 C.F.R. § 204.314(b)(1) and (2) state that there is no right to administratively appeal if the home study was not timely filed or if the Form I–800A was filed during any period in which the filing was barred.

G. Form I-800 Petition for the Child for "Hague Relative" Status

The Form I-800 (Petition to Classify Convention Adoptee as an Immediate Relative) should not be filed until after the Form I-800A has been approved, and after the applicant has obtained (in the foreign country) a proposed adoptive placement of a specific child with the assistance of a Hague-accredited provider. (Importantly, under 8 C.F.R. § 204.312(e), the home study that is submitted to the foreign country must be the same report that was submitted with the Form I-800 application.) However, the Form I-800 should be filed before an adoption is granted.

1. Who Qualifies as a "Child" in a Hague Adoption?

Information as to the specific child to be adopted is not required on the Form I-800A application. However, before filing such an application, one should learn what requirements the child must ultimately satisfy, and plan accordingly. According to 8 U.S.C. § 1101(b)(1)(G)(i), a "child" is a person who is younger than 16 years of age at the time an immigration visa petition is filed on the child's behalf, and who has been adopted in a Hague country, or who is emigrating from a Hague country to be adopted in the U.S. by a U.S. citizen and spouse jointly or by an unmarried U.S. citizen who is at least 25 years of age, provided that,

- the Secretary of Homeland Security is satisfied that proper care will be furnished the child if admitted to the United States;
- the child's natural parents (or parent, in the case of a child who has one sole or surviving parent because of the death or disappearance of, abandonment or desertion by, the other parent), or other persons or institutions that retain legal custody of the child, have freely given their written irrevocable consent to the termination of their legal relationship with the child, and to the child's emigration and adoption;
- in the case of a child having two living natural parents, the natural parents are incapable of providing proper care for the child;
- the Secretary of Homeland Security is satisfied that the purpose of the adoption is to form a bona fide parent-child relationship, and the parent-child relationship of the child and the natural parents has been terminated (and in carrying out both obligations under this subclause the Secretary of Homeland Security may consider whether there is a petition pending to confer immigrant status on one or both of such natural parents); and
- in the case of a child who has not been adopted—

    (aa) the competent authority of the foreign state has approved the child's emigration to the United States for the purpose of adoption by the prospective adoptive parent or parents; and

    (bb) the prospective adoptive parent or parents has or have complied with any pre-adoption requirements of the child's proposed residence; and However, 8 U.S.C. § 1101(b)(1)(G)(ii) states that no natural parent or prior adoptive parent of any such child shall thereafter, by virtue of such parentage, be accorded any statutory right, privilege, or status under this chapter.

Under 8 C.F.R. § 204.303(b), the child is deemed to be "habitually resident" in the country wherein the child has his or her citizenship.

According to 8 U.S.C. § 1101(b)(1)(G)(iii), a natural sibling of such a child also qualifies as a Hague child if that child –

- was adopted abroad, or is coming to the United States for adoption, by that same adoptive parent (or prospective adoptive parent) or parents of the sibling; and
- is younger than 18 years of age at the time the immigration visa petition is filed on his or her behalf.

2. Filing Deadline

According to 8 C.F.R. § 204.313(c), the petitioner must file the Form I-800 petition before the expiration of the notice of approval (i.e., the 15-month period) and before the child's 16th birthday. The 15-month validity period for a Form I–800A approval may be extended under certain circumstances pursuant to 8 C.F.R. § 204.312(e)(3).

3. Preparing and Filing the Form I-800 Petition

According to 8 C.F.R. § 204.313(a), once a Form I–800A has been approved and the Central Authority of the foreign country has proposed placing a child for adoption by the petitioner, the petitioner may file the Form I–800. The petitioner must complete it in accordance with the instructions that accompany the Form I–800, and must sign it personally. In the case of a married petitioner, one spouse cannot sign for the other, even under a power of attorney or similar agency arrangement. The petitioner may then file it with the stateside or overseas USCIS office or the visa issuing post that has jurisdiction under 8 C.F.R. § 204.308(b) to adjudicate the Form I–800, together with the required information and documents, as explained below.

If the Form I-800A has been approved, no additional filing fee is required for the filing of the first Form I-800 for a specifically identified child. However, if the petitioner seeks approval for a second child (requiring a second Form I-800) who is not sibling of the first, an additional $720 filing fee is required pursuant to 8 C.F.R. § 103.7(b)(1). On the other hand, there is no additional filing fee if the children are siblings.

4. What Documents Must Accompany the Petition?

According to 8 C.F.R. § 204.313(d), the petition must be accompanied by:

a) approval notice

The Form I–800A approval notice and any extensions thereof.

b) primary provider's declaration

A statement from the primary provider, signed under penalty of perjury under U.S. law, indicating that all of the required pre-placement preparation and training has been completed.

c) foreign country's central authority's report

The report by the foreign country's Central Authority (authenticated under penalty of perjury by the petitioner's primary provider) setting forth the child's name and date of birth (accompanied by the birth certificate or secondary evidence of the child's age), the reasons for the adoptive placement, and that the competent authority has:

(i) established that the child is eligible for adoption;

(ii) determined, after having given due consideration to the possibility of placing the child for adoption within the Convention country, that intercountry adoption is in the child's best interests;

(iii) ensured that the legal custodian, after having been counseled as required, concerning the effect of the child's adoption on the legal custodian's relationship to the child and on the child's legal relationship to his or her family of origin, has freely consented in writing to the child's adoption, in the required legal form (copies of the signed irrevocable consents must usually accompany the report, with certain exceptions);

(iv) ensured that if any individual or entity other than the legal custodian must consent to the child's adoption, this individual or entity, after having been counseled as required concerning the effect of the child's adoption, has freely consented in writing, in the required legal form, to the child's adoption;

(v) ensured that the child, after having been counseled as appropriate concerning the effects of the adoption; has freely consented in writing, in the required legal form, to the adoption, if the child is of an age that, under the law of the country of the child's habitual residence, makes the child's consent necessary, and that consideration was given to the child's wishes and opinions; and

(vi) ensured that no payment or inducement of any kind has been given to obtain the consents necessary for the adoption to be completed.

d) summary of child's medical and social history

A summary (which may be in a separate document or in the report by the foreign country's Central Authority) of the information given to the petitioner regarding the child's medical and social history. This summary (the "Article 16 Report") must include:

(A) A statement concerning whether, from any examination or for any other reason, there is reason to believe that the child has any medical condition that makes the child legally inadmissible into the U.S.; if the medical information that is available at the provisional approval stage is not sufficient to assess whether the child may be inadmissible, the submission of this information may be deferred until the petitioner seeks final approval of the Form I–800;

(B) If both of the child's birth parents were the child's legal custodians and signed the irrevocable consent, the factual basis for determining that they are incapable of providing proper care for the child;

(C) Information about the circumstances of the other birth parent's death, if applicable, supported by a copy of the death certificate, unless paragraph (d)(4)(ii) of this section makes it unnecessary to provide a copy of the death certificate;

(D) If a sole birth parent was the legal custodian, the circumstances leading to the determination that the other parent abandoned or deserted the child, or disappeared from the child's life; and

(E) If the legal custodian was the child's prior adoptive parent(s) or any individual or entity other than the child's birth parent(s), the circumstances leading to the custodian's acquisition of custody of the child and the legal basis of that custody.

e) primary provider's post-placement duties

According to 8 C.F.R. § 204.313(d)(4)(v), if the child will be adopted in the U.S., the primary provider's written report must detail the primary adoption service provider's plan for post-placement duties, as specified in 22 C.F.R. § 96.50.

f) application for waiver of ineligibility, if needed

If the specifically-identified child may be deemed ineligible to enter the U.S., a waiver of ineligibility may be sought. In such cases, 8 C.F.R. § 204.313(d)(5), the Form I-800 petition must include a properly completed waiver application for each such ground of actual or potential ineligibility. Due to the extreme complexity of the laws regarding ineligibility and waivers of ineligibility, the petitioner should retain an immigration law specialist for this purpose. Very briefly, under 8 U.S.C. § 1182(a), an alien may be deemed ineligible to enter the U.S. based on –

(1) health-related grounds,
(2) criminal activity and related grounds,
(3) national security and related grounds,
(4) the alien becoming a public charge,
(5) the absence of labor certification and qualifications for certain immigrants,
(6) being a prior illegal entrant and immigration violator,
(7) the failure to meet documentation requirements (which would not appear to apply),
(8) ineligibility for citizenship (such ineligibility including draft evaders),
(9) being an alien who was previously removed (i.e., deported), or
(10) miscellaneous reasons (none of which would appear to apply to a Hague child).

5. What Additional Information is Required?

According to 8 C.F.R. § 204.313(b)(1), the petitioner must specify either that:

- Whether the child will be adopted in the foreign country or in the U.S., the child will seek an immigrant visa, because the child will reside in the U.S. with the petitioner after the child's admission to the United States on the basis of the proposed adoption, or
- If the child will be adopted only in the foreign country, the child will seek a nonimmigrant visa, in order to travel to the U.S. to obtain naturalization, because the petitioner and the child will continue to reside abroad immediately following the adoption, rather than residing in the United States with the petitioner.

If the petitioner is stationed abroad as a member of the Armed Forces, the child will be deemed to be coming to the U.S. to reside in the United States with that petitioner.

H. Investigation and Adjudication of the Form I-800 Petition

1. Investigation

Under 8 C.F.R. § 204.313(f), filing of a completed Form I-800 prompts an investigation which includes document checks, telephone checks, interview(s) with the birth or prior adoptive parent(s), a field investigation, and any other appropriate investigatory actions. The materials from the Form I–800A proceeding will be included in the record of the Form I–800 proceeding. In any case in which there are significant differences between the facts in the Form I–800A or Form I–800 and the facts uncovered by the investigation, the office conducting the investigation may consult directly with the appropriate USCIS office. In any instance where the investigation reveals negative information sufficient to sustain a denial of the Form I–800 (including a denial of a Form I–800 that had been provisionally approved) or the revocation of the final approval of the Form I–800, the results of the investigation, including any supporting documentation, and the Form I–800 and its supporting documentation will be forwarded to the appropriate USCIS office.

Although USCIS is not precluded from denying final approval of a Form I–800 based on the results of an investigation under this paragraph, the grant of provisional approval and the fact that the Department of State has given the notice contemplated by article 5(c) of the Convention, shall constitute prima facie evidence that the grant of adoption or custody for purposes of adoption will, ordinarily, warrant final approval of the Form I–800. The Form I–800 may still be denied, however, if the Secretary of State declines to issue the certificate provided for under section 204(d)(2) of the Act or if the investigation under this paragraph establishes the existence of facts that clearly warrant denial of the petition.

2. Provisional Approval before Adoption / Custody Order

Under 8 C.F.R. § 204.313(g), the USCIS officer considers the evidence submitted with the Form I–800A and Form I–800, and the results of the investigation, "to determine whether the preponderance of the evidence shows that the child qualifies as a Convention adoptee" and that "the proposed adoption or grant of custody will meet the Convention requirements." The officer will then serve the petitioner (and the Department of State) with a written order provisionally approving the Form I–800. Pursuant to 22 C.F.R. § 42.24(e) and (f), the provisional approval may also be issued by a consulate officer (i.e., an employee of the State Department). The provisional approval will expressly state that the child will, upon adoption or acquisition of custody, be eligible for classification as a Convention adoptee, and direct the petitioner to obtain and present the evidence required to obtain final approval of the Form I–800.

Immediately after the provisional approval of the I-800 petition, the State Department (through the embassy or consulate) will send information to the petitioner concerning how to apply for the actual visa using the DS-230 form (Application for Immigrant Visa), as explained below. Under 22 C.F.R. § 42.24(g), after the Form I-800 petition has been provisionally approved, a completed visa application form (see below) must be submitted to the consular officer for a provisional review of visa eligibility. (The petitioner is thus working with two U.S. agencies at this point.)

According to 22 C.F.R. § 42.24(h) and (i), after reviewing the visa application (assuming it is satisfactory), the consular officer notifies the Convention country's Central Authority – using what is called an Article 5 Letter – that the petitioner is a suitable adoptive parent and that the child will be able to enter and reside permanently in the United States. The petitioner must not attempt to adopt or obtain custody of the child until after the consular officer issues the Article 5 letter. Article 5 of the Treaty states:

> "An adoption within the scope of the Convention shall take place only if the competent authorities of the receiving State –

a) have determined that the prospective adoptive parents are eligible and suited to adopt;

b) have ensured that the prospective adoptive parents have been counselled as may be necessary; and

c) have determined that the child is or will be authorised to enter and reside permanently in that State."

3. Final Approval after the Adoption or Custody Order

After the Article 5 letter is issued, the petitioner must then seek from the foreign court or tribunal an order of adoption or legal custody of the child. The foreign country will then issue what is called an Article 23 Certificate (or its equivalent), certifying that the adoption or grant of custody complies with the Hague Convention. The Article 23 Certificate is sent directly to the consular officer at the Embassy or Consulate.

The petitioner must also seek to obtain final approval of the provisionally approved Form I–800. To do so, the petitioner is required by 8 C.F.R. § 204.313(h) to submit to the officer at the State Department or at the USCIS copies of the following documents:

- If the child is adopted in the foreign country, the adoption decree or administrative order showing that the petitioner has adopted the child; in the case of a married petitioner, the decree or order must show that both spouses adopted the child; or
- If the child will be adopted in the United States:

  (A) The foreign decree or administrative order giving custody of the child for purposes of emigration and adoption to the petitioner or to an individual or entity acting on behalf of the petitioner. In the case of a married petitioner, an adoption decree that shows that the child was adopted only by one spouse, but not by both, will be deemed to show that the petitioner has acquired sufficient custody to bring the child to the United States for adoption by the other spouse;

  (B) If not already provided before the provisional approval (because, for example, the petitioner thought the child would be adopted abroad, but that plan has changed so that the child will now be adopted in the United States), a statement from the primary provider, signed under penalty of perjury under United States law, summarizing the plan for monitoring of the placement until the adoption is finalized in the United States;

  (C) If not already provided before the provisional approval (because, for example, the petitioner thought the child would be adopted abroad, but that plan has changed so that the child will now be adopted in the United States), a written description of the preadoption requirements that apply to adoptions in the State of the child's proposed residence and a description of when and how, after the child's immigration, the petitioner intends to complete the child's adoption. The written description must include a citation to the relevant State statutes or regulations and specify how the petitioner intends to comply with any requirements that can be satisfied only after the child arrives in the United States.

4. Denial of a Form I-800 Petition

Under 8 C.F.R. § 204.313(i), if the petition is to be denied, the USCIS officer will comply with the requirements of 8 C.F.R. § 103.2(b)(16), if required to do so under that provision, and may issue a request for evidence or a notice of intent to deny under 8 C.F.R. § 103.2(b)(8). The denial will be in writing, and will specify the reason(s) for the denial and notify the petitioner of the right to appeal. If a Department of State officer finds that the Form I–800 is "not clearly approvable," or that 8 C.F.R. § 204.309(b) warrants denial of the Form I–800, the Department of State officer will forward the to the USCIS office for review and decision.

According to 8 C.F.R. § 204.314(a)(1)(ii), the denial of a Form I-800 petition is administratively appealable. However, 8 C.F.R. § 204.314(b)(3) and (4) state that there is no right to administratively appeal if the Form I-800 was filed before the approval of the Form I-800A or after the expiration of the approval of the Form I-800A, or if the Form I-800 was filed during a period in which it was barred.

I. Obtaining Hague Certification and the "Hague Relative" Visa

1. Issuance of an IH-3 or IH-4 Visa

An IH-3 visa is issued for children with a full and final adoption decree from a foreign Hague Convention country, while an IH-4 visa is issued when the child is coming to the U.S. from a Hague Convention country to be adopted. The visa is obtained as follows:

Just after the petitioner receives provisional approval of the I-800 petition, the petitioner submits a completed DS-230 Application for Immigrant Visa to the State Department (through the embassy or consulate). Pursuant to 22 C.F.R. § 42.63(a)(2), if the child is under 14 years old or is physically incapable of completing the form, it may be executed by the child's parent or guardian, or, if the child has no parent or guardian, by any person having legal custody of, or a legitimate interest in, the child. Therefore, unless the child's parents are dead or have had their parental rights terminated, the child must sign the form, and do so before the consulate officer.

The application must be accompanied by –

- the visa processing fee ($230 per child at the time of publishing this book),
- a copy of the child's birth certificate,
- three full frontal photographs of the child,
- police, military, or prison records, if they exist (which is rare),
- the passport of the Convention adoptee, and
- the results of panel physician's medical exam.

After these materials are submitted, the child is fingerprinted pursuant to 22 C.F.R. § 42.67(c). A consular officer then reviews the application to determine whether the child appears to qualify for the visa. If the application is satisfactory, the Consular officer will send the "Article 5 letter" to the foreign central authority (see above).

After the Convention country then grants the adoption or custody rights and issues an "Article 23 Certificate," certifying that the order complies with the Convention, the order and the certificate may be sent directly to the consular officer at the U.S. Embassy or Consulate. The officer at the Embassy or Consulate will then schedule the final visa interview. The child must appear before the consular officer (if he or she did not do so at the time of the initial visa application review). During the interview, present the valid adoption or custody decree. Under 8 U.S.C. § 1154(d)(2), 42 U.S.C. § 14931(a)(1), and 22 C.F.R. § 42.24(j), the State Department official at the embassy or consulate then approves the I-800 petition, issues a Hague Certificate, and issues the visa.

2. Revocation of the Approval of a Visa Petition

a) Revocation upon Notice and Hearing

Under 8 U.S.C. § 1155 and 8 C.F.R. § 205.2(a), the USCIS may also revoke the approval of a visa petition upon notice to the petitioner on any ground other than those specified for automatic revocation, when the necessity for the revocation comes to the attention of the USCIS. The petitioner must first be given, under 8 C.F.R. § 205.2(b), notice and the opportunity to offer evidence in support of the petition and in opposition to the grounds alleged for revocation of the approval. Also, 8 U.S.C. § 1155 provides that no revocation shall have effect unless notice of the revocation is communicated to the beneficiary of the petition before such beneficiary commences his journey to the United States.

If, upon reconsideration of the petitioner's evidence, the approval previously granted is revoked, 8 C.F.R. § 205.2(c) requires the USCIS to provide the petitioner with a written notification of the decision that explains the specific reasons for the revocation. The petitioner is then entitled under 8 C.F.R. § 205.2(d) to appeal the USCIS's decision within 15 days after the service of the revocation notice to the Board of Immigration Appeals. From there, the petitioner would then be entitled to seek judicial review from the U.S. District Court if the administrative remedies are unavailing.

b) Automatic Revocation

As stated in 8 C.F.R. § 205.1, there are several situations in which the approval of the visa petition may be automatically revoked. According to 8 C.F.R. § 205.1(b), the USCIS is to promptly give written notice of the automatic revocation to the petitioner's last known address.

According to 8 C.F.R. § 205.1(a)(1), the USCIS's approval of a visa petition is automatically revoked, retroactively to the date of approval, if the U.S. Secretary of State terminates the child's registration pursuant to 8 U.S.C. § 1153(g) (which deals with the failure to apply for a visa within one year after alien registration). In addition, 8 C.F.R. § 205.1(a)(2) provides for automatic revocation if the filing fee and associated service charge are not paid within 14 days of the notification that the check or other financial instrument used to pay the filing fee has been returned as not payable.

Under 8 C.F.R. § 205.1(a)(3)(i), automatic revocation will result if, before the beneficiary's (i.e., the child's) journey to the U.S. commences, the petitioner files written notice of withdrawal of the petition with any USCIS officer who is authorized to grant or deny petitions, the petitioner dies (unless the U.S. Attorney General in his or her discretion determines that for humanitarian reasons revocation would be inappropriate), the petitioner's status as a lawful permanent resident terminates (unless the petitioner is or became a U.S. citizen), or the child reaches the age of 21 (however the approval of the petition will remain valid for the duration of the relationship with the petitioner to accord preferential status if the child remains unmarried, or to accord preferential status under 8 U.S.C. § 1153(a)(3) if he or she marries). According to 8 C.F.R. § 205.2(b), revocation on any other ground may not be made without giving the petitioner notice and an opportunity to be heard.

3. Judicial Review of Agency's Decision re the Visa

The courts may review the USCIS's revocation of a visa or denial of a preferential visa petition, to determine if the revocation or denial was an abuse of discretion. (See *Kaliski v. District Director of INS*, (9th Cir. 1980) 620 F.2d 214 [review of denial of petition], and *Kaho v. Ilchert*, (9th Cir. 1985) 765 F.2d 877 [review of revocation of visa].) In *Pascual v. O'Shea*, (D.Haw. 1976) 421 F.Supp. 80, it was held that if the petitioner's legal position is correct, the court even has the authority to direct the agency to classify the child as an immediate relative, if the facts underlying the petition are essentially undisputed.

As to what constitutes an "abuse of discretion," the courts have held that a USCIS decision denying "immediate relative" status is within the agency's broad discretion, and that courts will not find an abuse of discretion unless the decision (1) was made without a rational explanation, (2) inexplicably departed from established policies (such as those provided by statute or regulation), or (3) rested on an impermissible basis (such as an invidious discrimination against a particular race or group). See *Rogan v. Reno*, (E.D.N.Y. 1999) 75 F.Supp.2d 63 [citing *Sidhu v. Jenifer*, (6th Cir. 1996) 104 F.3d 361, and *Douglas v. INS*, (2d Cir. 1994) 28 F.3d 241]. *Kaliski* held that such an abuse also exists where the agency decision is based upon an improper understanding of the law.

Procedurally, the court in *Young v. Reno*, (9th Cir. 1997) 114 F.3d 879, held that the general provisions of the Federal Administrative Procedures Act apply. One of those provisions of the APA (specifically 5 U.S.C. § 553) require that regulations be enacted only after there has been an opportunity for the public to comment on proposed rules as set forth in published notices, such as those appearing in the Federal Register. In *Ruangswang v. INS*, (9th Cir. 1978) 591 F.2d 39, the court held that an abuse of discretion exists where the agency establishes and applies new legal standards in the adjudicatory process rather than by way of the APA rulemaking process. On the other hand, *Young* also held that since decisions by district directors do not constitute binding precedent, as opposed to decisions by the Board of Immigration Appeals, a decision by a district director would not violate the *Ruangswang* rule.

As far as the interpretation of the immigration statutes are concerned, the *Young* court applied the general rule of administrative law as declared in *Chevron, U.S.A., Inc. v. Natural Resources Defense Council, Inc.*, (1984) 467 U.S. 837. In *Chevron*, the Supreme Court set forth the two-step process for reviewing an agency's interpretation of a statute that it administers: The first step is to ask whether Congress has directly spoken to the precise question at issue. If the intent of Congress is clear, the courts and the agency must give effect to the unambiguously expressed intent of Congress. If the court determines that the statutes are silent or ambiguous as to the precise question at issue, the court then proceeds to the second step, which is to ask whether the agency's declarations of law are based on a permissible construction of the statutes. The courts do not simply impose their own construction of the statute, as would be necessary in the absence of an administrative interpretation. On the other hand, the Supreme Court in *INS v. Cardoza-Fonseca*, (1987) 480 U.S. 421, held that an agency interpretation of statute which conflicts with that agency's earlier interpretation is entitled to considerably less deference than a consistently held agency view.

Another aspect of administrative law was explained in *Young*, i.e., that 5 U.S.C. § 704 requires the petitioner to exhaust all mandatory administrative remedies within the agency before seeking judicial review of an adverse administrative decision. *Young* explains that where the APA applies, an appeal to a superior agency authority is a prerequisite to judicial review only when expressly required by statute or when an agency rule requires appeal before review and the administrative action is made inoperative pending that review. *Young* then notes that the federal district courts are granted jurisdiction under 8 U.S.C. § 1329 to review agency action taken pursuant to the Immigration and Naturalization Act, and that while a petitioner has the option of taking an appeal to the Board of Immigration Appeals, neither the statutes nor the regulations explicitly require a petitioner to administratively appeal prior to seeking judicial review.

J. "Automatic" U.S. Citizenship for the Hague Adoptee

1. If the Child was Issued an IH-3 Visa

Pursuant to 8 U.S.C. § 1431(b), in those cases where the child received a full and final adoption decree from the Hague country and then entered the U.S. pursuant to an IH-3 visa, the child automatically acquires U.S. citizenship if he or she enters (i.e., is admitted to) the United States prior to his or her 18th birthday. The U.S. Government will automatically send the child's Certificate of Citizenship to the adoptive parents' U.S. address without requiring additional forms or fees. In the case of adopting parents who are U.S. government or military personnel assigned overseas, the child automatically acquires citizenship as soon as he or she begins residing with the adoptive parents. If the U.S. State Department does not automatically issue a citizenship certificate for the child, an application for one can be filed. Such applications are discussed later in this chapter with regard to adopted orphans and alien relatives.

2. If the Child was Issued an IH-4 Visa

If the child came from a Hague country for the purpose of being adopted in the U.S., and did so pursuant to an IH-4 visa, the child will be deemed a "permanent resident" upon entry into the United States, and will automatically receive a permanent resident card (green card). The child will automatically acquire citizenship on the date of his or her adoption in U.S. if the adoption occurs before the child's 18th birthday.

Under 42 U.S.C. § 14931(c), in the case of a child who has entered the U.S. from another Convention country for the purpose of adoption (which is in the minority of cases), an order declaring the adoption final shall not be entered unless the Secretary of State has issued a certificate pursuant to 42 U.S.C. § 14931(a) that legal custody of the child has been granted to the citizen parent by the child's country of origin for purposes of emigration and adoption, and that the requirements of the Convention and federal law have been met with respect to the adoption

K. Outgoing Cases

An "outgoing case" is an adoption in which the child is emigrating from the U.S. to a foreign country. (22 C.F.R. § 96.) In an "outgoing case," the following rules apply:

1. California Agency's Duties to the Child

Under 42 U.S.C. § 14932(a)(1), the accredited agency must ensure that:

(A) a background study on the child is completed;

(B) reasonable efforts have been made to actively recruit and make a diligent search for prospective adoptive parents to adopt the child in the U.S., but that despite such efforts, it has not been able to place the child for adoption in the U.S. in a timely manner; and

(C) a determination is made that placement with the prospective adoptive parent or parents is in the best interests of the child.

Under 42 U.S.C. § 14932(a)(2)(A), the agency must document these matters to the court.

2. California Agency's Duties to the Adoptive Parents

Under 42 U.S.C. § 14932(a)(2), the accredited agency must furnish the following additional documents to the State court with jurisdiction over the case:

- a background report (home study) on the prospective adoptive parent or parents (including a criminal background check) prepared in accordance with the laws of the receiving country; and
- a declaration by the central authority (or other competent authority) of such other Convention country (i) that the child will be permitted to enter and reside permanently, or on the same basis as the adopting parent, in the receiving country; and (ii) that the central authority (or other competent authority) of such other Convention country consents to the adoption, if such consent is necessary under the laws of such country for the adoption to become final.

Family Code § 8902(a) states that "the licensed adoption agency shall provide" an "assessment of the suitability of the applicant's home," in addition to its duty under

Family Code § 8902(d) and federal law to submit a copy of the report to the court. However, it appears that Family Code § 8902(a) conflicts with 42 U.S.C. § 14932(a)(2), to the extent it requires the California agency to actually conduct the home study in an outgoing case, and it would appear counterintuitive to require a California agency to "assess" the foreign prospective adoptive parents and their home in the foreign country.

3. Conditions on State Court's Granting of the Adoption

Under 42 U.S.C. § 14932(b), the California court may not grant the adoption petition in an outgoing case unless it has –

- received and verified the material described in 42 U.S.C. § 14932(a)(2) [the background check on the child and the home study report on the prospective adoptive parents]; and satisfactory evidence that the requirements of Articles 4 and 15 through 21 of the Convention have been met; and
- determined that the adoptive placement is in the best interests of the child.

4. California Agency's Duties to U.S. Secretary of State

According to 42 U.S.C. § 14932(a)(3), the accredited agency must furnish the following additional documents to the U.S. Secretary of State:

> (A) official copies of State court orders certifying the final adoption or grant of custody for the purpose of adoption;
>
> (B) the documents concerning the background check on the child, to the extent required by the Secretary of State; and
>
> (C) any other information concerning the case required by the Secretary of State to perform the functions specified in 42 U.S.C. § 14932(c) or otherwise to carry out the duties of the U.S. central authority under the Convention.

5. The U.S. Secretary of State's Duties

According to 42 U.S.C. § 14932(c), in an outgoing case, the U.S. Secretary of State, on receipt and verification of the material and information described in 42 U.S.C. § 14932(a)(3) [see above], shall issue, as applicable, an official certification that the child has been adopted or a declaration that custody for purposes of adoption has been granted, in accordance with the Convention and this chapter.

V. ADOPTING A CHILD FROM A NON-HAGUE COUNTRY

A. Qualifying for a Visa for the Child under the "Orphan" Statute

As stated above, to adopt a child from a Hague country, one must meet the requirements of the Treaty and the implementing statutes and regulations. However, there are many affluent and well-populated countries, and some smaller ones, which have still not ratified the Hague Convention. Obtaining preferential immediate relative status for a child from a non-Hague country normally requires meeting the statutory definition of "orphan" or "alien relative," and submitting a satisfactory petition. Alien relative status is discussed below.

As for orphan status, in order to petition for an "immediate relative" preferential visa, one may use the standard forms published by the Bureau of Citizenship and Immigration Services. The forms include the I-600 "Petition to Classify Orphan as Immediate Relative" and the I-600A "Application for Advance Processing of Orphan Petition."

As set forth at 8 C.F.R. § 204.3(a)(2), petitioning for an orphan involves two distinct determinations. The first determination concerns the advanced processing application which focuses on the ability of the prospective adoptive parents to provide a proper home environment and on their suitability as parents. The second focuses on whether the child is an "orphan" under 8 U.S.C. § 1101(b)(1)(F). The prospective adoptive parents may submit the documentation necessary for each of these determinations separately or at one time, depending on when the child is identified. An orphan petition cannot be approved unless there is a favorable determination on the advanced processing application.

1. Children Who Qualify under the "Orphan" Statute

According to 8 U.S.C. § 1101(b)(1)(F)(i), a child qualifies as an immediate relative of the petitioner if that child (a) is under the age of sixteen at the time the visa petition is filed, (b) is an "orphan," and (c) has been adopted abroad or is coming to the U.S. for adoption and there has been compliance with the preadoption requirements, if any, of the child's proposed residence.

a) Age of the Child

As stated in 8 U.S.C. § 1101(b)(1)(F)(i), the child must be under the age of 16 years old at the time the petition is filed on behalf of the child. The "petition" would refer to the I-600 form, and not the I-600A application for advance processing, since the I-600A form is not intended to deal with a specific child. Also, the introductory language of 8 U.S.C. § 1101(b)(1) states that the child's "immediate relative" status only lasts until the child reaches 21 years old. Therefore, the processing of the petition needs to be completed before the child's 21st birthday. In addition, citizenship for the child should be obtained, as explained below, so as not to risk the revocation of the visa due to the loss of "immediate relative" status on the child's 21st birthday.

b) Loss of Parents (by Death, Abandonment, etc.)

The language of 8 U.S.C. § 1101(b)(1)(F)(i) specifically provides that immediate relative status is only available for those children who have become orphans because of the death or disappearance of, abandonment or desertion by, or separation or loss from, both parents, or for whom the sole or surviving parent is incapable of providing the proper care and has in writing irrevocably released the child for emigration and adoption.

(1) USCIS Regulations re Relinquishments

The provisions of 8 U.S.C. § 1101(b)(1)(F)(i) are interpreted in 8 C.F.R. § 204.3(b), which states that an "abandonment" does not exist merely by virtue of (1) a relinquishment or release by the parents to the prospective adoptive parents or for a specific adoption, (2) a relinquishment or release of the child by the parents to a third party for custodial care in anticipation of, or preparation for, adoption, unless the third party (such as a governmental agency, a court of competent jurisdiction, an adoption agency, or an orphanage) is authorized under the child welfare laws of the foreign-sending country to act in such a capacity, or (3) temporary placement of the child in an orphanage if the parents express an intention to retrieve the child, are contributing or attempting to contribute to the support of the child, or otherwise exhibit ongoing parental interest in the child. Additionally, *Rogan v. Reno*, (E.D.N.Y. 1999) 75 F.Supp.2d 63, holds that the abandonment must occur before the adoption petition is filed. However, 8 C.F.R. § 204.3(b) does state that "a child who has been given unconditionally to an orphanage shall be considered to be abandoned."

(2) Evidence of Orphan Status

With the petition, 8 C.F.R. § 204.3(d)(1)(iii) requires the petitioner to provide evidence that the child is an orphan as appropriate to the case. That substantiation may include (A) evidence that the orphan has been abandoned or deserted by, separated or lost from both parents, or that both parents have disappeared as those terms are defined in 8 C.F.R. § 204.3(b), (B) the death certificate(s) of the orphan's parent(s), if applicable, or (C) if the orphan has only a sole or surviving parent, as defined in 8 C.F.R. § 204.3(b), evidence of this fact and evidence that the sole or surviving parent is incapable of providing for the orphan's care and has irrevocably released the orphan for emigration and adoption.

(3) Monetary Transactions in the Placement

In addition, as is the policy of all of the states, 8 C.F.R. § 204.3(i) provides that an orphan petition will be denied if a prospective adoptive parent or an adoptive parent, or a person or entity working on their behalf, have given or will give money or other consideration either directly or indirectly to the child's parent(s), agent(s), other individual(s), or entity as payment for the child or as an inducement to release the child. However, 8 C.F.R. § 204.3(i) also states that the reasonable payment for necessary activities such as administrative, court, legal, translation, and/or medical services related to the adoption proceedings is not precluded.

c) Completed or Contemplated Adoption

According to 8 U.S.C. § 1101(b)(1)(F)(i), the petitioner must show that the child has been (a) adopted abroad by a U.S. citizen and spouse jointly, or by an unmarried U.S. citizen at least 25 years of age, who personally saw and observed the child prior to or during the adoption proceedings, or (b) is coming to the U.S. for adoption by a U.S. citizen and spouse jointly, or by an unmarried U.S. citizen at least 25 years of age, who have or has complied with the preadoption requirements, if any, of the child's proposed residence. As to the category dealing with children adopted abroad, the statutory and regulatory requirements are discussed below in the context of alien relative visa petitions. The second category is explained further as follows:

Under 8 U.S.C. § 1101(b)(1)(F)(i) and 8 C.F.R. § 204.3(f)(1), the state's preadoption requirements must be complied with in every case in which a child is coming to that state as an orphan to be adopted. California has requirements that must be satisfied before a child may be placed with a prospective adoptive parent, as set forth in the section below concerning state law on intercountry adoptions. Also, 8 C.F.R. § 204.3(f)(2) further provides that any preadoption requirements which by operation of state law cannot be met before filing the advanced processing application must be noted.

d) Assurance of Proper Care for the Child in U.S.

According to 8 U.S.C. § 1101(b)(1)(F)(i), there is a proviso that the "Attorney General is satisfied that proper care will be furnished the child if admitted to the United States." A related rule is provided at 8 U.S.C. § 1154(d), which states that a favorable home study must be completed before a visa petition will be approved. These two provisions are related, and are explained below in the discussion concerning the home study.

e) Severance of Child's Prior Relationships

Under 8 U.S.C. § 1101(b)(1)(F)(i), another proviso states that "no natural parent or prior adoptive parent of any such child shall thereafter, by virtue of such parentage, be accorded any right, privilege, or status under this chapter." As stated in *Young v. Reno*, (9th Cir. 1997) 114 F.3d 879, it would appear that adoptions generally have this effect by operation of law.

f) Orphan Sibling of Orphan / Alien Relative Child

As stated at 8 U.S.C. § 1101(b)(1)(F)(ii), "immediate relative" status is available to a child who (I) is a natural sibling of an "orphan" child or an "alien relative" child as described below and at 8 U.S.C. § 1101(b)(1)(E)(i), (II) has been adopted abroad, or is coming to the U.S. for adoption, by the adoptive parent or prospective adoptive parent or parents of the sibling "orphan" or "alien relative" child, and (III) fits the description of an "orphan" except that the child is under the age of 18 at the time a petition is filed in his or her behalf. In other words, a 17-year-old orphan can be the subject of a petition as long as that individual's younger brother or sister who is under 16 years old and who is also an orphan is also sought for adoption.

2. Hague Convention on International Child Abduction

The rules requiring the petitioner to show that the child is an "orphan" or an "alien relative" under 8 U.S.C. § 1101(b)(1)(E) or (F) clearly accommodate the operation of the international treaty prohibiting international kidnapping, which was made in The Hague, Netherlands and is called the Convention on the Civil Aspects of International Child Abduction. In addition to the civil remedies provided by this treaty, the International Parental Kidnapping Crime Act of 1993 (18 U.S.C. § 1204) provides for criminal penalties which may be prosecuted in federal court. See *United States v. Cummings*, (9th Cir. 2002) 281 F.3d 1046, for a further explanation of the treaty and the IPKCA.

3. The Home Study of the Petitioners

Under 8 U.S.C. §§ 1101(b)(1)(F)(i) and 1154(d), one who files an orphan petition must document that a favorable home study was completed so as to assure that proper care will be furnished for the child in the United States. According to 8 C.F.R. § 204.3(e)(9) and the introductory language of 8 C.F.R. § 204.3(e), one copy of a home study that is not more than six months old, and/or the most recent update to the home study, must be submitted to the USCIS for the orphan petition. In addition, 8 C.F.R. § 204.3(c)(2) provides that the documentation of the home study of the prospective adoptive parents may be submitted with the advanced processing application before an orphan is identified, thereby contemplating that a pre-placement home study may be completed in connection with the adoption. The details of the USCIS's specific requirements for the home study are described as follows:

a) Who May Conduct the Home Study

As set forth in 8 C.F.R. § 204.3(e)(7), the "home study preparer" must certify that he or she is licensed or otherwise authorized by the State of the orphan's proposed residence to research and prepare home studies. Under Family Code § 8811.5(a) and 22 California Code of Regulations § 35087(a), a public or private adoption agency may conduct a home study and certify a prospective adoptive parent in a preplacement evaluation that that person is suited to be an adoptive parent.

b) Pre-Filing Judicial Review of the Home Study

Under 8 C.F.R. § 204.3(e)(8), if the prospective adoptive parents reside in a State which requires the State to review the home study, such a review must occur and be documented before the home study is submitted to the USCIS. As to California law, one could interpret Family Code § 8917(a) and (b) as requiring judicial review of the home study. In addition, *In re Backhaus' Adoption*, (1962) 209 Cal.App.2d 13 (discussed in more detail in Chapter 2), held in the context of an intercountry adoption that the trial court has jurisdiction to review an unfavorable home study report, and to make its own independent determination of the suitability of the home of the petitioners for the adoption, without regard to whether the foreign agency and government have consented to the adoption, and without regard to whether an immigration visa would be issued. (See also *Adoption of Baby Girl B.*, (1999) 74 Cal.App.4th 43, for a discussion of the current California statutes on judicial review of home studies.) Moreover, under 8 C.F.R. § 204.3(e)(9)(ii), a home study may be "amended" before it is submitted to the USCIS, meaning that the court's judicial review of the home study could culminate in an order that the home study preparer amend the report.

c) Assessment of Petitioners' Residence

As set forth at 8 C.F.R. § 204.3(e)(3), the home study report must include a detailed description of the living accommodations where the prospective adoptive parents currently reside, and where the petitioners will reside if they are intending to move. In addition, 8 C.F.R. § 204.3(e)(9)(ii) contemplates that the adoptive parents could move from one state to another prior to the completion of the adoption. The description in the home study report must include an assessment of the suitability of accommodations for a child and a determination whether such space meets applicable State requirements.

d) Required Interviews of Petitioners' Household

Under 8 C.F.R. § 204.3(e)(1), the home study preparer must document with particularity that he or she conducted at least one interview in person, and at least one home visit, with the petitioner(s), and at least one in-person interview of each additional adult member of the prospective adoptive parents' household.

e) Assessment of Petitioners' Parenting Abilities

According to 8 C.F.R. § 204.3(e)(2), the home study report must discuss five specific aspects of the petitioners' capabilities to properly parent an orphan:

(1) Physical, Mental and Emotional Status

As set forth in 8 C.F.R. § 204.3(e)(2)(i) and (e)(4), the home study preparer must initially assess how the physical, mental, and emotional health of the prospective adoptive parents and each adult member of their household affects their ability to properly care for a child. If the home study preparer determines that there are areas beyond his or her expertise which need to be addressed, he or she shall refer the prospective adoptive parents to an appropriate licensed professional, such as a physician, psychiatrist, clinical psychologist, or clinical social worker for an evaluation. The home study report must then include the home study preparer's assessment of any potential problem areas, a copy of any outside evaluation(s), and the home study preparer's recommended restrictions, if any, on the characteristics of the child to be placed in the home.

(2) The Petitioners' Finances

Under 8 C.F.R. § 204.3(e)(2)(ii), the home study report must include a description of the income, financial resources, debts, and expenses of the prospective adoptive parents, and must state what evidence was considered to verify the income and financial resources. Any income designated for the support of one or more children in the care and custody of the prospective adoptive parents, such as funds for foster care, or any income designated for the support of another member of the household must not be counted towards the financial resources available for the support of a prospective orphan.

(3) History of Abuse and/or Violence

According to 8 C.F.R. § 204.3(e)(2)(iii)(A), the home study preparer must ask each prospective adoptive parent whether he or she has a history of substance abuse, sexual or child abuse, or domestic violence, even if it did not result in an arrest or conviction, and include the responses in the report. Therefore, the USCIS is concerned not only with child abuse, but substance abuse as well and related incidents, such as an arrest and/or conviction for driving while intoxicated. As for child abuse, the home study preparer must check the available child abuse registries to see if any report exists as to each prospective adoptive parent and each adult member of their household. The petitioners must cooperate with the home study preparer in complying with the requirements of state law for gaining access to any such registries. Under 8 C.F.R. § 204.3(e)(2)(iii)(D), the failure to cooperate and/or the failure to disclose an arrest, conviction, or history of substance abuse, sexual or child abuse, and/or domestic violence to the home study preparer may result in the denial of the advanced processing application or the orphan petition.

If the home study preparer becomes aware of any such abuse either by way of the petitioners' disclosure or other means, 8 C.F.R. § 204.3(e)(2)(iii)(B) requires the report to evaluate the suitability of the home for adoptive placement of an orphan in light of this history, and to include documentation as to all arrests or convictions and the final disposition thereof. Additionally, the individual at issue must submit a signed statement giving details including mitigating circumstances, if any, about each incident. Moreover, 8 C.F.R. § 204.3(e)(2)(iii)(C) requires the home study report to discuss whether the individual with the history has completed appropriate rehabilitation which demonstrates that the prospective adoptive parent is and will be able to provide proper care for the orphan, and the documentation thereof.

(4) Prior Unfavorable Home Studies

According to 8 C.F.R. § 204.3(e)(2)(iv), the home study preparer must ask each prospective adoptive parent and each adult member of the prospective adoptive parents' household whether there was any previous rejection as a prospective adoptive parent or unfavorable home study, and must include the responses to this question in the report. If there were, the reasons for such a finding must be set forth and a copy of each previous rejection and/or unfavorable home study must be attached to the favorable home study. Since all unfavorable home studies must be disclosed, judicial review of the home study must be obtained pursuant to *In re Backhaus' Adoption*, (1962) 209 Cal.App.2d 13, and Family Code § 8917(a) and (b), if it contains unfavorable information.

(5) Criminal History

According to 8 C.F.R. § 204.3(e)(2)(v), the prospective adoptive parents and the adult members of the prospective adoptive parents' household are expected to disclose to the home study preparer and the Service any history of arrest and/or conviction early in the advanced processing procedure, and the failure to do so may result in denial of the advanced processing application and the orphan petition. The regulation goes on to mention that the existence of prior arrests, even without convictions, will come to the attention of the USCIS by way of the fingerprint checks, and that it is in the petitioners' interests to disclose any criminal history at the soonest possible opportunity in order to resolve any issues early in the process.

f) Counseling re International Adoptions

Under 8 C.F.R. § 204.3(e)(5), the home study report must include a summary of the counseling given to prepare the prospective adoptive parents for an international adoption, such as a discussion of the processing, expenses, difficulties, and delays associated with international adoptions, and any plans for post-placement counseling.

g) Home Study Preparer's Approval of Petitioners

According to 8 C.F.R. § 204.3(e)(6), if the home study preparer's findings are favorable, the home study must contain his or her specific approval of the prospective adoptive parents for adoption and a discussion of the reasons for such approval. The home study must include the number of orphans which the prospective adoptive parents may adopt, and whether there are any specific restrictions to the adoption such as nationality, age, or gender of the orphan. (On the other hand, 42 U.S.C. § 1996b prohibits persons, entities and governments that are involved in adoption or foster care placements from denying any individual the opportunity to become an adoptive or a foster parent on the basis of the national origin of the child.) If the home study preparer has approved the prospective parents for a handicapped or special needs adoption, this fact must be clearly stated.

4. Application for Advanced Processing

According to 8 C.F.R. § 204.3(c), the prospective adoptive parents must file an I-600A advanced processing application before an orphan is identified in order to expedite and to secure the necessary clearance to file the orphan petition.

a) Supporting Documentation for the Application

Under 8 C.F.R. § 204.3(c)(1), the advanced processing application must be supported by (i) evidence of the petitioner's U.S. citizenship and (if the petitioner is married and the married couple is residing in the United States) of the spouse's U.S. citizenship or lawful immigration status, (ii) a copy of the petitioner's marriage certificate (if the petitioner is currently married), (iii) evidence of the legal termination of all previous marriages for the petitioner and/or spouse (if previously married), and (iv) evidence of compliance with preadoption requirements, if any, of the State of the orphan's proposed residence. The language of 8 C.F.R. § 204.3(c)(1) also mentions that any preadoption requirements which cannot be met at the time the advanced processing application is filed because of operation of state law must be noted and explained when the application is filed, and that preadoption requirements must be met at the time the petition is filed, except for those which cannot be met until the orphan arrives in the United States. Since the advanced processing application only applies where there is not yet a specific child identified, 8 C.F.R. § 204.3(c)(1) states that this rule does not apply where it is known that there will be no adoption abroad.

b) Documentation of Pre-Placement Home Study

To carry out the directives of 8 U.S.C. §§ 1101(b)(1)(F) and 1154(d), the language of 8 C.F.R. § 204.3(c)(2) provides that a copy of the home study must be submitted with the advanced processing application or within one year thereafter.

c) Fingerprints

According to 8 C.F.R. § 204.3(c)(3), after the receipt of a properly filed advanced processing application, the USCIS will fingerprint each adult member of the prospective adoptive parent's household.

5. Procedural Requirements for the Orphan Petition

As mentioned above, the petitioner submits an I-600 orphan petition form for the purpose of seeking an immigration visa for a specifically identified child. As explained below, the handling of the petition depends upon the status of the I-600A advance processing application.

a) Where I-600 Application Was Approved

As stated in the introductory language of 8 C.F.R. § 204.3(d), the prospective adoptive parents who have submitted an approved advanced processing application must file an orphan petition and all supporting documents within 18 months of the date of the approval of the advanced processing application. If they fail to do so, the advanced processing application shall be deemed abandoned and the petition shall be denied.

Under 8 C.F.R. § 204.3(d)(1), an orphan petition timely filed after approval of the advanced processing application shall be accompanied by the following supporting documentation: (i) the approval of the advanced processing application, (ii) the orphan's birth certificate (or other proof of identity and age if such a certificate is not available, and an explanation thereof), and (iii) evidence that the child is an orphan as appropriate to the case (as described above).

In addition, 8 C.F.R. § 204.3(d)(1)(iv) requires there to be evidence of adoption abroad or that the prospective adoptive parents have, or a person or entity working on their behalf has, custody of the orphan for emigration and adoption in accordance with the laws of the foreign-sending country. As to the first alternative, supporting documentation would consist of a legible, certified copy of the adoption decree, if the orphan has been the subject of a full and final adoption abroad, and evidence that the unmarried petitioner, or married petitioner and spouse, saw the orphan prior to or during the adoption proceeding abroad. As to the second alternative, 8 C.F.R. § 204.3(d)(1)(iv) may be satisfied by evidence (1) that the prospective adoptive parents have, or a person or entity working on their behalf has, secured custody of the orphan in accordance with the laws of the foreign-sending country, (2) of an irrevocable release of the orphan for emigration and adoption from the person, organization, or competent authority which had the immediately previous legal custody or control over the orphan if the adoption was not full and final under the laws of the foreign-sending country, (3) of compliance with all preadoption requirements, if any, of the State of the orphan's proposed residence (any such requirements that cannot be complied with prior to the orphan's arrival in the U.S. because of State law must be noted and explained), and (4) that the State of the orphan's proposed residence allows readoption or provides for judicial recognition of the adoption abroad if there was an adoption abroad which does not meet the requirements of 8 U.S.C. § 1101(b)(1)(F), because the unmarried petitioner, or married petitioner and spouse, did not personally see the orphan prior to or during the adoption proceeding abroad, and/or the adoption abroad was not full and final. As to the fourth element, Family Code § 8919 provides for readoption, and *Estate of O'Dea*, (1973) 29 Cal.App.3d 759, provides for judicial recognition of the adoption abroad.

b) Where I-600 Is Pending or Concurrent

According to the introductory language of 8 C.F.R. § 204.3(d), if an orphan has been identified for adoption and the advanced processing application is pending, the prospective adoptive parents may file the orphan petition at the Service office where the application is pending. Under 8 C.F.R. § 204.3(d)(2), where the advanced processing application is pending, the petition must be accompanied by (i) evidence that the advanced processing application has been filed such as a photocopy of the fee receipt or a statement including the date when the application was filed, (ii) the home study, if not already submitted, and (iii) the supporting documentation for an orphan petition required by 8 C.F.R. § 204.3(d)(1).

Under the introductory language of 8 C.F.R. § 204.3(d), prospective adoptive parents who do not have an advanced processing application approved or pending may file the application and petition concurrently on one Form I-600 if they have identified an orphan for adoption. As provided at 8 C.F.R. § 204.3(d)(3), the petitioner merely submits a signed and completed Form I-600, which will serve as both the advanced processing application and the orphan petition, meaning that the prospective adoptive parents should not file a separate Form I-600A. This regulation goes on to state that the petition must be accompanied by (i) the supporting documentation for an advanced processing application required by 8 C.F.R. § 204.3(c) (as described above), and the supporting documentation for an orphan petition required by 8 C.F.R. § 204.3(d)(1), as described immediately above.

6. Grant or Denial of the Orphan Petition

The grant of the I-600 petition results in the issuance of the visa. On the other hand, as stated in *Young v. Reno*, (9th Cir. 1997) 114 F.3d 879, the granting of the petition does not create any vested rights, since the approval may be subject to automatic revocation or revocation for cause, as explained above.

Where the petition is denied, 8 C.F.R. § 204.3(h)(12) requires the USCIS to state its reasons for the denial, and the petitioner may then file an administrative appeal to the Board of Immigration Appeals under 8 C.F.R. §§ 3.1(b)(5) and 103.3. According to 8 C.F.R. § 3.6(a), the agency will not execute a decision being appealed to the BIA.

B. Obtaining a Visa under the "Alien Relative" Statute

"Immediate relative" preferential status is also available for children who satisfy the "alien relative" requirements of 8 U.S.C. § 1101(b)(1)(E) and the related regulations. The USCIS publishes standard form I-130 for those who wish to submit an "alien relative" petition for an immigration visa for the child. Under 8 C.F.R. § 204.2(d)(1) and (d)(2)(vii), the petition may be filed by a U.S. citizen or "an alien lawfully admitted for permanent residence."

1. Children Who Qualify under "Alien Relative" Statute

Under 8 U.S.C. § 1101(b)(1)(E)(i), a child qualifies as the petitioner's immediate relative if at the time of filing the petition (a) the child is unmarried and under 21 years of age, (b) the child was adopted while under the age of 16 years old, (c) the child has been in the legal custody of, and has resided with, the adopting parent or parents for at least two years, and (d) the child's natural parents will not, by virtue of such parentage, be accorded any right, privilege, or status.

Unlike the orphan statute, the alien relative statute has no provision concerning the death of or abandonment by the parents, nor with regard to home studies or the preadoption requirements of the state of the proposed residence for the child, nor with assuring any government entity that the child will be given proper care in the U.S., nor with advanced processing of the petitioners, nor requiring that the petitioner be a U.S. citizen.

a) Age of the Child

Under 8 U.S.C. § 1101(b)(1)(E)(i) and 8 C.F.R. § 204.2(d)(2)(vii)(C), a petition for immediate relative classification may be filed on behalf of an unmarried child under 21 years of age who was adopted while under 16 years old. As for documenting age, 8 C.F.R. § 204.2(d)(5) appears to require a birth certificate, although this is not expressly mentioned as one of the items of "primary evidence" that 8 C.F.R. § 204.2(d)(2)(vii) requires to be submitted with the petition.

With regard to age, the court in *Kaliski v. District Director of INS*, (9th Cir. 1980) 620 F.2d 214, held that an unmarried, adopted person over 21 years of age may qualify for a second preference visa if he or she once satisfied the requirements of 8 U.S.C. § 1101(b)(1)(E).

b) Completed Adoption

The language of 8 U.S.C. § 1101(b)(1)(E) contemplates that an adoption had to have taken place prior to the filing of the petition. However, in *Kaho v. Ilchert*, (9th Cir. 1985) 765 F.2d 877, the court held that for an adoption to be valid under 8 U.S.C. § 1101(b)(1)(E), an adoption need not conform to the USCIS's or "Anglo-American" notions of adoption, but that the adoption need only be recognized under the law of the country where the adoption occurred. *Kaho* held that an adoption under Tongan law which did not carry with it the right of intestate succession could still be considered an "adoption" for purposes of 8 U.S.C. § 1101(b)(1)(E).

Kaho also held that the lack of a statutory procedure for the adoption of legitimate children does not compel a determination that common law or "customary" adoptions are not recognized under the foreign law. *Kaho* also says that it is not necessary for an adoption to be recognized by a judicial act before it can be recognized as valid for immigration purposes, in light of the immigration statutes' purpose to reunite families. However, *Kaho* did hold that the agency or the district court (whichever the case may be) must look to the specifics of the law of the foreign country to determine whether the adoption at issue actually exists.

Where the federal district court is required to determine what the foreign law is, Federal Rule of Civil Procedure 44.1 provides that the party intending to raise an issue of foreign law must give written notice of the intent to do so, and that the court may consider any relevant material or source, including testimony, whether or not submitted by a party or admissible under the Federal Rules of Evidence. In *Kaho*, the appellate court interpreted FRCP 44.1 as allowing a district court to consider material that was not considered by the agency when it made its administrative adjudication. *Kaho* also holds that since the USCIS is not charged with administering the foreign law, its interpretation of foreign law is likewise not entitled to judicial deference. (But see, *Mila v. District Director of Denver*, (10th Cir. 1982) 678 F.2d 123.)

c) In Adoptive Parent's Legal Custody Two Years

Under 8 U.S.C. § 1101(b)(1)(E), the petitioner must show that the child has been in the legal custody of the adopting parent(s) for two years. "Legal custody" is defined in 8 C.F.R. § 204.2(d)(2)(vii)(A), as the assumption of responsibility for a minor by an adult under the laws of the state and under the order or approval of a court of law or other appropriate government entity. An informal custodial or guardianship document, such as a sworn affidavit signed before a notary public, is insufficient for this purpose. The regulation goes on to require that a legal process involving the courts or other recognized government entity take place, but that if the adopting parent was granted legal custody by the court or recognized governmental entity prior to the adoption, that period may be counted toward fulfillment of the two-year legal custody requirement.

Thus, the child need not have been adopted for two years, only in the petitioner's legal custody for two years, as stated in 8 C.F.R. § 204.2(d)(2)(vii)(C). However, 8 C.F.R. § 204.2(d)(2)(vii)(A) provides that if custody was not granted prior to the adoption, the adoption decree shall be deemed to mark the commencement of legal custody. On the other hand, 8 C.F.R. § 204.2(d)(2)(vii)(C), legal custody and residence are accounted for in the aggregate, meaning that a break in legal custody or residence will not affect the time already fulfilled, although the petitioner still must establish that the child was adopted while under 16.

There is also nothing in the alien relative petition regulations disallowing the two-year residency period from occurring within the United States. In other words, if a foreign-born child found his or her way into the U.S. and then into California's dependency system (which occurred in *In re Stephanie M.*, (1994) 7 Cal.4th 295), someone who adopted the child after the termination of the parents' rights could conceivably file an alien relative petition. (However, it is clear from 8 C.F.R. § 204.2(d)(2)(vii) that the two-year period under 8 U.S.C. § 1101(b)(1)(E) would commence from the time of the adoption order, since a foster parent does not have "legal custody" over the child.) As explained later in this chapter, the granting of the visa could then qualify the child for citizenship.

As to children adopted outside the U.S., the child still may be required to have a medical examination under 8 U.S.C. § 1201(d) before being allowed to enter the United States, regardless of what kind of visa petition is filed. It would appear that in an orphan petition situation, the home study's evaluation of whether the petitioner is capable to parent the child would have to include the health status of the child, meaning that the medical examination would appear to be superfluous for the orphan, but possibly not for the alien relative child.

Importantly, the alien relative statutes and regulations say nothing about where the adoption had to have taken place. Furthermore, the regulations (8 C.F.R. § 204.2(d)(2)(vii)) plainly suggest that the adoption could have taken place anywhere in the world.

d) "Resided With" Adoptive Parent for Two Years

According to 8 U.S.C. § 1101(b)(1)(E), the petitioner must also show that the child has resided with the adopting parent(s) for two years. As stated in 8 C.F.R. § 204.2(d)(2)(vii)(B), documentary evidence must be submitted showing that the petitioner and the child resided together in a familial relationship wherein the petitioner had primary parental control. The regulation states that such documentation would include evidence that the adoptive parent owns or maintains the property where the child resides and provides financial support and day-to-day supervision of the child.

The evidence must clearly indicate the physical living arrangements of the adopted child, the adoptive parent(s), and the natural parent(s) for the period of time during which the adoptive parent claims to have met the residence requirement. When the adopted child continued to reside in the same household as a natural parent(s) during the period in which the adoptive parent petitioner seeks to establish his or her compliance with this requirement, the petitioner has the burden of establishing that he or she exercised primary parental control during that period of residence.

e) Alien Relative Sibling of an Orphan or Alien Relative Child

Just as with the Hague implementing statutes and the orphan statute, there is also a provision for siblings here: According to 8 U.S.C. § 1101(b)(1)(E)(ii), a child qualifies for immediate relative status if the child (I) is a natural sibling of an alien relative or orphan child, (II) was adopted by the adoptive parent or parents of the sibling alien relative or orphan, and (III) is otherwise himself or herself an "alien relative," except that the child was adopted while under the age of 18 years.

2. Processing of the I-130 Alien Relative Petition

As mentioned above, the petitioner must be a U.S. citizen or a lawful permanent resident, and the petition must provide evidence of that fact under 8 C.F.R. § 204.3(d)(2). As for the rules concerning the child, the procedural requirements are as follows:

a) "Primary Evidence" Requirements

Along with the I-130 form alien relative petition, 8 C.F.R. § 204.3(d)(vii) requires that, as primary evidence to be submitted for an adopted child, the petitioner provide a copy of an adoption decree issued by the civil authorities. In those rare cases where a country permits an informal "adoption" (i.e., one not decreed by court order), it would appear that *Kaho v. Ilchert*, (9th Cir. 1985) 765 F.2d 877, as explained above, would supersede 8 C.F.R. § 204.3(d)(vii). However, the petitioner would bear the burden of showing that the law of the foreign country recognizes such situations as "adoptions," and meeting this burden could actually be more expensive and risky than simply obtaining an adoption decree in what might turn out to be an uncontested proceeding. Furthermore, the lack of an adoption decree could make it more difficult to later obtain citizenship for the child, as explained below.

In addition, 8 C.F.R. § 204.2(d)(2)(vii)(A) and (B) require the petitioner to submit documentary evidence that the child has been in the legal custody of, and has resided with, the adopting parent(s) for two years. Where there has been a name change, which is often the case with an adopted child, 8 C.F.R. § 204.2(d)(5) requires that evidence of the name change (such as the legal document showing the name change) must accompany the petition. Most adoption decrees will list the name that the child will use.

b) Permissible "Secondary Evidence"

According to 8 C.F.R. § 204.2(d)(2)(v), when it is established that primary evidence is not available (according to specific rules promulgated by the U.S. State Department), secondary evidence may be acceptable, but will be evaluated for its authenticity and credibility. Secondary evidence may take the form of historical evidence which was issued contemporaneously with the event which it documents, and may include medical records, school records and religious documents. When affidavits are submitted, they must be sworn to by persons who have personal knowledge of the events to which they attest, and must contain the affiant's full name and address, date and place of birth, relationship to the party, if any, and complete details concerning how the affiant acquired knowledge of the events.

3. Grant or Denial of the Alien Relative Petition

Under 8 C.F.R. § 204.2(d)(3), if the petition is approved, it will be forwarded to the U.S. State Department's Processing Center if the child is outside the United States. If the child is in the U.S. and is eligible for a visa, the approved petition will be retained by the USCIS. As stated at 8 C.F.R. § 204.2(h)(1), the approval of an alien relative petition shall remain valid for the duration of the relationship to the petitioner and of the petitioner's status as established in the petition, unless the approval is terminated or revoked as explained above. If the petition is denied, 8 C.F.R. § 204.2(d)(3) provides that the petitioner will be notified of the reasons for the denial and of the right to appeal in accordance with USCIS regulations.

C. U.S. Citizenship for the Adopted Orphan or Alien Relative

Congress enacted the Child Citizenship Act ("CCA") to provide for automatic citizenship for the child in limited situations, and for a parent's petition for the child's citizenship in other cases. If the child does not qualify for citizenship under either method prescribed by the CCA, the child may seek naturalization through other means, as explained in immigration law treatises.

1. Qualifying for Automatic Citizenship for the Child

As stated at 8 U.S.C. § 1431(a), a child born outside the U.S. "automatically becomes a citizen of the United States" when (1) at least one parent of the child is a U.S. citizen, whether by birth or naturalization, (2) the child is under the age of 18 years, and (3) the child is residing in the U.S. in the legal and physical custody of the citizen parent pursuant to a lawful admission for permanent residence. According to 8 U.S.C. § 1431(b), an adopted child may be deemed to have met this three-part rule if the child was adopted by a U.S. citizen parent, and if the child satisfied the requirements applicable to adopted children under 8 U.S.C. § 1101(b)(1), which is the statutory definition of "child" for purposes of classification as an "immediate relative," as explained above with reference to "orphans" and "alien relatives."

Importantly, 8 U.S.C. § 1431(b) does not specify when the adoption had to have been ordered, nor does it expressly exclude a *nunc pro tunc* adoption from the application of the three-part rule for automatic citizenship. However, in *Hughes v. Ashcroft*, (9th Cir. 2001) 255 F.3d 752, the court strictly construed the CCA, and held that an adopted person who was over 40 years old when the CCA took effect was not entitled to automatic citizenship. The *Hughes* court applied the portion of the CCA (as provided at Pub.L. 106-395, Title I, § 104) that states that the Act applies to individuals who "satisfy the requirements" of the CCA "as in effect on such effective date (of February 27, 2001)." Although the person was adopted as a child and had been admitted to the U.S. pursuant to an approved orphan petition, he was not a child under 18 years old on February 27, 2001. (It would appear that the reasoning of *Hughes* would also apply to a CCA citizenship application under 8 U.S.C. § 1433, as explained below.)

In those situations where the adoption proceedings in the Superior Court become rather lengthy, it would be in the child's interests to have the adoption order granted nunc pro tunc back to the time of filing the adoption petition. In other words, Family Code § 8600 and various other adoption statutes mentioned in this book allow a petition to be filed as to an unmarried minor. In Family Code § 6500, "minor" is defined as someone under 18 years old.

2. Adoptive Parent's Application for Child's Citizenship

If a child born outside the U.S. has not acquired automatic citizenship according to 8 U.S.C. § 1431, then 8 U.S.C. § 1433(a) would permit a parent who is a U.S. citizen (or, if the citizen parent has died during the preceding 5 years, a citizen grandparent or citizen legal guardian) to apply for naturalization on behalf of the child. Since a child who was granted an "orphan" or "alien relative" visa would likely qualify for automatic citizenship, an application under 8 U.S.C. § 1433(a) would likely involve a child who came to the U.S. in some other capacity, such as a refugee (see 8 U.S.C. § 1157), or one who was granted asylum pursuant to 8 U.S.C. § 1158, or one who was paroled into the United States (see 8 U.S.C. § 1182(d)(5)).

Under 8 U.S.C. § 1433(a), a certificate of citizenship will be issued to the child upon satisfactory proof that five specified conditions have been fulfilled: First, at least one parent is (or, at the time of his or her death, was) a U.S. citizen, whether by birth or naturalization. Second, the U.S. citizen parent has been (or, at the time of his or her death, had been) (A) physically present in the U.S. or its outlying possessions for an aggregate period totaling at least five years, at least two of which were after attaining the age of 14 years, or (B) a citizen parent who has been physically present in the U.S. or its outlying possessions for a aggregate period totaling at least five years, at least two of which were after attaining the age of 14 years. Third, the child is under the age of 18 years. Fourth, the child is residing outside of the U.S. in the legal and physical custody of the applicant (or, if the citizen parent is deceased, an individual who does not object to the application). Fifth, the child is temporarily present in the U.S. pursuant to a lawful admission, and is maintaining such lawful status. According to 8 U.S.C. § 1433(c), an adopted child may be considered under this five-part rule if the child was adopted by a U.S. citizen parent, and if the child satisfies the requirements for "immediate relative" status as applicable to adopted children under 8 U.S.C. § 1101(b)(1). Again, under *Hughes v. Ashcroft*, (9th Cir. 2001) 255 F.3d 752, an application on behalf of one who was an adult as of February 27, 2001 would be rejected due to the inability to satisfy the third condition.

According to 8 U.S.C. § 1433(b), the child shall become a U.S. citizen and shall be furnished with a certificate of citizenship upon the approval of the application (which may be filed from abroad) and, except as provided in the last sentence of section 1448(a) of this title, upon taking and subscribing to the oath of allegiance (as required for naturalization applicants) before a USCIS officer within the United States.

At the time this book was written, very few regulations had been enacted with regard to the CCA. One such regulation is 8 C.F.R. § 322.5(b), which provides that if the district director denies the application for a certificate of citizenship, the applicant shall be furnished with the reasons for denial and advised of the right to file an appeal on Form I-290B to the Administrative Appeals Unit within 30 days of the denial. As with the denial of a visa application, it does not appear that an administrative appeal of the denial of a citizenship application is mandatory, and that the reasoning of *Young v. Reno*, (9th Cir. 1997) 114 F.3d 879, which permits judicial review of the district director's decision, would apply to an 8 C.F.R. § 322.5(b) denial as well.

VI. CALIFORNIA LAW GOVERNING INTERCOUNTRY ADOPTIONS

A. Introduction

"Intercountry adoption" is defined by Family Code § 8527 as "the adoption of a foreign-born child for whom federal law makes a special immigration visa available," and includes the "completion of the adoption in the child's native country or completion of the adoption in this state." Also, Family Code §§ 8900 through 8919 speak specifically to the procedures for intercountry adoptions, and contemplate that there will be interaction between the California agency and the federal immigration agency. Family Code § 8901 specifically authorizes the CDSS to enact regulations to administer the intercountry adoption program. While Family Code §§ 8527 and 8900 through 8919 have been in effect since 1994, no case law interpreting any of these code sections, nor of the interpretive regulations, existed at the time this book was written.

As stated in Family Code § 8900, intercountry adoption services may only be provided by private adoption agencies licensed by the CDSS specifically to provide these services. Family Code § 8905 states that adoption agencies licensed in California may work only with domestic and foreign adoption agencies with whom they have written agreements that specify the responsibilities of each. In addition, 22 California Code of Regulations § 35297(a)(1)) provides that prior to the placement of the child for purposes of an adoption that will be completed in California, the California adoption agency shall obtain documentation from the foreign agency that the child is legally free for adoption.

Based on these laws, an intercountry adoption in California essentially proceeds as a "dual-agency" adoption. As to the arrangements between the two agencies, 22 California Code of Regulations § 35243(a) provides that the agency in California shall have a written agreement with each foreign agency from which the California agency places children. As to the contents of that agreement, 22 California Code of Regulations § 35243(a)(1) states that the agreement shall specify (A) that the foreign agency is authorized to place children for intercountry adoption under the laws of the foreign agency's country, (B) the responsibility of the foreign agency for the care of the child including medical care and financial support, (C) the authority and responsibility of the foreign agency in relation to placement, disruptions, finalization of the intercountry adoption or return of the child to his or her native country, (D) that the agency shall notify the foreign agency in writing whenever the adoption cannot be finalized, (E) the supervision and reporting requirements of the foreign agency, (F) the policies and procedures for the selection of children through the foreign agency, and (G) responsibility for travel arrangements for the child's transportation from the child's native country to the final California destination.

B. Jurisdiction to Conduct the Adoption Proceeding

As set forth at Family Code § 9210(a)(5), the California courts have jurisdiction to conduct an adoption proceeding if it appears that no state would have jurisdiction to do so and the child's present or future care may be accommodated in California. Since Family Code § 145 defines "state" as a U.S. state, district, territory or possession, it would appear that the Family Code § 9210(a)(5) "vacuum jurisdiction" provision would apply to a petition for an intercountry adoption filed prior to the child coming to this country.

Regarding concurrent proceedings in the foreign country, Family Code § 3405(a) states that a foreign country is generally treated as if it were a state of the U.S. for purpose of applying the Uniform Child Custody Jurisdiction and Enforcement Act. Family Code § 3405(b) provides that a foreign country's child custody determination made under factual circumstances in substantial conformity with the UCCJEA must be recognized and enforced. And although Family Code § 3403 expressly states that the UCCJEA does not apply to adoptions, the UCCJEA does apply to guardianships, terminations of parental rights and other child custody orders.

C. Local Agency's Duties in a California Intercountry Adoption

Along with the matters mentioned above that are required by the immigration laws for the home study, California law imposes the following additional rules on the adoption agency:

1. Obtain and Disclose Information on the Child's History

Under Family Code § 8909(a), an agency may not place a child for adoption unless a written report on the child's medical background and, if available, the medical background of the child's biological parents so far as ascertainable, has been submitted to the prospective adoptive parents and they have acknowledged in writing the receipt of the report. Family Code § 8909(b) requires that report to contain all known diagnostic information, including current medical reports on the child, psychological evaluations, and scholastic information, as well as all known information regarding the child's developmental history and family life.

Family Code § 8909(c)(1) allows the biological parents to provide a blood sample, which is to be taken at an approved clinic or hospital, stored at an approved laboratory for 30 years, all of the purpose of providing a basis from which DNA testing can be done at a later date after entry of the order of adoption at the request of the adoptive parents or the adopted child. Family Code § 8909(d) sets forth confidentiality rules concerning the blood sample.

2. Obtain Applicants' Fingerprints and Criminal Record

According to Family Code § 8908(a), the California agency must require each person filing an application for adoption to be fingerprinted, and must secure from an appropriate law enforcement agency any criminal record of that person to determine whether the person has ever been convicted of a crime other than a minor traffic violation. Family Code § 8908(b) requires the California agency to take whatever criminal record that exists into consideration when evaluating the prospective adoptive parent, and to assess the effects of any criminal history on the prospective adoptive parent's ability to provide adequate and proper care and guidance to the child, and to report these findings to the court.

3. Complete Pre-Placement Home Study and Disclosures

According to 22 California Code of Regulations § 35297(a)(2), prior to placement of the child for purposes of adoption in California, the California agency must determine that the child's needs can be met by placement with the prospective adoptive parent by completing the assessment required by 22 California Code of Regulations § 35275 et seq., and by making the psychological and medical history form required by 22 California Code of Regulations § 35285 available to the prospective adoptive parent.

Pre-placement evaluations and certifications by licensed agencies as to the suitability of individuals to become adoptive parents are also authorized by Family Code § 8811.5(a). While Family Code § 8811.5(a) is located in that part of the code books dealing with independent adoptions, the language of the statute does not appear to be limited to independent adoptions, meaning that the CDSS would appear to have authority to enact regulations governing the specifics of pre-placement home studies. As provided in Family Code § 8811.5(c), the preplacement evaluation, whether it is conducted for the purpose of initially certifying prospective adoptive parents or for renewing that certification, shall be completed no more than one year prior to the signing of an adoption placement agreement. Furthermore, under 22 California Code of Regulations § 35180(b), an assessment completed in connection with merely a proposed domestic adoption shall not be used as the assessment for an intercountry adoption, until it has been updated by an agency licensed to provide intercountry adoption services.

4. Verify and Certify Compliance with Immigration Laws

Under 22 California Code of Regulations § 35297(a)(3) and (4), the California agency must, before the child is placed for purposes of an adoption to be completed in California, determine that all federal immigration requirements for a foreign-born child have been met, and certify to the federal immigration agency that the prospective adoptive parents have complied with California's preadoption requirements, such as the home study and the securing of a favorable report concerning the suitability of the prospective adoptive parents and their home.

5. Complete the Written Placement Agreement

According to 22 California Code of Regulations § 35297(a)(7), before the child is physically placed in the prospective adoptive parents' home, the California adoption agency and the prospective adoptive parents shall enter into an adoptive placement agreement, which shall include (A) general identifying information concerning the prospective adoptive parents, the agency, the first name and date of birth of the child, the anticipated date of the placement, and the amount of the agencies' fees, including the foreign agency's fees, (B) statements which summarize the parties' respective rights and duties during the placement (as explained below with reference to 22 California Code of Regulations § 35297(a)(5) and (6)), (C) a space for acknowledgement of receipt by the prospective adoptive parents of the information of the child's psychological and medical history (22 California Code of Regulations § 35297(a)(2)(C)), (D) a space for the prospective adoptive parents' signatures and the date thereof, and (E) a space for the agencies' representatives' signatures and the dates thereof (the written approvals by both agencies are required if the placement is a cooperative placement between two agencies).

a) Financial Responsibility for Child During Adoptive Placement

Family Code § 8906 specifically permits the licensed adoption agency and the prospective adoptive parents to enter into an agreement to share or transfer financial responsibility for the child. Family Code § 8907 also permits the agency to charge a fee to the prospective adoptive parents, as long as those fees are pre-approved by the CDSS. In addition, Family Code § 8908(c) allows the California agency to charge a fee for the fingerprinting and criminal record check.

Also, 22 California Code of Regulations § 35297(a)(5)(A)(1) states that if the agency enters into an agreement with the prospective adoptive parent to share or transfer financial responsibility for the child, the placement agreement shall include the nature of the responsibility assumed by the prospective adoptive parent, the duration of that responsibility and the effective date. It would also appear that the placement agreement could include provisions concerning the status of the child in the event the prospective adoptive parents are unable to complete the adoption, although this would be a matter for the court's ultimate determination, as explained below.

b) Filing Adoption Petition as a Condition to Adoptive Placement

Family Code § 8911 provides that "as a condition of placement," the prospective adoptive parents shall file the adoption petition "within 30 days of placement." Importantly, Family Code § 8911 does not specify whether the placement occurs before or after the petition is filed, nor do the statutes or regulations define exactly what an intercountry placement is.

As explained above and in Chapter 9, Family Code § 9210 contains several jurisdictional provisions allowing an adoption petition to be filed in a California court even as to a child who is not present in California. Also, as stated in Family Code § 8912, even though an intercountry adoption proceeds as a kind of dual-agency adoption, standing to file an adoption petition does not require placement as a statutory prerequisite.

Therefore, the "placement" that is described in Family Code § 8911 could consist merely of the completion of the adoptive placement agreement -- a kind of constructive placement of the child. In fact, the Family Code § 8539 definition of the verb "place for adoption" contemplates that the placement is fully recognized merely upon the selection of the adoptive parents and the completion of the placement agreement, and not the additional step of physically transferring the child into the adoptive parent's home. In addition, 22 California Code of Regulations § 35243(a)(1)(A) provides that the placement of the child might be handled through the foreign agency. Furthermore, while 22 California Code of Regulations § 35297(a)(5)(H) appears to contemplate a physical placement of the child prior to the filing of the adoption petition, the regulation does not foreclose the possibility of a constructive placement.

There is no case law interpreting Family Code § 8911. However, construing Family Code § 8911 so as to allow for constructive placement permits the adoption petition to be filed before the child arrives in California to live with the prospective adoptive parents. This interpretation of Family Code § 8911 would give the court jurisdiction to grant certain remedial relief as required (for example if there are difficulties with the home study), and would give the California court jurisdiction to communicate with the foreign agency and the judicial authorities in the foreign country, assuming foreign law permits. This interpretation of Family Code § 8911 would also allow the agency to be provided with some level of assurance, before the child actually comes to the U.S. and becomes the financial responsibility of the agency, that the prospective adoptive parents are committed to completing the adoption, and a forum for handling custody issues if the adoption efforts are unsuccessful.

D. Logistics of the Physical Placement of the Child for Adoption

1. California Agency's Role Where a Guardianship Exists

According to Family Code § 8903(b), if the child's native country requires and has given full guardianship to the prospective adoptive parents, the prospective adoptive parents shall assume all responsibilities for the child including care, custody, control, and financial support. In addition, 22 California Code of Regulations § 35297(a)(6) provides that if the prospective adoptive parent has received guardianship of the foreign-born child from the child's native country, the California agency must, prior to placing the child for purposes of an adoption to be completed in California, "discuss" the following matters with the prospective adoptive parent:

As provided in 22 California Code of Regulations § 35297(a)(6)(E), the agency must discuss with the prospective adoptive parents the matters explained above concerning concealment of the child within the county, removal of the child from the county, placing the child under the care of a licensed physician for routine health care, changes in the composition or place of residence of the adoptive family, the agency's duty to obtain court approval before removing the child from the adoptive home, the agency's duty to have a grievance review procedure and the prospective adoptive parents duty to file the adoption petition within 30 days of placement. Additional matters that must be discussed include the following:

a) Agency Duty to Routinely Meet with Petitioners

Under 22 California Code of Regulations § 35297(a)(6)(A), the agency shall routinely meet with the prospective adoptive parent and child until a final decree of adoption is granted.

b) Notifying Agency of Out-of-County Travel

As stated in 22 California Code of Regulations § 35297(a)(6)(B), the child shall not be removed from the county of residence of the prospective adoptive parent prior to filing an adoption petition without notifying the agency in writing.

c) Notifying Agency of Child's Injuries or Illnesses

According to 22 California Code of Regulations § 35297(a)(6)(C), the prospective adoptive parent shall inform the agency of any serious injury to or illness of the child.

d) Notifying Child Protective Services Agency of Neglect or Abuse

Under 22 California Code of Regulations § 35297(a)(6)(D), the agency will notify the local child protective services agency when the agency has determined that the child is in danger of cruelty, neglect, depravity or abuse.

2. Agencies' Roles Where There Is No Guardianship

Where a guardianship order has not been issued by the foreign country's court, Family Code § 8903(a) provides that for each intercountry adoption finalized in California, the California agency shall assume all responsibilities for the child including care, custody, and control as if the child had been relinquished for adoption in California (see Chapter 5 of this book) from the time the child left the child's native country. Of course, as explained above with regard to Family Code § 8906, the parties may agree to shift the financial burden of caring for the child to the adoptive parents. Also, 22 California Code of Regulations § 35243(a)(1)(B) envisions that the foreign agency might be permitted to share in the responsibility for the medical care and financial support of the child.

As to the specifics of the California agency's role, unless the prospective adoptive parent has received guardianship of the child from the child's native country, 22 California Code of Regulations § 35297(a)(5) provides that the California agency must, prior to placing the child for purposes of an adoption to be completed in California, "discuss" the following matters with the prospective adoptive parent:

a) Agency's Custody and Supervision of the Child

As stated above and in 22 California Code of Regulations § 35297(a)(5)(A), the agency shall retain legal custody of the child, supervise the adoptive placement, and routinely meet with the prospective adoptive parent and child until a final decree of adoption is granted.

b) Location of the Child Pending the Adoption Proceedings

According to 22 California Code of Regulations § 35297(a)(5)(B), (C) and (D), the agency must mention that the child shall not be concealed within the county prior to granting of the final decree of adoption, that the child shall not be removed from the county of residence of the prospective adoptive parent prior to filing an adoption petition without the prior written consent of the agency, and that after the adoption petition is filed the child shall not be removed from the county of residence of the prospective adoptive parent for a period exceeding 30 days without the approval of the court until a final decree of adoption is granted. These regulations are essentially a restatement of Family Code § 8910.

c) Health Care for the Child

Under 22 California Code of Regulations § 35297(a)(5)(E) and (F), the prospective adoptive parent shall place the child under the care of a licensed physician for routine health care of the child, and shall inform the agency of any serious injury to or illness of the child and shall obtain prior written consent for all nonemergency surgical and other nonroutine medical treatment.

d) Composition of Prospective Adoptive Family

As stated in 22 California Code of Regulations § 35297(a)(5)(G), the prospective adoptive parent shall inform the agency regarding any changes in the composition of the adoptive family or place of residence of the family. As explained Chapter 5 of this book, *Marten v. Thies*, (1979) 99 Cal.App.3d 161, held that, prior to the filing of the adoption petition, the failure to inform the adoption agency of the existence of marital difficulties in the home may constitute grounds for the agency to terminate the adoptive placement.

e) Agency's Right to Terminate the Placement

According to 22 California Code of Regulations § 35297(a)(5)(H) and (J), the adoptive placement may be terminated and the child removed from the prospective adoptive parent's home at the agency's discretion prior to the filing of the petition to adopt, but that after the adoptive petition has been filed the agency must obtain court approval to remove the child. See also *In re Adoption of Graham*, (1962) 58 Cal.2d 899, and *Department of Social Services v. Superior Court*, (1997) 58 Cal.App.4th 721. Also, the agency must, pursuant to 22 California Code of Regulations § 35297(a)(5)(I), give seven days written notice to the prospective adoptive parent of its intent to terminate the adoptive placement and remove the child unless the agency has determined that the child is in danger of cruelty, neglect, depravity or abuse, as was held in *C.V.C. v. Superior Court*, (1973) 29 Cal.App.3d 909.

f) Petitioners' Right to Terminate the Placement

As stated in 22 California Code of Regulations § 35297(a)(5)(K), the prospective adoptive parent have the right to terminate the adoptive placement and return the child to the agency at any time prior to the granting of the final decree of adoption. The status of the child upon the inability or failure to complete the adoption is discussed below.

g) Interstate Compact for Placement of Children

Under 22 California Code of Regulations § 35297(a)(5)(L), the agency must determine that all requirements under the Interstate Compact for the Placement of Children for an interstate placement have been met. As stated in Family Code § 7901, et seq., the ICPC only applies to placements from one state in the U.S. to another state in the U.S., and not to a country-to-country placement. Therefore, it would appear that this regulation would only apply in the rare case where the prospective adoptive parents moved to California from another state after the child had already been physically placed with them from the foreign country.

h) Administrative Grievance Process

According to 22 California Code of Regulations § 35297(a)(5)(M), the agency must provide a grievance review procedure and accord the prospective adoptive parent their right to file a grievance with the agency if the parent is dissatisfied with any action of the agency at any time before a petition for adoption is filed.

i) Prospective Adoptive Parents' Duty to File

As provided in 22 California Code of Regulations § 35297(a)(5)(N), the agency must discuss with the prospective adoptive parents that Family Code § 8911 requires that as a condition of placement the prospective adoptive parent shall file a petition to adopt the child within 30 days of placement, as explained above.

3. The Foreign Child's Rights

In *Plyler v. Doe*, (1982) 457 U.S. 202, which dealt with entitlement to educational benefits, it was held that even an illegal alien may assert a 14th Amendment "equal protection" claim, and that in certain circumstances there may not be a rational basis for a state statute that discriminates against persons who were not "legally admitted into the United States." Also, in *Rodriguez v. Kline*, (1986) 186 Cal.App.3d 1145, it was held that even an illegal alien could file suit in the California courts to seek damages for personal injuries suffered here. Based on *Plyler* and *Rodriguez*, it would appear that a foreign child would be able to assert all of the statutory and constitutional rights in the intercountry adoptive placement that an American child would be able to assert in a purely domestic agency adoption placement.

E. Procedural Considerations in an Intercountry Adoptions

1. Filing the Petition and Notifying the State

As stated in Family Code § 8912(a), "A person desiring to adopt a child may for that purpose file a petition in the county in which the petitioner resides." Unlike a domestic agency adoption (see Family Code § 8704(b)), the petition may be filed even if the child is not physically placed in the home of the prospective adoptive parents. Family Code § 8912(a) also provides that the court clerk shall immediately notify the CDSS in Sacramento in writing of the pendency of the proceeding and of any subsequent action taken.

As with all adoptions, Family Code § 8912(b) provides that the caption of the adoption petition shall contain the names of the petitioners, but not the child's name, but shall state the child's sex and date of birth. Likewise, Family Code § 8912(d) states that the order of adoption shall contain the child's adopted name, but not the name the child had before adoption.

Where there is a guardianship, Family Code § 8912(c) requires that the adoption petition shall state the child is the subject of a guardianship petition and shall include the caption and docket number or have attached a copy of the letters of the guardianship or temporary guardianship. The petitioners shall notify the court of any petition for guardianship or temporary guardianship filed after the adoption petition. The guardianship proceeding shall be consolidated with the adoption proceeding.

2. Joinder by the California Agency

The statutes do not expressly mandate that the agency file a joinder to the petition, but they contemplate that an agency joinder may be filed. Since the agency has financial responsibility for the child in the absence of a guardianship, and owes certain duties to the child even where a guardianship exists, it would appear to be in the agency's interests to file the joinder to the adoption petition, so as to make certain its status as a party to the case. Under Family Code § 8912(b), the name the child had before adoption shall appear in the joinder signed by the licensed adoption agency.

3. Agency's Report to the Court / Setting of the Hearing

Family Code § 8914 provides that if the licensed adoption agency is a party to or joins in the adoption petition, it shall submit a full report of the facts of the case to the court, and that the CDSS may also submit a report to the court. Family Code § 8915 provides that when any report or findings are submitted to the court by a licensed adoption agency, a copy of the report or findings, whether favorable or unfavorable, shall be given to the petitioner or to the petitioner's attorney. There does not appear to be any provision for expedited completion and service of the report where the recommendations are unfavorable to the prospective adoptive parents.

Family Code § 8917(a) provides that if the agency finds that the petitioners' home is not suitable for the child or that the required agency consents are not available and the agency recommends that the petition be denied, or if the petitioners desire to withdraw the petition and the agency recommends that the petition be denied, the clerk upon receipt of the report of the licensed adoption agency shall immediately refer it to the court for review. At that point, Family Code § 8917(b) requires the court to set a date for a hearing of the petition and give reasonable notice of the hearing to the agency and the petitioners. In addition, Family Code § 8916(a) provides that if the agency recommends against the proposed adoption, it shall file a full report with the court recommending a suitable plan for the child.

4. Appearance of the Parties at the Hearing

Under Family Code § 8913, the prospective adoptive parents and the child proposed to be adopted must appear before the court at the hearing on the adoption petition. There is no case on the issue of whether the court has the authority to approve of the adoption if Family Code § 8913 is not satisfied.

5. Agency's Representation of the Child

Family Code § 8917(c) states that the licensed adoption agency shall appear at the hearing to represent the child. It would also appear that the court would have the authority to act in the child's best interests by appointing independent counsel for the child, although there is no express provision for this in the intercountry adoption statutes.

6. Involvement of the Foreign Government in the Case

The intercountry adoption statutes do not contain any provision discussing the involvement of the foreign government in the California adoption proceeding. However, in *In re Stephanie M.*, (1994) 7 Cal.4th 295, which involved a juvenile court dependency proceeding concerning a Mexican-born child who had been brought to California by his mother and father, all three of whom had "entered the United States illegally," the California Supreme Court held that the juvenile court could keep the child in California's dependency system despite the Mexican government's objections.

The facts of *Stephanie M.* were that a Mexican court issued letters of guardianship for the child's grandmother in Mexico, and the juvenile court did not appear to have complied with the treaty between the U.S. and Mexico governing service of process. As to the effect of what was then the Uniform Child Custody Jurisdiction Act (i.e., *state* law), the juvenile court took jurisdiction of the child before the Mexican court ordered the conflicting guardianship, meaning that the juvenile court had UCCJA jurisdiction. Opposing the Mexican government's objections, the California foster parents were interested in remaining the child's caregivers and in terminating parental rights.

As to the issue of international comity, *Stephanie M.* held that the courts of this state may, but are not required to, execute the judgment of a foreign nation as a matter of comity in their discretion. *Stephanie M.* also held that it would violate the public policy of the U.S. to ignore the UCCJA so as to enforce a subsequent guardianship order issued by a foreign court.

7. Status of the Child if Adoption Cannot be Completed

Family Code § 8916(a) contemplates that the petitioners may move to withdraw the adoption petition or dismiss the proceeding. If this happens, the statute requires the court clerk to immediately notify the CDSS at Sacramento of the action. Family Code § 8916(a) also requires the licensed adoption agency to file a full report with the court recommending a suitable plan for the child and to appear before the court for the purpose of representing the child.

If the court sustains a recommendation that the child be removed from the home of the petitioners because the petitioners desire to withdraw the petition or the court dismisses the petition or the agency has recommended to deny the petition, Family Code § 8918 requires the court to commit the child to the care of the California agency for the agency to arrange adoptive placement or to make a suitable plan for the child, if the court decides not return the child to the child's parents.

Family Code § 8916(b) provides that notwithstanding the petitioners' withdrawal or dismissal, the court may retain jurisdiction over the child for the purpose of making any order for the child's custody that the court deems to be in the child's best interest. The court may take into consideration the provisions of the agreement between the California agency and the foreign agency, which is permitted under 22 California Code of Regulations § 35243(a)(1)(C) to return the child to his or her native country in the event of a disruption in the placement of the child. Moreover, as stated in Family Code § 8903(c), if the licensed adoption agency or prospective adoptive parents fail to meet their responsibilities for the child's care, custody, control, and financial support, and the child becomes a dependent of the court pursuant to Welfare & Institutions Code § 300, the state shall assume responsibility for the cost of care for the child. When the child becomes a dependent of the court and if, for any reason, is ineligible for AFDC under Welfare & Institutions Code § 14005.1 and loses Medi-Cal eligibility, the State Director of Health Services has authority to provide payment for the medical services to the child that are necessary to meet the child's needs.

F. Readoption in California

Under Family Code § 8919(a), each state resident who adopts a child through an intercountry adoption that is finalized in a foreign country shall readopt the child in this state if it is required by the federal immigration agency. As set forth at 8 C.F.R. § 204.3(d)(1)(iv)(B)(4), readoption may also be necessary where the adoption abroad does not meet statutory requirements of 8 U.S.C. § 1101(b)(1)(F), because the petitioners did not personally see the orphan prior to or during the adoption proceeding abroad. The readoption statutes were enacted before the Hague Convention was ratified, and it would appear to be unnecessary to readopt a child that was the subject of a Hague intercountry adoption.

As for non-Hague adoptions, as stated in Family Code § 8904(c), the California agency shall provide readoption services to the adoptive parents if a readoption is required by the federal immigration authorities. The USCIS may require the parties to complete a readoption pursuant to Family Code § 8919 and 8 C.F.R. § 204.3(d)(1)(iv)(B)(4) to perfect the visa where it appears that the order issued by the foreign country is merely a custody order and not a full and final adoption. In order to allow the child to enter the U.S. for the purpose of completing the readoption, the USCIS will issue an IR-4 visa.

If the immigration bureau does not require readoption, Family Code § 8919(b) still allows individuals who have adopted a child through an intercountry adoption that was finalized in a foreign country to readopt in California. Such a readoption would be advisable in order to obtain a California birth certificate (see Family Code § 8919(c), and Health & Safety Code § 103450) and/or if the adoptive parents decided to move to a state which did not recognize the enforceability of non-Hague foreign adoptions. The readoption would qualify as a court order that is entitled to enforceability under the Full Faith and Credit clause of the U.S. Constitution. In addition, since *In re Stephanie M.*, (1994) 7 Cal.4th 295, appears to suggest that it is discretionary with the California courts whether to recognize the enforceability of a foreign decree under the doctrine of comity, readoption would appear to be advisable even if all of the members of the adoptive family were to stay in California throughout their lifetimes.

Family Code § 8919(a) and (b) also provide that a readoption must include, but not be limited to, at least one postplacement in-home visit, the filing of the adoption petition, the intercountry adoption court report provided by the licensed California adoption agency, accounting reports, and the final adoption order. It would appear the readoption should proceed as essentially an uncontested proceeding if the natural parent's rights were terminated in the course of the adoption litigation that occurred in the foreign country. Thus, the issues at the readoption hearing would usually appear to be limited to whether the readoption was in the child's interests, such as securing nationwide recognition of the new parent-child relationship.

POST-ADOPTION ACCESS TO INFORMATION 12

In this chapter:

CONFIDENTIALITY OF RECORDS AS AGAINST THIRD PARTIES
- Documents in Court's and Adoption Agency's Case Files
  - Petitioner's Duties re Confidentiality in the Pleadings
  - Agencies' Duty to Keep Documents Confidential
    - Disclosure to the Department of Social Services
    - Inter-Agency Sharing of Information
    - "Promotion of Child's Welfare"
    - "Research Purposes"
  - General Governmental Privilege to Refuse Disclosure
  - Court's Duties re Confidentiality of Adoption Records
  - Who Are the "Parties?"
  - The Court's Duties in Indian Child Welfare Act Cases
- Special Rules for Medical Information and Blood Samples
  - Medical Reports
  - Blood Samples
  - Post-Adoption Contact with Birth Parent because of Medical Necessity
- Documents Maintained by the State Registrar
  - The California Court's Report of the Adoption
  - Adoption Reports Received from outside California
- Birth Certificates
  - New Birth Certificate / Name Change after Adoption
  - The Contents of the New Birth Certificate
  - Original Birth Certificate and Court Report
  - Petition for Judicial Modification of Birth Certificate
- Intercountry Adoptions
  - Access to Documents in a Hague Convention Case
  - Modification to Birth Certificate in Intercountry Case

RECORDS OPEN TO DISCLOSURE TO THE PARTIES
- Parties' Rights to Disclosure in the Context of Any Adoption
- Disclosure Rights Where Adoption Occurred After 1983
  - Adoptee's Right to Disclosure of Birth Parent Identity
  - Birth Parent's Right to Disclosure of the Adoptee Identity
- Special Rules Depending on the Type of Adoption Completed
  - Agency Adoptions
    - Limited Right to Know Status of the Adoption
    - The Parties' Right to Provide Information
    - The Rights of Parents with Terminated Rights
  - Independent Adoptions
  - Intercountry Adoptions

Stepparent Adoptions
The Right to Disclosure Concerning Biological Siblings
Release of Photographs, Letters and Personal Property

In 1955, a six month old baby who was later named Raymond Allen Liotta was relinquished to an orphanage in New Jersey. He was soon adopted by Alfred and Mary Liotta. In 1997, "Ray" Liotta hired a private investigator to track down his biological mother, and found out that she is not of Italian descent.

I. CONFIDENTIALITY OF RECORDS AS AGAINST THIRD PARTIES

A. Documents in Court's and Adoption Agency's Case Files

1. Petitioner's Duties re Confidentiality in the Pleadings

In any kind of adoption case, the petitioner must omit the child's full name given at birth from the petition and the proposed order. See Family Code §§ 8714(d) and (f), 8801.4(c) and (e), 8912(b) and (d), and 9000(c) and (e). Also, the adoption statutes do not require the name of the child's birth parents to be listed on the petition or order. Instead, they are referred to generically in the Judicial Council forms. Likewise, Family Code §§ 8614 and 9200(c) provide that, upon the request of the adoptive parents or the child, the court clerk shall issue a certificate of the adoption stating the date and place of the adoption, the birth date of the child, the names of the adoptive parents, and the name the child has taken, but not the names of the birth parents. In this way, the child's rights in a subsequent probate case or wrongful death suit, which are litigated in open court, may be proved by documents which do not divulge confidential facts.

2. Agencies' Duty to Keep Documents Confidential

Family Code § 9201(a) sets forth the general rule that neither the CDSS nor any licensed adoption agency (which may be public or private as explained in Chapter 5) shall release information that would identify persons who receive, or have received, adoption services. The statute then provides certain exceptions:

a) Disclosure to Department of Social Services

Family Code § 9201(b) states that the CDSS and agency employees shall release to the CDSS at Sacramento any requested information, including identifying information, for the purposes of recordkeeping and monitoring, evaluation, and regulation of the provision of adoption services.

b) Inter-Agency Sharing of Information

Under Family Code § 9201(d), an agency or the CDSS may, upon written authorization for the release of specified information by the subject of that information, share information regarding an adoptive parent or birth parent with other social service agencies, or health care providers as defined in Civil Code § 56.05 (which merely identifies licensed and certified health care providers).

c) "Promotion of Child's Welfare"

According to Family Code § 9201(e), an agency or the CDSS may furnish adoption information to "the juvenile court, county welfare department, public welfare agency, private welfare agency licensed by the CDSS, provider of foster care services, potential adoptive parent, or provider of health care," if it is "believed the child's welfare will be promoted thereby." The statute appears to apply a subjective standard as to whether the disclosure will promote the child's welfare; however this statute only allows disclosure to a finite group.

d) "Research Purposes"

Family Code § 9201(f) allows agencies and the CDSS to make adoption case records, including identifying information, available for research purposes, provided that the research will not result in the disclosure of the identity of the child or the parties to the adoption to anyone other than the entity conducting the research. The statutes do not define "research purposes," and do not limit the kinds of groups that may seek the information pursuant to this statute.

3. General Governmental Privilege to Refuse Disclosure

Evidence Code § 1040(b) states that a public entity may refuse to disclose official information, and to prevent another from disclosing official information, if the privilege is claimed by a person authorized by the public entity to do so and (1) disclosure is forbidden by a federal or California statute, or (2) disclosure of the information is against the public interest because there is a necessity for preserving the confidentiality of the information that outweighs the necessity for disclosure in the interest of justice.

As to California statutes forbidding the disclosure of adoption records, those statutes are explained later in this chapter. With regard to California statutes forbidding the disclosure of records in dependency cases, Welfare & Institutions Code § 10850(a) and (d) binds all departments, officials and employees of the State of California to keep all records maintained by the CDSS confidential, and to not allow examination for any purpose not directly connected with the administration of the dependency case.

As to the Evidence Code § 1040(b)(2) "public interest" ground for maintaining confidentiality, the code section itself states that in determining whether disclosure of the information is against the public interest, the public entity's interest as a party in the outcome of the proceeding may not be considered. In addition, *In re Maria V.*, (1985) 167 Cal.App.3d 1099, holds that the statute does not prohibit a court from allowing disclosure of relevant information, where the need for disclosure outweighs the public policy supporting nondisclosure. Evidence Code § 1040(b) also provides that the governmental privilege may be waived.

4. Court's Duties re Confidentiality of Adoption Records

As stated in previous chapters of this book, several kinds of documents, in addition to the petition and final order, must be submitted to the court in an adoption case. The home study is one such document. To maintain the confidentiality of these documents, Family Code § 9200(a) provides that petitions, relinquishments, consents, agreements, orders, reports to the court from investigating agencies, powers of attorney and depositions filed with the court in an adoption case are not open to inspection by any person other than the parties to the proceeding and their attorneys and the CDSS, except upon the written authority of the court. Family Code § 9200(a) also states that the court may not authorize anyone to inspect these documents or any portion thereof "except in exceptional circumstances and for good cause approaching the necessitous."

In *Hubbard v. Superior Court*, (1961) 189 Cal.App.2d 741, the court cited what is now Family Code § 9200, and held that the purpose and intent of the statute is to encourage and facilitate adoptions. The *Hubbard* court noted that, in an adoption proceeding, the birth parents – and many times the adoptive parents – must reveal private and embarrassing facts to government investigators; and also held that the statutes require the adoption proceedings to remain secret in order to avoid public censure of the parties.

Hubbard involved proceedings to administer a trust in New York and a will in Connecticut, wherein it was claimed that the decedent's surviving children, who had been adopted by the decedent in California, were not truly adopted due to alleged jurisdictional defects in the adoption proceedings, which if true would have negated the full faith and credit effect of the adoptions (see Chapter 9 of this book). The jurisdictional attack was that the decedent had allegedly fraudulently misrepresented to the California court that she was a California resident, and failed to disclose to the California court that she was suffering from cancer and that a Connecticut court had earlier ordered that her two previous children be removed from her care and custody. The appellate court in *Hubbard* held that even under these circumstances, the trial court abused its discretion in granting the third parties' petition to inspect the adoption records. *Hubbard* also held that the children did not waive the statutory privilege by attaching copies of certain documents from the adoption case (presumably the adoption order and possibly the adoption petition) to pleadings that were filed in the New York trust case.

Family Code § 3412(d) provides that the California courts shall preserve the pleadings, orders, decrees, records of hearings, evaluations, and other pertinent records with respect to a child custody proceeding until the child attains 18 years of age. Notwithstanding, under Family Code § 3412(d), which is part of the Uniform Child Custody Jurisdiction and Enforcement Act, it provides that upon an appropriate request by a court or law enforcement official of another state, the court shall forward a certified copy of those records. Importantly, Family Code § 3403 states that the UCCJEA does not apply to adoptions, meaning that a court might refuse to release "adoption" records. However, the UCCJEA does apply to guardianships, parentage issues, terminations of parental rights, and other questions which may be related to an adoption case.

Even if a third party is permitted to obtain adoption documents, a court may redact the documents before disclosing them. Family Code § 9200(b) provides that upon written request of any party to the proceeding and upon the order of any superior court judge, the clerk shall not provide any documents for inspection or copying, unless the child's birth parents' names or any information tending to identify the birth parents is deleted from the documents or copies thereof.

5. Who Are the "Parties?"

Under Family Code § 9200(a), only the "parties" to the proceeding, their attorneys or the CDSS may inspect the adoption records, unless leave of court is obtained. It would appear that the petitioners and the child would clearly be considered "parties" to the case. In addition, based on Family Code § 8506 and 8914, the agency would be a party to an agency adoption or an intercountry adoption to which it has filed a joinder, but not as to an independent adoption or a stepparent adoption. It is unclear whether a birth parent would be a party to the adoption for purposes of post-adoption access to records.

The court in *In re Maria V.*, (1985) 167 Cal.App.3d 1099, interpreted what is now Family Code § 9200, as well as the public policy of maintaining the confidentiality of adoption records, all in the context of a proceeding to free a child from parental custody. In *Maria V.*, an adoption case was apparently proceeding in anticipation of the termination of the birth parent's rights, and the *Maria V.* court held that the adoption file was conditionally privileged as against the birth mother. The *Maria V.* court concluded it was proper for the lower court to conduct an *in camera* review of the file and determine what documents would be relevant to the petition to free the child from parental custody. *Maria V.* does not mention whether the names and address of the foster parents were kept confidential from the birth mother, which the dependency laws permit.

In re Maria V. involved a proceeding under what is now Family Code § 7800 to free a child from parental custody following a foster placement, wherein the child was being considered for adoptive placement apparently with the child's foster parents, as opposed to the alternative placement with the child's maternal grandmother, as suggested by the birth mother. It appears that the county recommended against the placement with the child's maternal grandmother due to the presence in the home of the birth mother's brother, who had a juvenile delinquency record. The birth mother sought disclosure of the county's records from the juvenile delinquency case, and from the adoption case involving the foster parents. The birth mother's attorney had been permitted to fully inspect the County's file in the dependency proceedings.

Maria V. also held that the juvenile delinquency records were not discoverable since Welfare & Institutions Code § 827 limits the availability of documents in juvenile court proceedings to court personnel, the minor who is the subject of the proceeding, his or her parents or guardian, the attorneys for those parties and other persons designated by court order upon filing a petition therefor. In *T.N.G. v. Superior Court*, (1971) 4 Cal.3d 767, the court held that Welfare & Institutions Code § 827 gives the court the exclusive authority to determine whether disclosure of juvenile records to persons not specifically named in the statute is in the best interest of the minor.

6. The Court's Duties in Indian Child Welfare Act Cases

Under 25 U.S.C. § 1917, upon application by an Indian individual who has reached the age of 18 and who was the subject of an adoptive placement, the court which entered the final decree shall inform such individual of the tribal affiliation, if any, of the individual's biological parents and provide such other information as may be necessary to protect any rights flowing from the individual's tribal relationship.

B. Special Rules for Medical Information and Blood Samples

1. Medical Reports

Under Family Code § 9202(a), the CDSS or licensed adoption agency that issued a medical report required by Family Code §§ 8706, 8817 or 8909 shall provide a copy of the medical report, in the manner the CDSS regulations prescribe, to the following persons upon request: (1) the adoptee upon attaining 18 years of age or that person's marriage, and (2) the adoptive parent of a person under the age of 18 years. Under Family Code § 9202(c), the names and addresses of any persons contained in the report shall be removed unless the person requesting the report has previously received the information. If such a person is denied access to a medical report, Family Code § 9202(b) allows that person to petition the court for review of the reasonableness of the agency's decision.

2. Blood Samples

According to Family Code § 9202.5(a), the laboratory storing a blood sample pursuant to Family Code §§ 8706, 8817 or 8909 shall provide access to the blood sample to only the following individuals upon the person's request: (1) a person who has been adopted, and (2) the adoptive parent of a person under 18 years old, but then only after the entry of the adoption order. Family Code § 9202.5(c) states that no person other than the adoptive parent and the adoptee shall have access to the blood sample or any DNA test results related to the blood sample, unless the adoptive parent or the child authorizes another person or entity to have that access. However, Family Code § 9202.5(b) gives the birth parent or parents access to any DNA test results related to the blood sample.

3. Post-Adoption Contact with Birth Parent because of Medical Necessity

Upon the request of the adoptive parent of a person who is under 21 years of age, Family Code § 9203(a)(3) and (c) requires the CDSS or an agency to disclose the identity of a birth parent and the birth parent's most current address shown in the records of the CDSS or the agency if it finds that a medical necessity or other extraordinary circumstances justify the disclosure, unless the birth parent has indicated that he or she does not wish his or her name or address to be disclosed. Importantly, these provisions do not require the birth parent to have previously given consent to such contact, only that the birth parent can expressly prohibit the disclosure of identifying information.

In *Johnson v. Superior Court*, (2000) 80 Cal.App.4th 1050, the child was conceived from donated sperm and years later was diagnosed with a congenital kidney disease. The issue was whether the sperm bank was required to respond to a subpoena for information concerning the donor. The *Johnson* court began by holding that the donor was not the sperm bank's "patient" for purposes of the Evidence Code § 994 physician-patient privilege. *Johnson* then analyzed the argument by the anonymous donor (who made a special appearance by counsel in the action) that his anonymity was protected based on the sperm bank's contract with the child's parents, and that he was a third party beneficiary of that contract. The *Johnson* court agreed that the donor was a third party beneficiary, but held that the confidentiality clause in the agreement violated public policy based on Family Code § 7613(a), which allows the court to order the disclosure of certain information for good cause. On the other hand, the *Johnson* court ruled that, while the donor was required to provide documentation of his medical history and be deposed, his privacy was to be protected in that the identifying information as to himself and his family was not to be disclosed.

C. Documents Maintained by the State Registrar

1. The California Court's Report of the Adoption

Health & Safety Code § 102625 requires the court clerk to complete a report of the adoption and forward it to the State Registrar within five days after the decree has been entered by the court. Health & Safety Code § 102630 provides that such judicial adoption reports that are received by the State Registrar for children born outside California but within the United States or Canada shall be transmitted to the registration authority of the place of birth. Health & Safety Code § 102695 states that such court reports of adoption for children born outside the United States or Canada shall constitute a court order of delayed registration of birth, unless the court report contains a statement of the date and place of birth.

2. Adoption Reports Received from outside California

Under Health & Safety Code § 102690, where a court report of an adoption is received from an American court outside California, but which has jurisdiction of a child born in California and for whom no original record of birth is on file with the California

State Registrar, the court report of adoption shall constitute a court order of delayed birth registration, unless the court report contains a statement of the date and place of birth.

D. Birth Certificates

1. New Birth Certificate / Name Change after Adoption

In any kind of adoption in California, the petitioners are permitted to obtain a new birth certificate for the child. Health & Safety Code § 102640 provides that the new birth certificate shall supplant any birth certificate previously registered for the child and shall be the only birth certificate open to public inspection. Also, under Family Code § 8618, the child may take the name of the adoptive parent, meaning that the adoption and the issuance of the new birth certificate may actually effectuate a name change for the child. The process for obtaining the new birth certificate is as follows:

Under Health & Safety Code § 102635, a new birth certificate shall be established by the State Registrar upon receipt of a report of adoption from any court of record that has jurisdiction of the child in California, another state, the District of Columbia, any U.S. territory or any foreign country, for any child born in California and whose certificate of birth is on file in the office of the State Registrar. On the other hand, Health & Safety Code § 102640 provides that a new certificate shall not be established when so requested by the adopting parent or parents. The new birth certificate may be obtained by having the court clerk send certified copies of the adoption order and a "Court Report of Adoption" (State Registrar's Form VS 44) to the State Registrar's Office (with the proper fee enclosed if the child was born outside California).

2. The Contents of the New Birth Certificate

Under Health & Safety Code § 102645, the new birth certificate shall bear the child's name as shown in the court report, the names and ages of the adopting parents, and the date and place of birth, but no reference shall be made in the new birth certificate to the child's adoption. The new certificate shall be identical with a birth certificate registered for the birth of a child of natural parents, except, when requested by the adopting parents, the new birth certificate shall not include the name and address of the hospital or other facility where the birth occurred, the color and race of the parents, or both.

According to Health & Safety Code § 102650, when a child is adopted by an unmarried man or woman, the new certificate shall, if the adopting parent so requests, reflect the fact that it is a single-parent adoption. Also, Health & Safety Code § 102675 provides that at any time after the new birth certificate is issued, the adopting parents may request that an amended certificate be issued that omits any or all of the following: (a) the specific name and address of the hospital or other facility where the birth occurred, (b) the city and county of birth, and (c) the color and race of the parents.

3. Original Birth Certificate and Court Report

According to Health & Safety Code § 102700, the State Registrar is to maintain copies of the court report of adoption and the original record of birth. An adoptee may later learn about his or her birth parents by seeking out the original birth certificate and adoption records pursuant to Health & Safety Code § 102705. This statute (which was formerly numbered at Health & Safety Code § 10439) provides that the original birth and adoption records transmitted to the State Registrar shall be available upon the order of the superior court of the adopted child's county of residence or the superior court of the county granting the adoption order. Also, the courts have the authority to correct any erroneously stated fact on the original birth certificate. (*Wynn v. Superior Court* (2009) 176 Cal.App.4th 346.) There is no published case law interpreting Health & Safety Code § 102705 or its predecessors.

Health & Safety Code § 102705 provides that the court shall not grant such an order unless a verified petition setting forth facts showing the necessity of the order has been presented to the court, and good and compelling cause is shown for the granting of the order. The statute does not limit what persons may file such a petition. However, it provides that "great weight" is to be given to a petition that is by or on behalf of an adopted child who has attained majority (which is now 18 years old pursuant to Family Code § 6502(a)(2)), but the granting of any petition is solely within the sound discretion of the court.

When a petition pursuant to Health & Safety Code § 102705 is filed, the court clerk shall send a copy of the petition to the CDSS, which then has the duty to send to the court a copy of all records and information it has concerning the adopted person, with the name and address of the natural parents removed. The court must review these records before making an order. In addition, Health & Safety Code § 102705 provides that the natural parents' names and address shall be given to the petitioner only if he or she can demonstrate that the name and address, or either of them, are necessary to assist him or her in establishing a legal right.

4. Petition for Judicial Modification of Birth Certificate

Under Health & Safety Code § 103450, any beneficially interested person may file a verified petition to judicially establish the fact of, and the time and place of a birth, death or marriage that is not registered or for which a certified copy is not obtainable. The statute states that the petition is to be filed with the court in and for (a) the county in which the birth, death or marriage is alleged to have occurred, or (b) the county of residence of the person whose birth or marriage it is sought to be established, or (c) the county in which the person was domiciled at the date of death, if the person has died. It would appear that this statute would give the court the authority to order the State Registrar to modify its records in conformity with the court's order.

According to Health & Safety Code § 103455, the verified petition shall contain all the facts necessary to enable the court to determine the fact of and the time and place of the birth, death, or marriage upon the proofs adduced in behalf of the petitioner at the hearing. Health & Safety Code § 103460 provides that if the time and place of birth are not known, the petition shall contain all of the facts known to the petitioner or otherwise available and a statement of the probable time and place of birth as accurately as the circumstances permit.

E. Intercountry Adoptions

1. Access to Documents in a Hague Convention Case

According to 42 U.S.C. §§ 14902(11) and 14941(b), access to documents generated during the course of an intercountry adoption under the Hague Convention is strictly limited. On the other hand, 42 U.S.C. § 14942, provides that documents originating in any other Convention country (and thus not under federal control) and related to a Convention adoption case shall require no authentication in order to be admissible in any Federal, State, or local court in the United States, unless a specific and supported claim is made that the documents are false, have been altered, or are otherwise unreliable. Article 30 and 31 of the Hague Convention (and foreign law) would appear to limit access to documents in the custody of foreign authorities.

2. Modification to Birth Certificate in Intercountry Case

As of January 1, 2002, Family Code § 8919(c) allows for a new birth certificate to be issued under Health & Safety Code § 103450 (as explained above) for a child who was readopted in California. While the approved form for an adoption petition asks the petitioner to specify if the petition is for an intercountry adoption, it only requires the petitioner to specify the child's birthplace "if known." On the other hand, the State Registrar's Office maintains a policy that if the date and place of the child's birth is not included on the form, it will be returned to the court clerk for correction. Importantly, Health & Safety Code § 103450 and Family Code § 8919(c) do not require the State to obtain information from the federal immigration authorities in obtaining the new birth certificate.

II. RECORDS OPEN TO DISCLOSURE TO THE PARTIES

A. Parties' Rights to Disclosure in the Context of Any Adoption

As stated above, Health & Safety Code § 102705 allows an adoptee to seek a court order requiring the State Registrar to disclose the original birth certificate. Additionally, Family Code § 9200(a) allows the court to authorize an individual to inspect documents in the court's possession where he or she demonstrates that "exceptional circumstances" exist and that "good cause approaching the necessitous" supports the disclosure. Where such is not possible, the following methods of obtaining information about the adoption are available:

According to Family Code § 9204(a) and (b), if an adult adoptee and the adult adoptee's birth parents have each filed a written consent with the CDSS or licensed adoption agency on an approved form, the CDSS or licensed adoption agency may arrange for contact between those persons. On the CDSS's web site (http://www.dss.cahwnet.gov), the AD-904 form is provided for this purpose. However, Family Code § 9204(a) prohibits the CDSS and the agency from directly or indirectly soliciting the execution of a written consent.

Under Family Code § 9203(e), the CDSS shall announce the availability of the present method of arranging contact among an adult adoptee, the adult adoptee's birth parents, and adoptive parents authorized by Family Code § 9204, utilizing a means of communication appropriate to inform the public effectively. The "frequently asked questions" page of the CDSS's web site provides some information.

B. Disclosure Rights Where Adoption Occurred After 1983

1. Adoptee's Right to Disclosure of Birth Parent Identity

Family Code § 9203 provides the method for obtaining disclosure of the identity and whereabouts of the adoptee or the birth parents, where, according to Family Code § 9203(g), the relinquishment for or consent to the adoption was signed, or the birth parent's rights were involuntarily terminated by court action, on or after January 1, 1984. In addition, the Family Code § 9203 disclosure rules only apply to adoptions that were completed in California, but they apply to all types of adoptions.

Upon the request of an adoptee who is at least 21 years old, Family Code § 9203(a)(1), (c) and (d) require the CDSS or a licensed adoption agency to disclose, within 20 working days, the identity of the person's birth parent or parents and their most current address shown in the records of the CDSS or the agency, if the birth parent or parents have indicated written consent to the disclosure. The birth parent may also indicate that he or she does not wish his or her name or address to be disclosed. Such consent is explained below as to specific kinds of adoptions.

2. Birth Parent's Right to Disclosure of Adoptee Identity

Upon request by the birth parent of an adopted person who has attained 21 years of age, Family Code § 9203(a)(2), (c) and (d) require the CDSS or an agency to disclose, within 20 working days, the adopted name of the adoptee and the adoptee's most current address shown in the CDSS's or agency's records, if the adult adoptee has indicated in writing, under the CDSS's registration program, that the adult adoptee wishes the adult adoptee's name and address to be disclosed. The adoptee may also indicate that he or she does not wish his or her name or address to be disclosed. The details of the consent are explained below as to specific kinds of adoptions.

C. Special Rules Depending on the Type of Adoption Completed

1. Agency Adoptions

a) Limited Right to Know Status of the Adoption

According to Family Code § 8701, at or before the time a relinquishment is signed, the CDSS or licensed adoption agency shall advise the relinquishing birth parent, verbally and in writing, that the birth parent may, at any time in the future, request from the CDSS or agency all known information about the status of the child's adoption, except for personal identifying information about the adoptive family. The birth parent shall be advised that this information includes, but is not limited to: (a) whether the child has been placed for adoption, (b) the approximate date that an adoption was completed, and (c) if the adoption was not completed or was vacated, for any reason, whether adoptive placement of the child will again be considered.

b) The Parties' Right to Provide Information

Family Code § 8702(a) states that a CDSS-designed statement (see the AD-908 form that appears on the CDSS web site) shall be presented to the birth parents at the time a relinquishment is signed and to the prospective adoptive parents at the time of the home study. The statement is to communicate all the following facts: (1) It is in the child's best interest that the birth parent keep the CDSS or agency informed of any health problems that the parent develops that could affect the child, (2) It is extremely important that the birth parent keep an address current with the CDSS or agency to permit a response to inquiries as to medical or social history, (3) Family Code § 9203 authorizes a person who has been adopted and who attains 21 years of age to request the CDSS or the agency to disclose the name and address of the adoptee's birth parents (under the circumstances explained above), (4) The birth parent may change the decision whether to permit disclosure of the birth parent's name and address at any time by sending a notarized letter to that effect by certified mail return receipt requested to the CDSS or agency, and (5) The relinquishment will be filed in the office of the county clerk of the county in which the adoption takes place, but is not open to inspection by any persons other than the parties to the adoption proceeding, their attorneys, and the CDSS, except upon order of a superior court judge.

As to post-adoption contact, Family Code § 8702(b) provides that the CDSS form to be signed by the birth parents at the time of the relinquishment shall state: "Section 9203 of the Family Code authorizes a person who has been adopted and who attains the age of 21 years to make a request to the State Department of Social Services, or the licensed adoption agency that joined in the adoption petition, for the name and address of the adoptee's birth parents. Indicate by checking one of the boxes below whether or not you wish your name and address to be disclosed: /__/ YES /__/ NO /__/ UNCERTAIN AT THIS TIME; WILL NOTIFY AGENCY AT LATER DATE." Form AD-908 contains this language.

c) The Rights of Parents with Terminated Rights

Under Family Code § 8703, when parental rights are terminated pursuant to Family Code § 7660, Family Code § 7800, or Welfare & Institutions Code § 366.26, the CDSS or agency shall send a written notice to the birth parent – if the birth parent's address is known – that encourages the birth parent to keep the CDSS or agency informed of his or her current address, and to send the statement described above concerning rights under Family Code § 9203.

2. Independent Adoptions

Family Code § 8813 provides that at or before the time the consent to the adoption is signed, the CDSS or licensed adoption agency shall advise the consenting birth parent, verbally and in writing, that the birth parent may, at any time in the future, request from the CDSS or agency all known information about the status of the child's adoption, except for personal identifying information about the adoptive family. Also, Family Code § 8818 requires essentially the same statement to be given to the birth parent as is described in Family Code § 8702 (as explained above), but speaks with reference to the consent rather than to a relinquishment.

3. Intercountry Adoptions

The statutes specifically governing intercountry adoptions (Family Code §§ 8900, et seq.) are silent concerning post-adoption access to information. One must note that in an intercountry adoption, the adoptive parent normally obtains custody of the child through a foreign government or a foreign adoption agency, meaning that the child's and/or birth parents' post-adoption rights to (or prohibitions against) access to documents located in the foreign country are governed by foreign law. However, to the extent that the California agency obtains certain documentation, which the agency must retain pursuant to 22 California Code of Regulations § 35251, the agency must comply with Family Code § 9200, et seq.

4. Stepparent Adoptions

The statutes specifically governing stepparent adoptions (Family Code §§ 9000, et seq.) are also silent concerning post-adoption access to information. Importantly, in a stepparent adoption, there is usually no home study, meaning that there are usually no agency documents. On the other hand, as explained above in connection with *In re Maria V.*, (1985) 167 Cal.App.3d 1099, if a Family Code § 7800 proceeding to free the child from parental custody is commenced (in the event the non-custodial parent does not consent to the stepparent adoption), the case is investigated by public agencies, who generate documents in connection with the proceedings, and such documents are confidential. On the other hand, the rules concerning consent to post-adoption access to information would still appear to apply. Specifically, if there is a consent to an adoption, Family Code § 8818 would appear to require the non-custodial parent to receive the statement described above, and if parental rights are terminated, Family Code § 8703 (as explained above) would appear to apply, in spite of the location of these code sections.

D. The Right to Disclosure Concerning Biological Siblings

Family Code § 9205(a) provides that the CDSS or the agency that joined in the adoption petition shall release the names and addresses of biological siblings to one another if both of the siblings have attained the age of 21 years and have filed with the CDSS or agency (1) a current address, (2) a written request for contact with any biological sibling whose existence is known to the person making the request, and (3) a written waiver of the person's rights with respect to the disclosure of the person's name and address to the sibling, if the person is an adoptee. On the other hand, Family Code § 9205(c) states that an adoptee may revoke the statutory waiver by giving written notice of revocation to the CDSS or agency. Pursuant to Family Code § 9205(d), the CDSS's web site provides Form AD-904A for the purpose of allowing the written waiver to be memorialized. According to Family Code § 9205(b), upon inquiry and proof that a person is the biological sibling of an adoptee who has filed a waiver pursuant to this section, the CDSS or the agency may advise the sibling that a waiver has been filed by the adoptee. On the other hand, Family Code § 9205(e) prohibits the CDSS and the agency from soliciting the execution of a waiver, but allows the CDSS to publicly announce the availability of these procedures.

E. Release of Photographs, Letters and Personal Property

Family Code § 9206(a) allows the CDSS or licensed adoption agency to release any letters, photographs, or other items of personal property in its possession to an adoptee, birth parent, or adoptive parent, upon written request. The material may be requested by (1) the adoptee, if the adoptee has attained the age of 18 years, (2) the adoptive parent or parents, on behalf of an adoptee under the age of 18 years, as long as instructions to the contrary have not been made by the depositor, and (3) the birth parent or parents. However, Family Code § 9206(b) requires all identifying names and addresses to be deleted from the letters, photographs, or items of personal property before delivery to the requester. In addition, Family Code § 9206(f) actually defines "photograph" as a portrayal "of the person depositing the photograph or the person making the request for the release," thereby limiting the kinds of pictures that would be subject to the statute.

Letters, photographs, and other items of personal property deposited on or after January 1, 1985 are required by Family Code § 9206(c) to be accompanied by a release form or similar document signed by the person depositing the material, specifying to whom the material may be released. At its discretion, the CDSS or licensed adoption agency may refuse for deposit items of personal property that, because of value or bulk, would pose storage problems.

As to items deposited before January 1, 1985, Family Code § 9206(d) provides that only the following photographs, shall be released: (1) Photographs of the adoptee that have been requested by the adoptee, and (2) photographs that have been deposited by the adoptee, the adoptive parent or parents, or the birth parent or parents, and for which there is a letter or other document on file indicating that person's consent to the release of the photographs.

INDEX

ABOUT THE AUTHOR

Prof. Everett L. Skillman is a member of the adjunct faculty at the University of San Diego School of Law. He and his wife Shelley were foster parents for three years and adoptive parents for 12 years after that. At seminars conducted by social services agencies and private agencies, Prof. Skillman had the good fortune of meeting many wonderful, committed fellow foster parents, and learning how they overcame a wide variety of challenges. Prof. Skillman has been licensed to practice law since 1990; he has taught several courses on Adoption Law; he has helped many others complete their adoptions; and he has been certified since 2000 by the California State Bar as a specialist in appellate law. *Thank you for considering this book.*

www.ingramcontent.com/pod-product-compliance
Lightning Source LLC
LaVergne TN
LVHW062110200926
848484LV00007B/1634